Maternal and Infant Nutrition and Nurture

201

B13

D0550808

Note

Health and social care practice and knowledge are constantly changing and developing as new research and treatments, changes in procedures, drugs and equipment become available.

The authors, editor and publishers have, as far as is possible, taken care to confirm that the information complies with the latest standards of practice and legislation.

Maternal and Infant Nutrition and Nurture

Second edition

edited by

Victoria Hall Moran

QUAY
BOOKS

A division of MA Healthcare Ltd

Quay Books Division, MA Healthcare Ltd, St Jude's Church, Dulwich Road, London
SE24 0PB

British Library Cataloguing-in-Publication Data
A catalogue record is available for this book

ISBN-10: 1 85642 435 9
ISBN-13: 978 1 85642 435 6

Printed by Mimeo, Huntingdon, Cambridgeshire

Contents

Contents

Foreword

Fiona Dykes

The second edition of this book is very timely as we see maternal and child nutrition coming increasingly onto public health agendas across the globe, with a growing focus upon the interconnectedness of mother and child. The World Health Organization states:

> The health and nutritional status of mothers and children are intimately linked. Improved infant and young child feeding begins with ensuring the health and nutritional status of women, in their own right, throughout all stages of life and continues with women as providers for their children and families. Mothers and infants form a biological and social unit; they also share problems of malnutrition and ill-health. Whatever is done to solve these problems concerns both mothers and children together. (WHO, 2003, p. 5).

This book is particularly important, as it not only focuses upon the challenges to optimising maternal and child nutrition, but refers throughout to policy and practice related to this issue, thus bridging the gaps between rhetoric and reality. It also represents a positive move to disrupt disciplinary boundaries that have, in many cases, persisted with regard to maternal and infant nutrition, eating and feeding. It thus produces new ways of seeing within the field of maternal and child nutrition and nurture that connect the disciplines of nutrition, dietetics, midwifery, medicine and the social sciences.

In Chapter 1, Paula Williams and Hiten Mistry discuss the importance of specific antioxidant micronutrients and the crucial part that they play in the health and wellbeing of pregnant women and in early childhood. They argue that it is only by fully understanding the requirements for micronutrients during pregnancy that we will be able to evaluate the potential use of dietary antioxidant supplements as a way of preventing pathological pregnancy outcomes. They advocate that future strategies focusing upon providing nutritional guidance specifically to pregnant women will be pivotal in helping to ensure the optimal health of both mother and baby.

In Chapter 2, Victoria Hall Moran focuses upon nutrition in pregnant and breastfeeding adolescents. She highlights the specific nutritional needs of pregnant adolescents and examines the factors that influence their eating behaviours. She emphasises that overcoming the barriers in order to achieve improved nutrition in pregnancy among adolescents requires multidisciplinary collaborations of adolescent health care providers, academics, professional organisations, policy makers, industry and service users.

In Chapter 3, Kevin Hugill discusses the enormous challenges and debates that relate to optimising nutrition and nurture for preterm infants. His discussion ranges from emphasising nutritional and immunological aspects of feeding to issues related to support and relational considerations. This is a useful guide for practitioners in their endeavour to tailor the provision of infant nutrition to address the unique needs of preterm infants.

In Chapter 4, Sally Inch discusses the crucial components of breast milk for optimal infant feeding and then explores the risks of formula feeding babies and the ways in which breastfeeding has been fundamentally undermined by the multinational marketing of breast milk substitutes. These practices have contributed to a marginalisation of breastfeeding so that, in many communities across the world, it is no longer seen or experienced as the norm. The complex socio-cultural issues related to women's choices and decision making with regard to feeding method are illuminated.

In Chapter 5, Magda Sachs discusses the reasons why breastfeeding mothers weigh their babies. She draws upon her doctoral ethnographic research on the impact of routine weight monitoring on the feeding decisions of breastfeeding women in north-west England. Magda concludes that infant health and wellbeing could benefit from a change in the assumption that health is easily measured through physical weight gain, and that weight increases will happen in a linear, mechanical way. She refers to current policy recommendations centring upon building infant social and emotional capacity in order to ensure lifelong wellbeing and achievement and argues that an understanding of wellbeing wider than physical growth needs to be facilitated.

In Chapter 6, Nicola Crossland and Gill Thomson describe health professionals' views and experiences of working alongside breastfeeding peer supporters. They refer, in particular, to the notion of 'expertise' and discuss health professionals' attitudes towards the perceived 'expert' status of the peer supporters, together with the associated facilitators and tensions of integrating a breastfeeding peer support service in practice. They argue that suitable opportunities need to be provided for co-working between health professionals and peer supporters to encourage relationship formation, reassurance and knowledge transfer to ensure that the service is sensitively and meaningfully integrated into practice.

In Chapter 7, Katherine Ebisch-Burton reports on an analysis of discourse on breastfeeding in public in Western Europe. She concludes that the visibility of breastfeeding in the public space remains a profoundly controversial matter, with much debate revolving around its undisguised or uncensored visibility; this discourse seeks to establish relationships of responsibility between the breastfeeding mother and those around her in the public space, with the primary responsibility assigned to the former.

In Chapter 8, Tyra Gross and Alex Kojo Anderson highlight the enormous challenges and controversies for women and health practitioners in balancing the risk and benefits of breastfeeding in the context of HIV. They refer to the complex and culturally specific influences upon HIV-infected mothers' infant feeding decisions. They recommend that researchers and clinicians alike evaluate the feasibility of such guidelines in their own contexts and that WHO should continue to review their guidelines using experience from the field to ensure that HIV-infected mothers can make the best feeding decisions for their infants.

In Chapter 9, Gill Rapley focuses upon baby-led weaning; she illustrates the ways in which doctrine and cultural beliefs have led to ways of 'managing' complementary feeding that ignore the developmental readiness and needs of babies. She highlights that the best way in which to meet the WHO recommendations for exclusive breastfeeding to six months is to adopt a developmental approach to the introduction of complementary foods.

In Chapter 10, Wendy Hunt and Alexandra McManus focus upon seafood and omega-3 fatty acids for maternal and child mental health with particular emphasis on the role of maternal, gestational and childhood nutrition. They provide a review of research into mental health disorders and the positive role of seafood and marine sourced long chain polyunsaturated omega-3 fatty acid consumption. They argue that inclusion of seafood within a healthy diet, in conjunction with current best practice treatments, has the potential to significantly impact the burden of disease attributable to mental health disorders.

Understandings of maternal and child nutrition need to take account of the embodied, emotional and social nature of eating and feeding, the ways in which women negotiate these in a range of cultural contexts *and* the macro-political influences upon women in relation to their dietary and infant feeding practices. This collection of chapters provides a basis for making improvements in maternal and child nutrition through dietary recommendations, political activity and social policy. It presents a challenge to academics and health practitioners to become more strategically engaged with government agendas to bring about fundamental changes required to ensure that women have the information, resources and support to feed themselves and their infants in ways that optimise their health outcomes.

Reference

World Health Organization (WHO) (2003) *Global Strategy on Infant and Young Child Feeding*. WHO, Geneva.

Contributors

Nicola Crossland

Nicola Crossland is a research assistant in the Maternal and Infant Nutrition and Nurture Unit at the University of Central Lancashire. Prior to her work in infant feeding, Nicola's background was in biological sciences, particularly the neurobiology of mental health disorders. Nicola's research interests relate to the sociocultural aspects of women's experiences of infant feeding and early motherhood, maternal wellbeing, infant feeding and the family, and breastfeeding peer support.

Fiona Dykes

Fiona Dykes is Professor of Maternal and Infant Health and Director of the Maternal and Infant Nutrition and Nurture Unit (MAINN), School of Health, University of Central Lancashire. She is also Adjunct Professor at University of Western Sydney. Fiona has a particular interest in the global, socio-cultural and political influences upon infant and young child feeding practices. She is a member of the editorial board for *Maternal and Child Nutrition*, the Wiley-Blackwell published international journal (editorial office in MAINN) and a Fellow of the Higher Education Academy. Fiona has worked on WHO, UNICEF, European Union (EU Framework 6), Government (DH), NIIS, National Institute for Health and Clinical Excellence (NICE), TrusTECH® Service Innovation (UK), National Institute for Health Research (NIHR), Wellcome Trust, British Council and Australian Research Council (ARC) funded projects.

Katherine Ebisch-Burton

Katherine Ebisch-Burton conducts research into discourses on breastfeeding in the UK and Germany, and has collaborated with members of the Maternal and Infant Nutrition and Nurture Unit at the University of Central Lancashire. She holds a DPhil in German literature and lives in Germany, where she works as an academic translator and editor and lectures at various universities.

Tyra Gross

Tyra Gross is a doctoral candidate in the Department of Health Promotion and Behaviour at the University of Georgia in the USA. Her research interests include maternal and child health disparities, with a particular focus on breastfeeding in African-American women. Tyra Gross was a fellow for both the American Public Health Association Maternal and Child Section and the Albert Schweitzer Fellow, New Orleans chapter in 2008–2009.

Victoria Hall Moran

Victoria Hall Moran is Associate Professor in Maternal and Child Nutrition in the Maternal and Infant Nutrition and Nurture Unit (MAINN) at the University of Central Lancashire, Preston. Her research has focused on micronutrient requirements, with a particular interest in zinc, and the nutritional needs of women during pregnancy and lactation. Recent work includes a review of dietary zinc requirements and associated health outcomes within the European Commission funded 'Eurreca' Network of Excellence; whose aim is to harmonise the approach to setting European micronutrient recommendations with specific focus on vulnerable populations such as infants, pregnant and lactating women, and the elderly. Victoria is a Fellow of the Higher Education Academy and Senior Editor of *Maternal & Child Nutrition* (a Wiley-Blackwell journal).

Kevin Hugill

Kevin Hugill is a senior lecturer and neonatal courses lead at the University of Central Lancashire in Preston. His nursing background is predominantly in neonatal care and he has worked in a number of different neonatal units and higher education institutions in England. His PhD research was concerned with the emotion work of fathers after their baby's admission to a neonatal unit. He has a particular interest in preterm infant feeding and its connections with nurturance. His present research activity focuses upon parent–infant closeness in neonatal units. In addition he has served as a member of Data Monitoring Committees for randomised controlled trials and more recently a trial steering committee concerning neonatal skin care.

Wendy Hunt

Doctor Wendy Hunt is the Senior Food Scientist at the Centre of Excellence for Science Seafood and Health, Curtin University. She holds a Bachelor of Science (Health Science), an advanced Master of Business Administration (Marketing) and a Doctor of Philosophy (Food Science) and is a professional member of The

Australian Institute of Food Science and Technology, The Australian Society of Microbiology and The Australian Institute of Management. Wendy has expertise in food science and food microbiology across a range of industry sectors and specialises in science communication. Her research interests have centred on new product development, food safety and the importance of seafood to human health.

Sally Inch

Since 1997 Sally Inch has been employed by the Oxford University Hospitals Trust as their Infant Feeding Specialist and as Baby Friendly Initiative (BFI) and Human Milk Bank coordinator. As the Infant Feeding Specialist she runs a hospital-based drop-in breastfeeding clinic. As BFI coordinator Sally led the three midwife-led units in the Trust to obtain the Global Baby Friendly award in 2001. For the last 20 years Sally has written widely on aspects of birth and breastfeeding, and was both a contributor to and Editor of *Successful Breastfeeding*, the RCM Handbook, now in its third edition (Harcourt 2001) and published in 11 languages. She also authored the chapter on Infant Feeding in the last three editions of *Myles Textbook for Midwives*. From 2001–2003 Sally worked with the University of Coventry (on a Department of Health funded multi-centred randomised controlled trial – the Best Start Breastfeeding Project), where she is now a visiting Research Fellow.

Alex Kojo Anderson

Alex Kojo Anderson is an Associate Professor of Foods and Nutrition at the University of Georgia in the USA, with a research interest in maternal and child nutrition, and a particular interest in health promotion related to breastfeeding, child feeding and maternal health. He also teaches courses on Optimal Nutrition for the Life Span, Public Health Dietetics, and Nutrition Epidemiology.

Alexandra McManus

Professor Alexandra McManus is Director of Centre of Excellence for Science Seafood and Health, Curtin University. She is also Deputy Director of the International Institute Agrifood Security and Professor with the Curtin Health Innovation Research Institute. Alexandra has a Bachelor of Science (Health Promotion/Human Biology), Master of Public Health and a Doctor of Philosophy (Sports Medicine). Additionally, she holds several Executive Committee and Board Memberships including those for Research Australia and Kidsafe WA. Alexandra's research expertise encompasses many aspects of public health and sports medicine with specific emphasis on the management and evaluation of health interventions. Alexandra's commitment to public health is demonstrated in her research outputs of: 133 national and international conference presentations, 54 peer reviewed journal articles, 48 major research reports, 47 invited presentations, 15 education and training resources and 12 book chapters/online training courses between 2000 and 2012.

Hiten D. Mistry

Hiten D. Mistry is a Postdoctoral Associate in the Division of Women's Health, Women's Health Academic Centre, KHP, King's College London, UK. Dr. Mistry received a first class BSc (Hons) in Biochemistry with Industrial Experience from University of Manchester Institute of Science and Technology (UMIST). He then went on to complete a PhD entitled 'Selenium, selenoproteins and factors which might interact with them relating to oxidative stress, in normal and pre-eclamptic pregnancies'. Dr. Mistry's primary research interests are focussed on the influences of antioxidant micronutrients in relation to the pathophysiology of the hypertensive diseases of pregnancy and intrauterine growth restriction. He has published widely in the field, including peer reviewed scientific articles, expert reviews, book chapters and abstracts.

Gill Rapley

Over a 35-year career Gill Rapley has practised as a health visitor, midwife and voluntary breastfeeding counsellor, and has been a certified lactation consultant (IBCLC). Latterly, she worked for 14 years with the UNICEF UK Baby Friendly Initiative, while pursuing her interest in infant development as it relates to infant feeding as the basis of a Masters degree. She is currently studying further the process and means by which infants are introduced to solid foods, with the aim of gaining a PhD. She is credited with pioneering the concept of 'baby-led weaning', although she does not claim to have invented it – rather, with the help of her co-author, Tracey Murkett, she has 'brought it out of the closet'.

Magda Sachs

Magda Sachs qualified as a volunteer breastfeeding counsellor in 1988, and is currently a Breastfeeding Supporter with The Breastfeeding Network. Magda was awarded her PhD in 2005: this examined the impact of routine weighing of babies on breastfeeding mothers' feeding decisions. In 2008 she joined the Growth Chart Working Group convened by the Royal College of Paediatrics and Child Health, which developed the UK–World Health Organization 0–4 growth charts. Magda conducted parent focus groups and staff consultation workshops which informed the design of these charts, wording of chart instructions, and parental information for the Personal Child Health Record (red book). She took up the position of public health manager with NHS Salford in 2009, and continues in that capacity at Salford City Council.

Gill Thomson

Gill Thomson is currently working as a Research Fellow within the Maternal and Infant Nutrition and Nurture Unit (MAINN), University of Central Lancashire (UCLan). Gill is a social scientist with a psychology academic background and has worked within the public, private and voluntary sectors. Since completing her Masters in the Psychology of Child Development in 1998, she has been employed on a number of consultation projects, the majority of which involved engaging with vulnerable population groups. Following successful completion of her PhD at the end of 2007 she has been employed by UCLan and has been involved in a number of research/evaluation based projects to explore biopsychosocial influences and experiences towards maternity services and infant feeding issues. Gill's research interests relate to maternal wellbeing across the perinatal period. She also has a particular specialism in the interpretive phenomenological based research.

Paula J. Williams

Paula J. Williams studied for her PhD in reproductive immunology at the University of Newcastle working under the supervision of Professor Stephen Robson, Dr Judith Bulmer and Dr Roger Searle. After completing her PhD in 2005 she continued her research moving into the field of the role of nutrition in successful pregnancy working at the University of Nottingham. She has published a number of papers looking at the novel roles of folic acid in placental development and is interested in the role of nutrition in preventing the obstetric disorder pre-eclampsia.

CHAPTER 1

Antioxidant micronutrients in pregnancy and early childhood

Paula J. Williams and Hiten D. Mistry

Introduction

Pregnancy is a period of increased metabolic demands due to the changes occurring within the woman's physiology and the requirements of her growing fetus. During this time, insufficient stores or intake of vitamins or minerals, referred to as micronutrients, can have adverse effects on the pregnant mother, including complications such as anaemia, hypertensive disorders of pregnancy, complications of labour and even death. The fetus can also be affected, leading to stillbirth, preterm delivery, fetal growth restriction, congenital malformations, abnormal organ development, childhood disorders and even effects that do not become apparent until later in life, including obesity.

The essential nature of micronutrients has been recognised through the identification of clinical conditions associated with severe deficiencies of particular micronutrients, and through subsequent animal experiments. While the importance of deficiencies of iodine and folate during pregnancy is now well recognised, the role of many other micronutrient deficiencies during this crucial phase has only more recently become appreciated. Gaining an understanding of the importance of micronutrients is complicated by the finding that micronutrient deficiencies often coexist, and that deficiencies of specific vitamins and minerals vary by stage of life, season, year, ethnic group and economic status, and among individuals within the same community. Variability in micronutrient status can be attributed to consumption of diets with differing content and bioavailability of micronutrients and differing losses and requirements for micronutrients at different stages, with enhanced levels being required to support pregnancy. It is also important to note that micronutrients can have either positive or negative interactions, and that these interactions may not be the same for all possible consequences of deficiencies.

The possible occurrence of multiple micronutrient deficiencies in pregnant women, particularly in developing countries, and the presence of numerous confounding factors (Ramakrishnan *et al.*, 1999), have meant that observational studies related to micronutrients and pregnancy outcomes are of only limited value. The best causal evidence for micronutrients and adverse outcomes of pregnancy comes from randomised controlled trials, and to date these have largely been carried out for individual vitamins or minerals. Although these results can be very informative, it is also possible that correction of a single micronutrient deficiency, when one or more other limiting deficiencies are present, may not demonstrate the effects of that micronutrient. There are also issues surrounding interpretation of results when correction of multiple micronutrient deficiencies has been demonstrated in pregnancy whilst continuing to consume a diet that is inadequate in macronutrients, such as calories and protein, therefore leading to poor outcome results, such as fetal growth restriction.

What are antioxidants?

Antioxidants are substances that either have inherent antioxidant activity or are part of antioxidant enzyme systems involved in the disposal of potentially harmful free radicals. Oxidative stress is defined as a disturbance in the balance between antioxidants and (pro)oxidants (free radical species) in favour of the latter. Oxidative stress occurs when levels of free radicals exceed the capacity of antioxidant defences due to an inadequate dietary intake of antioxidants or by an increase of cellular oxidants, which can be defined as substances with one or more unpaired electrons (Davidge, 1998). Free radicals take the form of reactive oxygen species (ROS, such as oxygen ions and peroxides), reactive nitrogen species (RNS) and reactive chlorine species (RCS) and are produced during normal metabolism. Physiological ROS/RNS/RCS production is, in fact, necessary for proper health; for example, it helps the body's immune system to kill microorganisms. Optimal health is therefore a balance between the two: antioxidants serve to regulate the levels of free radicals, permitting them to perform useful biological functions without too much damage (Halliwell and Gutteridge, 2006).

Thus antioxidants are essential to maintain homeostasis. An imbalance in the equilibrium between anti- and pro-oxidants can result in oxidative stress, which is a key pathophysiological mechanism involved in a number of diseases (Agarwal, 2008). Harmful effects of ROS can be bought about through their ability to oxidise DNA, lipids and proteins, causing cellular injury and cell death. Many antioxidants are obtained from dietary sources, including vitamins C and E and beta-carotene and a number of dietary micronutrients are essential co-factors of

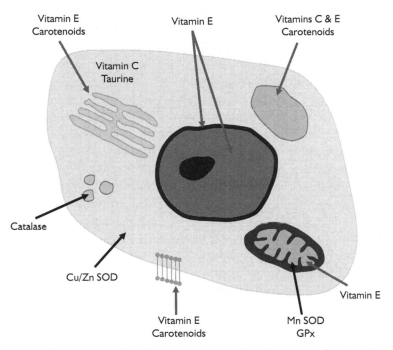

Figure 1.1 Endogenous (black) and exogenous (grey) sources of antioxidants and their places of action within the cell.

antioxidant enzymes; these include selenium (which is a co-factor for glutathione peroxidases; GPxs) and copper, zinc and manganese (which are co-factors for superoxide dismutase; Cu/Zn/Mg-SOD). Zinc is also an essential co-factor for metallothionein and copper is needed for the enzyme ceruloplasmin. Figure 1.1 shows the endogenous and exogenous sources of antioxidants and their places of action within the cell.

How antioxidants work: prevention, inception and repair

ROS are oxidants, being atoms of oxygen that can oxidise a substrate; they are reduced during this reaction. They are able to damage several key cellular components such as membrane lipids, nucleic acids, carbohydrates and proteins, thereby severely disturbing major cellular and organic physiological functions. This type of damage occurs when the host's antioxidants are quantitatively and/or qualitatively unable to counteract the production and effects of oxidants themselves. The antioxidant defence system provides protection against oxidative reactions and is organised at the levels of prevention, interception and repair.

Prevention comprises strategies that avoid the generation of ROS, RNS and RCS, for example diminished light exposure to lower photo-oxidative reactions or caloric restriction to decrease side reactions in the sequence of the respiratory chain. Proteins that tightly bind metal ions which otherwise catalyse pro-oxidant reactions are also involved in prevention.

Interception involves a network of antioxidant enzymes (i.e. exogenous and endogenous molecules) that are available to scavenge ROS, RNS and RCS once they are generated. Superoxide dismutase, catalase, glutathione and glutathione-dependent enzymes, as well as sulphur- or selenium-containing proteins and low molecular weight compounds, are produced for defence. Small molecular weight compounds with antioxidant properties such as ascorbate (vitamin C), alpha-tocopherol (vitamin E) and carotenoids, instead, are provided through the diet, particularly fruit and vegetables, and are therefore called antioxidant micronutrients. These dietary factors are an essential component of the antioxidant defence network; an inadequate supply within the diet has been epidemiologically correlated with increased risk of a number of oxidative stress related diseases.

Repair is the domain of enzymes, which recognise oxidatively damaged molecules and initiate repair, degradation or removal. The interplay of all processes and compounds in the network provides optimal protection.

Antioxidant micronutrients

It is often difficult to correlate a dietary deficiency with clinical symptoms that may arise, because many vitamins and minerals have multiple roles in metabolism (Stahl *et al.*, 2002). For example, vitamin metabolites exhibit both antioxidant and pro-oxidative activity (Yeum and Russell, 2002). Further illustrating this is the observation that in general, at low ascorbate concentrations ascorbate is prone to be a pro-oxidant, yet at high concentrations it will tend to be an antioxidant.

Antioxidant micronutrients are able to exert non-antioxidant biological activities in addition to their free radical-scavenging capacity. For example, vitamin C, due to its participation in hydroxylation reactions and involvement in collagen synthesis, has been suggested to be important in the prevention of pressure sores in the elderly (Selvaag *et al.*, 2002), and vitamin E exerts regulation on cell proliferation and shows a beneficial effect in improving glucose transport and insulin sensitivity (Yu *et al.*, 1998).

The fact that there are a multitude of oxidants and antioxidants which have overlapping reactivity renders a biochemically rigorous assessment of the implications of oxidative stress difficult. Moreover, helpful as epidemiological studies can be, sometimes there is a confounding of associations with cause–

effect relationships, leading to erroneous conclusions. The results of observational studies, be these ecological or based on comparisons between individuals, might therefore be difficult to interpret because there is usually an abundance of possible confounding factors, such as diet, lifestyle and physical activity. Inter-individual variations should also be taken into account; similar mean intakes of vitamin E, for instance, do not relate to similar mean plasma alpha-tocopherol concentrations (Stahl *et al.*, 2002). Geographical issues may also be extremely relevant, as the consumption and processing of antioxidant-rich foods vary considerably from country to country (de Lorgeril *et al.*, 2002).

Even when attempts are made to carefully and rigorously control as many variables as possible in a randomised controlled trial, a statistically significant relationship between two parameters (such as a biological compound and a clinical marker of disease) does not always allow a cause–effect relationship to be elucidated. There may be several explanations for the conflicting results obtained in such trials, such as inappropriate design, lack of control of confounding factors, insufficient treatment duration, type of antioxidant used (synthetic versus natural), and the absence of evaluation of markers of oxidative stress as intermediate end-points. With respect to this latter point, it is essential to measure biomarkers of lipid peroxidation or DNA oxidation in nutritional studies (Halliwell, 2000; Mayne 2003) to confirm that antioxidant vitamins are materially able to decrease disease-related oxidative damage (McCall and Frei, 1999).

Oxidative stress and pregnancy

In the non-pregnant state endometrial stromal cells produce ROS as part of normal cellular metabolism. Antioxidant protection is provided by expression of both manganese superoxide dismutase (Mn-SOD) and copper/zinc superoxide dismutase (Cu/Zn-SOD). During formation of the maternal–fetal boundary and consequently fetal growth, O_2 tension, a function of uterine blood flow, plays an important role. Increased lipid peroxidation is a normal phenomenon of pregnancy (Hubel, 1999). The early embryo, however, is particularly vulnerable to the damaging effects that ROS can have on its DNA and proteins and therefore it is imperative that adequate antioxidant protection is provided. This protection is afforded by the embryonic supply of enzymatic antioxidant systems including Cu/Zn and Mn-SOD, catalase, GPx and peroxiredoxins (Donnay and Knoops, 2007), as well as non-enzymatic systems including vitamin E and beta-carotene (Yu, 1994), which all serve to directly protect from ROS-mediated damage (Guerin et al., 2001). Placental expression of all the major antioxidant systems, including Mn and Cu/Zn-SOD, catalase, GPx and vitamins C and E, further serves to provide

5

long-term protection from the damaging effects of locally produced and circulating ROS (Myatt and Cui, 2004).

Oxidative stress is increased as a part of normal pregnancy due to the increase in both placental and maternal metabolism. This increased metabolism is essential for the continued growth and development of the fetus, but it also leads to increased oxidative stress, which is associated with an increase in lipid peroxidation (Myatt and Cui, 2004). Early stages of placental (and embryonic) development take place in a hypoxic environment relative to the uterus (Red-Horse *et al.*, 2004); thus the placenta limits rather than facilitates O_2 supply to the fetus during organogenesis (Jauniaux *et al.*, 2003). The onset of uteroplacental blood flow at around 10 weeks of pregnancy into the intervillous space further adds to the generation of oxidative stress during normal pregnancy when the cytotrophoblast cells of the placenta come into direct contact with maternal blood. This causes the mean local O_2 pressure to rise as high as 90–100 mm Hg (Jauniaux *et al.*, 2000).

Although often considered to be harmful, the generation of all of these ROS is important in regulating placental function, including trophoblast differentiation, proliferation and vascular reactivity (Figure 1.2) (Harris *et al.*, 2008). In addition to their effects on the trophoblast cells of the placenta, ROS are important vasoactive factors which are essential for the vascular remodelling that occurs during placentation. RCS are also generated by macrophages within the placenta and decidua. Decidual macrophages are important in regulating trophoblast cell apoptosis, which is essential for the successful invasion and establishment of the placenta (Abrahams *et al.*, 2004). Decidual macrophages are also important in

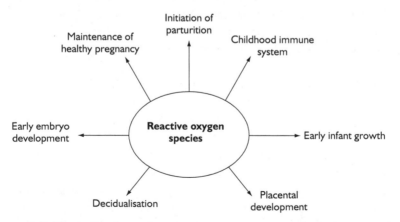

Figure 1.2 The role of reactive oxygen species in normal pregnancy and early childhood.

protecting the developing fetus from intrauterine infection via the production of oxide ions and the proinflammatory cytokine tumour necrosis factor alpha (Singh *et al.*, 2005). Increased expression of antioxidant enzymes has also been shown in sheep placentomes during early pregnancy, again indicating that this is an important protective mechanism against oxidative stress-mediated damage during placental development and early fetal growth, reinforcing the critical importance of early pregnancy for both maternal and fetal health (Garrel *et al.*, 2010).

The placenta is thus placed in the middle of the materno-fetal oxygen gradient and is exposed to major changes in O_2 concentration from conception to delivery (Jauniaux *et al.*, 2003). It has been suggested that it has a real protective role against the damaging effects of ROS (Lista *et al.*, 2010). Antioxidant regulation of ROS is crucial for successful embryogenesis and placentation to occur, as it has been shown that ROS-induced oxidative stress can alter embryonic development (Dennery, 2007).

Furthermore, by both direct and indirect mechanisms, antioxidants are able to modulate aspects of the immune system and the cytokine-mediated response to pregnancy. Under normal conditions, the placental antioxidant defence systems, which have the capacity to induce conversion of ROS to water and molecular oxygen, prevent ROS overproduction as a consequence of increased metabolic activity of placental mitochondria throughout gestation.

In summary, as described above, a level of controlled oxidative stress in pregnancy, particularly during placental development, is required. Antioxidants provide regulation to ensure that the levels of oxidative stress are not raised to harmful levels.

Oxidative stress and parturition

Parturition is an inflammatory event. During term pregnancy, a massive influx of neutrophils and monocytes into the uterine myometrium and cervix is thought to be essential for the stimulation of labour (Golightly *et al.*, 2007). An increased expression of cervical and myometrial cytokines triggers leucocyte migration at labour and these pro-inflammatory cytokines also serve to trigger myometrial contractility and cervical ripening (Romero *et al.*, 2006).

The increase in ROS concentrations around parturition seems to be involved in prostaglandin and cytokine release. Thus labour can be considered an event during which a positive feedback and a synergism of action occur between ROS and mediators of inflammation (Jenkin and Young, 2004). Therefore the increase in ROS generation during labour is a predictable event, because ROS levels are known to increase markedly, especially in conditions of high metabolic demand.

It has also been suggested that the increased expression of Mn-SOD mRNA by fetal membranes at term labour may represent a fetal mechanism of antioxidant defence during this inflammatory process (Than *et al.*, 2009). Furthermore, the marked increase in enzymatic antioxidants in the last phase of pregnancy has been suggested to serve as preparation for life in an environment rich in oxygen (O'Donovan and Fernandes, 2004). There is some controversy in studies investigating oxidative stress in women delivering vaginally versus caesarean section, with some studies reporting higher oxidative stress parameters in caesarean section in both the maternal and fetal circulation (Paamoni-Keren *et al.*, 2007; Nabhan *et al.*, 2009; Mutlu *et al.*, 2011), while others show no differences (Mehmetoglu *et al.*, 2002). Although such studies indicate that both the mother and her baby may be exposed to increased levels of oxidative stress during caesarean section, the consequences of this exposure on their health has not been examined in detail.

Antioxidants and asthma in early childhood

In the field of paediatrics, allergic disease represents the largest category of chronic disease and its prevalence has increased since the mid-20th century (Jonsson, 2010). Several recent reviews have suggested that maternal diet during pregnancy is one of the main contributing factors that may influence specific immune maturation events, allergic sensitisation and incidence of childhood allergic disease (Ramankrishnan and Huffman, 2008; Allen *et al.*, 2009; Ramakrishnan *et al.*, 2009). Airway development occurs predominantly antenatally, commencing approximately 24 days after fertilisation with the pre-acinar airway branching pattern being completed by about 17 weeks' gestation (Devereux, 2007).

There is growing recognition that, in addition to genetic factors, environmental elements during pregnancy and the first years of life are also implicated in alterations to the likelihood of disease development (Bhutta *et al.*, 2008), and particularly strong associations have been found to exist between nutritional adequacy, immune maturation and the onset of paediatric allergies (Gera *et al.*, 2009; Eilander *et al.*, 2010). More specifically, suboptimal fetal nutrient status antenatally adversely affects respiratory epithelial and mesenchymal development, resulting in suboptimal early-life airway function, which is associated with an increased risk of wheezing and asthma in later childhood (Menon *et al.*, 2007).

In 1994 Seaton *et al.* hypothesised that the increased prevalence of asthma had resulted from increasing population susceptibility rather than the air becoming more toxic or allergenic (Seaton *et al.*, 1994). This hypothesis arose from the parallel changes in the UK diet, particularly by them becoming more deficient in antioxidants, potentially resulting in a decline in lung antioxidant defences and thus increased oxidant-induced airway damage, airway inflammation and asthma (Seaton *et al.*, 1994). Associations between several antioxidant micronutrients during pregnancy with asthma, wheezing and eczema during early childhood have been shown in a recent systematic review (Patelarou *et al.*, 2011). In addition, studies have revealed that consuming a Mediterranean diet, which has a high antioxidant content (fruit, vegetables, legumes, nuts and whole-grain cereals) has been linked with a reduced likelihood of asthma, wheezing and allergic rhinitis (Bjorksten, 2008).

Antioxidant micronutrients and outcomes in pregnancy and childhood

Selenium

Selenium was first discovered in 1817 by Jöns Jacob Berzelius when investigating the chemicals responsible for outbreaks of ill health among workers in a Swedish sulphuric acid plant, which had switched from expensive, imported sulphur to a local product (Oldfield, 1987). The local product contained a contaminant which he named Selēnē, after the Greek goddess of the Moon (McKenzie *et al.*, 1998). In 1957, Klaus Schwarz proved that selenium is an essential nutrient necessary for both normal growth and reproduction through experiments demonstrating that minute amounts of selenium were protective against a form of liver necrosis in laboratory rats fed diets containing torula yeast as a protein source (Schwarz and Foltz, 1957). Today, selenium is recognised as an essential trace element of importance to human biology and health, and supplementation is now recommended as part of public health policy in geographical areas with severe selenium deficiency in soil.

Plant foods are the major dietary sources of selenium in most countries (Combs, 2001). Surveys suggest that wheat is the most efficient selenium accumulator of the common cereals, and is one of the most important selenium sources for humans (Lyons *et al.*, 2003). The content in food depends on the selenium content of the soil where plants are grown or animals are raised (Mistry *et al.*, 2012a). There appears to be no homeostatic control of selenium absorption, which is unusual in contrast, for example, to the complex regulation of iodine absorption (Kohrle, 2005). Selenium is stored in the tissues in varying density: 30% in the liver, 30% in muscle, 15% in the kidney, 10% in the plasma and the remaining 15% throughout other organs (Levander, 1987). Concentrations of free selenium are greatest in the renal cortex and pituitary gland, followed by the thyroid gland, adrenals, testes, ovaries, liver, spleen and cerebral cortex (Drasch *et al.*, 2000). The main foods

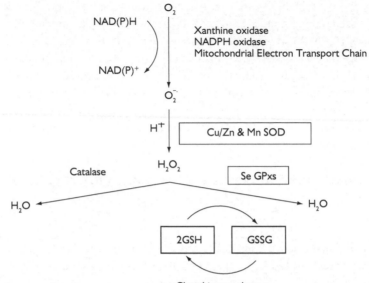

Figure 1.3 Major pathways of reactive oxygen species generation and metabolism. Superoxide can be generated by specialised enzymes, such as the xanthine or NADPH oxidases, or as a byproduct of cellular metabolism, particularly the mitochondrial electron transport chain. Superoxide dismutase (SOD) (both Cu/Zn and Mn SOD) then converts the superoxide to hydrogen peroxide (H_2O_2), which has to be rapidly removed from the system. This is generally achieved by catalase or peroxidases, such as the selenium-dependent glutathione peroxidases (GPxs) which use reduced glutathione (GSH) as the electron donor (adapted from Mistry and Williams, 2011, with permission).

that make a substantial contribution to selenium intake in northern Europe are meat, poultry, and fish (a total of about 36% in the UK) (Ministry of Agriculture, Fisheries and Food, 1997).

Of particular importance to pregnancy are the six antioxidant GPxs which play a pivotal role in reducing hydrogen peroxide (H_2O_2) and lipid peroxides to harmless products (water and alcohols; Figure 1.3), thereby dampening the propagation of damaging ROS (Brigelius-Flohe *et al.*, 2003). This pathway may also offer protection against development of several chronic diseases in which oxidative damage has been implicated, including atherosclerosis and certain cancers (Rayman, 2002; Brigelius-Flohe, 2008).

The optimal range of selenium intake to ensure biological benefit appears to be narrow and has still not been determined with certainty. Assessments of requirements, adequacy and intakes of selenium have been reviewed previously in detail (Thomson, 2004; Rayman, 2008) and summarised in Table 1.1. The USA recommended dietary allowance/UK reference nutrient intake (RDA/RNI) values have been determined from the intake believed necessary to maximise the activity of the antioxidant GPx in plasma, whereas the NR is based on selenium intake needed to achieve two-thirds of maximum activity of erythrocyte GPx (Thomson, 2004).

Normal pregnancy

During normal pregnancy, the selenium requirement is increased as a result of demands from the growing fetus (Mistry *et al.*, 2012a) and both inorganic and organic forms of selenium cross the placenta in humans and experimental animals (Shennan, 1988; Nandakumaran *et al.*, 2003). The RDA of selenium in pregnancy in the USA, calculated based on a fetal deposition of 4 μg/day throughout pregnancy, is 60 μg/day (Institute of Medicine, 2000). It has been observed that infants on average have lower selenium concentrations compared to the mother (maternal selenium: 58.4 μg/L; umbilical cord selenium: 42.1 μg/L) (Gathwala *et al.*, 2000, Mistry *et al.*, 2008), which is expected, as selenium is transported via the placenta across a concentration gradient via an anion exchange pathway, shared with sulphate (Shennan, 1988).

Numerous reports implicate selenium deficiency in several reproductive and obstetric complications including male and female fertility, miscarriage, pre-eclampsia, fetal growth restriction, preterm labour, gestational diabetes and obstetric cholestasis (intrahepatic cholestasis of pregnancy) (Mariath *et al.*, 2011; Mistry *et al.*, 2012a). Recurrent early pregnancy loss has been associated with reduced serum selenium concentrations compared to healthy controls in two observational studies from the UK (Barrington *et al.*, 1997) and Turkey (Kocak *et al.*, 1999). It has therefore been suggested that reduced selenium concentration results in reduced GPx activity, culminating in reduced antioxidant protection of biological membranes and DNA during the early stages of embryonic development (Barrington *et al.*, 1997; Zachara *et al.*, 2001). Although speculative and requiring larger placebo-controlled randomised trials, women with recurrent early pregnancy loss may benefit from optimisation of selenium status.

Table 1.1 Requirement of micronutrient intakes for selenium, copper, zinc, manganese, vitamin C, vitamin E and folate.

	Selenium (μg/d)	Copper (μg/d)	Zinc (mg/d)	Manganese (mg/d)	Vitamin C (mg/d)	Vitamin E (μg/d)	Folate (μg/d)
RDA Male adult	55	900	11	2.3	90	15	400
Female adult	55	900	8	1.8	75	15	400
Pregnancy	60	1,000	11	2	85	15	600–800
Infants 0–6 months	15	200	2	0.003	40	4	65
Infants 7 months–3 years old	20	340	3	1.2	15	6	150
Children 4–8 years old	30	440	5	1.5	25	7	200
Upper limit	400	10,000	40	11	2,000	1,000	1,000
RNI Male adult	75	1,200	9.5	1.4	40	–	400
Female adult	60	1,200	7	1.4	40	–	400
Pregnancy	75	1,500	7	–	50	–	600
Infants 0–6 months	10	200	4	–	25	–	50
Infants 7 months–3 years old	15	400	5	–	30	–	70
Children 4–8 years old	20	600	6.5	–	30	–	100
NR Male adult	40	1,350	1.4	–	–	–	400
Female adult	30	1,350	1	–	–	–	400

Table 1.1 (*continued*)

	Selenium (µg/d)	Copper (µg/d)	Zinc (mg/d)	Manganese (mg/d)	Vitamin C (mg/d)	Vitamin E (µg/d)	Folate (µg/d)
Pregnancy	–	1,150	2	–	–	–	800
Infants 0–6 months	9	370	4	–	–	–	–
Infants 7 months–3 years old	20	560	5	–	–	–	–
Children 4–8 years old	25	750	5	–	–	–	–

RDA: Recommended Dietary Allowance, USA; RNI: Reference Nutrient Intakes, UK and NR: Normative Requirement Estimate, World Health Organization.
Values taken from Institute of Medicine (2000, 2001), Department of Health (1991) and WHO/FAO/IAEA (1996).
– indicates no recommended values at present.

Pre-eclampsia

Recently, retrospective studies have demonstrated associations between low serum selenium concentrations and reduced antioxidant function of the associated antioxidant GPx enzymes in women with pre-eclampsia (defined as de novo proteinuric hypertension) (Mistry *et al.*, 2008, 2010; Maleki *et al.*, 2011; Katz *et al.*, 2012). It has been suggested that adequate selenium status is important for antioxidant defence and may be a potential factor in women at risk of pre-eclampsia; this hypothesis has been further supported by the reduced expression and activities of GPx found in maternal, fetal and placental samples taken from 25 pre-eclamptic pregnancies when compared to 27 normal controls in our recent cross-sectional retrospective study (Mistry *et al.*, 2008). Dawson *et al.* also completed a retrospective study in the USA and reported lower amniotic fluid selenium concentrations in 29 pre-eclamptics delivering between 33 and 36 weeks' gestation compared to 48 gestation-matched controls (10 ± 1 vs. 7 ± 0.7 µg/L respectively) (Dawson *et al.*, 1999). A study of data from around the world found that increasing serum/plasma selenium concentration correlated with a reduction in pre-eclampsia incidence; the authors also noted that countries with serum/plasma selenium concentration ≥ 95 µg/L (selenium sufficient) had a significant reduction in incidence (Vanderlelie and Perkins, 2011). This study also highlighted that the reduction in pre-eclampsia incidence coincided with an increase in serum/plasma selenium concentrations following government interventions to increase selenium intakes in countries such as New Zealand and Finland (Vanderlelie and Perkins, 2011), contributing to the evidence that supplementation of selenium may be beneficial in reducing oxidative stress in women at risk of pre-eclampsia.

To date there have been a limited number of small placebo-controlled randomised controlled trials on selenium supplementation, reporting lower rates of pre-eclampsia and/or pregnancy-induced hypertension in the supplemented groups (Han and Zhou, 1994; Rumiris *et al.*, 2006 Tara *et al.*, 2010a). It must be noted that none of these studies adequately addressed the role of supplementation on the incidence of pre-eclampsia. Currently the 'Selenium in Pregnancy Intervention Trial' (SPRINT) is under way in the UK, run jointly by the Universities of Surrey and Oxford. This is a small randomised controlled trial of selenium supplementation (60 µg a day). While it is not powered to demonstrate clinical benefit, it will provide insight into the impact of selenium supplements on laboratory measurements of circulating factors that are relevant to the development of pre-eclampsia. If the study is successful a much larger multicentre trial will be needed to further explore clinical benefit.

Preterm labour

Among the few studies to have investigated selenium and preterm labour (delivery < 37 weeks' gestation), Dobrzynski *et al.* reported lower maternal selenium concentrations and reduced maternal and cord plasma GPx activities in 46 women who delivered preterm compared to 42 women delivering at term (Dobrzynski *et al.*, 1998). In addition, a potential association with selenium and preterm premature (pre-labour) rupture of membranes has been highlighted through a small prospective double-blind placebo-controlled randomised controlled trial in which 166 primigravid pregnant women were randomised in the first trimester of pregnancy to receive 100 μg/day selenium or placebo until delivery (Tara *et al.*, 2010b). The supplemented group demonstrated a significant increase in the mean serum selenium concentration and a reduction in the incidence of preterm premature (pre-labour) rupture of membranes (Tara *et al.*, 2010b). Once again, reduction in oxidative stress as a result of increased selenium concentrations is likely to play an important role.

Fetal growth restriction

Fetal growth restriction or delivery of a small-for-gestational-age infant is defined as an individualised birth weight ratio below the 10th percentile (Cetin *et al.*, 2004). Correlations between selenium concentrations and fetal growth restriction are inconsistent. A retrospective study reported low placental selenium concentrations in 49 mothers affected by fetal growth restriction, compared to 36 healthy normal birth weight controls (Klapec *et al.*, 2008), whereas others have reported higher (Osada *et al.*, 2002; Zadrozna *et al.*, 2009) or unchanged concentrations (Llanos and Ronco, 2009). Another retrospective study also demonstrated that in 81 small-for-gestational-age babies, infant plasma selenium concentrations were significantly lower compared to controls (Strambi *et al.*, 2004). A retrospective study on an adolescent cohort (Baker *et al.*, 2009) found lower maternal plasma selenium concentrations in 28 mothers who delivered small-for-gestational-age babies compared to 143 healthy controls (Mistry *et al.*, 2012a). Further studies are warranted to fully investigate the potential link between selenium deficiency and fetal growth restriction.

Obstetric cholestasis

Selenium has also been associated with obstetric cholestasis (also known as intrahepatic cholestasis of pregnancy) a serious complication of pregnancy which affects approximately 4,500 women per year in the UK (Gurung *et al.*, 2009). Selenium was first linked with obstetric cholestasis in 1987 when Kauppila *et al.*

demonstrated that serum selenium concentrations were significantly lower in 12 Finnish women with obstetric cholestasis when compared to 12 normal pregnancies during the last trimester and postpartum (Kauppila *et al.*, 1987). Furthermore, they also showed GPx activities to be decreased, showing a significant positive correlation with selenium concentration (Kauppila *et al.*, 1987). Thus it has been hypothesised that inadequate antioxidant protection may lead to hepatocyte oxidative damage and reduce excretion of bile (Akerboom *et al.*, 1984). These initial results have been confirmed and extended in a study of 21 women with obstetric cholestasis in Chile, also showing that the decrease in prevalence of obstetric cholestasis in Chile during the last decade coincided with an increase in plasma selenium concentrations (Reyes *et al.*, 2000).

Gestational diabetes mellitus

Gestational diabetes mellitus, defined as a deficient insulin supply relative to the increased demands that are characteristic of pregnancy, is an increasing problem with an incidence of 7.6% (Lawrence *et al.*, 2010). Animal studies have highlighted a link between selenium and glucose metabolism (McNeill *et al.*, 1991; Becker *et al.*, 1996). Several studies from China, Kuwait, Turkey and the USA have shown a decrease in maternal plasma selenium concentrations in women with gestational diabetes mellitus (Tan *et al.*, 2001; Al-Saleh *et al.*, 2004; Hawkes *et al.*, 2004; Kilinc *et al.*, 2008). Bo *et al.* (2005) completed a retrospective study investigating selenium intakes through dietary questionnaires in 504 pregnant women (210 with hyperglycaemia and 294 healthy controls) as well as measuring serum concentrations in a second cohort (71 hyperglycaemic and 123 controls). A lower dietary intake of selenium was observed in the hyperglycaemic group, and in the second cohort selenium concentrations were significantly lower in the women who had impaired glucose tolerance; both dietary intakes and selenium concentrations were negatively associated with gestational hyperglycaemia in a multiple regression model (odds ratios 0.97 and 0.92 respectively) (Bo *et al.*, 2005).

An inverse relationship between selenium concentrations and blood glucose concentrations has also been observed (Tan *et al.*, 2001; Hawkes *et al.*, 2004; Kilinc *et al.*, 2008), but was not accompanied by changes in insulin (Hawkes *et al.*, 2004), suggesting that selenium may affect glucose metabolism downstream from insulin, or possibly through independent energy regulating pathways such as thyroid hormones (Hawkes *et al.*, 2004). This relationship is unique to pregnancy; diabetes in non-pregnant subjects is associated with higher blood selenium concentrations (Laclaustra *et al.*, 2009).

Children

Selenium deficiency has also been linked with complications in early childhood. Low selenium concentrations and GPx activities in the blood of preterm infants have been proposed to contribute to respiratory distress syndrome, retinopathy of prematurity, increased haemolysis or other prematurity-related conditions (Dobrzynski *et al.*, 1998). Several studies have observed significantly low mean plasma/serum selenium concentrations in very preterm (gestational age <32 weeks, birth weight < 1500 g) compared to healthy term infants (Mask and Lane, 1993; Sievers *et al.*, 2001; Iranpour *et al.*, 2009). Maternal plasma selenium concentrations during pregnancy are inversely associated with wheezing in children at 2 years of age (Devereux *et al.*, 2007). In addition, low selenium concentrations in umbilical cord plasma have been observed in children with wheezing compared to controls (Shaheen *et al.*, 2004; Devereux *et al.*, 2007). This has been further confirmed by measurements of selenium in nails from children at 12 years of age; those children with the highest quintile of nail selenium concentrations presented a five-fold decrease in the prevalence ratio of asthma, whereas those in the lowest selenium quintile presented with an almost 2.5-fold increase (Carneiro *et al.*, 2011). Lower plasma selenium concentrations have also been found in children at 12 years of age with childhood asthma compared to healthy age-matched controls (Kocyigit *et al.*, 2004).

Zinc

Zinc is an essential constituent of over 200 metalloenzymes participating in carbohydrate and protein metabolism, nucleic acid synthesis and antioxidant functions (through Cu/Zn-SOD; Figure 1.3) (Izquierdo Alvarez *et al.*, 2007). In addition, zinc is required for cellular division and differentiation, making it essential for successful embryogenesis. Total body zinc content is estimated to be 2 g and plasma zinc has a rapid turnover, representing approximately 0.1% body zinc content (WHO/FAO/IAEA, 1996). The body does not store zinc, thus a constant dietary intake is essential. The main dietary sources of zinc include meat, seafood, pulses, legumes and whole grain cereals (FAO/WHO, 2004). It has been highlighted that in many parts of the world, including the Latin American countries, 40% of the population is at risk for inadequate zinc intake (Brown *et al.*, 2004). Zinc deficiency has increased over the last decade due to a trend towards zinc-poor diets, based on processed foods and soy-based substitutes, as well as food grown in zinc-poor soil (Tahan and Karakukcu, 2006); current recommended intakes are shown in Table 1.1. In addition, mean plasma zinc concentrations are lower in African-American compared to Caucasian women, and multiparous compared to nulliparous women (Neggers *et al.*, 1996).

17

During pregnancy, zinc assists fetal brain development. It has been estimated that the total amount of zinc retained during pregnancy is ~100 mg (Swanson and King, 1987). The requirement of zinc during the third trimester is approximately twice as high as that of non-pregnant women (WHO/FAO/IAEA, 1996). Plasma zinc concentrations decline as pregnancy progresses and increase towards delivery (Izquierdo Alvarez *et al.*, 2007; Liu *et al.*, 2010). Alteration in zinc homeostasis may have devastating effects on pregnancy outcome, including prolonged labour, fetal growth restriction, or embryonic or fetal death (King, 2000; Simpson *et al.*, 2011).

Many zinc supplementation studies have been conducted in developing countries where the incidence of zinc deficiency is high, and these women are often selected as they are less well-nourished or have low plasma zinc levels (Goldenberg *et al.*, 1995; Black, 2001). Benefits of supplementation include reduced incidence of pregnancy-induced hypertension, low birth weight (Goldenberg *et al.*, 1995) and preterm birth (Mahomed *et al.*, 2007). Such studies suggest benefits of zinc supplementation in developing countries where zinc deficiency is likely, although for developed countries there is conflicting data as to the benefits (Garg *et al.*, 1993; Caulfield *et al.*, 1999; Osendarp *et al.*, 2000). However, zinc-containing multivitamins have been shown to reduce preterm birth incidence in an intervention study in the USA (Goldenberg *et al.*, 1995). Moreover, a US study in a cohort of low-income urban girls and women observed a low intake of zinc early in pregnancy was associated with a greater than three-fold increased risk of preterm birth preceded by premature rupture of membranes, after controlling for other known risks (OR 3.5, 95% CI 1.0–11.5) (Scholl *et al.*, 1993).

Pre-eclampsia

Zinc deficiency has been associated with pre-eclampsia since the 1980s (Kiilholma *et al.*, 1984). Placental zinc concentration has been shown to be lower in pre-eclampsia in a cross-sectional retrospective study of 11 pre-eclamptic and 15 healthy pregnancies with placental zinc values positively correlating with birth weight (Diaz *et al.*, 2002). More recently lower serum concentrations of zinc have been associated with pre-eclampsia in two relatively small retrospective studies from Turkey (Kumru *et al.*, 2003; Kolusari *et al.*, 2008). The authors suggested that this may be useful for early diagnosis, as lower plasma zinc concentrations have been associated with increased lipid peroxidation in rat studies (Yousef *et al.*, 2002). Moreover, a retrospective study in India reported reduced serum zinc concentrations in mild and severe pre-eclamptic mothers compared to controls; the authors suggested that the reduction may not only affect antioxidant protection, but could also contribute to a rise in blood pressure (Jain *et al.*, 2010). The lower serum zinc concentrations in mothers who develop pre-eclampsia have been suggested to at least be partly due to reduced oestrogen and zinc binding-protein levels (Bassiouni *et al.*, 1979).

Zinc is transported across the placenta via active transport from the mother to the fetus. The fetus has notably higher zinc concentrations compared to the mother, even in cases of pre-eclampsia (Kiilholma *et al.*, 1984) and higher fetal arterial and venous blood zinc concentrations in severe pre-eclampsia (Katz *et al.*, 2012), indicating that the fetus itself can maintain adequate zinc homeostasis. In contrast, two case-control studies in Iran (Bahadoran *et al.*, 2010) and Israel (Katz *et al.*, 2012), showed no differences in third trimester maternal zinc concentrations between pre-eclampsia and control women, although Bahadoran *et al.* (2010) did observe an association between lower zinc concentrations and severity of pre-eclampsia, suggesting that zinc status may still be a useful clinical marker for severity. It must be noted that, as with all these micronutrients, the concentration early in pregnancy in relation to the development of pregnancy complications remains to be established.

Allergies

As with some of the other antioxidant micronutrients, maternal zinc intake during pregnancy could also influence early life immune responses to allergens, which has been shown using human and murine experimental models (Prasad, 2000; Richter *et al.*, 2003). Animal studies report that zinc deficiency results in impaired lung maturation, with the lungs of pups born to zinc-deficient rats being smaller, having reduced DNA levels, and smaller lumina of alveolar ducts (Vojnik and Hurley, 1977). Maternal zinc intake during pregnancy has been shown to be negatively associated with childhood asthma status at 5 years of age in a Scottish study (Devereux *et al.*, 2006). A similar observation has been reported in a large US cohort study (Project Viva), with reduced maternal zinc intake being associated with increased likelihood of childhood wheezing and asthma at 2 years of age (Litonjua *et al.*, 2006). Also, a zinc-dependent metalloprotease (ADAM33) has been identified as a putative asthma susceptibility gene (Van Eerdewegh *et al.*, 2002) and has been shown to be expressed in embryonic lungs, increasing with gestation (Haitchi *et al.*, 2005). Thus the associations demonstrated between maternal zinc intake and childhood asthma may potentially be mediated through ADAM33 by zinc modulating ADAM33 activity, thus influencing lung development (Devereux *et al.*, 2006; Devereux, 2007).

Children

Infants and young children are particularly vulnerable to zinc deficiency because of the higher zinc requirement for rapid growth, and growth-limiting zinc deficiency can exist in otherwise healthy infants (Solomons, 1988). Lower zinc concentrations in children suffering from wheezing and asthma have been observed using both nail (Carneiro *et al.*, 2011) and hair (Tahan and Karakukcu, 2006) samples compared to controls. Bahl *et al.*'s observational study provide some evidence of higher risks of infectious diseases in children with low plasma zinc concentrations (Bahl *et al.*, 1998). Zinc deficiency is thought to increase infections of the respiratory tract, possibly through defects in T-cell immunity, as zinc regulates the balance between CD4+ and CD8+ T-cells and between Th1 and Th2 subsets (Soutar *et al.*, 1997; Prasad, 2000). It has been suggested that zinc deficiency causes a shift towards a Th2-dependent response, which possibly promotes the production of inflammatory cytokines and mucosal IgE in asthma (Zalewski, 1996). This deficiency may also increase eicosanoid production, which could lead to promoting airway inflammation (Tahan and Karakukcu, 2006). Zinc supplementation in populations with low zinc intake, during pregnancy and for vulnerable infants may be beneficial, as it has been suggested that physiological supplementation of zinc for 1–2 months restores immune responses and reduces the incidence of infection (Ferencik and Ebringer, 2003).

Manganese

Manganese is a free element in nature (often in combination with iron) and is abundantly present in the environment. Manganese(II) ions function as cofactors for a number of enzymes; the element is thus a required trace mineral for all known living organisms. About 80% of the known world manganese resources are found in South Africa; other important manganese deposits are in Ukraine, Australia, India, China, Gabon and Brazil (Corathers, 2009). While essential to human health, overexposure to manganese is associated with devastating irreversible neurological impairment (Aschner *et al.*, 2009).

The classes of enzymes that have manganese cofactors are very broad, and include oxidoreductases, transferases, hydrolases, lyases, isomerases, ligases, lectins and integrins. One of the most well-known manganese enzymes is the antioxidant Mn-SOD (Figure 1.3) which may protect the placenta from oxidative stress by detoxifying superoxide anions (Ademuyiwa *et al.*, 2007). The human body contains about 12 mg of manganese, which is stored mainly in the bones; in the tissue it is mostly concentrated in the liver and kidneys (Emsley, 2001).

In the human brain, manganese is bound to manganese metalloproteins, most notably glutamine synthetase in astrocytes (Takeda, 2003). Current requirements for manganese, although less studied compared to other micronutrients, are shown in Table 1.1.

Little is known about the effects of deficiency or excess of manganese on the developing human fetus or pregnancy outcome (Wood, 2009). This is further hampered by the fact that at present sensitive biomarkers of manganese exposure and nutritional status are not available (Wood, 2009). Manganese, upon absorption, is primarily sequestered in tissue and intracellular compartments and thus blood manganese concentrations do not always provide a good estimate of manganese levels in targeted tissues (Zheng *et al.*, 2011).

In various animal studies, Mn-SOD has been shown to play a contributing role in hypertension. Mice lacking Mn-SOD die of cardiomyopathy within 10 days of birth and mice lacking one of the alleles (Mn-SOD$^{+/-}$ mice) develop hypertension (Rodriguez-Iturbe *et al.*, 2007). In addition, overexpression of Mn-SOD improves endothelial function, as well as reducing hypertension and oxidative stress in angiotensin II-induced hypertensive mice (Dikalova *et al.*, 2010). These studies highlight the importance of manganese in relation to Mn-SOD in regulating mitochondrial O_2 production and endothelial function.

Fetal growth restriction

Circulating whole blood manganese concentrations have been shown to be lower in women with fetal growth restriction compared to healthy controls indicating that this micronutrient may be important in maintaining fetal growth (Vigeh *et al.*, 2008). This study also found that manganese concentrations were higher in umbilical samples from fetal growth restriction cases compared to controls, suggesting that manganese contributes different effects on birth weight in healthy mothers (Vigeh *et al.*, 2008). Zota *et al.*'s (2009) retrospective study in the USA reported a non-linear relationship between manganese concentrations and birth weights in a cohort of 470 full term (delivered at > 37 weeks' gestation) infants further indicating the potential effect on fetal growth. A small retrospective study of African-American mothers reported reduced umbilical cord whole blood manganese concentrations in neonates born to mothers with pre-eclampsia compared to controls (Jones *et al.*, 2010). Furthermore, this study found that, like other micronutrients, umbilical cord blood from smoking mothers had reduced manganese concentrations (Jones *et al.*, 2010). Increased fetal membrane Mn-SOD mRNA expression has also been demonstrated in women with preterm labour (Than *et al.*, 2009). Manganese is one of the least studied micronutrients and at present no supplementation trial has been published, which may reflect the lack of data on manganese concentrations in pregnancy.

Children

Manganese deficiency has also been linked with an increased risk of childhood asthma. A case-control study from Turkey reported significantly lower plasma manganese concentrations in children (aged 2–13 years) suffering from asthma compared to age-matched controls (Kocyigit *et al.*, 2004). Only one other study has investigated manganese concentrations in an adult population, showing that dietary manganese intake was inversely related to bronchial activity and the lowest intake of manganese (and vitamin C) was associated with a five-fold increase in risk of bronchial reactivity (Soutar *et al.*, 1997). At present, an explanation for this association is unclear, but it can be speculated that, as with the other antioxidant micronutrients, reducing levels of oxidative stress may play an important contributory factor. Future studies are required to elucidate potential factors as well as whether manganese deficiency during pregnancy has any influence on the prevalence of childhood wheezing and asthma.

Copper

Copper is an essential trace element and a cofactor for a number of enzymes involved in metabolic reactions, angiogenesis, oxygen transport and antioxidant protection, including catalase, superoxide dismutase (Figure 1.3) and cytochrome oxidase (Gambling *et al.*, 2008). During pregnancy, plasma copper concentrations significantly increase from the first to the third trimester, returning to normal non-pregnant values after delivery (Izquierdo Alvarez *et al.*, 2007; Liu *et al.*, 2010). The increase in copper with progression of pregnancy could be partly related to synthesis of ceruloplasmin, a major copper binding protein, due to altered levels of oestrogen (Liu *et al.*, 2010). Approximately 96% of plasma copper is strongly bound to ceruloplasmin, a protein with antioxidant ferroxidase properties (Shakour-Shahabi *et al.*, 2010). The dietary intake of copper in women aged 19–24 years is generally below the recommended levels (Table 1.1) (Institute of Medcine, 2001), which may cause problems during pregnancy when requirements increase (McArdle *et al.*, 2008).

Copper is essential for embryonic development (Kambe *et al.*, 2008). Maternal dietary deficiency can result in both short-term consequences (including early embryonic death and gross structural abnormalities) and long-term consequences, such as increased risk of cardiovascular disease risk and reduced fertilisation rates

(Keen *et al.*, 2003; Gambling *et al.*, 2008); current recommendations on intakes are summarised in Table 1.1.

Normal pregnancy

Cu/Zn-SOD is an important antioxidant known to be expressed in both maternal and fetal tissues (Ali Akbar *et al.*, 1998). Copper concentration has been shown to be higher in maternal plasma than in umbilical cord plasma (Krachler *et al.*, 1999). It has been suggested that the placenta acts as a blockade in the transfer of copper from the mother to the fetus (Krachler *et al.*, 1999; Rossipal *et al.*, 2000). An observational Turkish study on 61 placentae from healthy pregnancies between 37 and 40 weeks' gestation found that copper concentrations positively correlated with neonatal weight; the authors suggested that copper may have interactive connections in human placenta (Ozdemir *et al.*, 2009), and this requires further studies to fully elucidate its role. It is known that copper is transferred across the placenta via high-affinity carriers (Ctr1) which have been shown to be expressed early in pregnancy. It is also thought that placental copper transport is related to iron transport, but the mechanism is unknown (McArdle *et al.*, 2008).

Pre-eclampsia

Retrospective studies have shown elevation of maternal serum copper levels in pre-eclampsia after clinical onset of the disease (Serdar *et al.*, 2006; Kolusari *et al.*, 2008; Katz *et al.*, 2012). It is thought that as copper is a redox-active transition metal and can participate in single electron reactions and catalyse the formation of free radicals, including undesirable hydroxyl radicals, it could contribute to the oxidative stress which is characteristic of pre-eclampsia (Serdar *et al.*, 2006). This illustrates that copper itself appears to act as a pro-oxidant, but when associated in Cu/Zn-SOD it functions as an antioxidant. Furthermore, studies have reported increased levels of serum concentrations and placental expression of ceruloplasmin in women with pre-eclampsia; this is positively correlated with serum malondialdehyde, indicating an increased production of this antioxidant protein as an adaptation to increased lipid peroxidation (Aksoy *et al.*, 2003; Serdar *et al.*, 2006; Guller *et al.*, 2008). These abnormal levels of copper may also interfere with the ascorbic acid/copper balance in pre-eclampsia, thus compromising normal nitric oxide release (Gandley *et al.*, 2005). However, it must be remembered that concentrations early in pregnancy have yet to be determined and data on copper status in normal human pregnancies are sparse. This is further hampered by the fact that at present there is no reliable biomarker for copper status, so whether deficiency is a significant public health problem remains unclear (Arredondo and Nunez, 2005).

Children

Copper nutrition in infants and children is not usually considered as an area for concern unless the infant is born prematurely. Umbilical cord blood copper (Perveen *et al.*, 2002) and ceruloplasmin concentrations have been reported to be lower in preterm infants compared to full-term newborns, with a consistent rise in concentrations as gestation increases from weeks 26 to 42 (Galinier *et al.*, 2005). Lower copper concentrations and Cu/Zn-SOD activities have been reported in both preterm and fetal growth restricted placentae (Sutton *et al.*, 1985; Zadrozna *et al.*, 2009). A study that followed preterm children up to 100 days of life noted that plasma copper concentrations and erythrocyte SOD levels were constantly and significantly lower in preterm compared to term children at all time points measured (Nassi *et al.*, 2009). Newborns often exhibit reduced activities of antioxidant enzymes, which may be associated with a deficiency of their constitutive elements, the availability of which appears to be less sufficient the lower the gestational age and/or birthweight <1000 g (Nassi *et al.*, 2009).

Vitamin C and E

Vitamin C (ascorbic acid and dihydroascorbic acid) is an essential water-soluble vitamin found widely in fruit and vegetables; it has important roles in collagen synthesis, wound healing and prevention of anaemia, and as an antioxidant as it can quench a variety of reactive oxygen species and reactive nitrogen species in aqueous environments (Buettner, 1993). Vitamin C is commonly included in low doses (< 200 mg/day) within multivitamin preparations for pregnancy, but has also been given in higher doses (up to 1000 mg/day) as a supplement, alone or in combination with vitamin E (Poston *et al.*, 2011). Smoking has been shown to increase oxidative stress and metabolic turnover of vitamin C; thus the requirement for smokers is increased by 35 mg/day (Institute of Medicine, 2000).

Vitamin E (alpha-tocopherol) is a lipid-soluble vitamin acting with the lipid membrane and with synergistic interactions with vitamin C (Packer *et al.*, 1979). Vitamin E functions primarily as a chain-breaking antioxidant that prevents propagation of lipid peroxidation, including inhibition of NAD(P)H oxidase activation and the inflammatory response (Chappell *et al.*, 1999; Poston *et al.*, 2011).

Pre-eclampsia

Considerable interest exists regarding prevention of maternal and perinatal morbidity with vitamins C and E given the abnormally low plasma vitamin C and E concentrations reported in women with pre-eclampsia. However, the most recent meta-analysis of ten trials (6,533 women) of antioxidant supplementation (including vitamin C and E but also other supplements such as lycopene) showed no difference in the relative risk (RR) of pre-eclampsia (RR 0.73, 95% CI 0.51–1.06), preterm birth (before 37 weeks) (RR 1.10, 95% CI 0.99–1.22), small-for-gestational-age infants (RR 0.83, 95% CI 0.62–1.11) or any baby death (RR 1.12, 95% CI 0.81–1.53) (Rumbold *et al.*, 2008). Considerable heterogeneity between the trials was seen, reflecting the different supplements studied, the varying risk criteria used for entry into the studies, and the study sizes. Two subsequent multicentre double-blind randomised trials of a combination of vitamin C and E (Roberts *et al.*, 2010; Xu *et al.*, 2010) also found that supplementation did not reduce the rate of pre-eclampsia or gestational hypertension and, similar to the 'Vitamins In Pre-eclampsia trial' (Poston *et al.*, 2006), increased the risk of fetal loss or perinatal death and preterm prelabour rupture of membranes. Another multicentre placebo-controlled trial of vitamin C and E in women with type 1 diabetes in pregnancy (DAPIT) also reported no differences in the rates of pre-eclampsia between supplemented or placebo groups (McCance *et al.*, 2010).

Further investigations are required, as the concentrations of these vitamins remain significantly reduced in women with pre-eclampsia, but in the absence of further evidence routine supplementation with higher dose vitamin C and E is not recommended as they can be potentially dangerous in high concentrations. Whether these trials suggest that oxidative stress is not part of the pathogenesis of pre-eclampsia, or that the dose, timing of supplementation and/or choice of antioxidant prophylaxis is inappropriate, is unknown.

Children

Epidemiological data of children and adults have reported associations between asthma and reduced intake and blood levels of dietary nutrients such as antioxidant vitamins (vitamin C and E) (Bodner *et al.*, 1999; Hijazi *et al.*, 2000; Gilliland *et al.*, 2003; Harik-Khan *et al.*, 2004). Several studies have reported reduced maternal vitamin E concentration associated with increased incidence of wheezing and asthma in children at both 2 and 5 years of age (Devereux *et al.*, 2006; Litonjua *et al.*, 2006; De Luca *et al.*, 2010). However, supplementation with vitamin E has not been consistently associated with improved asthma outcomes (Fogarty *et al.*, 2003; Pearson *et al.*, 2004; Ram *et al.*, 2004; Greenough *et al.*, 2012). It is thought that these inconsistencies may be due to dietary antioxidants which primarily influence the development of asthma during the critical period early in life (Devereux *et al.*, 2006).

Folate

Folic acid, the synthetic form of folate, is a micronutrient found in green leafy vegetables, dairy products, poultry and meat, seafood, fruits and cereal products (Tamura and Picciano, 2006). Folate is involved in a number of important functions within the body, including synthesis of proteins required for DNA and RNA and as an essential substrate for a range of enzymatic reactions needed for amino acid synthesis and vitamin metabolism; as such, folate is essential for cell multiplication and differentiation processes (Friso and Choi, 2002; Fox and Stover, 2008). Although not a classical antioxidant, studies have highlighted the potential antioxidant capacity of folate (Joshi *et al.*, 2001) and thus it is considered in this chapter.

Normal pregnancy

It is well established that there is an increased demand for folate associated with pregnancy, mainly caused by the growth of the fetus and its placenta (Jauniaux *et al.*, 2007). Current knowledge suggests that nutrient transfer via the placenta from the maternal circulating pool must in most cases supply the demands of fetoplacental growth, but information on human placental transfer is limited (Jauniaux *et al.*, 2007). Several studies have shown that folate levels drop slightly as pregnancy progresses (Qvist *et al.*, 1986; Megahed and Taher, 2004) and have been shown to remain decreased up to six weeks after delivery (Cikot *et al.*, 2001).

Neural tube defects

The importance of folate in the prevention of neural tube defects has long been known (MRC, 1991). However, folate may also have important roles in other physiological pathways needed for successful pregnancy, including angiogenesis and vasculogenesis (Sasaki *et al.*, 2003), methylation of the harmful, sulphur-containing homocysteine (Ciaccio *et al.*, 2008), antioxidant protection (Joshi *et al.*, 2001; Gori and Munzel, 2011) and endothelial-dependent vascular relaxation (Griffith *et al.*, 2005). These processes are essential for the establishment of fetoplacental circulation, enabling successful pregnancy outcome. We have recently shown folic acid to possibly play a direct role in extravillous trophoblast invasion, angiogenesis and secretion of matrix metalloproteinase (Williams *et al.*, 2011).

Interest in folic acid supplementation followed observational studies linking decreased red blood cell folate (Smithells *et al.*, 1976) and lower maternal dietary folate intake (Bower and Stanley, 1989) with neural tube defects. A number of randomised controlled trials of periconceptional supplementation with a variety of multivitamins followed (MRC, 1991). Due to its roles in DNA synthesis, repair and methylation, folate intake is increased five- to tenfold during pregnancy, indicating that an adequate supply of folate is important in the implantation and development of both the placenta and fetus (Williams *et al.*, 2011). Folate supplementation is now recommended peri-conceptually at a dose of 400 µg/day to prevent neural tube defects (MRC, 1991). However, few studies have examined how extending folic acid supplementation may also benefit later stages of pregnancy.

Meta-analyses have reported that maternal folic acid supplementation is also associated with decreased risk of other congenital anomalies, including cardiovascular defects (OR 0.61, 95% CI 0.40–0.92) and limb defects (OR 0.57, 95% CI 0.38–0.85) (Goh *et al.*, 2006) and some paediatric cancers including leukaemia, paediatric brain tumours and neuroblastoma (Goh *et al.*, 2007). Concern has been expressed over an increase in twin births associated with periconceptional folic acid supplementation. The two largest studies have given discrepant findings, with one showing no association (OR 0.91, 95% CI 0.82–1.00) (Li *et al.*, 2003) and the other showing tentative evidence of a possible relationship (adjusted OR 1.26, 95% CI 0.91–1.73) (Vollset *et al.*, 2005).

Pre-eclampsia

Folate deficiency is associated with recurrent miscarriage, placental abruption, fetal growth restriction and pre-eclampsia (Kupferminc *et al.*, 1999). Studies have shown supplementation with multivitamins containing folic acid to reduce the occurrence of pre-eclampsia (Bodnar *et al.*, 2006; Wen *et al.*, 2008). The exact mechanism by which folic acid supplementation leads to this reduction in pre-eclampsia remains to be elucidated; however, a number of mechanisms have been suggested, including improvement of endothelial function, direct or indirect lowering of blood homocysteine, or via antioxidant mechanisms through increasing nitric oxide bioavailability or contributing to reducing ROS-induced endothelial dysfunction (Ray and Laskin, 1999; Joshi *et al.*, 2001). There is evidence to indicate that folic acid supplementation in pregnancy reduces the risk of pre-eclampsia (Ray and Laskin, 1999; Sanchez *et al.*, 2001). However, there are also a number of contradictory studies in which no association has been found between folate deficiency and pre-eclampsia (Rajkovic *et al.*, 1997; Powers *et al.*, 1998; Makedos *et al.*, 2007; Mistry *et al.*, 2011). Nor was folic acid supplementation associated with a reduction of pre-eclampsia (Ray and Mamdani, 2002). Furthermore, increasing parity has been shown to reduce folate concentrations, especially in mothers who have previously had pre-eclampsia (Mistry *et al.*, 2011); this area requires further investigation. This raises the question of whether the standard recommended folic acid supplementation of 400 µg/day may be of too low a dose to be effective in pre-eclampsia.

A systematic review estimated the use of periconceptional folic acid in the UK to be 21–48%, with awareness of the health prevention message at 66–81% (Stockley and Lund, 2008), rates similar to those in Europe, the USA and Australasia. The authors highlighted a package of interventions relevant to increasing uptake, particularly for those groups with lowest use (lower income and young women), but acknowledge the considerable difficulties of any approach, particularly in the light of the significant unplanned pregnancy rate in the UK. The NICE guideline 'Antenatal care: routine care for the healthy pregnant woman' advises folic acid supplementation at a dose of 400 µg/day before conception and up to 12 weeks' gestation (NICE, 2008).

Multivitamin and multinutrient supplementation

There has been much interest in the potential benefits of antioxidant multivitamin or multinutrient supplementation, but the substantial majority of these trials have been undertaken in resource-limited countries with undernourished populations (Haider *et al.*, 2011). Although the practice of multivitamin supplementation in pregnancy is widespread among women in developed countries, contemporaneous evidence for benefit is sparse. It has been suggested that there is a link between maternal diet during pregnancy, preterm birth and cardiovascular disease in offspring at least 50 years after their births (Barker, 1999, Klebanoff *et al.*, 1999), but at present it remains unknown whether women who use supplements before and during pregnancy have children with fewer chronic diseases at middle age.

Accurate assessment of the prevalence of multivitamin and/or folic acid use is fraught with difficulties. The frequent use of case-control studies increases the likelihood of recall bias and the retrospective recollection of multivitamin use in early pregnancy may also lead to inaccuracies. Many preparations are available over the counter and thus use cannot easily be cross-referenced with prescription databases. The definition of multivitamin use varies, with many studies concentrating on folic acid as the main constituent. A small double-blind placebo-randomised control trial of daily antioxidant supplementation (including vitamin C and E, folic acid, copper, selenium, zinc and manganese) in pregnant women presenting with low antioxidant status at 8–12 weeks' gestation reported significant reductions in pre-eclampsia rates in the supplementation group compared to the control group (Rumiris *et al.*, 2006). The authors also commented on increased perinatal outcomes, with a reduced number of fetal growth restricted fetuses (Rumiris *et al.*, 2006). Although these results are positive, caution must be exercised, as the numbers used in this study were low and the study was probably underpowered; this is further highlighted by a Cochrane review of antioxidant trials (mainly with vitamin C and E, but also including other antioxidants) that reported no significant benefit of supplementation in pregnancy in relation to relative risk of pre-eclampsia, preterm birth or fetal growth restriction (Rumbold *et al.*, 2008).

Conclusions

Micronutrient status is increasingly recognised to play an important role in the health and wellbeing of pregnant women and in early childhood. Increased knowledge about the importance of these specific antioxidant micronutrients and the crucial part that they have in maintaining successful pregnancy and determining both the long- and short-term health of both mother and baby needs to be addressed and made a key focus for future health strategies in improving pregnancy outcomes. The importance of meeting and maintaining the desirable intakes of these vitamins and micronutrients is essential to sustain a balance between antioxidants and pro-oxidants. This is particularly important with regard to pre-eclampsia and fetal growth restriction during pregnancy and also for childhood asthma, where oxidative stress is an essential component of the aetiology of these conditions, and so these specific antioxidant micronutrient deficiencies may play a contributing role. Micronutrient deficiencies during pregnancy can undoubtedly have profound influences on the health of both the mother and her child; however, conflicting evidence hinders the development of robust public health guidance.

Only by fully understanding the requirements for micronutrients during pregnancy will we be able to evaluate the potential use of these dietary antioxidant supplements as a way of preventing pathological pregnancy outcomes. At present, there is a need for adequately powered, randomised controlled trials, including long follow-up periods to elucidate causality, as well as the best formulation, dose, duration and period of supplementation during pregnancy. Furthermore, the influences of these trials on the health of the child both early and later in life must also be considered. However, it must also be remembered that these antioxidant and other micronutrients can be obtained via a healthy diet, thereby negating the need for supplementation. Future strategies focusing on providing nutritional guidance specifically to pregnant women will be pivotal in helping to ensure optimal health of both mother and baby.

References

Abrahams, V. M., Kim, Y. M., Straszewski, S. L., Romero, R. and Mor, G. (2004) Macrophages and apoptotic cell clearance during pregnancy. *American Journal of Reproductive Immunology*, **51**, 275–82.

Ademuyiwa, O., Odusoga, O. L., Adebawo, O. O. and Ugbaja, R. N. (2007) Endogenous antioxidant defences in plasma and erythrocytes of pregnant women during different trimesters of pregnancy. *Acta Obstetricia et Gynecologica Scandinavica*, 86(10), 1175–82.

Agarwal, A., Gupta, S., Sekhon, L. and Shah, R. (2008) Redox considerations in female reproductive function and assisted reproduction: from molecular mechanisms to health implications. *Antioxidants & Redox Signaling*, **10**, 1375–403.

Akerboom, T.P., Bilzer, M. and Sies, H. (1984) Relation between glutathione redox changes and biliary excretion of taurocholate in perfused rat liver. *Journal of Biological Chemistry*, **259**, 5838–43.

Aksoy, H., Taysi, S., Altinkaynak, K., Bakan, E., Bakan, N. and Kumtepe, Y. (2003) Antioxidant potential and transferrin, ceruloplasmin, and lipid peroxidation levels in women with preeclampsia. *Journal of Investigative Medicine*, **51**, 284–7.

Al-Saleh, E., Nandakumaran, M., Al-Shammari, M., Al-Falah, F. and Al-Harouny, A. (2004) Assessment of maternal-fetal status of some essential trace elements in pregnant women in late gestation: relationship with birth weight and placental weight. *Journal of Maternal and Fetal Neonatal Medicine*, **16**, 9–14.

Ali Akbar, S., Nicolaides, K. H. and Brown, P. R. (1998) Measurement of Cu/Zn SOD in placenta, cultured cells, various fetal tissues, decidua and semen by ELISA. *Journal of Obstetrics and Gynaecology*, **18**, 331–5.

Allen, L. H., Peerson, J, M. and Olney, D. K. (2009) Provision of multiple rather than two or fewer micronutrients more effectively improves growth and other outcomes in micronutrient-deficient children and adults. *Journal of Nutrition*, **139**, 1022–30.

Arredondo, M. and Nunez, M. T. (2005) Iron and copper metabolism. *Molecular Aspects of Medicine*, **26**, 313–27.

Aschner, M., Erikson, K. M., Herrero Hernandez, E. and Tjalkens, R. (2009) Manganese and its role in Parkinson's disease: from transport to neuropathology. *Neuromolecular Medicine*, **11**, 252–66.

Bahadoran, P., Zendehdel, M., Movahedian, A. and Zahraee, R. H. (2010) The relationship between serum zinc level and preeclampsia. *Iranian Journal of Nursing and Midwifery Research*, **15**, 120–4.

Bahl, R., Bhandari, N., Hambidge, K. M. and Bhan, M. K. (1998) Plasma zinc as a predictor of diarrheal and respiratory morbidity in children in an urban slum setting. *American Journal of Clinical Nutrition*, **68**, 414S–417S.

Baker, P. N., Wheeler, S. J., Sanders, T. A., Thomas, J. E., Hutchinson, C. J., Clarke, K. *et al.* (2009) A prospective study of micronutrient status in adolescent pregnancy. *American Journal of Clinical Nutrition*, **89**, 1114–24.

Barker, D. J. (1999) Fetal origins of cardiovascular disease. *Annals of Medicine*, **31**(Suppl. 1), 3–6.

Barrington, J. W., Taylor, M., Smith, S. and Bowen-Simpkins, P. (1997) Selenium and recurrent miscarriage. *Journal of Obstetrics and Gynaecology*, **17**, 199–200.

Bassiouni, B. A., Foda, A. I. and Rafei, A. A. (1979) Maternal and fetal plasma zinc in pre-eclampsia. *European Journal of Obstetrics & Gynecology and Reproductive Biology*, **9**, 75–80.

Becker, D. J., Reul, B., Ozcelikay, A. T., Buchet, J. P., Henquin, J. C. and Brichard, S. M. (1996) Oral selenate improves glucose homeostasis and partly reverses abnormal expression of liver glycolytic and gluconeogenic enzymes in diabetic rats. *Diabetologia*, **39**, 3–11.

Bhutta, Z. A., Ahmed, T., Black, R. E., Cousens, S., Dewey, K., Giugliani, E. *et al.* (2008) What works? Interventions for maternal and child undernutrition and survival. *Lancet*, **371**, 417–40.

Bjorksten, B. (2008) Environmental influences on the development of the immune system: consequences for disease outcome. *Nestlé Nutrition Workshop Series. Pediatric Program*, **61**, 243–54.

Black, R. E. (2001) Micronutrients in pregnancy. *British Journal of Nutrition*, **85**(Suppl. 2), S193–7.

Bo, S., Lezo, A., Menato, G., Gallo, M. L., Bardelli, C., Signorile, A. *et al.* (2005) Gestational hyperglycemia, zinc, selenium, and antioxidant vitamins. *Nutrition*, **21**, 186–91.

Bodnar, L. M., Tang, G., Ness, R. B., Harger, G. and Roberts, J. M. (2006) Periconceptional multivitamin use reduces the risk of preeclampsia. *American Journal of Epidemiology*, **164**, 470–7.

Bodner, C., Godden, D., Brown, K., Little, J., Ross, S. and Seaton, A. (1999) Antioxidant intake and adult-onset wheeze: a case-control study. Aberdeen WHEASE Study Group. *European Respiratory Journal*, **13**, 22–30.

Bower, C. and Stanley, F. J. (1989) Dietary folate as a risk factor for neural-tube defects: evidence from a case-control study in Western Australia. *Medical Journal of Australia*, **150**, 613–19.

Brigelius-Flohe, R. (2008) Selenium compounds and selenoproteins in cancer. *Chemistry and Biodiversity*, **5**, 389–95.

Brigelius-Flohe, R., Banning, A. and Schnurr, K. (2003) Selenium-dependent enzymes in endothelial cell function. *Antioxidants & Redox Signaling*, **5**, 205–15.

Brown, K. H., Rivera, J. A., Bhutta, Z., Gibson, R. S., King, J. C., Lonnerdal, B. *et al.* (2004) International Zinc Nutrition Consultative Group (IZiNCG) technical document #1. Assessment of the risk of zinc deficiency in populations and options for its control. *Food and Nutrition Bulletin*, **25**, S99–203.

Buettner, G. R. (1993) The pecking order of free radicals and antioxidants: lipid peroxidation, alpha-tocopherol, and ascorbate. *Archives of Biochemistry and Biophysics*, **300**, 535–43.

Carneiro, M. F., Rhoden, C. R., Amantea, S. L. and Barbosa, F., Jr (2011) Low concentrations of selenium and zinc in nails are associated with childhood asthma. *Biological Trace Element Research*, **144**, 244–52.

Caulfield, L. E., Zavaleta, N., Figueroa, A. and Leon, Z. (1999) Maternal zinc supplementation does not affect size at birth or pregnancy duration in Peru. *Journal of Nutrition*, **129**, 1563–8.

Cetin, I., Foidart, J. M., Miozzo, M., Raun, T., Jansson, T., Tsatsaris, V. *et al.* (2004) Fetal growth restriction: a workshop report. *Placenta*, **25**, 753–7.

Chappell, L. C., Seed, P. T., Briley, A. L., Kelly, F. J., Lee, R., Hunt, B. J. *et al.* (1999) Effect of antioxidants on the occurrence of pre-eclampsia in women at increased risk: a randomised trial. *Lancet*, **354**, 810–16.

Cherry, F. F., Bennett, E. A., Bazzano, G. S., Johnson, L. K., Fosmire, G. J. and Batson, H. K. (1981) Plasma zinc in hypertension/toxemia and other reproductive variables in adolescent pregnancy. *American Journal of Clinical Nutrition*, **34**, 2367–75.

Ciaccio, M., Bivona, G. and Bellia, C. (2008) Therapeutical approach to plasma homocysteine and cardiovascular risk reduction. *Therapeutics and Clinical Risk Management*, **4**, 219–24.

Cikot, R. J., Steegers-Theunissen, R. P., Thomas, C. M., de Boo, T. M., Merkus, H. M. and Steegers, E. A. (2001) Longitudinal vitamin and homocysteine levels in normal pregnancy. *British Journal of Nutrition*, **85**, 49–58.

Combs, G. F., Jr (2001) Selenium in global food systems. *British Journal of Nutrition*, **85**, 517–47.

Corathers, L. A. (2009) *Mineral Commodity Summaries 2009: Manganese*. United States Geological Survey.

Davidge, S. T. (1998) Oxidative stress and altered endothelial cell function in preeclampsia. *Seminars in Reproductive Endocrinology*, **16**, 65–73.

Dawson, E. B., Evans, D. R. and Nosovitch, J. (1999) Third-trimester amniotic fluid metal levels associated with preeclampsia. *Archives of Environmental Health*, **54**, 412–15.

de Lorgeril, M., Salen, P., Paillard, F., Laporte, F., Boucher, F. and de Leiris, J. (2002) Mediterranean diet and the French paradox: two distinct biogeographic concepts for one consolidated scientific theory on the role of nutrition in coronary heart disease. *Cardiovascular Research*, **54**, 503–15.

De Luca, G., Olivieri, F., Melotti, G., Aiello, G., Lubrano, L. and Boner, A. L. (2010) Fetal and early postnatal life roots of asthma. *Journal of Maternal and Fetal Neonatal Medicine*, **23**(Suppl. 3), 80–3.

Dennery, P. A. (2007) Effects of oxidative stress on embryonic development. *Birth Defects Research Part C: Embryo Today*, **81**, 155–62.

Devereux, G. (2007) Early life events in asthma – diet. *Pediatric Pulmonology*, **42**, 663–73.

Devereux, G., McNeill, G., Newman, G., Turner, S., Craig, L., Martindale, S. *et al.* (2007) Early childhood wheezing symptoms in relation to plasma selenium in pregnant mothers and neonates. *Clinical & Experimental Allergy* **37**, 1000-1008.

Devereux, G, Turner, SW, Craig, LC, McNeill, G, Martindale, S, Harbour, PJ, *et al.* (2006) Low maternal vitamin E intake during pregnancy is associated with asthma in 5-year-old children. *Am J Respir Crit Care Med* **174**, 499-507.

Diaz, E, Halhali, A, Luna, C, Diaz, L, Avila, E & Larrea, F (2002) Newborn birth weight correlates with placental zinc, umbilical insulin-like growth factor I, and leptin levels in preeclampsia. *Arch Med Res* **33**, 40-47.

Dikalova, AE, Bikineyeva, AT, Budzyn, K, Nazarewicz, RR, McCann, L, Lewis, W, *et al.* (2010) Therapeutic targeting of mitochondrial superoxide in hypertension. *Circ Res* **107**, 106-116.

Dobrzynski, W, Trafikowska, U, Trafikowska, A, Pilecki, A, Szymanski, W & Zachara, BA (1998) Decreased selenium concentration in maternal and cord blood in preterm compared with term delivery. *Analyst* **123**, 93-97.

Donnay, I & Knoops, B (2007) Peroxiredoxins in gametogenesis and embryo development. *Subcell Biochem* **44**, 345-355.

Drasch, G, Mail der, S, Schlosser, C & Roider, G (2000) Content of non-mercury-associated selenium in human tissues. *Biological Trace Element Research* **77**, 219-230.

Eilander, A, Gera, T, Sachdev, HS, Transler, C, van der Knaap, HC, Kok, FJ, *et al.* (2010) Multiple micronutrient supplementation for improving cognitive performance in children: systematic review of randomized controlled trials. *American Journal of Clinical Nutrition* **91**, 115-130.

Emsley, J (2001) *"Manganese". Nature's building blocks: An A-Z guide to elements.* Oxford University Press, Oxford.

FAO/WHO (2004) Zinc. In: Vitamins and mineral requirement in human nutrition. 2nd edn. World Health Organisation and Food and Agriculture Organisation of the United Nations.

Ferencik, M & Ebringer, L (2003) Modulatory effects of selenium and zinc on the immune system. *Folia Microbiol (Praha)* **48**, 417-426.

Fogarty, A, Lewis, SA, Scrivener, SL, Antoniak, M, Pacey, S, Pringle, M, *et al.* (2003) Oral magnesium and vitamin C supplements in asthma: a parallel group randomized placebo-controlled trial. *Clinical & Experimental Allergy*, **33**, 1355–9.

Fox, J. T. and Stover, P. J. (2008) Folate-mediated one-carbon metabolism. *Vitamins and Hormones*, **79**, 1–44.

Friso, S. and Choi, S. W. (2002) Gene-nutrient interactions and DNA methylation. *Journal of Nutrition*, **132**, 2382S–2387S.

Galinier, A., Periquet, B., Lambert, W., Garcia, J., Assouline, C., Rolland, M. *et al.* (2005) Reference range for micronutrients and nutritional marker proteins in cord blood of neonates appropriated for gestational ages. *Early Human Development*, **81**, 583–93.

Gambling, L., Andersen, H. S. and McArdle, H. J. (2008) Iron and copper, and their interactions during development. *Biochem Society Transactions*, **36**, 1258–61.

Gandley, R. E., Tyurin, V. A., Huang, W., Arroyo, A., Daftary, A., Harger, G. *et al.* (2005) S-nitrosoalbumin-mediated relaxation is enhanced by ascorbate and copper: effects in pregnancy and preeclampsia plasma. *Hypertension*, **45**, 21–7.

Garg, H. K., Singhal, K. C. and Arshad, Z. (1993) A study of the effect of oral zinc supplementation during pregnancy on pregnancy outcome. *Indian Journal of Physiology & Pharmacology*, **37**, 276–84.

Garrel, C., Fowler, P. A. and Al-Gubory, K. H. (2010) Developmental changes in antioxidant enzymatic defences against oxidative stress in sheep placentomes. *Journal of Endocrinology*, **205**, 107–16.

Gathwala, G., Yadav, O. P., Singh, I. and Sangwan, K. (2000) Maternal and cord plasma selenium levels in full-term neonates. *Indian Journal of Pediatrics*, **67**, 729–31.

Gera, T., Sachdev, H. P. and Nestel, P. (2009) Effect of combining multiple micronutrients with iron supplementation on Hb response in children: systematic review of randomized controlled trials. *Public Health Nutrition*, **12**, 756–73.

Gilliland, F. D., Berhane, K. T., Li, Y. F., Gauderman, W. J., McConnell, R. and Peters, J. (2003) Children's lung function and antioxidant vitamin, fruit, juice, and vegetable intake. *American Journal of Epidemiology*, **158**, 576–84.

Goh, Y. I., Bollano, E., Einarson, T. R. and Koren, G. (2006) Prenatal multivitamin supplementation and rates of congenital anomalies: a meta-analysis. *Journal of Obstetrics and Gynaecology of Canada*, **28**, 680–9.

Goh, Y. I., Bollano, E., Einarson, T. R. and Koren, G. (2007) Prenatal multivitamin supplementation and rates of pediatric cancers: a meta-analysis. *Clinical Pharmacology & Therapeutics*, **81**, 685–91.

Goldenberg, R. L., Tamura, T., Neggers, Y., Copper, R. L., Johnston, K. E., DuBard, M. B. *et al.* (1995) The effect of zinc supplementation on pregnancy outcome. *Journal of the American Medical Association*, **274**, 463–8.

Golightly, E., Jabbour, H. N. and Norman, J. E. (2011) Endocrine immune interactions in human parturition. *Molecular and Cellular Endocrinology*, **335**, 52–9.

Gori, T. and Munzel, T. (2011) Oxidative stress and endothelial dysfunction: therapeutic implications. *Annals of Medicine*, **43**, 259–72.

Greenough, A., Shaheen, S. O., Shennan, A., Seed, P. T. and Poston, L. (2012) Respiratory outcomes in early childhood following antenatal vitamin C and E supplementation. *Thorax*, **65**, 998–1003.

Griffith, T. M., Chaytor, A. T., Bakker, L. M. and Edwards, D. H. (2005) 5-Methyltetrahydrofolate and tetrahydrobiopterin can modulate electrotonically mediated endothelium-dependent vascular relaxation. *Proceedings of the National Academy of Sciences of the USA*, **102**, 7008–13.

Guerin, P., El Mouatassim, S. and Menezo, Y. (2001) Oxidative stress and protection against reactive oxygen species in the pre-implantation embryo and its surroundings. *Human Reproduction Update*, **7**, 175–89.

Guller, S., Buhimschi, C. S., Ma, Y. Y., Huang, S. T., Yang, L., Kuczynski, E. *et al.* (2008) Placental expression of ceruloplasmin in pregnancies complicated by severe preeclampsia. *Laboratory Investigation*, **88**, 1057–67.

Gurung, V., Williamson, C., Chappell, L., Chambers, J., Briley, A., Broughton Pipkin, F. *et al.* (2009) Pilot study for a trial of ursodeoxycholic acid and/or early delivery for obstetric cholestasis. *BMC Pregnancy and Childbirth*, **9**, 19.

Haider, B. A., Yakoob, M. Y. and Bhutta, Z. A. (2011) Effect of multiple micronutrient supplementation during pregnancy on maternal and birth outcomes. *BMC Public Health*, **11**(Suppl. 3), S19.

Haitchi, H. M., Powell, R. M., Shaw, T. J., Howarth, P. H., Wilson, S. J., Wilson, D. I. *et al.* (2005) ADAM33 expression in asthmatic airways and human embryonic lungs. *American Journal of Critical Care Medicine*, **171**, 958–65.

Halliwell, B. (2000) Why and how should we measure oxidative DNA damage in nutritional studies? How far have we come? *American Journal of Clinical Nutrition*, **72**, 1082–7.

Halliwell, B. and Gutteridge, J. M. C. (2006) *Free Radicals in Biology and Medicine*, 4th edn. Clarendon Press, Oxford.

Han, L. and Zhou, S. M. (1994) Selenium supplement in the prevention of pregnancy induced hypertension. *Chinese Medical Journal (English)*, **107**, 870–1.

Harik-Khan, R. I., Muller, D. C. and Wise, R. A. (2004) Serum vitamin levels and the risk of asthma in children. *American Journal of Epidemiology*, **159**, 351–7.

Harris, A., Devaraj, S. and Jialal, I. (2002) Oxidative stress, alpha-tocopherol therapy, and atherosclerosis. *Current Atherosclerosis Reports*, **4**, 373–80.

Harris, L. K., McCormick, J., Cartwright, J. E., Whitley, G. S. and Dash, P. R. (2008) S-nitrosylation of proteins at the leading edge of migrating trophoblasts by inducible nitric oxide synthase promotes trophoblast invasion. *Experimental Cell Research*, **314**, 1765–76.

Hawkes, W. C., Alkan, Z., Lang, K. and King, J. C. (2004) Plasma selenium decrease during pregnancy is associated with glucose intolerance. *Biological Trace Element Research*, **100**, 19–29.

Hijazi, N., Abalkhail, B. and Seaton, A. (2000) Diet and childhood asthma in a society in transition: a study in urban and rural Saudi Arabia. *Thorax*, **55**, 775–9.

Hubel, C. A. (1999) Oxidative stress in the pathogenesis of preeclampsia. *Proceedings of the Society for Experimental Biology and Medicine*, **222**, 222–35.

Institute of Medicine (2000) Food and nutrition board. In: *Dietary Reference Intakes for Vitamin C, Vitamin E, Selenium, and Carotenoids*. National Academy Press Washington DC.

Institute of Medicine (2001) *Dietary Reference Intakes for Vitamin A, Vitamin K, Arsenic, Boron, Chromium, Copper, Iodine, Iron, Manganese, Molybdenum, Nickel, Silicon, Vanadium, and Zinc*. National Academy Press.

Iranpour, R., Zandian, A., Mohammadizadeh, M., Mohammadzadch, A., Balali-Mood, M. and Hajiheydari, M. (2009) Comparison of maternal and umbilical cord blood selenium levels in term and preterm infants. *Zhongguo Dang Dai Er Ke Za Zhi*, **11**, 513–16.

Izquierdo Alvarez, S., Castanon, S. G., Ruata, M. L., Aragues, E. F., Terraz, P. B., Irazabal, Y. G. *et al.* (2007) Updating of normal levels of copper, zinc and selenium in serum of pregnant women. *Journal of Trace Elements in Medicine and Biology*, **21**(Suppl. 1), 49–52.

Jain, S., Sharma, P., Kulshreshtha, S., Mohan, G. and Singh, S. (2010) The role of calcium, magnesium, and zinc in pre-eclampsia. *Biological Trace Element Research*, **133**, 162–70.

Jauniaux, E., Gulbis, B. and Burton, G. J. (2003) The human first trimester gestational sac limits rather than facilitates oxygen transfer to the foetus – a review. *Placenta*, **24**(Suppl. A), S86–93.

Jauniaux, E., Johns, J., Gulbis, B., Spasic-Boskovic, O. and Burton, G. J. (2007) Transfer of folic acid inside the first-trimester gestational sac and the effect of maternal smoking. *American Journal of Obstetrics and Gynecology*, **197**, 58.e1–6.

Jauniaux, E., Watson, A. L., Hempstock, J., Bao, Y. P., Skepper, J. N. and Burton, G. J. (2000) Onset of maternal arterial blood flow and placental oxidative stress. A possible factor in human early pregnancy failure. *American Journal of Pathology*, **157**, 2111–22.

Jenkin, G. and Young, I. R. (2004) Mechanisms responsible for parturition; the use of experimental models. *Animal Reproduction Science*, **82–3**, 567–81.

Jones, E. A., Wright, J. M., Rice, G., Buckley, B. T., Magsumbol, M. S., Barr, D. B. *et al.* (2010) Metal exposures in an inner-city neonatal population. *Environment International*, **36**, 649–54.

Jonsson, U. (2010) The rise and fall of paradigms in world food and nutrition policy. *World Nutrition*, **1**(3), 128–58.

Joshi, R., Adhikari, S., Patro, B. S., Chattopadhyay, S. and Mukherjee, T. (2001) Free radical scavenging behavior of folic acid: evidence for possible antioxidant activity. *Free Radicals in Biology and Medicine*, **30**, 1390–9.

Kambe, T., Weaver, B. P. and Andrews, G. K. (2008) The genetics of essential metal homeostasis during development. *Genesis*, **46**, 214–28.

Katz, O., Paz-Tal, O., Lazer, T., Aricha-Tamir, B., Mazor, M., Wiznitzer, A. *et al.* (2012) Severe pre-eclampsia is associated with abnormal trace elements concentrations in maternal and fetal blood. *Journal of Maternal and Fetal Neonatal Medicine*, **25**(7), 1127–30.

Kauppila, A., Korpela, H., Makila, U. M. and Yrjanheikki, E. (1987) Low serum selenium concentration and glutathione peroxidase activity in intrahepatic cholestasis of pregnancy. *British Medical Journal (Clinical Research Edition)*, **294**, 150–2.

Keen, C. L., Hanna, L. A., Lanoue, L., Uriu-Adams, J. Y., Rucker, R. B. and Clegg, M. S. (2003) Developmental consequences of trace mineral deficiencies in rodents: acute and long-term effects. *Journal of Nutrition*, **133**, 1477S–1480S.

Kiilholma, P., Paul, R., Pakarinen, P. and Gronroos, M. (1984) Copper and zinc in pre-eclampsia. *Acta Obstetricia et Gynecologica Scandinavica*, **63**, 629–31.

Kilinc, M., Guven, M. A., Ezer, M., Ertas, I. E. and Coskun, A. (2008) Evaluation of serum selenium levels in Turkish women with gestational diabetes mellitus, glucose intolerants, and normal controls. *Biological Trace Element Research*, **123**, 35–40.

King, J. C. (2000) Determinants of maternal zinc status during pregnancy. *American Journal of Clinical Nutrition*, **71**, 1334S–1343S.

Klapec, T., Cavar, S., Kasac, Z., Rucevic, S. and Popinjac, A. (2008) Selenium in placenta predicts birth weight in normal but not intrauterine growth restriction pregnancy. *Journal of Trace Elements in Medicine and Biology*, **22**, 54–8.

Klebanoff, M. A., Secher, N. J., Mednick, B. R. and Schulsinger, C. (1999) Maternal size at birth and the development of hypertension during pregnancy: a test of the Barker hypothesis. *Archives of Internal Medicine*, **159**, 1607–12.

Kocak, I., Aksoy, E. and Ustun, C. (1999) Recurrent spontaneous abortion and selenium deficiency. *International Journal of Gynaecology & Obstetrics*, **65**, 79–80.

Kocyigit, A., Armutcu, F., Gurel, A. and Ermis, B. (2004) Alterations in plasma essential trace elements selenium, manganese, zinc, copper, and iron concentrations and the possible role of these elements on oxidative status in patients with childhood asthma. *Biological Trace Element Research*, **97**, 31–41.

Kohrle, J. (2005) Selenium and the control of thyroid hormone metabolism. *Thyroid*, **15**, 841–53.

Kolusari, A., Kurdoglu, M., Yildizhan, R., Adali, E., Edirne, T., Cebi, A. *et al.* (2008) Catalase activity, serum trace element and heavy metal concentrations, and vitamin A, D and E levels in pre-eclampsia. *Journal of International Medical Research*, **36**, 1335–41.

Krachler, M., Rossipal, E. and Micetic-Turk, D. (1999) Trace element transfer from the mother to the newborn – investigations on triplets of colostrum, maternal and umbilical cord sera. *European Journal of Clinical Nutrition*, **53**, 486–94.

Kumru, S., Aydin, S., Simsek, M., Sahin, K., Yaman, M. and Ay, G. (2003) Comparison of serum copper, zinc, calcium, and magnesium levels in preeclamptic and healthy pregnant women. *Biological Trace Element Research*, **94**, 105–12.

Kupferminc, M. J., Eldor, A., Steinman, N., Many, A., Bar-Am, A., Jaffa, A. *et al.* (1999) Increased frequency of genetic thrombophilia in women with complications of pregnancy. *New England Journal of Medicine*, **340**, 9–13.

Laclaustra, M., Navas-Acien, A., Stranges, S., Ordovas, J. M. and Guallar, E. (2009) Serum selenium concentrations and diabetes in U.S. adults: National Health and Nutrition Examination Survey (NHANES) 2003–2004. *Environmental Health Perspectives*, **117**, 1409–13.

Law, M. R. and Morris, J. K. (1998) By how much does fruit and vegetable consumption reduce the risk of ischaemic heart disease? *European Journal of Clinical Nutrition*, **52**, 549–56.

Lawrence, J. M., Black, M. H., Hsu, J. W., Chen, W. and Sacks, D. A. (2010) Prevalence and timing of postpartum glucose testing and sustained glucose dysregulation after gestational diabetes mellitus. *Diabetes Care*, **33**, 569–76.

Levander, O. A. (1987) Selenium. In: *Trace Elements in Human and Animal Nutrition.* Academic Press, London.

Li, Z., Gindler, J., Wang, H., Berry, R. J., Li, S., Correa, A. *et al.* (2003) Folic acid supplements during early pregnancy and likelihood of multiple births: a population-based cohort study. *Lancet*, **361**, 380–4.

Lista, G., Castoldi, F., Compagnoni, G., Maggioni, C., Cornelissen, G. and Halberg, F. (2010) Neonatal and maternal concentrations of hydroxil radical and total antioxidant system: protective role of placenta against fetal oxidative stress. *Neuro Endocrinology Letters*, **31**, 319–24.

Litonjua, A. A., Rifas-Shiman, S. L., Ly, N. P., Tantisira, K. G., Rich-Edwards, J. W., Camargo, C. A., Jr *et al.* (2006) Maternal antioxidant intake in pregnancy and wheezing illnesses in children at 2 y of age. *American Journal of Clinical Nutrition*, **84**, 903–11.

Liu, J., Yang, H., Shi, H., Shen, C., Zhou, W., Dai, Q. *et al.* (2010) Blood copper, zinc, calcium, and magnesium levels during different duration of pregnancy in Chinese. *Biological Trace Element Research*, **135**, 31–7.

Llanos, M. N. and Ronco, A. M. (2009) Fetal growth restriction is related to placental levels of cadmium, lead and arsenic but not with antioxidant activities. *Reproductive Toxicology*, **27**, 88–92.

Lyons, G., Stangoulis, J. and Graham, R. (2003) Nutriprevention of disease with high-selenium wheat. *Journal of Australasian College of Nutritional Medicine*, **22**, 3–9.

Mahomed, K., Bhutta, Z. and Middleton, P. (2007) Zinc supplementation for improving pregnancy and infant outcome. *Cochrane Database of Systematic Reviews*, CD000230.

Makedos, G., Papanicolaou, A., Hitoglou, A., Kalogiannidis, I., Makedos, A., Vrazioti, V. *et al.* (2007) Homocysteine, folic acid and B12 serum levels in pregnancy complicated with preeclampsia. *Archives of Gynecology and Obstetrics*, **275**, 121–4.

Maleki, A., Fard, M. K., Zadeh, D. H., Mamegani, M. A., Abasaizadeh, S. and Mazloomzadeh, S. (2011) The relationship between plasma level of Se and preeclampsia. *Hypertension in Pregnancy*, **30**(2), 180–7.

Mariath, A. B., Bergamaschi, D. P., Rondo, P. H., Tanaka, A. C., Hinnig Pde, F., Abbade, J. F. *et al.* (2011) The possible role of selenium status in adverse pregnancy outcomes. *British Journal of Nutrition*, **105**, 1418–28.

Mask, G. and Lane, H. W. (1993) Selected measures of selenium status in full-term and preterm neonates, their mothers and non-pregnant women. *Nutrition Research*, **13**, 901–11.

Mayne, S. T. (2003) Antioxidant nutrients and chronic disease: use of biomarkers of exposure and oxidative stress status in epidemiologic research. *Journal of Nutrition*, 133(Suppl. 3), 933S–940S.

McArdle, H. J., Andersen, H. S., Jones, H. and Gambling, L. (2008) Copper and iron transport across the placenta: regulation and interactions. *Journal of Neuroendocrinology*, **20**, 427–31.

McCall, M. R. and Frei, B. (1999) Can antioxidant vitamins materially reduce oxidative damage in humans? *Free Radical Biology & Medicine*, **26**, 1034–53.

McCance, D. R., Holmes, V. A., Maresh, M. J., Patterson, C. C., Walker, J. D., Pearson, D. W. *et al.* (2010) Vitamins C and E for prevention of pre-eclampsia in women with type 1 diabetes (DAPIT): a randomised placebo-controlled trial. *Lancet*, **376**, 259–66.

McKenzie, R. C., Rafferty, T. S. and Beckett, G. J. (1998) Selenium: an essential element for immune function. *Immunology Today*, **19**, 342–5.

McNeill, J. H., Delgatty, H. L. and Battell, M. L. (1991) Insulin-like effects of sodium selenate in streptozocin-induced diabetic rats. *Diabetes*, **40**, 1675–8.

Megahed, M. A. and Taher, I. M. (2004) Folate and homocysteine levels in pregnancy. *British Journal of Biomedical Science*, **61**, 84–7.

Mehmetoglu, I., Kart, A., Caglayan, O., Capar, M. and Gokce, R. (2002) Oxidative stress in mothers and their newborns in different types of labour. *Turkish Journal of Medical Sciences*, **32**, 427–9.

Menon, P., Ruel, M. T., Loechl, C. U., Arimond, M., Habicht, J. P., Pelto, G. *et al.* (2007) Micronutrient sprinkles reduce anemia among 9- to 24-mo-old children when delivered through an integrated health and nutrition program in rural Haiti. *Journal of Nutrition*, **137**, 1023–30.

Ministry of Agriculture Fisheries and Food (1997) *Dietary Intake of Selenium*. (ed. Joint Food Safety and Standards Group). HMSO, London.

Mistry, H. D. and Williams P. J. (2011) The importance of antioxidant micronutrients in pregnancy. *Oxidative Medicine and Cellular Longevity*. Doi: 10.1155/2011/841749.

Mistry, H. D., Wilson, V., Ramsay, M. M., Symonds, M. E. and Broughton Pipkin, F. (2008) Reduced selenium concentrations and glutathione peroxidase activity in pre-eclamptic pregnancies. *Hypertension*, **52**, 881–8.

Mistry, H. D., Kurlak, L. O., Williams, P. J., Ramsay, M. M., Symonds, M. E. and Broughton Pipkin, F. (2010) Differential expression and distribution of placental glutathione peroxidases 1, 3 and 4 in normal and preeclamptic pregnancy. *Placenta*, **31**, 401–8.

Mistry, H. D., Mather, J., Ramsay, M. M., Kurlak, L. O., Symonds, M. E. and Broughton Pipkin, F. (2011) Homocysteine and folate plasma concentrations in mother and baby at delivery after pre-eclamptic or normotensive pregnancy: influence of parity. *Pregnancy Hypertension*, **1**, 150–5.

Mistry, H. D., Broughton Pipkin, F., Redman, C. W. and Poston, L. (2012a) Selenium in reproductive health. *American Journal of Obstetrics and Gynecology*, **206**, 21–30.

Mistry, H. D., Kurlak, L. O., Young, S. D., Briley, A. L., Broughton Pipkin, F., Baker, P. N. and Poston, L. (2012b) Maternal selenium, copper and zinc concentrations in pregnancy associated with small-for-gestational-age infants. *Maternal & Child Nutrition.* DOI: 10.1111/j.1740-8709.2012.00430.x.

MRC (1991) Prevention of neural tube defects: results of the Medical Research Council Vitamin Study. MRC Vitamin Study Research Group. *Lancet,* **338**, 131–7.

Mutlu, B., Aksoy, N., Cakir, H., Celik, H. and Frel, O. (2011) The effects of the mode of delivery on oxidative-antioxidative balance. *Journal of Maternal and Fetal Neonatal Medicine,* **24**, 1367–70.

Myatt, L. and Cui, X. (2004) Oxidative stress in the placenta. *Histochemistry and Cell Biology,* **122**, 369–82.

Nabhan, A. F., El-Din, L. B., Rabie, A. H. and Fahmy, G. M. (2009) Impact of intrapartum factors on oxidative stress in newborns. *Journal of Maternal and Fetal Neonatal Medicine,* **22**, 867–72.

Nandakumaran, M., Dashti, H. M., Al-Saleh, E. and Al-Zaid, N. S. (2003) Transport kinetics of zinc, copper, selenium, and iron in perfused human placental lobule in vitro. *Molecular and Cell Biochemistry,* **252**, 91–6.

Nassi, N., Ponziani, V., Becatti, M., Galvan, P. and Donzelli, G. (2009) Anti-oxidant enzymes and related elements in term and preterm newborns. *Pediatrics International,* **51**, 183–7.

Neggers, Y. H., Dubard, M. B., Goldenberg, R. L., Tamura, T., Johnston, K. E., Copper, R. L. *et al.* (1996) Factors influencing plasma zinc levels in low-income pregnant women. *Biological Trace Element Research,* **55**, 127–35.

NICE (2008) *Improving the Nutrition of Pregnant and Breastfeeding Mothers in Low-income Households.* NICE Public Health Guidance, London.

O'Donovan, D. J. and Fernandes, C. J. (2004) Free radicals and diseases in premature infants. *Antioxidants & Redox Signaling,* **6**, 169–76.

Oldfield, J. E. (1987) The two faces of selenium. *Journal of Nutrition,* **117**, 2002–8.

Osada, H., Watanabe, Y., Nishimura, Y., Yukawa, M., Seki, K. and Sekiya, S. (2002) Profile of trace element concentrations in the feto-placental unit in relation to fetal growth. *Acta Obstetricia et Gynecologica Scandinavica,* **81**, 931–7.

Osendarp, S. J., van Raaij, J. M., Arifeen, S. F., Wahed, M., Baqui, A. H. and Fuchs, G. J. (2000) A randomized, placebo-controlled trial of the effect of zinc supplementation during pregnancy on pregnancy outcome in Bangladeshi urban poor. *American Journal of Clinical Nutrition,* **71**, 114–19.

Ozdemir, Y., Borekci, B., Levet, A. and Kurudirek, M. (2009) Assessment of trace element concentration distribution in human placenta by wavelength dispersive X-ray fluorescence: effect of neonate weight and maternal age. *Applied Radiation and Isotopes,* **67**, 1790–5.

Paamoni-Keren, O., Silberstein, T., Burg, A., Raz, I., Mazor, M., Saphier, O. *et al.* (2007) Oxidative stress as determined by glutathione (GSH) concentrations in venous cord blood in elective cesarean delivery versus uncomplicated vaginal delivery. *Archives of Gynecology and Obstetrics,* **276**, 43–6.

Packer, J. E., Slater, T. F. and Willson, R. L. (1979) Direct observation of a free radical interaction between vitamin E and vitamin C. *Nature,* **278**, 737–8.

Patelarou, E., Giourgouli, G., Lykeridou, A., Vrioni, E., Fotos, N., Siamaga, E. *et al.* (2011) Association between biomarker-quantified antioxidant status during pregnancy and infancy and allergic disease during early childhood: a systematic review. *Nutrition Reviews*, **69**, 627–41.

Pearson, P. J., Lewis, S. A., Britton, J. and Fogarty, A. (2004) Vitamin E supplements in asthma: a parallel group randomised placebo controlled trial. *Thorax*, **59**, 652–6.

Perveen, S., Altaf, W., Vohra, N., Bautista, M. L., Harper, R. G. and Wapnir, R. A. (2002) Effect of gestational age on cord blood plasma copper, zinc, magnesium and albumin. *Early Human Development*, **69**, 15–23.

Poston, L., Briley, A. L., Seed, P. T., Kelly, F. J. and Shennan, A. H. (2006) Vitamin C and vitamin E in pregnant women at risk for pre-eclampsia (VIP trial): randomised placebo-controlled trial. *Lancet*, **367**, 1145–54.

Poston, L., Igosheva, N., Mistry, H. D., Seed, P. T., Shennan, A. H., Rana, S. *et al.* (2011) Role of oxidative stress and antioxidant supplementation in pregnancy disorders. *American Journal of Clinical Nutrition*, **94**, 1980S–1985S.

Powers, R. W., Evans, R. W., Majors, A. K., Ojimba, J. I., Ness, R. B., Crombleholme, W. R. *et al.* (1998) Plasma homocysteine concentration is increased in preeclampsia and is associated with evidence of endothelial activation. *American Journal of Obstetrics and Gynecology*, **179**, 1605–11.

Prasad, A. S. (2000) Effects of zinc deficiency on Th1 and Th2 cytokine shifts. *Journal of Infectious Diseases*, **182**(Suppl. 1), S62–8.

Qvist, I., Abdulla, M., Jagerstad, M. and Svensson, S. (1986) Iron, zinc and folate status during pregnancy and two months after delivery. *Acta Obstetricia et Gynecologica Scandinavica*, **65**, 15–22.

Rajkovic, A., Catalano, P. M. and Malinow, M. R. (1997) Elevated homocyst(e)ine levels with preeclampsia. *Obstetric Gynecology* **90**, 168–71.

Ram, F. S., Rowe, B. H. and Kaur, B. (2004) Vitamin C supplementation for asthma. *Cochrane Database of Systematic Reviews*, CD000993.

Ramakrishnan, U., Manjrekar, R., Rivera, J., Gonzales-Cossio, T. and Martorell, R. (1999) Micronutrients and pregnancy outcome: a review of the literature. *Nutrition Research*, **19**, 103–59.

Ramakrishnan, U., Neufeld, L. M., Flores, R., Rivera, J. and Martorell, R. (2009) Multiple micronutrient supplementation during early childhood increases child size at 2 y of age only among high compliers. *American Journal of Clinical Nutrition*, **89**, 1125–31.

Ramankrishnan, U. and Huffman, S. L. (2008) Multiple micronutrition malnutrition: what can be done? In: *Nutrition and Health in Developing Countries*, 2nd edn (eds. R. D. Semba and M. Bloom). Humanan Press, Totowa.

Ray, J. G. and Laskin, C. A. (1999) Folic acid and homocyst(e)ine metabolic defects and the risk of placental abruption, pre-eclampsia and spontaneous pregnancy loss: a systematic review. *Placenta*, **20**, 519–29.

Ray, J. G. and Mamdani, M. M. (2002) Association between folic acid food fortification and hypertension or preeclampsia in pregnancy. *Archives of Internal Medicine*, **162**, 1776–7.

Rayman, M. P. (2002) The argument for increasing selenium intake. *Proceedings of the Nutrition Society*, **61**, 203–15.

Rayman, M. P. (2008) Food-chain selenium and human health: emphasis on intake. *British Journal of Nutrition*, **100**, 254–68.

Rayman, M. P., Bode, P. and Redman, C. W. (2003) Low selenium status is associated with the occurrence of the pregnancy disease preeclampsia in women from the United Kingdom. *American Journal of Obstetrics and Gynecology*, **189**, 1343 9.

Red-Horse, K., Zhou, Y., Genbacev, O., Prakobphol, A., Foulk, R., McMaster, M. *et al.* (2004) Trophoblast differentiation during embryo implantation and formation of the maternal–fetal interface. *Journal of Clinical Investigation*, **114**, 744–54.

Reyes, H., Baez, M. E., Gonzalez, M. C., Hernandez, I., Palma, J., Ribalta, J. *et al.* (2000) Selenium, zinc and copper plasma levels in intrahepatic cholestasis of pregnancy, in normal pregnancies and in healthy individuals, in Chile. *Journal of Hepatology*, **32**, 542–9.

Richter, M., Bonneau, R., Girard, M. A., Beaulieu, C. and Larivee, P. (2003) Zinc status modulates bronchopulmonary eosinophil infiltration in a murine model of allergic inflammation. *Chest*, **123**, 446S.

Roberts, J. M., Myatt, L., Spong, C. Y., Thom, E. A., Hauth, J. C., Leveno, K. J. *et al.* (2010) Vitamins C and E to prevent complications of pregnancy-associated hypertension. *New England Journal of Medicine*, **362**, 1282–91.

Rodriguez-Iturbe, B., Sepassi, L., Quiroz, Y., Ni, Z., Wallace, D. C. and Vaziri, N. D. (2007) Association of mitochondrial SOD deficiency with salt-sensitive hypertension and accelerated renal senescence. *Journal of Applied Physiology*, **102**, 255–60.

Romero, R., Espinoza, J., Goncalves, L. F., Kusanovic, J. P., Friel, L. A. and Nien, J. K. (2006) Inflammation in preterm and term labour and delivery. *Seminars in Fetal and Neonatal Medicine*, **11**(5), 317–26.

Rossipal, E., Krachler, M., Li, F. and Micetic-Turk, D. (2000) Investigation of the transport of trace elements across barriers in humans: studies of placental and mammary transfer. *Acta Paediatrica*, **89**, 1190–5.

Rumbold, A., Duley. L., Crowther, C. A. and Haslam, R. R. (2008) Antioxidants for preventing pre-eclampsia. *Cochrane Database of Systematic Reviews*, Issue 1. Art. No.: CD004227; DOI: 10.1002/14651858.

Rumiris, D., Purwosunu, Y., Wibowo, N., Farina, A. and Sekizawa, A. (2006) Lower rate of preeclampsia after antioxidant supplementation in pregnant women with low antioxidant status. *Hypertension in Pregnancy*, **25**, 241–53.

Sanchez, S. E., Zhang, C., Rene Malinow, M., Ware-Jauregui, S., Larrabure, G. and Williams, M. A. (2001) Plasma folate, vitamin B(12), and homocyst(e)ine concentrations in preeclamptic and normotensive Peruvian women. *American Journal of Epidemiology*, **153**, 474–80.

Sasaki, K., Duan, J., Murohara, T., Ikeda, H., Shintani, S., Shimada, T. *et al.* (2003) Rescue of hypercholesterolemia-related impairment of angiogenesis by oral folate supplementation. *Journal of the American College of Cardiology*, **42**, 364–72.

Scholl, T. O., Hediger, M. L., Schall, J. I., Fischer, R. L. and Khoo, C. S. (1993) Low zinc intake during pregnancy: its association with preterm and very preterm delivery. *American Journal of Epidemiology*, **137**, 1115–24.

Schwarz, K. and Foltz, C. M. (1957) Selenium as an integral part of factor 3 against dietary necrotic liver degeneration. *Journal of the American Chemical Society*, **79**, 3292–3.

Seaton, A., Godden, D. J. and Brown, K. (1994) Increase in asthma: a more toxic environment or a more susceptible population? *Thorax*, **49**, 171–4.

Selvaag, E., Bohmer, T. and Benkestock, K. (2002) Reduced serum concentrations of riboflavine and ascorbic acid, and blood thiamine pyrophosphate and pyridoxal-5-phosphate in geriatric patients with and without pressure sores. *Journal of Nutrition Health Aging*, **6**, 75–7.

Serdar, Z., Gur, E. and Develioglu, O. (2006) Serum iron and copper status and oxidative stress in severe and mild preeclampsia. *Cell Biochemistry and Function*, **24**, 209–15.

Shaheen, S. O., Newson, R. B., Henderson, A. J., Emmett, P. M., Sherriff, A. and Cooke, M. (2004) Umbilical cord trace elements and minerals and risk of early childhood wheezing and eczema. *European Respiratory Journal*, **24**, 292–7.

Shakour-Shahabi, L., Abbasali-Zadeh, S. and Rashtchi-Zadeh, N. (2010) Serum level and antioxidant activity of ceruloplasmin in preeclampsia. *Pakistan Journal of Biological Sciences*, **13**, 321–7.

Shennan, D. B. (1988) Selenium (selenate) transport by human placental brush border membrane vesicles. *British Journal of Nutrition*, **59**, 13–19.

Sievers, E., Arpe, T., Schleyerbach, U., Garbe-Schonberg, D. and Schaub, J. (2001) Plasma selenium in preterm and term infants during the first 12 months of life. *Journal of Trace Elements in Medicine and Biology* **14**, 218-222.

Simpson, J. L., Bailey, L. B., Pietrzik, K., Shane, B. and Holzgreve, W. (2011) Micronutrients and women of reproductive potential: required dietary intake and consequences of dietary deficiency or excess. Part II – vitamin D, vitamin A, iron, zinc, iodine, essential fatty acids. *Journal of Maternal and Fetal Neonatal Medicine*, **24**, 1–24.

Singh, U., Nicholson, G., Urban, B. C., Sargent, I. L., Kishore, U. and Bernal, A. L. (2005) Immunological properties of human decidual macrophages – a possible role in intrauterine immunity. *Reproduction*, **129**, 631–7.

Smithells, R. W., Sheppard, S. and Schorah, C. J. (1976) Vitamin dificiencies and neural tube defects. *Archives of Disease in Childhood*, **51**, 944–50.

Solomons, N. W. (1988) Zinc and copper. In: *Modern Nutrition in Health and Disease*, 7th edn (eds. M. E. Shils and V. R. Young). Lea and Febiger, Philadelphia.

Soutar, A., Seaton, A. and Brown, K. (1997) Bronchial reactivity and dietary antioxidants. *Thorax*, **52**, 166–70.

Stahl, W., van den Berg, H., Arthur, J., Bast, A., Dainty, J., Faulks, R. M. *et al.* (2002) Bioavailability and metabolism. *Molecular Aspects of Medicine* **23**, 39–100.

Stockley, L. and Lund, V. (2008) Use of folic acid supplements, particularly by low-income and young women: a series of systematic reviews to inform public health policy in the UK. *Public Health Nutrition*, **11**, 807–21.

Strambi, M., Longini, M., Vezzosi, P., Berni, S. and Buoni, S. (2004) Selenium status, birth weight, and breast-feeding: pattern in the first month. *Biological Trace Element Research*, **99**, 71–81.

Sutton, A. M., Harvie, A, Cockburn, F, Farquharson, J & Logan, RW (1985) Copper deficiency in the preterm infant of very low birthweight. Four cases and a reference range for plasma copper. *Archives of Disease in Childhood*, **60**, 644–51.

Swanson, C. A. and King, J. C. (1987) Zinc and pregnancy outcome. *American Journal of Clinical Nutrition*, **46**, 763–71.

Tahan, F. and Karakukcu, C. (2006) Zinc status in infantile wheezing. *Pediatric Pulmonology*, **41**, 630–4.

Takeda, A. (2003) Manganese action in brain function. *Brain Research Reviews*, **41**, 79–87.

Tamura, T. and Picciano, M. F. (2006) Folate and human reproduction. *American Journal of Clinical Nutrition*, **83**, 993–1016.

Tan, M., Sheng, L., Qian, Y., Ge, Y., Wang, Y., Zhang, H. *et al.* (2001) Changes of serum selenium in pregnant women with gestational diabetes mellitus. *Biological Trace Element Research*, **83**, 231–7.

Tara, F., Maamouri, G., Rayman, M. P., Ghayour-Mobarhan, M., Sahebkar, A., Yazarlu, O. *et al.* (2010a) Selenium supplementation and the incidence of preeclampsia in pregnant Iranian women: a randomized, double-blind, placebo-controlled pilot trial. *Taiwanese Journal of Obstetrics and Gynecology*, **49**, 181–7.

Tara, F., Rayman, M. P., Boskabadi, H., Ghayour-Mobarhan, M., Sahebkar, A., Yazarlu, O. *et al.* (2010b) Selenium supplementation and premature (pre-labour) rupture of membranes: a randomised double-blind placebo-controlled trial. *Journal of Obstetrics and Gynaecology*, **30**, 30–4.

Than, N. G., Romero, R., Tarca, A. L., Draghici, S., Erez, O., Chaiworapongsa, T. *et al.* (2009) Mitochondrial manganese superoxide dismutase mRNA expression in human chorioamniotic membranes and its association with labor, inflammation, and infection. *Journal of Maternal and Fetal Neonatal Medicine*, **22**, 1000–13.

Thomson, C. D. (2004) Assessment of requirements for selenium and adequacy of selenium status: a review. *European Journal of Clinical Nutrition*, **58**, 391–402.

Van Eerdewegh, P., Little, R. D., Dupuis, J., Del Mastro, R. G., Falls, K., Simon, J. *et al.* (2002) Association of the ADAM33 gene with asthma and bronchial hyperresponsiveness. *Nature*, **418**, 426–30.

Vanderlelie, J. and Perkins, A. V. (2011) Selenium and preeclampsia: a global perspective. *Pregnancy Hypertension*, **1**, 213–24.

Vigeh, M., Yokoyama, K., Ramezanzadeh, F., Dahaghin, M., Fakhriazad, E., Seyedaghamiri, Z. *et al.* (2008) Blood manganese concentrations and intrauterine growth restriction. *Reproductive Toxicology*, **25**, 219–23.

Vojnik, C. and Hurley, L. S. (1977) Abnormal prenatal lung development resulting from maternal zinc deficiency in rats. *Journal of Nutrition*, **107**, 862–72.

Vollset, S. E., Gjessing, H. K., Tandberg, A., Ronning, T., Irgens, L. M., Baste, V. *et al.* (2005) Folate supplementation and twin pregnancies. *Epidemiology*, **16**, 201–5.

Wen, S. W., Chen, X. K., Rodger, M., White, R. R., Yang, Q., Smith, G. N. *et al.* (2008) Folic acid supplementation in early second trimester and the risk of preeclampsia. *American Journal of Obstetrics and Gynecology*, **198**, 45, e41–7.

WHO/FAO/IAEA (1996) *Trace Elements in Human Nutrition and Health*. World Health Organization, Geneva.

Williams, P. J., Bulmer, J. N., Innes, B. A. and Broughton Pipkin, F. (2011) Possible roles for folic acid in the regulation of trophoblast invasion and placental development in normal early human pregnancy. *Biology of Reproduction*, **84**, 1148–53.

Wood, R. J. (2009) Manganese and birth outcome. *Nutrition Reviews*, **67**, 416–20.

Xu, H., Perez-Cuevas, R., Xiong, X., Reyes, H., Roy, C., Julien, P. *et al.* (2010) An international trial of antioxidants in the prevention of preeclampsia (INTAPP). *American Journal of Obstetrics and Gynecology*, **202**, 239.e1–239.e10.

Yeum, K. J. and Russell, R. M. (2002) Carotenoid bioavailability and bioconversion. *Annual Review of Nutrition*, **22**, 483–504.

Yousef, M. I., El-Hendy, H. A., El-Demerdash, F. M. and Elagamy, E. I. (2002) Dietary zinc deficiency induced-changes in the activity of enzymes and the levels of free radicals, lipids and protein electrophoretic behavior in growing rats. *Toxicology*, **175**, 223–34.

Yu, B. P. (1994) Cellular defenses against damage from reactive oxygen species. *Physiological Reviews*, **74**, 139–62.

Yu, B. P., Kang, C. M., Han, J. S. and Kim, D. S. (1998) Can antioxidant supplementation slow the aging process? *Biofactors*, **7**, 93–101.

Zachara, B. A., Dobrzynski, W., Trafikowska, U. and Szymanski, W. (2001) Blood selenium and glutathione peroxidases in miscarriage. *BJOG*, **108**, 244–7.

Zadrozna, M., Gawlik, M., Nowak, B., Marcinek, A., Mrowiec, H., Walas, S. *et al.* (2009) Antioxidants activities and concentration of selenium, zinc and copper in preterm and IUGR human placentas. *Journal of Trace Elements in Medicine and Biology*, **23**, 144–8.

Zalewski, P. D. (1996) A review. Zinc and immunity: implications for growth, survival and function of lymphoid cells. *Journal of Nutrition Immunology*, **4**, 39–101.

Zheng, W., Fu, S. X., Dydak, U. and Cowan, D. M. (2011) Biomarkers of manganese intoxication. *Neurotoxicology*, **32**, 1–8.

Zota, A. R., Ettinger, A. S., Bouchard, M., Amarasiriwardena, C. J., Schwartz, J., Hu, H. *et al.* (2009) Maternal blood manganese levels and infant birth weight. *Epidemiology*, **20**, 367–73.

CHAPTER 2

Nutrition in pregnant and breastfeeding adolescents: a biopsychosocial perspective

Victoria Hall Moran

Introduction

Teenage pregnancy is a major global public health challenge. More than 10% of all births worldwide are to adolescent mothers, accounting for 14–15 million births per year (World Health Organization (WHO), 2006). Over the past 20 years the general trend in Europe is of declining adolescent pregnancy. Teenage pregnancy statistics for England and Wales from the Office of National Statistics revealed that conceptions in girls aged under 18 years fell by 9.5% in 2010 to 34,633 compared with 38,259 in 2009 (ONS, 2012). Pregnancies in adolescents aged under 16 years also declined by 6.8% to 6,674 from 7,158 the previous year. Overall this represents the lowest teenage pregnancy rate in England and Wales for over 40 years; nevertheless, UK rates remain higher than those of other western European countries.

Compared to women who give birth in their twenties and thirties, adolescents who become pregnant face a number of additional obstetric, medical and social challenges. Adolescents account for 13% of maternal deaths worldwide and most at risk are mothers under the age of 15 and those living in low-income countries, where girls aged 15–19 years are twice as likely to die in childbirth as women in their twenties (WHO, 2006). Teenage pregnancy has been associated with a number of negative outcomes for the infants and children of teenage mothers, although there is some conflict in the current research (Chen *et al.*, 2007). The majority of studies from high- and low-income countries have consistently reported that teenage pregnancy is associated with an increased risk for preterm delivery (Fraser *et al.*, 1995; Gortzak-Uzan *et al.*, 2001; Igwegbe and Udigwe,

2001; Jolly *et al.*, 2000; Gilbert *et al.*, 2004; Chen *et al.*, 2007), low birth weight (Bacci *et al.*, 1993; Satin *et al.*, 1994; Gortzak-Uzan *et al.*, 2001; Igwegbe and Udigwe 2001; Gilbert *et al.*, 2004; Chen *et al.*, 2007) and small for gestational age births (Fraser *et al.*, 1995; Gortzak-Uzan *et al.*, 2001; Smith and Pell, 2001; Conde-Agudelo *et al.*, 2005), although some studies have failed to find such an association (Lubarsky *et al.*, 1994; Olausson *et al.*, 1997; Zabin and Kiragu 1998; Olausson *et al.*, 1999; Bukulmez and Deren, 2000). Infants born to adolescent mothers have also been found to be at increased risk of neonatal mortality (Zabin and Kiragu 1998; Olausson *et al.*, 1999; Gilbert *et al.*, 2004; Chen *et al.*, 2007), whilst this has not been found in other studies (Satin *et al.*, 1994; Smith and Pell, 2001; Conde-Agudelo *et al.*, 2005).

There is some debate over whether the observed association between teenage pregnancy and adverse birth outcomes is causally related to biological immaturity or whether it is largely attributable to the deleterious sociodemographic environment that many pregnant teenagers confront (Smith and Pell, 2001). For example, teenage mothers are more likely than older mothers to come from unskilled manual backgrounds or live in areas with higher social deprivation; have mothers who were teenage mothers themselves; have low self-esteem; and have low educational achievement (Teenage Pregnancy Unit, 2004). Adolescents and young women from social class V have around ten times the risk of becoming teenage mothers as those from social class I and young people with below-average achievement levels at ages 7 and 16 have been found to be at significantly higher risk of becoming parents in adolescence (Kiernan, 1995). Teenage mothers are nearly six times more likely to smoke throughout pregnancy compared to mothers aged 35 or over (35% versus 6%) (Health & Social Care Information Centre, 2012). Pregnant adolescents are more likely to enter prenatal care late and are less likely to obtain an adequate quantity of care compared to adults (Stevens-Simon *et al.*, 1992) and adolescent mothers are less likely than older mothers to breastfeed their infants. In the UK, breastfeeding rates are lowest among mothers under the age of 20 (58%), compared to 87% mothers aged 30 and above (Health & Social Care Information Centre, 2012). Such social disadvantages, it has been suggested, are a result of teenage mothers' greater social adversity, rather than because of their age *per se* (DH, 2007), and there is growing recognition that socio-economic disadvantage can be both a cause and a consequence of teenage motherhood (Swann *et al.*, 2003).

Teenage pregnancy is also associated with adverse outcomes for the adolescent herself and may result in significant public costs. The teenage mother is at increased risk of developing anaemia, pre-eclampsia and postnatal depression

(Wilson, 1995; Irvine *et al.*, 1997). It is estimated that the cost to the NHS alone of pregnancy among under-18-year-olds is over £63 million per year (DfES, 2006). In addition, around 70% of mothers aged 16–19 years claim income support, equating to around £26 million in benefits per year (Teenage Pregnancy Associates, 2011). A US study reported that a third of young teenage mothers leave school before gaining their college degree or high school diploma, and less than 2% of teenage mothers earn a degree by the time they turn 30. As teenage pregnancy deters continued education, it is estimated that over the course of his or her lifetime, a single high school dropout costs the nation approximately $260,000 in lost earnings, taxes and productivity; equating to $154 billion in lost income to the US economy per year (Shuger, 2012). It is clear, therefore, that compared to older women, becoming pregnant during adolescence is consistently associated with increased risks of poor social, economic and health outcomes for both mother and child.

It has been argued that the biological risk associated with young maternal age has been exaggerated due to inadequate control of such sociodemographic factors in research (Anderson *et al.*, 2000). For example, Casanueva and colleagues (1991) investigated the effect of late prenatal care on nutritional status of 163 pregnant adolescents aged 11–17 years and found that late prenatal care (accessed when ≥25 weeks pregnant) was associated with increased risk of maternal anaemia (57% compared to 20% of adolescents accessing prenatal care before 25 weeks), iron deficiency and zinc deficiency. Other research has shown, however, that the association between poor fetal and maternal outcomes persists even after sociodemographic factors were controlled for (Fraser *et al.*, 1995; Chen *et al.*, 2007).

Some researchers have attributed the poor pregnancy outcomes of adolescent mothers to an independent factor related to some aspect of the woman's physiology, such as gynaecological immaturity, competition for nutrients, or the growth and nutritional status of the mother (King, 2003). A plausible explanation for the negative effect of young gynaecological age on pregnancy outcome is the competition for nutrients between the mother and fetus. The competition for nutrients hypothesis was first proposed by Naeye (1981). Further support for the hypothesis was provided by a study that reported that infants born to young, growing Peruvian mothers were smaller than those born to adult women (Frisancho *et al.*, 1983). Scholl *et al.* (1990, 1994) reported that many pregnant adolescents continue to grow during gestation, as assessed by measuring knee height length, and that these adolescents give birth to smaller infants (about 155 g less) despite a tendency to gain more weight during pregnancy and retain more weight postpartum than nongrowing adolescents. This is in contrast to adults where, generally, an increased weight gain during pregnancy is associated with larger birth weights (King, 2003). In their subsequent research, Scholl *et al*. (2000) found that growing teenagers have a surge in maternal leptin concentrations during the last trimester, which may reduce the rate of maternal fat breakdown during late pregnancy and thereby increase the mother's use of glucose for energy. This would result in less energy being available for fetal growth. It looks possible, therefore, that the pregnant teenager partitions metabolic fuels to enable more energy to become available for maternal growth (and therefore higher maternal fat gains) at the expense of that available for fetal growth (resulting in lower birth weights).

The importance of maternal nutrition for the achievement of maternal and infant wellbeing is well documented. This chapter will begin with a discussion of the role of maternal nutrition in pregnancy and lactation, describing the specific nutrient needs of mothers who are pregnant and breastfeeding with particular reference to adolescents. Nutrient requirements will be discussed in the context of their impact on maternal, fetal and infant wellbeing.

Adolescence is a critical period during which lifetime habits are established (Cavadini *et al*., 2000) and, as adolescents are particularly susceptible to certain risk behaviours, including unhealthy eating, the impact that their eating behaviour has on both their short- and long-term nutritional status is considerable. This chapter discusses the eating behaviours and barriers to healthy eating in the adolescent population, with particular reference to how these behaviours may relate to other 'risky' behaviours often seen in this population. 'Adolescence' can be described as the transitional stage of development between childhood and adulthood. It is a cultural and social phenomenon, and therefore its endpoints are not easily defined. The World Health Organization (WHO, 1998) defines adolescence as a person between 10 and 19 years of age. For reasons of clarity, throughout this chapter 'adolescence' refers to the ages 10–19 years inclusive (unless otherwise stated).

Nutrition during pregnancy and lactation

Nutritional needs are increased during pregnancy and lactation in order to support fetal and infant growth and development, along with alterations in maternal body composition, metabolism and physiological systems. During this period, the maternal diet must provide sufficient nutrients to meet this increased demand and to ensure maternal wellbeing and the growth of a healthy, thriving infant. The requirement for several nutrients is higher during pregnancy and lactation than in the non-pregnant state, although the lack of congruity between countries and committees as to the appropriate magnitude of this increase is stark (Tables 2.1 and 2.2). Maternal nutrient intake and nutritional status are known to influence birth outcome. There is controversy, however, as to whether the adverse effects of suboptimal nutrition affect only the welfare of the mother and the fetus *in utero* of the chronically undernourished woman. Many studies in habitually well-nourished women have shown that optimal weight gain during pregnancy and good obstetric outcome can be achieved over a wide range of habitual dietary intake with or without any increase in dietary intake during pregnancy (Matthews *et al.*, 1999; Ramachandran, 2002).

It has been suggested that impaired intrauterine growth and development may 'programme' the fetus for cardiovascular, metabolic, or endocrine disease in adult life (Barker and Osmond, 1986). Epidemiological associations have been found to exist between lower birth size and a greater risk of death in later life from cardiovascular disease (Barker and Osmond, 1986) and type 2 diabetes mellitus (Ravelli *et al.*, 1998). The 'Developmental Origins of Adult Disease Hypothesis' describes the origin of adult disease in terms of fetal developmental 'plasticity', or the ability of the fetus to respond to environmental cues (such as poor *in utero* conditions) by choosing a trajectory of development that often has adaptive advantage. This, then, alters the development of the organism to such an extent that it affects its capacity to cope with the environment of adult life and therefore influences disease risk (Gluckman *et al.*, 2005). Intrauterine growth restriction, which may result from perturbations in placental blood flow, poor maternal nutrition, or maternal exposure to toxins (Hendrix and Berghella, 2008; Neerhof and Thaete, 2008; Kinzler and Vintzileos, 2008), provides a useful model for the examination of the developmental origins hypothesis. The subtle adjustments needed to ensure developmental plasticity in intrauterine growth restriction are brought about by epigenetic modulation of critical genes (Joss-Moore and Lane, 2009).

It should be remembered that birth outcome is influenced by an array of interrelated factors. These include sociodemographic factors (e.g. age, parity, ethnic background and socioeconomic status); nutritional factors (e.g. pre-pregnancy weight and BMI, height, lean body mass and body fat); genetics; health and illness (e.g. diabetes, hypertension, chronic disease, systemic or genital tract infections); environmental factors (e.g. geography, climate); behavioural factors (e.g. stress, anxiety and drug, alcohol and cigarette use, dietary taboos associated with pregnancy); and adequacy of prenatal care (Institute of Medicine, 1990; Garza and Rasmussen 2000). Clearly maternal and infant wellbeing should always be considered within this broader context.

Table 2.1 Micronutrient reference values during pregnancy.

	UK DRV[1] – RNI	US DRI[2-6] – RDA	WHO/FAO[7]
Vitamin A	700 μg RE/d ↑ 100 μg RE/d	750 μg RE/d (age 14–18 y) 770 μg RE/d (age 19–50 y) ↑ 50–70 μg RE/d	800 g RE/d ↑ 200 μg RE/d (age 10–18 y) ↑ 300 μg RE/d (age 19–50 y)
Vitamin D	10 μg/d ↑ 10 μg/d	15 μg/d No increment	5 μg/d No increment
Vitamin E	None set	15 mg/d No increment	None set
Vitamin K	None set	75 μg/d (age 14–18 y) (AI) 90 μg/d (age 19–50 y) No increment	55 μg/d No increment
Vitamin C	50 mg/d ↑ 10 mg/d (last trimester only)	80 mg/d (age 14–18 y) ↑ 15 mg/d 85 mg/d (age 19–50 y) ↑ 10 mg/d	55 mg/d ↑ 10 mg/d
Riboflavin	1.4 mg/d ↑ 0.3 mg/d	1.4 mg/d ↑ 0.4 mg/d (age 14–18 y) ↑ 0.3 mg/d (age 19–50 y)	1.4 mg/d ↑ 0.4 mg/d (age 14–18 y) ↑ 0.3 mg/d (age 19–50 y)
Thiamin	0.4 mg/1000 kcal (no increment)	1.4 mg/d ↑ 0.4 mg/d (age 14–18 y) ↑ 0.3 mg/d (age 19–50y)	1.4 mg/d ↑ 0.3 mg/d
Niacin	6.6 mg/d No increment	18 mg/d ↑ 4 mg/d	18 mg/d NE ↑ 2 mg/d (age 14–18 y) ↑ 4 mg/d (age 19–50 y)
Vitamin B$_6$	15 μg/g protein/d No increment	1.9 mg/d ↑ 0.7 mg/d (age 14–18 y) ↑ 0.6 mg/d (age 19–50 y)	1.9 mg/d ↑ 0.7 mg/d (age 14–18 y) ↑ 0.6 mg/d (age 19–50 y)
Folate	300 μg/d ↑ 100 μg/d	600 μg/d ↑ 200 μg/d	600 μg/d ↑ 200 μg/d
Vitamin B$_{12}$	1.5 μg/d No increment	2.6 μg/d ↑ 0.2 μg/d	2.6 μg/d ↑ 0.2 μg/d
Pantothenic acid	None set	6 mg/d (AI) ↑ 1 mg/d	6 mg/d ↑ 1 mg/d
Biotin	None set	30 μg/d (AI) ↑ 5 μg/d (age 14–18 y) No increment for women aged 19–50 y	30 μg/d (AI) ↑ 5 μg/d (age 14–18 y) No increment for women aged 19–50 y
Choline	None set	450 mg/d (AI) ↑ 50 mg/d (age 14–18 y) ↑ 25 mg/d (age 19–50 y)	None set
Calcium	800 mg/d (age 15–18y) 700 mg/d (age 19–50y) No increment	1300 mg/d (age 14–18y) 1000 mg/d (age 19–50y) No increment	800 mg/d ↑ 50 mg/d in last trimester (NPNL adolescents 1000 mg/d particularly during the growth spurt)

Table 2.1 (*continued*)

	UK DRV[1] – RNI	US DRI[2–6] – RDA	WHO/FAO[7]
Iron	14.8 mg/d No increment	27 mg/d ↑ 12 mg/d (age 14–18 y) ↑ 9 mg/d (age 19–50 y)	No figures are given for dietary iron requirements in pregnant women because the iron balance in pregnancy depends on the properties of the diet and on the amounts of stored iron
Phosphorus	634 mg/d* No increment	1250 mg/d (age 14–18 y) 700 mg/d (age 19–50 y) No increment	None set
Magnesium	300 mg/d (age 15–18 y) 270 mg/d (age 19–50 y) No increment	400 mg/d (age 14–18 y) 350 mg/d (age 19–30 y) 360 mg/d (age 31–50 y) ↑ 40 mg/d	220 mg/d No increment
Zinc	7.0 mg/d No increment	12 mg/d (age 14–18 y) 11 mg/d (age 19–50 y) ↑ 3 mg/d	Depending on bioavailability of zinc: 3.4–11.0 mg/d (1st trimester) 4.2–14.0 mg/d (2nd trimester) 6.0–20.0 (3rd trimester) NPNL adolescents 4.3–14.4 mg/d NPNL women 3.0–9.8 mg/d
Copper	1.0 mg/d (age 15–16 y) 1.2 mg/d (age 18–50 y) No increment	1.0 mg/d ↑ 0.1 mg/d	None set
Selenium	60 µg/d No increment	60 µg/d ↑ 5 µg/d	28 µg/d (2nd trimester) ↑ 2 µg/d 30 µg/d (3rd trimester) ↑ 4 µg/d
Iodine	140 µg/d No increment	220 µg/d ↑ 70 µg/d	200 µg/d ↑ 50 µg/d
Potassium	3.5 g/d No increment	4.7 g/d (AI) No increment	None set
Manganese	None set	2.0 mg/d (AI) ↑ 0.4 mg/d (age 14–18 y) ↑ 0.2 mg/d (age 19–50 y)	None set
Molybdenum	None set	50 µg/d ↑ 7 µg/d (age 14–18 y) ↑ 5 µg/d (age 19–50 y)	None set

↑ represents the amount of increase from non-pregnant, non-lactating levels.
↓ represents the amount of decrease from non-pregnant, non-lactating levels.
DRV: dietary reference value; RNI: reference nutrient intake; DRI: dietary reference intakes; RDA: recommended daily allowance; RE: retinol equivalents; NE: niacin equivalents; AI: average intake; NPNL: non-pregnant, non-lactating
*RNI for phosphorus set to equal the RNI for calcium in mmol. The increment for pregnancy/lactation therefore reflects the increment set for calcium
(*See Table 2.2 for numbered footnotes*)

Table 2.2 Micronutrient reference values during lactation.

	UK DRV[1] – RNI	US DRI[2-6] – RDA	WHO/FAO[7]
Vitamin A	950 µg RE/d ↑ 350 µg RE/d	1200 µg RE/d (age 14–18 y) ↑ 500 µg RE/d 1300 µg RE/d (age 19–50 y) ↑ 600 µg RE/d	850 µg RE/d ↑ 350 µg RE/d
Vitamin D	10 µg/d ↑ 10 µg/d	15 µg/d No increment	5 µg/d No increment
Vitamin E	None set	19 mg/d ↑ 4 mg/d	None set
Vitamin K	None set	75 µg/d (age 14–18 y) 90 µg/d (age 19–50 y) No increment	55 µg/d No increment
Vitamin C	70 mg/d ↑ 30 mg/d	115 mg/d (age 14–18 y) ↑ 50 mg/d 120 mg/d (age 19–50 y) ↑ 45 mg/d	70 mg/d ↑ 25 mg/d
Riboflavin	1.6 mg/d ↑ 0.5 mg/d	1.6 mg/d ↑ 0.6 mg/d (age 14–18 y) ↑ 0.5 mg/d (age 19–50 y)	1.6 mg/d ↑ 0.5 mg/d
Thiamin	0.4 mg/1000 kcal No increment	1.4 mg/d ↑ 0.4 mg/d (age 14–18 y) ↑ 0.3 mg/d (age 19–50 y)	1.5 mg/d ↑ 0.4 mg/d
Niacin	8.9 mg/d ↑ 2.3 mg/d	17 mg/d ↑ 3 mg/d	17 mg/d NE ↑ 3 mg/d
Vitamin B_6	15 µg/g protein/d No increment	2.0 mg/d ↑ 0.8 mg/d (age 14–18 y) ↑ 0.7 mg/d (age 19–50 y)	2.0 mg/d ↑ 0.7 mg/d
Folate	260 µg/d ↑ 60 µg/d	500 µg/d ↑ 100 µg/d	500 µg/d ↑ 100 µg/d
Vitamin B_{12}	2.0 µg/d ↑ 0.5 µg/d	2.8 µg/d ↑ 0.4 µg/d	2.8 µg/d ↑ 0.4 µg/d
Pantothenic acid	None set	7 mg/d (AI) ↑ 2 mg/d	7 mg/d ↑ 2 mg/d
Biotin	None set	35 µg/d (AI) ↑ 10 µg/d (age 14–18 y) ↑ 5 µg/d (age 19–50 y)	35 µg/d ↑ 5 µg/d
Choline	None set	550 mg/d (AI) ↑ 150 mg/d(age 14–18 y) ↑ 125 mg/d (age 19–50 y)	None set
Calcium	1350 mg/d (age 15–18 y) 1250 mg/d (age 19–50 y) ↑ 550 mg/d	1300 mg/d (age 14–18 y) 1000 mg/d (age 19–50 y) No increment	750 mg/d No increment (NPNL adolescents 1000 mg/d particularly during the growth spurt)

Table 2.2 (*continued*)

	UK DRV[1] – RNI	US DRI[2–6] – RDA	WHO/FAO[7]
Iron	14.8 mg/d No increment	10 mg/d (age 14–18y) ↓ 5 mg/d 9 mg/d (age 19–50 y) ↓ 9 mg/d	10–30 mg/d depending on bioavailability of iron (a decrease of around 50% of NPNL values)
Phosphorus	990 mg/d* ↑ 440 mg/d	1250 mg/d (age 14–18 y) 700 mg/d (age 19–50 y) No increment	None set
Magnesium	350 mg/d (age 15–18 y) 320 mg/d (age 19–50 y) ↑ 50 mg/d	360 mg/d (age 14–18 y) 310 mg/d (age 19–30 y) 320 mg/d (age 31–50 y) No increment	270 mg/d ↑ 50 mg/d
Zinc	13 mg/d (0–4 months) 9.5 mg/d (4+ months) ↑ 2.5–6 mg/d	13 mg/d (age 14–18 y) 12 mg/d (age 19–50) ↑ 4 mg/d	Depending on bioavailability of zinc: 5.8–19 mg/d (0–3 months) 5.3–17.5 mg/d (3–6 months) 4.3–14.4 (7–12 months) NPNL adolescents 4.3–14.4 mg/d NPNL women 3.0–9.8 mg/d
Copper	1.3 µg/d (age 15–16 y) 1.5 µg/d (age 18–50 y) ↑ 0.3 µg/d	1.3 µg/d ↑ 0.4 µg/d	None set
Selenium	75 µg/d ↑ 15 µg/d	70 µg/d ↑ 15 µg/d	35 µg/d (0–6 months) ↑ 9 µg/d 42 µg/d (7–12 months) ↑ 16 µg/d
Iodine	140 µg/d No increment	290 µg/d ↑ 140 µg/d	200 µg/d ↑ 50 µg/d
Potassium	3.5 g/d No increment	5.1 g/d (AI) ↑ 0.4 g/d	None set
Manganese	None set	2.6 mg/d (AI) ↑ 1.0 mg/d (age 14–18 y) ↑ 0.8 mg/d (age 19–50 y)	None set
Molybdenum	None set	50 µg/d ↑ 7 µg/d (age 14–18 y) ↑ 5 µg/d (age 19–50 y)	None set

[1]Committee on Medical Aspects of Food Policy (COMA) (1991)
[2]Institute of Medicine, Food and Nutrition Board (1997)
[3]Institute of Medicine, Food and Nutrition Board (1998)
[4]Institute of Medicine, Food and Nutrition Board (2000)
[5]Institute of Medicine, Food and Nutrition Board (2001)
[6]Institute of Medicine, Food and Nutrition Board (2004)
[7]WHO/FAO (2004)
(*See Table 2.1 for symbols and abbreviations*)

Lactation has a nutritive burden considerably greater than that of pregnancy: the energy required to produce 1 litre of breast milk is estimated to be 700 kcal, and the energy needed for a woman to breastfeed for 4 months is approximately equivalent to the total energy cost of pregnancy (Cervera and Ngo, 2001; Picciano, 2003). Although some of this energy will be sourced from the nutrients stored by the mother during pregnancy, there is a need for breastfeeding mothers to increase their food intake in order to meet the elevated energy and micronutrient requirements (Cervera and Ngo, 2001). The exact nature of this increased need, however, is contentious, with diverse dietary recommendations during lactation (as with pregnancy) between countries and committees (Table 2.2) (Hall Moran *et al.*, 2010).

The duration and intensity of lactation (whether the infant is breastfed exclusively or only partially) is likely to influence the nutritional needs of breastfeeding women as an exclusively breastfeeding woman has much greater energy and nutrient needs (with the exception of iron attributed to the potential protective effect of lactational amenorrhoea) than a woman who is only partially breastfeeding (Dewey, 2004). These aspects of breastfeeding, however, are rarely considered in studies of the nutritional impact of lactation in women. While the WHO recommends that infants should be exclusively breastfed for the first 6 months of life with breastfeeding continuing for up to 2 years of age or beyond (WHO, 2001), in reality, there are wide deviations from this recommended norm in terms of both duration and intensity, especially in industrialised countries, challenging the meaningfulness of setting standard recommendations of nutrient intakes for lactation (Hall Moran *et al.*, 2010).

Dietary recommendations during pregnancy and lactation

Nutrient recommendations are part of the basis for food policy and food-based dietary guidelines. The way in which these are defined vary between countries. In the UK, the Department of Health published Dietary Reference Values (DRVs) for Food Energy and Nutrients in 1991 (DH, 1991). DRVs can be divided into three main categories:

- RNI – Reference Nutrient Intake (97.5% of the population's requirement is met)
- EAR – Estimated Average Requirement (50% of the population's requirement is met)
- LRNI – Lower Recommended Nutritional Intake (2.5% of the population's requirement is met)

The terminology used to describe reference values varies between countries, making comparisons difficult. For example, the UK's RNI is equivalent to the population reference intake (PRI) used by the European Union (EU) and the recommended daily allowance (RDA) used in the USA. Such divergent terminology and concepts can lead to confused messages that may have a serious impact on policy and significant health consequences (Pavlovic *et al.*, 2007).

As already mentioned, requirements increase for several nutrients during pregnancy and lactation, although there is a lack of consensus among committees as to the nature of these increments with recommendations varying both qualitatively and quantitatively (Tables 2.1 and 2.2). For example, the UK Department of Health recommends increments of six vitamins and minerals during pregnancy (vitamins A, D, C, riboflavin, folate and phosphorus) and 13 in lactation (vitamin B_{12}, niacin, calcium, magnesium, zinc, copper and selenium, in addition to those increased in pregnancy) (DH, 1991). In comparison the USA recommend increments of up to 20 vitamins and minerals during pregnancy and lactation (IOM, 1997, 1998, 2000, 2001, 2004). There is also little recognition of increased requirements for adolescents in the UK recommendations, and no additional increments are recommended for pregnant or breastfeeding adolescents specifically. In contrast, the US recommendations identify several nutrients for which there are differential requirements in pregnant and breastfeeding adolescents compared to older pregnant and breastfeeding women (e.g. vitamin A, vitamin C, calcium, magnesium and zinc). Such disparities in recommendations have arisen from the use of different concepts and sometimes different data, and because the expert committees who set the standard often base their decisions on judgements concerning the quality of the available research (Pijls *et al.*, 2009). As national reference values are reviewed at different time points, decisions may also be based on different scientific data (Doets *et al.*, 2008).

As the metabolic data upon which estimates of requirements are based are often lacking for physiological states such as pregnancy and lactation due to the practical difficulties or ethical limitations of conducting research on women during these reproductive stages, differences between values can also be partly ascribed to differences in methodological approaches and how these approaches are applied (Atkinson and Koletzko, 2007). It has been argued that the limited systematic physiological difference in populations and climate across Western countries (with the possible exception of difference in sunlight exposure and consequent vitamin D recommendations) does not justify the existing disparities in nutrient recommendations. To address this problem, a network of excellence was established in 2007 (European Micronutrients Recommendations Aligned Network – http://www.eurreca.org/) to provide a common framework that uses consistent terminology in order to develop and maintain nutrient recommendations across Europe that are based on the best current evidence (Pijls *et al.*, 2009).

Although signs of overt deficiency are now rare in the UK, suboptimal nutrient intake and status is relatively common in pregnant and breastfeeding adolescents (Buttriss, 2002). There follows a discussion of some of the key micronutrients that have been identified for increased requirement during pregnancy and lactation with specific reference to the needs of adolescents who are pregnant or breastfeeding. Few prospective studies have been carried out that investigate the nutrition of pregnant or breastfeeding adolescents (Hall Moran, 2007a,b; Hall Moran *et al.*, 2010), and only two studies have described the diets of pregnant adolescents in the UK (Burchett and Seeley, 2003; Baker *et al.*, 2009). Evidence of adolescent eating patterns will be supplemented by citing data from the National Diet and Nutrition Survey (NDNS), a continuous cross-sectional survey, designed to assess the diet, nutrient intake and nutritional status of the general population aged 18 months upwards living in private households in the UK (Gregory *et al.*, 2000; Bates *et al.*, 2010).

Vitamin A

Vitamin A is needed for the growth and differentiation of cells and tissues and plays a key role in infant development (Strobe *et al.*, 2007). Vitamin A deficiency is a major public health problem in developing countries and it is estimated that, globally, 140–250 million children under the age of 5 years are affected by vitamin A deficiency. These children suffer a dramatically increased risk of death, blindness and illness, especially from measles and diarrhoea. Although high doses of vitamin A should not be consumed during pregnancy (to avoid teratogenesis), high dose supplementation of postpartum women with vitamin A has been shown to be an effective way of ensuring adequate supplies to the infant through breast milk (Sommer *et al.*, 2002) and preventing deficiency. Some caution should be exercised before providing universal high-dose vitamin A supplementation, however, as vitamin A (retinol) has been found to have a modulating effect on colostrum vitamin E (alpha-tocopherol) in human breast milk. Breastfeeding women not at risk of vitamin A deficiency enrolled in such supplementation programmes may exhibit reduced bioavailability of alpha-tocopherol in their breast milk, thereby compromising their infant's nutritional status (de Lira *et al.*, 2011).

Recommended intakes for vitamin A range from 700–800 µg/retinol equivalent (RE)/day during pregnancy and 850–1300 µg/RE/day when breastfeeding based on UK, US and WHO/FAO reference values (Tables 2.1 and 2.2). Evidence of significant deficit in the vitamin A intake of young women is inconclusive. In a study of 500 pregnant adolescents in the UK, Baker *et al.* (2009) reported vitamin A consumption that was 85% of the RNI. Research from the USA and Australia, however, have suggested that vitamin A intakes of pregnant adolescents are adequate (Hall Moran, 2007a). UK NDNS data reported that the median vitamin intake of adolescent girls did not meet the UK RNI of 600 µg/RE/day (non-pregnant, non-lactating level) (Bates *et al.*, 2010), but Haggarty *et al.*, (2009) found no evidence of low intake in socially deprived mothers (*n* = 1461) living in Aberdeen, UK.

Folate

Since 1992, the UK Department of Health has advised women who could become pregnant to take a daily folic acid supplement of 400 µg/d, in addition to ensuring their diet is rich in foods providing folates and folic acid (DH, 1992). US and WHO recommendations are higher at 600 µg/d (Table 2.1). Insufficient intake of folate in the early stages of pregnancy is linked to increased risk of neural tube defects in infants. Folate deficiency during pregnancy has also been linked to megaloblastic anaemia, high rates of spontaneous abortion, toxaemia, intrauterine growth retardation, premature delivery and antepartum haemorrhage (Garza and Rasmussen, 2000). During infancy, folate is critical to the rapid growth and development of the early years of life and poor folate status has been shown to be an independent risk factor for respiratory infections in young children (Strand *et al.*, 2007). Infant serum folate has been positively associated with exclusive breastfeeding and breastfed infants are usually well protected against folate deficiency (Hay *et al.*, 2008).

In the UK, nearly 40% of adolescents aged 15–18 years have red cell folate levels considered to indicate marginal status (< 13.0 nmol/L), with an average folate intake from food and supplement sources of 215 µg/day (Gregory *et al.*, 2000). Baker and colleagues (2009) found that median folate intakes (249 µg/day) of pregnant adolescents in the UK were below UK, US and WHO/FAO recommended amounts and 12% had serum folate indicative of deficient status (<7.0 nmol/L). Adolescents who smoked had a lower folate status than those who did not (it is well recognised that smoking status lowers serum and red blood cell folate), despite no differences in dietary intake. Furthermore, poor folate intake and status were was associated with increased risk of having a small for gestational age infant, even after controlling for confounding factors (Baker *et al.*, 2009). Gadowsky *et al.* (1995) also found that 7% and 17.5% of the 58 pregnant adolescents in their Canadian study had plasma concentrations indicative of deficient and marginal status respectively. A more recent US study found little evidence of folate deficiency among their study of 60 pregnant adolescents (Iannotti *et al.*, 2005). This may be due in part to the US policy introduced in 1998 for the mandatory fortification of cereals with folic acid (Klee, 200). At present there is no folic acid fortification programme in the UK, due to concerns about masking vitamin B_{12} deficiency, despite evidence that countries who have fortified food with folic acid report up to 19% reduction in neural tube defect birth prevalence (Honein *et al.*, 2001).

Riboflavin

The requirements for riboflavin are increased during pregnancy and when breastfeeding (1.4 mg/d and 1.6 mg/d respectively) (Tables 2.1 and 2.2). The UK NDNS in 2000 reported that 95% of adolescents aged 15–18 years had biochemical values normally considered to indicate riboflavin deficiency and 21% had riboflavin intakes that fell below the LRNI (Gregory *et al.*, 2000), although this latter figure has fallen to 12% in recent years (Bates *et al.*, 2010). Most dietary riboflavin occurs as the coenzymes flavin mononucleotide (FMN) and flavin adenine dinucleotide (FAD), which are involved in oxidation–reduction reactions in a number of metabolic pathways and affect cellular respiration. Riboflavin coenzymes are required in the metabolism of other nutrients, such as tryptophan, folic acid and in the absorption of iron (Thurnham *et al.*, 2000).

It has been suggested that, due to the increased energy demand during adolescence, more riboflavin, thiamin and niacin are necessary to facilitate the release of energy from carbohydrates (Lifshitz *et al.*, 1993). Because of the importance of riboflavin in metabolism, particularly folate metabolism, and due to the increased demand for riboflavin in adolescence, any deficiency occurring in adolescent pregnancy may have serious implications for birth outcome. As yet the riboflavin status of pregnant or breastfeeding adolescents remains unstudied. However, riboflavin intakes of pregnant adolescents in the USA and UK appear to be above recommended reference values (Pobocik *et al.*, 2003; Baker *et al.*, 2009).

Vitamin B_6

In the UK, biochemical evidence of vitamin B_6 deficiency has been reported in 8% of adolescents aged 15–18 years (Gregory *et al.*, 2000). The increased protein needs during pregnancy and the role of pyridoxal phosphate and pyridoxamine phosphate as coenzymes of transamination and other products of protein metabolism may increase the requirements of this vitamin during pregnancy. There is, however, limited direct evidence to support this hypothesis at present (Garza and Rasmussen, 2000). Inadequate maternal vitamin B_6 status has been associated with toxaemia, low birth weight and poor general conditions of infants at birth (IOM, 1990).

No studies to date have investigated the vitamin B_6 status of pregnant or breastfeeding adolescents, but a US study of 46 pregnant adolescents enrolled in the WIC programme (The Special Supplemental Nutrition Program for Women, Infants, and Children, which provides supplemental foods, health care referrals and nutrition education for low-income pregnant, breastfeeding and non-breastfeeding postpartum women) found that vitamin B_6 intakes were below the US DRI of 1.9 mg/day (Endres *et al.*, 1985). Evidence from the UK, however, suggests that B_6 intake in pregnant teenagers is well above the UK RNI of 15 µg/g protein/day (Baker *et al.*, 2009).

Vitamin B$_{12}$

Vitamin B_{12}, also known as cobalamin, is a water-soluble vitamin which plays a key role in the normal functioning of the brain and nervous system and red blood cell formation. It is involved in the metabolism of every cell of the human body, especially affecting DNA synthesis and regulation, and also has a role in fatty acid synthesis and energy production. Vitamin B_{12} deficiency that is undetected and untreated in infants can result in severe and permanent neurological damage (IOM, 1998). Vitamin B_{12} crosses the placenta during pregnancy and is present in breast milk. Exclusively breastfed infants of vegetarian women may have very limited reserves of vitamin B_{12} and can develop vitamin B_{12} deficiency within months of birth (von Schenck *et al.*, 1997). Vegetarian mothers should be advised to take a cobalamin supplement during pregnancy and lactation, and to ensure that complementary foods are rich in cobalamin (Hay *et al.*, 2008).

Vitamin B_{12} intakes have been found to be above the UK RNI of 1.5 µg/day in pregnant adolescents (Baker *et al.*, 2009). Serum cobalamin levels were negatively associated with smoking, although no association has been found to exist between serum cobalamin and pregnancy outcome (Baker *et al.*, 2009). An American study of pregnant adolescents found no evidence of serum B_{12} depletion (Ianotti *et al.*, 2005). No studies to date have investigated the vitamin B_{12} status of pregnant or breastfeeding vegetarian adolescents.

Vitamin D

Vitamin D is essential for bone metabolism. Most bone mineral deposition occurs during adolescence, with up to 50% of bone mass being acquired during this period of development (Buttriss, 2000). Peak bone mass in the spine and proximal femur, for example, is reached at the age of 16 years (Albertson *et al.*, 1997). There is also increasing evidence that links vitamin D deficiency to a number of chronic diseases such as hypertension, immune dysfunction, cancer, diabetes and cardiovascular disease (Hyppönen *et al.*, 2001; Prentice, 2008; Saintonge *et al.*, 2009).

Vitamin D deficiency has gained a lot of interest in recent years, with the resurgence in the prevalence of rickets, particularly among South Asian immigrants to western Europe (Alfaham *et al.*, 1995; Gillie, 2004). Vitamin D deficiency in pregnancy has been associated with reduced birth weight and neonatal hypocalcaemia and tetany (Garza and Rasmussen, 2000). As vitamin D is essential for calcium absorption, poor vitamin D status also has implications for adolescents, who are still growing themselves, and their infants. Recent research has found that both maternal 25(OH)D concentration (a biomarker for vitamin D status) and dietary calcium intake influences fetal bone growth (Young *et al.*, 2012). A significant interaction between the two nutrients was evident, with higher calcium intakes compensating or suboptimal vitamin D status and vice versa, suggesting that attainment of either may attenuate the deficits in fetal long bone growth and neonatal length at birth observed in pregnant adolescents who are calcium/vitamin D deficient (Young *et al.*, 2012).

Human breast milk typically contains a concentration of 25 IU/L vitamin D or less although limited sunlight exposure has been shown to prevent rickets in many breastfed infants. However, breastfed infants who do not receive supplemental vitamin D or adequate sunlight exposure may be at increased risk of developing vitamin D deficiency or rickets (Gartner and Greer, 2003).

In the UK, public health guidance has been provided which recommends that pregnant and breastfeeding women increase their vitamin D intake to 10 µg/day (NICE, 2011). As there are few dietary sources of vitamin D available to meet this recommended target vitamin D supplements should be taken. Many individual and environmental factors interfere with the ability to have sufficient sunlight exposure to produce vitamin D endogenously, so special care should be given to groups who are particularly vulnerable to vitamin D deficiency. Reduced UV exposure from sunlight due to the prevalent use of sunscreen creams, sunlight avoidance or the wearing of traditional Muslim dress can contribute to vitamin D deficiency in pregnant and lactating mothers, which can lead to lowered breast milk concentrations (Se*th et al.*, 2009). Other factors which influence the amount of UV exposure available for the synthesis of vitamin D include the amount of skin pigmentation, body mass, degree of latitude, season, the amount of cloud cover, the extent of air pollution and the amount of skin exposed. Thus the current UK NICE guidance states:

> Health professionals should take particular care to check that women at greatest risk of deficiency are following advice to take a vitamin D supplement during pregnancy and while breastfeeding. These include women who are obese, have limited skin exposure to sunlight or who are of South Asian, African, Caribbean or Middle Eastern descent. (NICE 2011, p. 9)

NICE does not specifically identify adolescent mothers as 'at risk', despite evidence from the UK which revealed that many pregnant adolescents have poor vitamin D intake and status (30% had serum 25(OH)D levels < 25 nmol/L) and less than 2% reporting to take supplements containing vitamin D (Baker *et al.*, 2009). Although supplements containing folic acid, vitamin C and vitamin D are now freely available to all pregnant adolescents in the UK, more needs to be done to improve uptake in this age group.

Calcium

From the age of around 10–17 years there is a striking increase in the rate of skeletal calcium accretion, with calcium retention peaking at 300–400 mg/day (WHO/FAO). UK, US and WHO/FAO dietary recommendations state that adolescents should consume more calcium than women aged 19+ years during this peak growth phase to cover the requirements of skeletal growth (DH, 1991; IOM, 1997; WHO/FAO, 2004). As the growing fetus obtains its calcium requirements from the maternal skeleton, it has been suggested that pregnant adolescents may be particularly at risk of bone fragility and osteoporosis in later life (Lytle, 2002).

Calcium supplementation during pregnancy has been associated with a reduced risk of gestational hypertension, preterm delivery and possibly preeclampsia (Repke and Villar, 1991), emphasising the importance of adequate calcium intake during pregnancy. When breastfeeding, women typically lose 280–400 mg/day of calcium through breast milk. To meet this increased demand the mother must mobilise calcium from her own stores, and calcium supplementation has been found to have no significant benefit in terms of breast milk calcium concentration, even in those with low dietary intakes of calcium (300–400 mg/d) and low breast milk concentrations (Jarjou *et al.*, 2006). Whilst there is evidence that adolescents experience bone mineral density loss during lactation, this effect seems to be transient, with subsequent repletion of bone mineral density once breastfeeding is ceased (Bezerra *et al.*, 2004). Further, it has been found that adolescents experience less bone resorption associated with lactation compared to adults, potentially contributing to protection against excessive bone loss (Bezerra *et al.*, 2002). There is also emerging evidence of a link between vitamin D receptor gene polymorphisms and bone mass in lactating adolescent women, with some genotypes having better bone status than others in a population with habitually low calcium intakes (Bezerra *et al.*, 2007).

UK NDNS data indicate that 11% of adolescents in the UK currently have calcium intakes below the LRNI in the UK (Bates *et al.*, 2010). UK dietary recommendations do not specify an increment in calcium intake during pregnancy, but do recommend an additional 550 mg Ca/d (to 1250 mg/d) to be consumed if breastfeeding (DH, 1991). For contrast, US recommendations state that adolescents should consume 1300 mg calcium per day whether they are pregnant, breastfeeding or not (IOM, 1997) (Tables 2.1 and 2.2).

Iron

Iron requirements in pregnancy total approximately 800–900 mg (Garza and Rasmussen, 2000). The UK dietary reference values for iron during pregnancy are the same as in non-pregnant women (14.8 mg/day; DH, 1991), although the US DRI for pregnancy is almost twice that at 27 mg/day (IOM, 1997). WHO/FAO provide no data for dietary iron requirements for pregnant women because 'the iron balance in pregnancy depends not only on the properties of the diet but also and especially on the amounts of stored iron' (WHO/FAO, 2004, p. 271).

Iron is needed for the rapid expansion of maternal blood volume and the deposition of iron in fetal tissues. Reduced oxygen-carrying capacity of the maternal blood can cause poor oxygenation in the fetus (Reifsnider and Gill, 2000). Iron deficiency anaemia (defined as haemoglobin (Hb) concentration <110 g/L in first trimester, < 105 g/L in second and third trimesters and < 100 g/L in postpartum period) is the most common nutrient deficiency in pregnancy and is associated with an increased risk of preterm delivery, low birth weight (Scholl and Hediger, 1995) and perinatal mortality (Ward, 2000; Tomashek *et al.*, 2006). Impaired psychomotor and/or mental development are well described in infants with iron deficiency anaemia (Perez *et al.*, 2005). Iron deficiency may contribute to maternal morbidity through effects on immune function, with increased susceptibility or severity of infections (Ekiz *et al.*, 2005*)*, poor work capacity and performance (Haas *et al.*, 2001) and disturbances of postpartum cognition and emotions (Beard *et al.*, 2005). Although iron deficiency is thought to affect up to 50% of women of childbearing age in the UK (Williamson, 2006), routine iron supplementation for all women in pregnancy is not recommended. Rather UK guidelines state that non-anaemic women identified to be at increased risk of iron deficiency (such as those with previous anaemia, multiple pregnancy, consecutive pregnancies with less than a year's interval between, adolescents and vegetarians) should have a serum ferritin checked early in pregnancy and be offered oral supplements if ferritin is < 30 ug/L (British Committee for Standards in Haematology, 2011).

After pregnancy, red cell mass contracts helping iron stores return to normal. Breastfeeding further protects against iron loss through lactational amenorrhoea. To reflect this US and WHO/FAO maternal dietary recommendations for iron decline during breastfeeding by around 50% from the levels recommended during pregnancy (Table 2.2). Mothers may still become anaemic in the postpartum period, mainly due to inadequate stores prior to pregnancy, but factors such as inflammation and infection may play a role (Lozoff *et al.*, 2006).

Controversy surrounds the adequacy of breast milk to provide the exclusively breastfed infant with sufficient iron for the six months recommended by WHO (2001). The WHO recommendations are based on a systematic review conducted by Kramer and Kakuma (2002), who concluded that, on the basis of available studies, children exclusively breastfed for six months were not adversely affected in terms of growth and allergy or asthma risk and had a reduced infection risk compared to infants exclusively breastfed for 3–4 months. Fewtrell *et al.* (2011) have challenged this evidence, claiming that there is insufficient evidence to confidently recommend exclusive breastfeeding for six months for infants in developed countries, and called for large randomised trials to be carried out to rule out the development of iron deficiency in 'susceptible' infants. A recent ransomised controlled trial of 100 infants in Iceland reported that adding a small amount of complementary food in addition to breast milk to infants' diets from four months had no effect on growth, but did reveal a small but statistically significant positive effect on iron status at six months (Jonsdottir *et al.*, 2012). The implications of this small study, however, have yet to be elucidated, and the weight of evidence still lies firmly behind the current WHO recommendations to breast feed exclusively until six months, and thereafter introduce appropriate complementary foods whilst continuing to breastfeed for at least two years (WHO, 2001).

Iron deficiency is fairly common in adolescence, especially among older adolescent females, lower socio-economic groups and pregnant adolescents (Looker *et al.*, 1987). Adolescents who consume vegetarian diets are also at risk. Iron deficiency during adolescence is partly related to rapid growth: the sharp

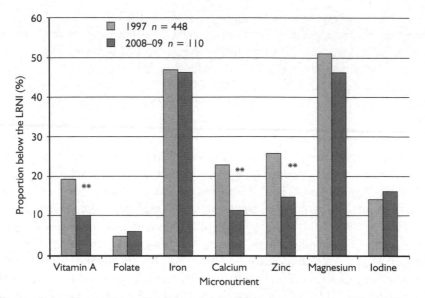

Figure 2.1 Proportion of girls aged 11–18 years with mean daily intakes of selected micronutrients from food sources only below the LRNI, by survey year. ****Proportion was significantly different from that of in the 1997 survey (*p* < 0.0001). From Whitton *et al.* (2011)

increases in lean body mass, blood volume and red cell mass increase iron needs for myoglobin in muscle and haemoglobin in blood (Lifshitz *et al.*, 1993). Systematic reviews have reported that pregnant adolescents' diets are suboptimal in iron, and iron deficiency anaemia is prevalent (Hall Moran, 2007a,b). More recently, pregnant adolescents in the UK have been reported to have median iron intakes that are lower than UK and US recommended amounts, and over half had iron deficiency anaemia. Interestingly, the risk of small for gestational age birth was significantly higher in adolescents with low food iron intake, but not when intake included iron from supplements (Baker *et al.*, 2009). The UK NDNS reported that a large proportion of adolescents aged 11–18 years had intakes below the LNRI for iron, and this situation (unlike that for other nutrients) has remained unchanged from previous surveys (Figure 2.1) (Bates *et al.*, 2010). Iron intakes in the UK have declined over the past few decades, which may be linked to changes in the consumption of specific foods, such as the offal meats liver and kidney, which are rich in iron but whose popularity has waned in recent years (Fairweather-Tait, 2004; Whitton *et al.*, 2011).

Magnesium

Magnesium acts as a cofactor of several enzymes involved in energy metabolism, protein synthesis, RNA and DNA synthesis, and maintenance of the electrical potential of nervous tissues and cell membranes (WHO/FAO, 2004). Magnesium is important throughout all life stages; in adolescence magnesium (together with calcium) is needed for bone formation and growth. There are relatively few studies carried out on the role of magnesium on maternal/fetal wellbeing, but a systematic review has shown a neuroprotective role for antenatal magnesium sulphate therapy given to women at risk of preterm birth for the preterm fetus, with reduced rates of cerebral palsy and substantial gross motor dysfunction in their infants (Doyle *et al.*, 2009). An earlier meta-analysis of randomised controlled trials indicated that oral magnesium treatment may result in lower risk of preterm birth, low birth weight and infants who are small for gestational age compared with placebo treatment. However, the authors could not recommend dietary magnesium supplementation of pregnant women for routine clinical practice due to the poor methodological quality of the evidence (Makrides and Crowther, 2001).

UK NDNS data revealed that 40% of adolescent females aged 11–18 years were below the LRNI for magnesium (Figure 2.1) (Bates *et al.*, 2011) and several studies have found that pregnant adolescents have magnesium intakes below recommended intakes (Skinner *et al.*, 1992; Dunn *et al.*, 1994; Giddens *et al.*, 2000; Pobocik *et al.*, 2003; Baker *et al.*, 2009). As the evidence on magnesium supplementation is not yet sufficiently robust, adolescents should be encouraged to eat sufficient amounts of magnesium-rich foods, such as dairy products, breads and cereals.

Zinc

Zinc plays a critical role in a variety of complex mechanisms during cell replication, maturation and adhesion, such as DNA and RNA metabolism, signal recognition and transduction, gene expression, and hormone regulation (Donangelo and King, 2012). Consequently, an adequate supply of zinc is essential for the normal growth and development of the fetus, and mammary gland function for milk synthesis and secretion. Adolescents who are still growing may also have an increased demand for zinc during pregnancy and lactation (Institute of Medicine, 2001). Despite the importance of zinc in a number of functions, observational data relating zinc deficiency to adverse fetal outcome have produced conflicting results. This is likely to be due, in part, to the problematic nature of assessing zinc status, as a sensitive, specific biomarker for zinc has not yet been identified (King, 2011). Studies of zinc supplementation in pregnancy and have failed to document a consistent beneficial effect on fetal growth, duration of gestation, and early neonatal survival (Shah and Sachdev, 2008) and plasma zinc concentrations have not been found to be associated with small for gestational age in pregnant adolescents (Mistry *et al.*, 2012). Evidence is emerging, however, on a possible protective role of supplemental zinc on neonatal immune status and infant morbidity from infectious diseases (Shah and Sachdev, 2008).

The UK DH recommends that zinc intake should increase for women who breastfeed to 13 mg/d (0–4 months of lactation) and 9.5 mg/d (4+ months of lactation). The high level of zinc in colostrum, which is 17 times higher than that in blood, illustrates the importance of zinc in development of newborn (Almeida *et al.*, 2008). Zinc concentration of milk declines rapidly in the first 3 months postpartum from 59.4 to 16.7 $\mu mol/L$ (Krebs *et al.*, 1995) and the high zinc needs of early breastfeeding may be met partially by mobilising maternal zinc pools. It has been estimated that about 4–6% of maternal bone mass is lost during six months of full lactation enabling maternal bone to contribute about 20% of the breast milk zinc over a six-month period (Moser-Veillon, 1995). A number of studies of lactating women with marginal zinc status have revealed that homeostatic mechanisms can compensate for low maternal dietary zinc intakes. The proportion of dietary zinc absorbed in such women has been shown to increase by over 70% compared to non-lactating women or pre-conception values (Jackson *et al.*, 1988; Sian *et al.*, 2002).

Although the prevalence of severe zinc deficiency is rare, mild to moderate zinc deficiency is common in pregnant and lactating women in several regions of the world (Brown *et al.*, 2004). Caulfield and colleagues (1998) have estimated that 82% of pregnant women in the world have zinc intakes below recommended values. Evidence from the UK NDNS suggests that 15% of adolescents had zinc intakes below the LRNI (Gregory *et al.*, 2000). In pregnant adolescents mean zinc intake (8.1 ± 2.9 mg) has been found to be above the UK RNI, but only 80% of the US EAR (Baker *et al.*, 2009). Less is known, however, about the zinc status of adolescents during pregnancy and lactation and a systematic review concluded that 'due to limited research, conclusions cannot be drawn about the zinc status of pregnant adolescents' (Hall Moran, 2007a, p. 74). Clearly further research is needed within this specific population.

Iodine

Insufficient intake of iodine during pregnancy and the immediate postpartum period increases the risk of neurologic and psychological deficits in children. In the children of women living in iodine-deficient areas, child IQ tend to be lower and attention deficit and hyperactivity disorders more prevalent compared to those in iodine-replete regions (Leung *et al.*, 2011). For women with marginal iodine status, the demands of pregnancy and lactation can precipitate clinical and biochemical symptoms including increased thyroid volume, altered thyroid hormone levels and impaired mental function (Dorea, 2002; Zimmermann and Delange, 2004).

Thyroidal iodine turnover rate is more rapid in infants (Zimmermann, 2009), so adequate breast milk iodine levels are particularly important for neuro-development in breastfed infants. A 33% increase in iodine intake is needed to accommodate the changes in maternal thyroid metabolism to support lactation and to supply sufficient iodine for milk to meet the needs for growth and development of the infant (WHO/FAO, 2004). In order to ensure that pregnant and lactating women do not suffer from iodine deficiency postpartum and that there is sufficient iodine in their breast milk, WHO recommends a dietary iodine intake of 200 µg per day (WHO, 2007) and the IOM in the US recommend intakes of 220 µg/d in pregnancy and 290 µg/day when breastfeeding (IOM, 2001).

Iodine deficiency affects more than 2.2 billion individuals (38% of the world's population) (ICCIDD, 2011) and remains the leading cause of preventable mental retardation worldwide. Although iodine deficiency is certainly much more common in low-income countries it is not confined only to them. A study of 737 teenage girls from nine areas of the UK found that half had a mild iodine deficiency while nearly a fifth (18%) of girls had moderate iodine deficiency with urinary iodine levels of below 50 µg/L rather than the acceptable minimum of 100 µg/L (Vanderpump *et al.*, 2011). Similar patterns have been seen in Europe, USA, Australia and New Zealand, where national surveys confirmed a re-emergence of the problem (Zimmermann and Delange, 2004; Leung *et al.*, 2011).

Many experts condone preventive salt iodisation as a cost-effective and sustainable solution to the issue. Since 1993 the WHO has conducted a global programme of salt iodisation to boost dietary levels and prevent deficiency, focusing largely on low-income countries. Although some European countries, including Switzerland and Denmark, have signed up to the WHO programme, it is currently not compulsory for manufacturers in the UK to add iodine to salt.

Adolescents' breastfeeding behaviour

Breastfeeding confers critical health benefits and contributes to reduced risk of short-term as well as chronic diseases in children and their mothers. Among the demographic risk factors for low initiation, continuation and exclusivity of breastfeeding, the greatest is being an adolescent mother, even after controlling for modifiable risk factors such as income, education and lack of prenatal care (Feldman-Winter and Shaikh, 2007). The 2010 UK Infant Feeding Survey revealed that breastfeeding rates were lowest among mothers aged 20 or under (58%) and highest in mothers aged 30 or over (87%). Older mothers were more likely than younger mothers to breastfeed for longer, and at six months only 13% of mothers aged under 20 were still breastfeeding compared with 33% of mothers aged 25–29 years, and 43% of mothers aged 35 or over. A clear relationship was also found between mother's age and timing of introducing solids. While only 36% of mothers aged 35 or over had begun weaning to solids by four months, 74% of infants of teenage mothers were weaned by this stage (Health and Social Care Information Centre, 2012).

Adolescent mothers and their infants may stand to gain the most benefit from breastfeeding. Parenting decisions of adolescents, such as mode of infant feeding, may be influenced by conditions that may also affect the neurobiology of the developing infant, such as maternal depression, substance abuse, and other high-risk behaviours (Azar *et al.*, 2007). It has been suggested that breastfeeding may reduce the deleterious effects of such conditions in adolescent mothers by increasing their self-efficacy and modifying the biological response to stress in mothers and their infants (Feldman-Winter and Shaikh, 2007; Flacking *et al.*, 2012).

There is a growing body of evidence which is helping us to understand the reasons why adolescents choose not to breastfeed. Perceived barriers to breastfeeding include a concern about the potential for excessive attachment between the teenage mother and her baby (Hannon, 2000); limited knowledge about breastfeeding, particularly in relation to the mother's own health (Swanson, 2006; Health and Social Care Information Centre, 2012); the perception of breastfeeding as painful (Nelson, 2009); being more exposed to bottle feeding than breastfeeding in day-to-day life and in the media (Swanson *et al.*, 2006); not being breastfed themselves (Mossman *et al.*, 2008; Swanson *et al.*, 2006); and embarrassment while breastfeeding in front of others or outside the home. In a UK study of teenage mothers, breastfeeding was viewed as 'morally inappropriate behaviour', with formula feeding being perceived as the appropriate behaviour (Dyson *et al.*, 2010, p. 114).

The evidence base for 'what works' in terms of supporting teenage mothers to breastfeed is limited, and further research is urgently needed to strengthen this evidence base. Adolescents who continue to breastfeed for longer find emotional, esteem and network components of support most helpful, with support from the adolescents' mothers being particularly powerful. There is also evidence to suggest that targeted breastfeeding educational programmes, specifically designed for the adolescent learner, may be successful in improving breastfeeding initiation and continuation rates in this population (Hall Moran *et al.*, 2007). It is clear that breastfeeding promotion in adolescents should be developmentally appropriate, adolescent focused and linked to multidimensional support, and challenges should be addressed by individually tailored and culturally sensitive counselling (Feldman-Winter and Shaikh, 2007).

Adolescent nutrition

Adolescence is a time of physiological, psychological and social development. It is one of the most dynamic and complex transitions in the lifespan. During puberty, teenagers gain 50% of their adult weight, 50% of their skeletal mass and 20% of their adult height. In females, puberty results in twice as much body fat deposition as males (Wahl, 1999). Total nutrient needs are higher in adolescence than at any other time in the life cycle (Story *et al.*, 2002).

Inadequate intake of nutrients during adolescence can potentially affect growth and delay sexual maturity (Story, 1992), as well as having an impact on major health problems such as cardiovascular disease, hypertension, diabetes and some cancers (Lenders *et al.*, 2000; Croll *et al.*, 2001). More immediate effects of poor nutrition during adolescence include iron deficiency, eating disorders, obesity, under-nutrition and dental caries (Story, 1992). The increased physical activity of adolescents places intense demands on the body, whilst at the same time it has been reported that approximately 60% of female adolescents claim to be trying to lose weight (Wahl, 1999).

Furthermore, dietary habits acquired during adolescence have the potential to enhance or undermine health throughout life. For example, high fat intake during adolescence and into adulthood is associated with an increased risk of heart disease, and low calcium intake during adolescence is associated with low bone density and an increased risk of osteoporosis in later life (Lytle, 2002). Such disordered eating habits are behaviours that may carry over into pregnancy (Neumark-Sztainer *et al.*, 2008).

Adolescent eating practices

Adolescents' nutritional status can be affected by specific aspects of the adolescent lifestyle. It has been reported that adolescents frequently miss meals and eat away from home, and that convenience and fast foods, which tend to be high in total and saturated fat, cholesterol and sodium, are popular choices among this population (Lifshitz *et al.*, 1993; Croll *et al.*, 2001; Neumark-Sztainer *et al.*, 2008).

Breakfast is an important component of a healthy diet and has been shown to have a positive impact on adolescents' health and wellbeing. Missing breakfast, however, is highly prevalent in children and adolescents, with cited incidences ranging from 12–34% and breakfast being the most commonly missed meal of the day in this population (Rampersaud *et al.*, 2005). Pregnant adolescents have also been shown to regularly miss breakfast (Burchett and Seeley, 2003; Stang *et al.*, 2005). A review of 47 studies examining the association of breakfast consumption with nutritional adequacy, body weight and academic performance in children and adolescents found that those who reported eating breakfast on a consistent basis tended to have superior nutritional profiles, consumed more calories and were less likely to be overweight than non-breakfast eaters (Rampersaud *et al.*, 2005). A number of studies have found that breakfast-skipping behaviour was associated with other risk behaviours, such as smoking, sexual behaviour in females, frequent alcohol use, behavioural disinhibition and missing school (e.g. Barker *et al.*, 2000; Kleinman *et al.*, 2002; Keski-Rahkonen *et al.*, 2003; Sjoberg *et al.*, 2003).

Snacking is a common phenomenon among adolescents, with up to 90% of teenagers reporting eating between meals (Bigler-Doughten and Jenkins, 1987). Snacking may fulfil an important role in an adolescent's diet. A US nationwide dietary survey revealed that snacks provided up to a third of adolescents' daily energy intake, as well as providing significant amounts of calcium, magnesium and vitamin C (US Department of Health, 1989). Indeed, reduced snacking, missing meals, or restriction to very low calorie snacks can result in poor weight gain and growth (Lifshitz and Moses, 1989). Wisely chosen snacks, therefore, appear to be a potential asset to an adolescent's diet (Lifshitz *et al.*, 1993). A US survey of adolescents' views of healthy eating in pregnancy found that pregnant adolescents were interested in healthy eating for their own wellbeing and that of their infants and ate healthy foods at meal times, but that their snacks generally consisted of unhealthy food choices (Wise and Arcamore, 2011).

Influences on adolescents' food choices

Financial constraints have been found to have an important influence on pregnant adolescents' food choices, particularly those living away from family (Burchett and Seeley, 2003). As money becomes scarce, pregnant adolescents consume more 'cheap fillers' and have less variety and less fresh produce in their diet. This is reflected in the NDNS of young people aged 4–18 years, with those from households in receipt of benefits being more likely to consume whole milk, table sugar and sugar confectionary, and consume significantly less protein, total carbohydrate, total sugars, non-milk extrinsic sugars, non-starch polysaccharides, vitamin C and biotin compared with those not receiving benefits (Gregory *et al.*, 2000). The influence of the family on food choices and eating behaviours has been found to be particularly strong for adolescents, whether pregnant (Burchett and Seely, 2003; Wise and Arcamore 2011) or not (Ambrosini *et al.*, 2009). Whilst this influence has been found to be mainly positive, dependence on the family means that the teenagers eat the same as the rest of the family, which may be less healthy than they would have wished (Burchett and Seely, 2003).

Over recent years in the UK there have been a number of programmes aimed at improving diet quality, such as the Food and Health Action Plan (DH, 2005) and the Food in Schools Programme (DH, 2010) in England and the Scottish Diet Action Plan (Scottish Executive, 2004), Hungry for Success (Scottish Executive, 2002) school meals policy in Scotland, and the Department of Health's Five-a-Day programme with its goal to increase fruit and vegetable consumption and improve public awareness (DH, 2001). The extent to which these programmes have influenced the eating patterns of pregnant adolescents, however, is not yet understood.

Conceptual framework for understanding adolescent eating behaviour

Conceptual theories are useful in helping to understand and explain the dynamics of health behaviours, the processes for changing behaviours and the effects of external influences on such behaviours (Story *et al.*, 2002). Unhealthy eating has been described a 'risk behaviour' in the adolescent population (Irwin *et al.*, 1997). It is helpful to evaluate the nature of risk behaviour in order to understand why adolescents behave this way.

Risk behaviours often associated with adolescents include unhealthy eating, dangerous driving, alcohol and drug use, sexual behaviour and injury-related behaviours. A survey of 1516 teenagers aged 14–15 years in the UK found that 23% smoked, 35% had been drunk in the previous three months, 64% considered they ate unhealthily and 39% took little exercise (Walker *et al.*, 2002). Risk behaviours have a developmental trajectory; typically they increase in prevalence over the adolescent years, with rates peaking in late adolescence and declining in young adulthood (Irwin *et al.*, 1997). These potentially health-damaging behaviours, established during adolescence, often have lasting deleterious effects throughout life. Negative health outcomes of risk-taking behaviours include sexually transmitted diseases, unplanned pregnancy, failure at school, habituation, premature cardiovascular disease, hypertension, obesity and its associated medical sequelae, physical and psychological disability and death (Irwin *et al.*, 1997). Risk-taking behaviours have been defined by Irwin *et al.* (1997, p. 2):

> Risk-taking behaviours can be distinguished from developmentally appropriate exploratory behaviour by their potentially serious, long-term, and negative consequences. Whereas adolescence exploratory behaviour in a safe or positive context enhances competence and confidence, risk-taking behaviours jeopardise health and wellbeing. Some risk-taking behaviours are defined by their adolescent age of onset. For example, sexual activity, certain eating behaviours, driving a car, drinking alcohol, or leaving home may be considered risk-taking behaviours at age 13, but may not be at age 21. Some behaviours are risky regardless of age such as unhealthy eating behaviours, promiscuous sexual behaviour, cocaine use, or driving under the influence of alcohol.

It is difficult to attribute an absolute reason why adolescents have an increased likelihood of risky behaviour, together with the associated negative nutritional outcomes. As with all health problems, there is a complex relationship between the individual and a variety of biopsychosocial and environmental factors that are associated with an increased likelihood of engaging in risky behaviours.

Interrelationship between risk behaviours

There is evidence to suggest that involvement in one type of risk behaviour increases the likelihood of becoming involved in other risk behaviours. Risk-taking behaviours cluster and interact with one another. For example, research has shown that adolescents who have sexual intercourse also engage in other risk behaviours, such as smoking and drug and alcohol use (Mott and Haurin, 1988). Even when socio-demographic variables (such as race, religion, parental education, family structure and personality) are controlled for, the association remains. Other research has shown that adolescents who have sexual intercourse are less likely to aspire to advanced education and less likely to report being very religious (Miller and Simon, 1974). There has been limited research that focuses specifically on the covariance of eating behaviours and other risk behaviours. A study of 36,284 adolescents found that, after controlling for socio-demographic and personal variables, male and female adolescents who engaged in health-promoting behaviours were less likely to have unhealthy eating behaviours, while those engaging in risk-taking behaviours were more likely to have unhealthy eating behaviours (Neumark-Sztainer *et al.*, 1997). A US study of school children found that students in the 8th grade who reported making less healthy food choices had lower physical activity patterns and were more likely to smoke cigarettes, and these behaviours persisted until the 12th grade (Lytle *et al.*, 1995). It has also been reported that adolescents who have sex, drink and smoke are more likely to eat high salt, high fat and high sugar foods (Irwin *et al.*, 1997). While several explanations for this clustering of behaviours have been proposed (Story *et al.*, 2002), the most frequently cited and tested explanation is that these behaviours cluster because they share a common aetiology: i.e. they are each a manifestation of a general predisposition towards unconventionality (Elliot, 1994).

It seems clear that eating behaviours are related to other behaviours often displayed in adolescents and should not be viewed in isolation. Adolescents who engage in a wide range of health-compromising behaviours may be particularly at risk of unhealthy eating. The interactive relationship between risk behaviours impacts on how health education for adolescents should be structured and delivered. It suggests that health education efforts should address a lifestyle approach, rather than specific individual health behaviours. Thus, health education should promote healthy lifestyles through health-enhancing curricula and personal, behavioural and environmental conditions conducive to healthful behaviours (Lytle and Roski, 1997). This will empower students with a sense of personal responsibility, decision-making skills and a clear understanding of the benefits of making healthy lifestyle decisions. Furthermore, it may be possible to identify high-risk adolescents and target and tailor health promotion programmes to them.

Improving pregnant and breastfeeding adolescents' diets

The nutritional challenges that face the pregnant adolescent are unique. The increased nutrient demands of pregnancy and lactation, together with the increased nutrient demands of the still-growing adolescent, may generate competition for nutrients between mother and fetus. Although relatively limited, the current research seems to suggest that pregnant and breastfeeding adolescents' diets are suboptimal. The most common dietary deficits appear to be in iron, zinc, calcium, folate and magnesium. Many pregnant adolescents do not consume the recommended amount of fruit and vegetables and may consume too much salt, saturated fat and sugar.

A 'one-size fits all' approach has not been shown to be particularly effective in modifying food choice in the general population. In a review of the factors that influence food choice, Buttriss and colleagues (2004) suggested that tailored approaches for different cultural settings should be a key consideration. For example, peer-led interventions have been shown to be successful for adolescents and 'hard to reach' groups (e.g. Fitzgibbon *et al.*, 1996). Hands-on practical interventions, such as 'cook and eat' classes, have been shown to appeal to low-income groups (e.g. Weaver *et al.*, 1999). For sustainability of positive changes, Buttriss *et al.* (2004) emphasise the need for message reinforcement.

An important factor that should be considered when developing appropriate and effective strategies to promote healthy eating in pregnant adolescents is the heterogeneity of the group. Factors affecting food choices vary considerably, depending on the individual's particular circumstances. Family and peers are likely to have a strong influence on the eating habits of most pregnant adolescents. Poverty is a significant factor that limits the ability of the pregnant adolescent to eat a healthy diet, even in those who aspire to it.

As many adolescents do not plan pregnancy, the issue of periconceptional nutrition is problematic. A UK survey of 674 adolescents (aged 14–15 years) on their perceptions of what constitutes a healthy pregnancy revealed that 70% of respondents thought that the optimum time to initiate changes in what a woman eats and drinks to ensure a healthy pregnancy was when pregnancy had been confirmed (Edwards *et al.*, 1997). This suggests that the benefits of preconceptual nutrition are not well understood by this population. A small associated pilot study also revealed that, whilst most adolescents thought that vitamin supplements were 'good for the baby', few thought that folic acid tablets were beneficial, suggesting that participants did not recognise folic acid as a vitamin (Parker, 1998). A further complication is that many teenagers may be unaware of their pregnancy or may not have accessed services in their first trimester, so providing the appropriate support to these individuals may be difficult.

Growth, adolescent eating behaviours and psychosocial factors must be considered when recommendations are made for the optimal nutritional care for this vulnerable population. The multiple psychosocial and economic stressors of prospective adolescent mothers often interfere with their ability to follow recommendations regarding nutrient intake. Effective interventions will need to go beyond education alone in order to tackle these barriers. For example, financial issues and food poverty are significant barriers, particularly in those adolescents who live away from family. Therefore initiatives and policies that aim to improve the financial circumstances or limit the effects of food poverty on pregnant adolescents could be much more effective in improving diets than any other intervention (Burchett and Seely, 2003).

At present there are very few projects that aim to improve pregnant adolescents' nutrition in the UK. The few that have been conducted have been subjected to short-term funding and have not been formally evaluated. Without proper evaluation it is impossible to provide evidence of their effectiveness (or otherwise), thus making progress in this area problematic. It is clear that more research in this area is urgently needed. Research should seek to further clarify the barriers to dietary improvements in pregnant adolescents. This information could then inform the development of effective nutritional programs that are targeted to suit this particularly vulnerable population.

Conclusion

Teenage pregnancy is one of the major public health challenges in the UK. Each year in the UK, around 35,000 adolescents under 18 years of age conceive. Although teenage pregnancy rates appear to be falling, rates are still much higher than in most other European countries. Teenage pregnancy has been associated with a number of negative outcomes for the infants and children of teenage mothers, such as infant mortality and morbidity, maternal morbidity and negative impacts on various socio-economic outcomes.

Nutrition in adolescent pregnancy must be viewed within a biopsychosocial context, since it has consistently been shown that there are multiple influencing factors that play a role in the eating behaviour and subsequent nutritional status of the pregnant adolescent. Eating behaviours are likely to be related to other, often 'risky', behaviours displayed in adolescents and should not be viewed in isolation. Achieving dietary change in this particularly vulnerable section of the population, many of who are from disadvantaged backgrounds, presents a major public health challenge. Biopsychosocial factors often experienced by such groups, including low levels of disposable income, unemployment, poor housing, sub-optimal mental and physical health and limited access to a wide variety of reasonably priced foods, all contribute to difficulties in tacking behavioural change (Symon and Wrieden, 2003).

Given the multiple factors that have the potential to influence nutrient intake in pregnant adolescents, interventions should perhaps use a lifestyle approach, rather than focus specifically on eating behaviours. Feasibility studies of potential interventions in this population are essential. A study in Dundee confirmed that compliance among pregnant teenagers invited to attend a nutrition education intervention programme was very poor – only 16 of 120 invited attended (Wrieden and Symon, 2003). There are numerous barriers to optimal nutrition in adolescent pregnancy, and any intervention should consider these carefully.

Overcoming the barriers in order to achieve improved nutrition in pregnancy among adolescents requires multidisciplinary collaborations of adolescent health care providers, academics, professional organisations, policy makers, industry and service users. Certainly, more needs to be done at a policy level, both with regard to enabling adolescents to be able to afford good nutrition and in modifying the nutrition message that adolescents receive. For example, the UK government could ensure that there is consistency in the food and nutrition message in schools, to include the curriculum, food provision in the canteen, vending machine policies, breakfast clubs, snacking and lunchbox policies, and so on. Although supplements are freely available to all pregnant women in the UK, as are food vouchers and dietary advice, it is clear that these are not adequately taken up by this group. Strategies developed through consultation with adolescents may ultimately lead to better compliance and improved outcomes for both mother and child (Baker *et al.*, 2009). Only once such actions have been achieved can adolescent nutrition, and adolescent nutrition in pregnancy and lactation, be significantly and sustainably optimised.

References

Albertson, A. M., Tobelmann, R. C. and Marquart, L. (1997) Estimated dietary calcium intake and food sources for adolescent females: 1980–92. *Journal of Adolescent Health*, **20**, 20–6.

Alfaham, M., Woodhead, S., Pask, G. and Davies, D. (1995) Vitamin D deficiency: a concern in pregnant Asian women. *British Journal of Nutrition*, **73**(6), 881–7.

Almeida, A. A., Lopes, C. M., Silva, A. M. and Barrado, E. (2008) Trace elements in human milk: correlation with blood levels, inter-element correlations and changes in concentration during the first month of lactation. *Journal of Trace Elements in Medicine & Biology*, **22**, 196–205.

Ambrosini, G. L., Oddy, W. H., Robinson, M., O'Sullivan, T. A., Hands, B. P., De Klerk, N. H., *et al.* (2009) Adolescent dietary patterns are associated with lifestyle and family psycho-social factors. *Public Health Nutrition*, **12**(10), 1807–15.

Anderson, N. E., Smiley, D. V., Flick, L. H., Lewis, C. Y. (2000) Missouri Rural Adolescent Pregnancy Project (MORAPP). *Public Health Nursing*, **17**, 355–62.

Atkinson, S. A. and Koletzko, B. (2007) Determining lifestage groups and extrapolating nutrient intake values (NIV). *Food and Nutrition Bulletin*, **28** (Suppl.), 61–76.

Azar, R., Paquette, D., Zoccolillo, M., Baltzer, F. and Tremblay, R. E. (2007) The association of major depression, conduct disorder, and maternal overcontrol with a failure to show a cortisol buffered response in 4-month-old infants of teenage mothers. *Biological Psychiatry*, **62**(6), 573.

Bacci, A., Manhica, G. M., Machungo, F., Bugalho, A. and Cuttini, M. (1993) Outcome of teenage pregnancy in Maputo, Mozambique. *International Journal of Gynaecology and Obstetrics*, **40**, 19–23.

Baker, P. N., Wheeler, S. J., Sanders, T. A., Thomas, J. E., Hutchinson, C. J., Clarke, K., *et al.* (2009) A prospective study of micronutrient status in adolescent pregnancy. *American Journal of Clinical Nutrition*, **89**(4), 1114–24.

Barker, D. J. and Osmond, C. (1986) Infant mortality, childhood nutrition, and ischaemic heart disease in England and Wales. *Lancet*, **327**(8489), 1077–81.

Barker, M., Robinson, S., Wilman, C. and Barker, D. J. P. (2000) Behaviour, body composition and diet in adolescent girls. *Appetite*, **35**, 161–70.

Bates, B., Lennox, A. and Swan, G. (2010) *NDNS Headline Results from Year 1 of the Rolling Programme (2008/2009)*. Available at: http://www.food.gov.uk/multimedia/pdfs/publication/ndnsreport0809year1results.pdf (accessed February 2013).

Beard, J. L., Hendricks, M. K., Perez, E. M., Murray-Kolb, L. E., Berg, A., Vernon-Feagans, L., *et al.* (2005) Maternal iron deficiency anemia affects postpartum emotions and cognition. *Journal of Nutrition*, **135**, 267–72.

Bezerra, F. F., Laboissiere, F. P., King, J. C., Donangelo, C. M. (2002) Pregnancy and lactation affect markers of calcium and bone metabolism differently in adolescent and adult women with low calcium intakes. *Journal of Nutrition*, **132**, 2183–7.

Bezerra, F. F., Mendonca, L. M. C., Lobato, E. C., O'Brien, K. O., Donangelo, C. M. (2004) Bone mass is recovered from lactation to postweaning in adolescent mothers with low calcium intakes. *American Journal of Clinical Nutrition*, **80**, 1322–6.

Bezerra, F. F., Cabello, G. M. K., Mendonca, L. M. C. and Donangelo, C. M. (2007) Bone mass and breast milk calcium are associated with vitamin D receptor gene polymorphisms in adolescent mothers. *Journal of Nutrition*, **138**, 277–81.

Bigler-Doughten, S. and Jenkins, R. M. (1987) Adolescent snacks: nutrient density and nutritional contribution to total intake. *Journal of the American Dietetic Association*, **87**, 1678–9.

British Committee for Standards in Haematology (2011) *UK Guidelines on the Management of Iron Deficiency in Pregnancy*. Available at: http://www.bcshguidelines.com/documents/UK_Guidelines_iron_deficiency_in_pregnancy.pdf (accessed 18 February 2013).

Brown, K. H., Rivera, J. A., Bhutta, Z., Gibson, R. S., King, J. C., Lönnerdal, B. and Hotz, C. (2004). International Zinc Nutrition Consultative Group (IZiNCG) technical document# 1. Assessment of the risk of zinc deficiency in populations and options for its control. *Food and Nutrition Bulletin*, **25**(1 Suppl. 2), S99.

Bukulmez, O. and Deren, O. (2000) Perinatal outcome in adolescent pregnancies: a case-control study from a Turkish University hospital. *European Journal of Obstetrics and Gynecology and Reproductive Biology*, **88**, 207–12.

Burchett, H. and Seeley, A. (2003) *Good Enough to Eat? The Diet of Pregnant Teenagers*. Maternity Alliance/Food Commission, London.

Buttriss, J. (2000) Diet and nutritional status of 4–18-year-olds: public health implications. *Nutrition Bulletin*, **25**, 209–17.

Buttriss, J. (2002) Nutrition, health and schoolchildren. *Nutrition Bulletin*, **27**, 275–305.

Buttriss, J., Stanner, S., McKevith, B., Nugent, A. P., Kelly, C., Phillips, F. and Theobald, H. E. (2004) Successful ways to modify food choice: lessons from the literature. *Nutrition Bulletin*, **29**, 333–43.

Casanueva, E., Magana, L., Pfeffer, F. and Baez, A. (1991) Incidence of premature rupture of membranes in pregnant women with low leukocyte levels of vitamin C. *European Journal of Clinical Nutrition*, **45**, 401–5.

Caulfield, L. E., Zavaleta, N., Shanker, A. H. and Merialdi, M. (1998) Potential contribution of maternal zinc supplementation during pregnancy to maternal and child survival. *American Journal of Clinical Nutrition*, **68**, 499–508.

Cavadini, C., Siega-Riz, A. M. and Popkin, B. M. (2000) US adolescent food intake trends from 1965 to 1996. *Archives of Disease in Childhood*, **83**, 18–24.

Cervera, P. and Ngo, J. (2001) Dietary guidelines for the breast-feeding woman. *Public Health Nutritionition*, **4**, 1357–62.

Chen, X. K., Wen, S. W., Fleming, N., Demissie, K., Rhoads, G. G. and Walker, M. (2007) Teenage pregnancy and adverse birth outcomes: a large population based retrospective cohort study. *International Journal of Epidemiology*, **36**, 368–73.

Committee on Medical Aspects of Food Policy (COMA) (1991) *Dietary Reference Values for Food Energy and Nutrients for the United Kingdom*. Stationery Office, London.

Conde-Agudelo, A., Belizan, J. M. and Lammers, C. (2005) Maternal-perinatal morbidity and mortality associated with adolescent pregnancy in Latin America: cross-section study. *American Journal of Obstetrics and Gynecology*, **192**, 342–49.

Croll, J. K., Neumark-Sztainer, D. and Story, M. (2001). Healthy eating: what does it mean to adolescents? *Journal of Nutrition Education*, **33**(4), 193–8.

de Lira, L. Q., Lima, M. S. R., de Medeiros, J. M. S., da Silva, I. F. and Dimenstein, R. (2011) Correlation of vitamin A nutritional status on alpha-tocopherol in the colostrum of lactating women. *Maternal & Child Nutrition*, DOI: 10.1111/j.1740-8709.2011.00376.x

Dewey, K. G. (2004) Impact of breastfeeding on maternal nutritional status. *Advances in Experimental Medicine & Biology*, **554**, 91–100.

Department of Health (1991) *Dietary Reference Values of Food Energy and Nutrients for the United Kingdom*. Stationery Office Books, London.

Department of Health (1992). *Folic Acid and the Prevention of Neural Tube Defects. Report from an Expert Advisory Group*. (Available from DH, PO Box 410, Wetherby LS23 7LN).

Department of Health (1999) *Saving Lives, Our Healthier Nation*. Available at: http://webarchive.nationalarchives.gov.uk/+/www.dh.gov.uk/en/Publicationsandstatistics/Publications/PublicationsPolicyAndGuidance/DH_4008701 (accessed 24 February 2013).

Department of Health (2001) *Five-a-day Update*. Available at: http://www.dh.gov.uk/prod_consum_dh/groups/dh_digitalassets/@dh/@en/documents/digitalasset/dh_4074293.pdf (accessed 24 February 2013).

Department of Health (2005) *Choosing a Better Diet: a Food and Health Action Plan*. Available at: http://www.dh.gov.uk/prod_consum_dh/groups/dh_digitalassets/@dh/@en/documents/digitalasset/dh_4105709.pdf (accessed 24 February 2013).

Department of Health (2007) *Teenage Parents Next Steps: Guidance for Local Authorities and Primary Care Trust on Improving Outcomes for Teenage Parents and their Children*. Available at: https://www.education.gov.uk/publications/standard/publicationdetail/page1/DCSF-00597-2007 (accessed 24 February 2013).

Department of Health (2010) *Food in Schools Programme*. Available at: http://webarchive.nationalarchives.gov.uk/+/www.dh.gov.uk/en/Publichealth/Healthimprovement/Foodinschoolsprogramme/index.htm (accessed June 2010).

Department for Education and Science (2006) *Teenage Pregnancy Next Steps: Guidance for Local Authorities and Primary Care Trusts on Effective Delivery of Local Strategies*.

Available at: https://www.education.gov.uk/publications/eOrderingDownload/6597-DfES-ECM-TeenPreg.pdf (accessed 18 February 2013).

Doets, E. L., deWit, L. S., Dhonukshe-Rutten, R. A., Cavelaars, A. E., Raats, M. M., Timotijevic, L. *et al.* (2008) Current micronutrient recommendations in Europe: towards understanding their differences and similarities. *European Journal of Nutrition*, **47**(Suppl. 1), 17–40.

Donangelo, C. M. and King, J. C. (2012) Maternal zinc intakes and homeostatic adjustments during pregnancy and lactation. *Nutrients*, **4**(7), 782–98.

Dorea, J. G. (2002) Iodine nutrition and breast feeding. *Journal of Trace Elements in Medicine & Biology*, **16**, 207–20.

Doyle, L. W., Crowther, C. A., Middleton, P., Marret, S. and Rouse, D. (2009) Magnesium sulphate for women at risk of preterm birth for neuroprotection of the fetus. *Cochrane Database of Systematic Reviews*, Issue 1. Art. No.: CD004661. DOI: 10.1002/14651858. CD004661.pub3.

Dunn, C., Kolasa, K., Dunn, P. C. and Ogle, M. B. (1994) Dietary intake of pregnant adolescents in a rural southern community. *Journal of the American Dietetic Association*, **94**, 1040–1.

Dyson, L., Green, J. M., Renfrew, M. J., McMillan, B. and Woolridge, M. (2010) Factors influencing the infant feeding decision for socioeconomically deprived pregnant teenagers: the moral dimension. *Birth*, **37**(2), 141–9.

Edwards, G., Stainistreet, M. and Boyes, E. (1997) Adolescents' ideas about the health of the fetus. *Midwifery*, **13**, 17–23.

Endres, J. M., Poell-Odenwald, K., Sawicki, M. and Welch, P. (1985) Dietary assessment of pregnant adolescents participating in a supplemental-food program. *Journal of Reproductive Medicine*, **30**, 10–17.

Ekiz, E., Agaoglu, L., Karakas, Z., Gurel, N. and Yalcin, I. (2005) The effect of iron deficiency anemia on the function of the immune system. *Hematology Journal*, **5**, 579–583.

Elliot, D. S. (1994) Health-enhancing and health-compromising life-styles. In: *Promoting the Health of Adolescents: New Directions for the Twenty-First Century* (eds S. G. Millstein, A. C. Peteresen and E. O. Nightingale). Oxford University Press, Oxford.

Fairweather-Tait, S. J. (2004) Iron nutrition in the UK: getting the balance right. Proceedings of the Nutrition Society, **63**, 519–28.

Feldman-Winter, L. and Shaikh, U. (2007) Optimizing breastfeeding promotion and support in adolescent mothers. *Journal of Human Lactation*, **23**(4), 362–7.

Fewtrell, M., Wilson, D. C., Booth, I., Parsons, L. and Lucas A. (2011) Six months of exclusive breast feeding: how good is the evidence? *British Medical Journal*, **342**, c5955.

Fitzgibbon, M. L., Stolley, M. R., Avellone, M. E., Sugerman, S. and Chavez, N. (1996) Involving parents in cancer risk reduction: a program for Hispanic American families. *Health Psychology*, **15**, 413–22.

Flacking, R., Lehtonen, L., Thomson, G., Axelin, A., Ahlqvist, S., Strand, H., Hall Moran, V., Ewald, U., Dykes, F. and the SCENE group (2012) Closeness and separation in neonatal intensive care. *Acta Pediatrica*, **101**(10), 1032–7.

Fraser, A. M., Brokert, J. E. and Ward, R. H. (1995) Association of young maternal age with adverse reproductive outcomes. *New England Journal of Medicine*, **332**, 1113–17.

Frisancho, A. R., Matos, J. and Flegel, P. (1983) Maternal nutritional status and adolescent pregnancy outcome. *American Journal of Clinical Nutrition*, **38**, 739–46.

Gadowsky, S. L., Gale, K., Wolfe, S. A., Jory, J., Gibson, R. and O'Connor, D. L. (1995) Biochemical folate, B$_{12}$ and iron status of a group of pregnant adolescents accessed through the public health system in Southern Ontario. *Journal of Adolescent Health*, **16**, 465–74.

Gartner, L. M. and Greer, F. R. (2003) Prevention of rickets and vitamin D deficiency: new guidelines for vitamin D intake. *Pediatrics*, **111**(4), 908–10.

Garza, C. and Rasmussen, K. M. (2000) Pregnancy and lactation. In: *Human Nutrition and Dietetics*, 10th edn (eds. J. S. Garrow, W. P. T. James and A. Ralph), pp. 437–48. Churchill Livingstone, Edinburgh.

Giddens, J. B., Krug, S. K., Tsang, R. C., ShuMei, G., Miodovnik, M. and Prada, J. A. (2000) Pregnant adolescent and adult women have similarly low intakes of selected nutrients. *Journal of the American Dietetic Association*, **100**(11), 1334–40.

Gilbert, W., Jandial, D., Field, N., Bigelow, P. and Danielsen, B. (2004) Birth outcomes in teenage pregnancies. *Journal of Maternal and Fetal Neonatal Medicine*, **16**, 265–70.

Gillie, O. (2004) Sunlight robbery. *Health Research Forum Occasional Reports*: No. 1, p. 20. Available at: http://www.healthresearchforum.org.uk/reports/public_health.pdf (accessed 19 March 2013).

Gluckman, P. D., Hanson, M. A. and Pinal, C. (2005) The developmental origins of adult disease. *Maternal and Child Nutrition*, **1**, 130–41.

Gortzak-Uzan, L., Hallak, M., Press, F., Katz, M. and Shoham-Vardi, I. (2001) Teenage pregnancy: risk factors for adverse perinatal outcome. *Journal of Maternal–Fetal Medicine*, **10**, 393–7.

Gregory, J., Lowe, S., Bates, C., Prentice, A., Jackson, L., Smithers, G., Wenlock, R. and Farron, M. (2000) Report of the Diet and Nutrition Survey volume 1: *National Diet and Nutrition Survey: Young People Aged 4 to 18 Years*. Stationery Office, London.

Griffin, I. J. and Abrams, S. A. (2001) Iron and breastfeeding. *Pediatric Clinics of North America*, **48**(2), 401.

Haas, J. D. and Brownlie, T. (2001) Iron deficiency and reduced work capacity: a critical review of the research to determine a causal relationship. *Journal of Nutrition*, **131**, 676S–690S.

Haggarty, P., Campbell, D. M., Duthie, S., Andrews, K., Hoad, G., Piyathilake, C. and McNeill, G. (2009) Diet and deprivation in pregnancy. *British Journal of Nutrition*, **102**(10), 1487–97.

Hall Moran, V. (2007a) A systematic review of dietary assessments of pregnant adolescents in industrialised countries. *British Journal of Nutrition*, **97**, 411–25.

Hall Moran, V. (2007b) Nutritional status in pregnant adolescents: a systematic review of biochemical markers. *Maternal & Child Nutrition*, **3**, 74–93.

Hall Moran, V., Lowe, N., Berti, C., Cetin, I., Hermoso, M., Koletzko, B. and Dykes, F. (2010) The EURRECA project: towards EU alignment for micronutrient reference values during lactation. *Maternal & Child Nutrition*, **6**(suppl. 2), 39–54.

Hall Moran, V., Edwards, J., Dykes, F. C. and Downe, S. (2007) A systematic review of the nature of support for breastfeeding adolescent mothers. *Midwifery*, **23**, 157–71.

Hall Moran, V., Lowe, N., Berti, C., Cetin, I., Hermoso, M., Koletzko, B. *et al.* (2010) Nutritional requirements during lactation. Towards European alignment of reference values: the EURRECA network. *Maternal & Child Nutrition*, **6**, 39–54.

Hannon, P. R., Willis, S. K., Bishop-Townsend, V., Martinez, I. M. and Scrimshaw, S. C. (2000) African-American and Latina adolescent mothers' infant feeding decisions and breastfeeding practices: a qualitative study. *Journal of Adolescent Health*, **26**(6), 399–407.

Hay, G., Johnston, C., Whitelaw, A., Trygg, K. and Refsum, H. (2008) Folate and cobalamin status in relation to breastfeeding and weaning in healthy infants. *The American Journal of Clinical Nutrition*, **88**(1), 105–114.

Health and Social Care Information Centre, IFF Research (2012) *Infant Feeding Survey 2010*. Information Centre for Health and Social Care, London.

Hendrix, N. and Berghella, V. (2008) Nonplacental causes of intrauterine growth restriction. *Seminars in Perinatology*, **32**, 161–5.

Honein, M. A., Paulozzi, L. J., Mathews, T. J., Erickson, J. D. and Wong L. C. (2001) Impact of folic acid fortification of the US food supply on the occurrence of neural tube defects. *Journal of the American Medical Association*, **285**, 2981–8.

Hyppönen, E., Läärä, E., Reunanen, A., Järvelin, M. R. and Virtanen, S. M. (2001) Intake of vitamin D and risk of type 1 diabetes: a birth-cohort study. *Lancet*, **358**(9292), 1500–3.

Igwegbe, A. O. and Udigwe, G. O. (2001) Teenage pregnancy: still an obstetric risk. *Journal of Obstetrics and Gynaecology*, **21**, 478–81.

Institute of Medicine (IOM) (1990) *Nutrition During Pregnancy*. National Academy Press, Washington DC.

Institute of Medicine, Food and Nutrition Board (1997) *Dietary Reference Intakes for Calcium, Phosphorus, Magnesium, Vitamin D and Fluoride*. National Academy Press, Washington DC.

Institute of Medicine, Food and Nutrition Board (1998) *Dietary Reference Intakes for Thiamin, Riboflavin, Niacin, Vitamin B_6, Folate, Vitamin B_{12}, Pantothenic Acid, Biotin, and Chlorine*. National Academy Press, Washington DC.

Institute of Medicine, Food and Nutrition Board (2000) *Dietary Reference Intakes for Vitamin C, Vitamin E, Selenium, and Carotenoids*. National Academy Press, Washington DC.

Institute of Medicine, Food and Nutrition Board (2001) *Dietary Reference Intakes for Vitamin A, Vitamin K, Arsenic, Boron, Chromium, Copper, Iodine, Iron, Manganese, Molybdenum, Nickel, Silicon, Vanadium, and Zinc*. National Academy Press, Washington DC.

Institute of Medicine, Food and Nutrition Board (2004) *Dietary Reference Intakes for Water, Potassium, Sodium, Chloride, and Sulphate*. National Academy Press, Washington DC.

Iannotti, L. L., O'Brien, K. O., Chang, S.-C., Mancini, J., Schulman Nathanson, M., Liu S. *et al.* (2005) Iron deficiency anemia and depleted body iron reserves are prevalent among pregnant African-American adolescents. *Journal of Nutrition*, **135**, 2572–7.

International Council for the Control of Iodine Deficiency Disorders (ICCIDD) (2013) http://www.iccidd.org/pages/iodine-deficiency.php (accessed 18 February 2013).

Irvine, H., Bradley, T., Cupples, M. and Boohan M. (1997)The implications of teenage pregnancy and motherhood for primary health care: unresolved issues. *British Journal of General Practice*, **47**, 323–6.

Irwin, C. E., Igra, V., Eyre, S. and Millstein, S. (1997) Risk-taking behavior in adolescents: the paradigm. *Annals of the New York Academy of Sciences*, **817**, 1–35.

Jackson, M. J., Giugliano, R., Giugliano, L. G., Oliveira, E. F., Shrimpton, R. and Swainbank, I. G. (1988) Stable isotope metabolic studies of zinc nutrition in slum-dwelling lactating women in the Amazon valley. *British Journal of Nutrition*, **59**, 193–203.

Jarjou, L. M., Prentice, A., Sawo, Y., Laskey, M. A., Bennett, J., Goldberg, G. R. and Cole, T. J. (2006) Randomized, placebo-controlled, calcium supplementation study in pregnant Gambian women: effects on breast-milk calcium concentrations and infant birth weight, growth, and bone mineral accretion in the first year of life. *American Journal of Clinical Nutrition*, **83**(3), 657–66.

Jolly, M. C., Sebire, N., Harris, J., Robinson, H. S. and Regan, L. (2000) Obstetric risk of pregnancy in women less than 18 years old. *Obstetrics & Gynecology*, **96**, 962–6.

Jonsdottir, O. H., Thorsdottir, I., Hibberd, P. L., Fewtrell, M. S., Wells, J. C., Palsson, G. I., Lucas, A., Gunnlaugsson, G. and Kleinman, R. E. (2012) Timing of the introduction of complementary foods in infancy: a randomized controlled trial. *Pediatrics*, **130**(6), 1038–45.

Joss-Moore, L. A. and Lane, R. H. (2009) The developmental origins of adult disease. *Current Opinion in Pediatrics*, **21**(2), 230.

Keski-Rahkonen, A., Kaprio, J., Rissanen, A., Virkkunen, M. and Rose, R. J. (2003) Breakfast skipping and health-compromising behaviors in adolescents and adults. *European Journal of Clinical Nutrition*, **57**, 842–53.

Kiernan, K. (1995) Transition to parenthood: young mothers, young fathers – associated factors and later life experiences. *LSE Discussion paper WSP/113*.

King, J. C. (2003) The risk of maternal nutritional depletion and poor outcomes increases in early or closely spaced pregnancies. *Journal of Nutrition*, **133**, 1732S–1736S.

King, J. C. (2011) Zinc: an essential but elusive nutrient. *American Journal of Clinical Nutrition*, **94**, 679S–684S.

Kinzler, W. L. and Vintzileos, A. M. (2008) Fetal growth restriction: a modern approach. *Current Opinion in Obstetrics and Gynecology*, **20**, 125–31.

Klee, G. C. (2000) Cobalamin and folate evaluation: measurement of methylalonic acid and homocysteine vs vitamin B_{12} and folate. *Clinical Chemistry*, **46**, 1277–83.

Kleinman, R. E., Hall, S., Green, H., Korzec-Ramirez, D., Patton, K., Pagano, M. E. and Murphy, J. M. (2002) Diet, breakfast and academic performance in children. *Annals of Nutrition and Metabolism*, **46**(Suppl. 1), 899–907.

Kramer, M. S. and Kakuma, R. (2002) The optimal duration of exclusive breastfeeding. A systematic review. World Health Organization, Geneva.

Krebs, N. F., Reidinger, C. J., Hartley, S., Robertson, A. D. and Hambidge, K. M. (1995) Zinc supplementation during lactation: effects on maternal status and milk zinc concentrations. *American Journal of Clinical Nutrition*, **61**, 1030–6.

Lenders, C. M., McElrath, T. F. and Scholl, T. O. (2000) Nutrition in adolescent pregnancy. *Current Opinion in Pediatrics*, **12**, 291–6.

Leung, A. M., Pearce, E. N. and Braverman, L. E. (2011) Iodine nutrition in pregnancy and lactation. *Endocrinology and Metabolism Clinics of North America*, **40**, 765.

Lifshitz, F. and Moses, N. (1989) Growth failure. A complication of dietary treatment of hypercholesterolemia. *American Journal of Diseases in Childhood*, **143**, 537–42.

Lifshitz, F., Tarim, O. and Smith, M. M. (1993) Nutrition in adolescence. *Adolescent Endocrinology*, **22**, 673–83.

Looker, A. C., Sempos, C. T., Johnson, C. L. and Yetley, E. A. (1987) Comparison of dietary intakes and iron status of vitamin-mineral supplement users and nonusers aged 1 to 19 years. *American Journal of Clinical Nutrition*, **46**, 655–72.

Lozoff, B., Kaciroti, N. and Walter, T. (2006) Iron deficiency in infancy: applying a physiologic framework for prediction. *American Journal of Clinical Nutrition*, **84**(6), 1412–21.

Lubarsky, S. L., Schiff, E., Friedman, S. A., Mercer, B. M. and Sibai, B. M. (1994) Obstetric characteristics among nulliparous under age 15. *Obstetrics & Gynecology*, **84**, 365–8.

Lytle, L. A. (2002) Nutritional issues for adolescents. *Journal of the American Dietetic Association*, **102**(Suppl.), S8–12.

Lytle, L. A. and Roski, J. (1997) Unhealthy eating and other risk-taking behavior: are they related? *Annals of the New York Academy of Sciences*, **817**, 49–65.

Lytle, L., Kelder, S., Perry, C. and Klepp, K. (1995) Covariance of adolescent health behaviours: the class of 1989 study. *Health Education Research: Theory & Practice*, **19**, 133–46.

Makrides, M. and Crowther, C. A. (2001) Magnesium supplementation in pregnancy. *Cochrane Database of Systematic Reviews*, Issue 4. Art. No.: CD000937. DOI: 10.1002/14651858.CD000937.

Matthews, F., Yudkin, P. and Neil, A. (1999) Influence of maternal nutrition on outcome of pregnancy: prospective cohort study. *British Medical Journal*, **319**, 339–43.

Miller, P. Y. and Simon, W. (1974) Adolescent sexual behaviour: context and change. *Social Problems*, **22**, 58–76.

Mistry, H. D., Kurlak, L. O., Young, S. D., Briley, A. L., Broughton Pipkin, F., Baker, P. N., and Poston, L. (2012) Maternal selenium, copper and zinc concentrations in pregnancy associated with small-for-gestational-age infants. *Maternal & Child Nutrition*. DOI: 10.1111/j.1740-8709.2012.00430.x.

Moser-Veillon, P. B. (1995) Zinc needs and homeostasis during lactation. *Analyst*, **120**, 895–7.

Mossman, M., Heaman, M., Dennis, C. L. and Morris, M. (2008) The influence of adolescent mothers' breastfeeding confidence and attitudes on breastfeeding initiation and duration. *Journal of Human Lactation*, **24**(3), 268–77.

Mott, E. L. and Haurin, R. J. (1988) Linkages between sexual activity and alcohol and drug use among American adolescents. *Family Planning Perspectives*, **20**, 108–28.

MRC Vitamin Study Research Group (1991) Prevention of neural tube defects: results of the Medical Research Council Vitamin Study. *Lancet*, **338**, 131–7.

Naeye, R. L. (1981) Teenage and pre-teenaged pregnancies: consequences of the fetal-maternal competition for nutrients. *Pediatrics*, **67**, 146–59.

Nelson, A. M. (2009) Adolescent attitudes, beliefs, and concerns regarding breastfeeding. *MCN: American Journal of Maternal/Child Nursing*, **34**(4), 249.

Neerhof, M. G. and Thaete, L. G. (2008) The fetal response to chronic placental insufficiency. *Seminars in Perinatology*, **32**, 201–5.

Neumark-Sztainer, D., Story, M., Toporoff, E., Himes, J. H., Resnick, M. D. and Blum, R. W. (1997) Covariations of eating behaviors with other health-related behaviors among adolescents. *Journal of Adolescent Health*, **20**, 450–8.

Neumark-Sztainer, D., Eisenberg, M. E., Fulkerson, J. A., Story, M. and Larson, N. I. (2008) Family meals and disordered eating in adolescents: longitudinal findings from project EAT. *Archives of Pediatrics & Adolescent Medicine*, **162**(1), 17.

NICE (2011) *Guidance for Midwives, Health Visitors, Pharmacists and Other Primary Care Services to Improve the Nutrition of Pregnant and Breastfeeding Mothers and Children in Low Income Households*. Public Heath Guidance. DH, London. http://guidance.nice.org.uk/PH11

Office for National Statistics (2012) *Conceptions in England and Wales 2010*. Available at: http://www.ons.gov.uk/ons/dcp171778_258291.pdf (accessed 18 February 2013).

Olausson, P. M., Cnattingius, S. and Goldenbery, R. L. (1997) Determinants of poor pregnancy outcomes among teenagers in Sweden. *Obstetrics & Gynecology*, **89**, 451–7.

Olausson, P. O., Cnattingius, S. and Haglund, B. (1999) Teenage pregnancies and risk of late foetal death and infant mortality. *British Journal of Obstetrics and Gynaecology*, **106**, 116–21.

Parker, T. (1998) Vitamins and pregnancy: teenagers' beliefs. *The Practising Midwife*, **1**, 23–4.

Pavlovic, M., Prentice, A., Thorsdottir, I., Wolfram, G. and Branca, F. (2007) Challenges in harmonising energy and nutrient recommendations in Europe. *Annals of Nutrition and Metabolism*, **51**, 108–14.

Perez, E. M., Hendricks, M. K., Beard, J. L., Murray-Kolb, L. E., Berg, A., Tomlinson, M., *et al.* (2005) Mother infant Interactions and infant development are altered by maternal iron deficiency anemia. *Journal of Nutrition*, **135**, 850–5.

Picciano, M. F. (2003) Pregnancy and lactation: physiological adjustments, nutritional requirements and the role of dietary supplements. *Journal of Nutrition*, **133**, 1997S–2002S.

Pijls, L., Ashwell, M. and Lambert, J. (2009) EURRECA – a network of excellence to align European micronutrient recommendations. *Food Chemistry*, **113**, 748–53.

Pobocik, R. S., Benavente, J. C., Boudreau, N. S. and Spore, C. L. (2003) Pregnant adolescents in Guam consume diets low in calcium and other micronutrients. *Journal of the American Dietetic Association*, **103**, 611–14.

Prentice, A. (2008) Vitamin D deficiency: a global perspective. *Nutrition Reviews*, **66**(s2), S153–S164.

Ramachandran, P. (2002) Maternal nutrition – effect on fetal growth and outcome of pregnancy. *Nutrition Reviews*, **60**, S26–S34.

Rampersaud, G. C., Pereira, M. A., Girard, B. L., Adams, J. and Metzl, J. D. (2005) Breakfast habits, nutritional status, body weight, and academic performance in children and adolescents. *Journal of the American Dietetic Association*, **105**, 743–60.

Ravelli, A. C., van der Meulen, J. H., Michels, R. P., Osmond, C., Barker, D. J., Hales, C. N. and Bleker, O. P. (1998) Glucose tolerance in adults after prenatal exposure to famine. *Lancet*, **351**, 173–7.

Reifsnider, E. and Gill, S. L. (2000) Nutrition for the childbearing years. *Journal of Obstetric, Gynecologic, & Neonatal Nursing*, **29**, 43–55.

Repke, J. T. and Villar, J. (1991) Pregnancy-induced hypertension and low birth weight: the role of calcium. *American Journal of Clinical Nutrition*, **54**, 237S–241S.

Saintonge, S., Bang, H. and Gerber, L. M. (2009) Implications of a new definition of vitamin D deficiency in a multiracial us adolescent population: the National Health and Nutrition Examination Survey III. *Pediatrics*, **123**(3), 797–803.

Satin, A. J., Leveno, K. J., Sherman, M. L., Reedy, N. J., Lowe, T. W. and McIntire, D. D. (1994) Maternal youth and pregnancy outcome: middle school versus high school age groups compared with women beyond teen years. *American Journal of Obstetrics and Gynecology*, **171**, 184–7.

Scholl, T. O., Hediger, M. L. and Ances, I. G. (1990) Maternal growth during pregnancy and decreased birth weight. *American Journal of Clinical Nutrition*, **51**, 790–3.

Scholl, T. O. and Hediger, M. L. (1994) Anemia and iron-deficiency anemia: compilation of data on pregnancy outcome. *American Journal of Clinical Nutrition*, **59**, 492S–501S.

Scholl, T. O. and Hediger, M. L. (1995) Weight gain, nutrition, and pregnancy outcome: findings from the Camden study of teenage and minority gravidas. *Seminars in Perinatology*, **19**, 171–81.

Scholl, T. O., Hediger, M. L., Schall, J. I., Khoo, C. S. and Fischer, R. L. (1994) Maternal growth during pregnancy and competition for nutrients. *American Journal of Clinical Nutrition*, **60**, 183–8.

Scholl, T. O., Stein, T. P. and Smith, W. K. (2000) Leptin and maternal growth during adolescent pregnancy. *American Journal of Clinical Nutrition*, **72**, 1542–7.

Scottish Executive (2002) *Hungry for Success. A Whole School Approach to School Meals in Scotland*. Available at: http://www.scotland.gov.uk/Publications/2003/02/16273/17566 (accessed June 2010).

Scottish Executive (2004) *Eating for Health – Meeting the Challenge*. Available at: http://www.scotland.gov.uk/Resource/Doc/47060/0012960.pdf (accessed June 2010).

Seth, A., Marwaha, R. K., Singla, B., Aneja, S., Mehrotra, P., Sastry, A. *et al.* (2009) Vitamin D nutritional status of exclusively breast fed infants and their mothers. *Journal of Pediatric Endocrinology*, **22**, 241–6.

Shah, D. and Sachdev, H. P. S. (2006) Zinc deficiency in pregnancy and fetal outcome. *Nutrition Reviews*, **64**(1), 15–30.

Shuger, L. (2012) *Teen Pregnancy and High School Dropout: What Communities are Doing to Address These Issues*. The National Campaign to Prevent Teen and Unplanned Pregnancy and America's Promise Alliance, Washington, DC. Available at: http://www.thenationalcampaign.org/resources/pdf/teen-preg-hs-dropout.pdf (accessed 18 February 2013).

Sian, L., Krebs, N. F., Westcott, J. E., Fengliang, L., Tong, L., Miller, L. V. *et al.* (2002) Zinc homeostasis during lactation in a population with a low zinc intake. *American Journal of Clinical Nutrition*, **75**, 99–103.

Sjoberg A, Hallberg L, Hoglund D, Hulthen L (2003) Meal patter, food choice, nutrient intake and lifestyle factors in The Goteborg Adolescence Study. *European Journal of Clinical Nutrition* 57: 1569-1578

Skinner, J. D., Carruth, B. R., Pope, J., Varner, L. and Goldberg, D. (1992) Food and nutrient intake of white, pregnant adolescents. *Journal of the American Dietetic Association*, **92**, 1127–30.

Smith, G. C. S. and Pell, J. P. (2001) Teenage pregnancy and risk of adverse perinatal outcomes associated with first and second births: population based retrospective cohort study. *British Medical Journal*, **323**, 476–9.

Sommer, A., Davidson, F. R. and Annecy, A. (2002) Assessment and control of vitamin A deficiency: the Annecy Accords. *Journal of Nutrition*, **132** (Suppl.) 2850S.

Stang, J., Story, M. and Feldman, S. (2005) Nutrition in adolescent pregnancy. *International Journal of Childbirth Education*, **20**(2), 4.

Stevens-Simon, C., Fullar, S. and McAnarney, E. R. (1992) Tangible differences between adolescent-oriented and adult-oriented prenatal care. *Journal of Adolescent Health*, **13**, 298–302.

Story, M. (1992) Nutritional requirements during adolescence. In: *Textbook of Adolescent Medicine* (eds. E. R. McAnarney, R. E. Kreipe, D. E. Orr and G. D. Comerci), pp. 75–84. WB Saunders, Philadelphia.

Story, M., Neumark-Sztainer, D. and French, S. (2002) Individual and environmental influences on adolescent eating behaviors. *Journal of the American Dietetic Association*, **102**(Suppl.), S40–S51.

Strand, T. A., Taneja, S., Bhandari, N. *et al.* (2007) Folate, but not vitamin B-12 status, predicts respiratory morbidity in north Indian children. *American Journal of Clinical Nutrition*, **86**, 139–44.

Swann, C., Bowe, K., McCormick, G. and Kosmin, M. (2003) *Teenage Pregnancy and Parenthood: a Review of Reviews*. Health Development Agency, London.

Swanson, V., Power, K., Kaur, B., Carter, H. and Shepherd, K. (2006) The impact of knowledge and social influences on adolescents' breast-feeding beliefs and intentions. *Public Health Nutrition*, **9**(3), 297.

Symon, A. G. and Wrieden, W. L. (2003) A qualitative study of pregnant teenagers' perceptions of the acceptability of a nutritional education intervention. *Midwifery*, **19**, 140–7.

Teenage Pregnancy Associates (2011) *Teenage Pregnancy: The Evidence*. Teenage Pregnancy Associates, London. Available at: http://teenagepregnancyassociates.co.uk/tpa-evidence.pdf (accessed 18 February 2013).

Teenage Pregnancy Unit (2004) *Teenage Pregnancy: an Overview of the Research Evidence*. Health Development Agency, London.

Thurnham, D. I., Bender, D. A., Scott, J. and Halsted, C. H. (2000) Water-soluble vitamins. In: *Human Nutrition and Dietetics*, 10th edn (eds. J. S. Garrow, W. P. T. James and A. Ralph), pp. 249–87. Churchill Livingstone, Edinburgh.

Tomashek, K. M., Ananth, C. V. and Cogswell, M. E. (2006) Risk of stillbirth in relation to maternal haemoglobin concentration during pregnancy. *Maternal & Child Nutrition*, **2**(1), 19–28.

US Department of Health, American School Health Association, Association for the Advancement of Health Education, Society for Public Health Education, Inc (1989) *The National Adolescent Student Health Survey: a Report of the Health of America's Youth*. Third Party, Oakland.

Vanderpump, M. P., Lazarus, J. H., Smyth, P. P., Laurberg, P., Holder, R. L., Boelaert, K. and Franklyn, J. A. (2011) Iodine status of UK schoolgirls: a cross-sectional survey. *Lancet*, **377**(9782), 2007–12.

von Schenck, U., Bender-Götze, C. and Koletzko, B. (1997). Persistence of neurological damage induced by dietary vitamin B-12 deficiency in infancy. *Archives of Disease in Childhood*, **77**(2), 137–9.

Wahl, R. (1999) Nutrition in the adolescent. *Pediatric Annals*, **28**, 107–111.

Walker, Z., Townsend, J., Oakley, L., Donovan, C., Smith, H., Hurst, Z., Bell, J. and Marshall, S. (2002) Health promotion for adolescents in primary care: randomised controlled trial. *British Medical Journal*, **326**, 524–9.

Ward, B. (2000) Sandwell report in note 31. In: *Poverty in Plenty: A Human Development Report for the UK* (ed. J. Seymour). Earthscan, London.

Weaver, M., Poehlitz, M. and Hutchinson, S. (1999) 5 a day for low-income families: evaluation of an advertising campaign and cooking events. *Journal of Nutrition Education*, **31**, 161–9.

Whitton, C., Nicholson, S. K., Roberts, C., Prynne, C. J., Pot, G. K., Olson, A., Fitt, E., Cole, D., Teucher, B., Bates, B., Henderson, H., Pigott, S., Deverill, C., Swan, G. and Stephen, A. M. (2011) National Diet and Nutrition Survey: UK food consumption and nutrient intakes from the first year of the rolling programme and comparisons with previous surveys. *British Journal of Nutrition*, **106**(12), 1899.

Williamson, C. S. (2006) Nutrition in pregnancy. *Nutrition Bulletin*, **31**(1), 28–59.

Wilson, J. (1995) Maternity policy. Caroline: a case of a pregnant teenager. *Professional Care of Mother and Child*, **5**, 139–42.

Wise, N. J. and Arcamone, A. A. (2011) Survey of adolescent views of healthy eating during pregnancy. *MCN: The American Journal of Maternal/Child Nursing*, **36**(6), 381.

World Health Organization (WHO) (1998) *The Second Generation*. WHO, Geneva.

WHO (2001) *The Optimal Duration of Exclusive Breastfeeding. Report of an Expert Consultation*. WHO, Geneva.

WHO/FAO (2004) *Expert Consultation on Human Vitamin and Mineral Requirements*. WHO/FAO, Geneva.

WHO (2006) *Pregnant Adolescents. Delivering on Global Promises of Hope*. WHO, Geneva.

WHO (2007) *Assessment of Iodine Deficiency Disorders and Monitoring their Elimination. A Guide for Program Managers*, 3rd edn. WHO, Geneva.

Wrieden, W. L. and Symon, A. (2003) The development and pilot evaluation of a nutrition education intervention programme for teenage women (food for life). *Journal of Human Nutrition and Dietetics*, **16**, 67–71.

Young, B. E., McNanley, T. J., Cooper, E. M., McIntyre, A. W., Witter, F., Harris, Z. L. and O'Brien, K. O. (2012) Maternal vitamin D status and calcium intake interact to affect fetal skeletal growth *in utero* in pregnant adolescents. *American Journal of Clinical Nutrition*, **95**(5), 1103–12.

Zabin, L. S. and Kiragu, K. (1998) The health consequences of adolescent sexual and fertility behaviour in sub-Saharan Africa. *Studies in Family Planning*, **29**, 210–32.

Zimmermann, M. and Delange, F. (2004) Iodine supplementation of pregnant women in Europe: a review and recommendations. *European Journal of Clinical Nutrition*, **58**, 979–84.

Zimmermann, M. B. (2009) Iodine deficiency. *Endocrinology Review*, **30**(4), 376–408.

CHAPTER 3

Feeding the preterm infant: current challenges and debates

Kevin Hugill

Introduction

Infants who are born preterm make up a relatively small, but highly vulnerable, group of newborns. These infants have significantly greater mortality and morbidities than those born at term. Effective neonatal care improves the likelihood of good outcomes for preterm infants; however, determining which strategies are best for this population can be problematic. In this chapter the term 'oral feeding' refers to all modes of providing infants with milk feeds, including breastfeeding, cup feeds, bottle feeding and all approaches to gavage feeding.

The relationship between preterm diet, growth, development and wellbeing, in both the short and long term, is a subject of considerable scrutiny and debate. Human milk (ideally the mother's own) is undoubtedly the pre-eminent choice of nourishment for all newborn infants regardless of gestation at birth. Nevertheless, achieving this ideal and simultaneously ensuring optimal nutrition for the preterm-born infant can be challenging. The rewards, however, can be considerable. There is persuasive and enduring data that preterm infants can gain greater benefits from breastfeeding and breast milk than those born at term, particularly in the areas of cognition, neurodevelopmental and immunological outcome measures (Lucas *et al.*, 1992; Anderson *et al.*, 1999; Boyd *et al.*, 2007; Edmond and Bahl, 2007; Vohr *et al.*, 2007; Meinzen-Derr *et al.*, 2009; Isaacs *et al.*, 2010; Moore *et al.*, 2011).

In recent decades improved understanding of preterm nutritional physiology and better dietary management have contributed to increased survival and reductions in morbidity. In an era of low breastfeeding prevalence and breast milk utilisation in many neonatal units, the 1980s saw the introduction of commercial low birth weight (LBW: 2.5 kg) preterm milks. These milks were engineered to better replicate preterm breast milk and apply the understandings gained from laboratory and clinical studies about the inadequacies of term formulations for preterm infants' nutritional needs. These technological advances have continued apace, and more recently further differentiation is evident, exemplified by attempts to mimic fat ratios seen in preterm breast milk (which are important in neuronal cell membrane structure) and the design of milks suitable for post-hospital discharge needs. Each of these advances has often stimulated considerable clinical and academic debate: a situation we now see over the use of macro- and complex micronutrient fortification and supplementation of human and formula milks and the inclusion of prebiotics and probiotics into preterm nutritional management. These subjects will be considered in more detail later in this chapter.

Importantly, in parallel with these developments in formula milk, there is an ongoing drive to articulate the benefits of human breast milk for preterm infants and promote greater prevalence of breastfeeding. This is an argument that goes beyond immediate nutritional concerns and includes immunological, relational and longer term developmental and health benefits for mothers and infants. This chapter will discuss some of these challenges and emerging debates about how best to tailor the provision of infant nutrition to address the unique needs of preterm infants.

Challenges of prematurity

Preterm infants – those born before 37 weeks' completed gestation – are a distinct group of newborns but with considerable variation in the severity of disorders associated with prematurity and outcomes. Factors that link them together include relative immaturity of virtually all organ systems; limited behavioural repertoires; and inadequate nutritional reserves for sustaining postnatal life compared with those born at term. Preterm infants are born during a time of rapid fetal growth and development: at birth all organ systems are immature and post-birth they mature at differential rates. Development of the fetal gut is anatomically complete by around the 24th week of gestation, but functional development continues beyond birth (Premji, 1998). Some functions, such as increased mucosal lactase activity, are moderated by birth and oral feeding. Others seem to be intrinsically programmed to occur in line with gestational maturity: for example coordination of suck/swallow reflexes (around 33–36 weeks' gestation) and organised intestinal motility (28 and beyond weeks' gestation), seemingly regardless of birth timing (Neu, 2007).

The time taken to establish full oral feeds is variable; it can take many weeks and is not without risk. The early nutritional support of preterm infants, particularly those born at lower gestations, can be critical to survival and can constitute a clinical emergency. In situations where full oral nutrition is not possible or contraindicated then intravenous, parenteral, nutrition becomes essential. The management of parenteral nutrition is guided by similar nutritional concerns to that of oral. The provision and management of the transition from parenteral nutritional strategies to establishing full oral feeding is beyond the scope of this chapter. For some insights into this topic area see Koletzko *et al.* (2005), Valentine and Puthoff (2007) and Morgan (2011).

Many preterm infants, particularly those born very preterm, suffer from a significant fall-off in predicted growth velocity (based on *in utero* projections) during the first few weeks of life (Claas *et al.*, 2011) and these growth deficits are accumulative (Embleton and Tinnion, 2009). Promoting optimal outcomes for these infants is a major goal of neonatal health care. In this chapter the term 'nutritional management' is used to describe those interventions and nourishments that affect preterm infant growth, development, clinical recovery and cognitive and psychosocial outcomes.

Feeding the preterm infant

Our diet, how we eat it, and how we relate to our food are ultimately products of our environment and are social and cultural artefacts. These perspectives also reflect how we see infant feeding, particular in relation to mothers' feeding choices and decisions.

Aims of preterm nutrition

The aims of neonatal nutrition have in recent years become increasingly diverse and multifaceted. In part this diversity reflects the unique nutritional challenges and morbidities that preterm infants and their parents experience. The historic focus on nutrition as providing sufficient calories and nutrients to promote weight gain has become more nuanced. Nutritional aims include a number of infant-focused perspectives, but others also feature that relate to relational or wider public health concerns (Box 3.1). In part this reflects increased recognition that preterm infant nutrition is not solely the preserve of clinicians, and that other factors, desires and influences come into play. In reality, most practitioners seek to combine these aims, although their exact prioritisations might vary.

Choice of milk

When deciding about preterm oral nutritional management strategies, judgments need to be made about what milk to feed, how much milk to give and by what route of administration. There is universal acknowledgement that the mother's breast milk is nutritionally adequate for term infants during the first six months after birth (Butte *et al.*, 2002; Kramer and Kakuma, 2002) and that breastfeeding can

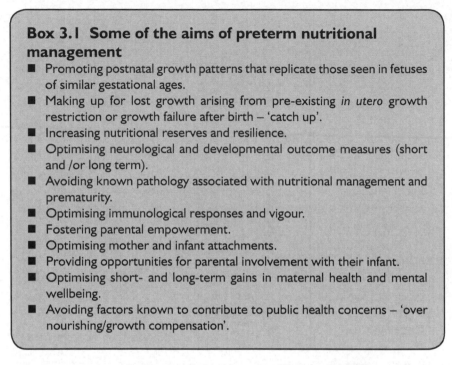

Box 3.1 Some of the aims of preterm nutritional management

- Promoting postnatal growth patterns that replicate those seen in fetuses of similar gestational ages.
- Making up for lost growth arising from pre-existing *in utero* growth restriction or growth failure after birth – 'catch up'.
- Increasing nutritional reserves and resilience.
- Optimising neurological and developmental outcome measures (short and /or long term).
- Avoiding known pathology associated with nutritional management and prematurity.
- Optimising immunological responses and vigour.
- Fostering parental empowerment.
- Optimising mother and infant attachments.
- Providing opportunities for parental involvement with their infant.
- Optimising short- and long-term gains in maternal health and mental wellbeing.
- Avoiding factors known to contribute to public health concerns – 'over nourishing/growth compensation'.

make important contributions to the health and wellbeing of children and mothers (Dykes, 2011). This view has been transcribed into national and international policy.

As a global public health recommendation, infants should be exclusively breastfed for the first six months of life to achieve optimal growth, development and health. (World Health Organization, 2003, pp. 7–8).

This position is endorsed by a wide range of lay, professional and governmental bodies. In the UK the Department of Health (2010) states:

Breastfeeding is the healthiest way to feed your baby. Exclusive breastfeeding (that means giving your baby breastmilk only, with no other food or drink) is recommended for around the first six months of your baby's life. Breastmilk provides all the nutrients your baby needs and helps to protect them from infections and diseases (Department of Health, 2010, p. 4).

The messages to parents of term infants are clear and unambiguous, but the situation is less clear for parents of preterm infants. In general, promoting breastfeeding remains the optimal choice, although with the caveat endorsed by the European Society for Paediatric Gastroenterology, Hepatology and Nutrition committee on nutrition (ESPGHAN) that those preterm infants weighing less than 1.8 kg receiving expressed breast milk (own mother or donor) should have it fortified (Agostoni *et al.*, 2010). However, for preterm infants not receiving breast milk the current advice is to use one of the specialist preterm milks which are formulated to meet published nutritional guidance, for example Tsang *et al.* (2005), Aggett *et al.* (2006) and Agostoni *et al.* (2010).

This subtle variation in guidance for preterm infants is perhaps understandable given the wide range of gestations and birth weights that infants can be born at. Many neonatal units differentiate their nutritional management approaches based upon weight and gestation at birth, age post-birth and growth trajectories; the availability of high-quality evidence to inform these guidelines is variable. Unpicking Agostoni *et al.*'s (2010) commentary reveals further complexities. This guideline offers advice related to the quantity and quality of nutrients for particular groups of preterm infants; specifically infants who are born weighing more than 1 kg and up to a weight of 1.8 kg. It is less clear how the nutritional needs of preterm infants of more than 1.8 kg or less than 1 kg should be best managed, and clinical judgment becomes essential. This situation reflects the availability of research and the gaps in our knowledge to make definitive recommendations, but also an understanding that infants of different gestations and weights at birth need different nutrition.

The focus upon ensuring adequate energy and increased amounts protein in the diet in published guidance (Tsang *et al.*, 2005; Aggett *et al.*, 2006; Agostoni *et al.*, 2010) reflects research knowledge that suggests these can be limiting factors in ensuring optimal growth in the preterm infant (Premji *et al.*, 2006; Ehrenkranz, 2007; Kashyap, 2007; Vlaardingerbroek *et al.*, 2009; Claas *et al.*, 2011). However, it is also supportive of a widely held aim of preterm nutrition, namely that nutritional management strategies should strive to achieve postnatal growth rates approximating that seen in fetuses of the same gestational age (Hay, 2008; De Curtis and Rigo, 2012).

The infant formula market is dynamic and companies often reformulate their products to meet emerging legislation, new knowledge and insights, or as part of a strategy of market segment diversification (Crawley and Westland, 2011). The use of commercial formula milk as a breast milk substitute for newborns can be contentious and it is a topic that generates considerable emotional intensity amongst some health professionals, mothers and others. Decisions and discussions about how best to feed preterm infants are not immune from these influences.

Nonetheless, in situations where mothers choose not to breastfeed or express breast milk or in circumstances which prevent its use then specialist preterm formulas can make important contributions to preterm diet.

For healthy term infants current recommendations suggest on demand (*ad libitum*) feeding regardless of milk source (Royal College of Nursing, 2007; Department of Health, 2010). For preterm infants the situation is less clear. There is some limited evidence which should be interpreted with caution that using infant hunger cues can help to reduce the time taken to establish full oral feeding and reduce the length of hospital stay (McCormick *et al.*, 2010a). In contrast, more structured feeding regimes can improve feeding tolerance and transition to full oral feeding and possibly avoid some pathologies (McCain, 2003; Bombell and McGuire, 2008; Krishnamurthy *et al.*, 2009; Morgan *et al.*, 2011b). To illustrate, beginning with small volume (variously described as 'sub-nutritional', 'trophic', 'gut priming' or 'minimal enteral feeding') milk feeds using the mother's expressed fresh breast milk in the days shortly after birth, regardless of the infant's ability to gain nourishment from milk feeds, can be beneficial in terms of intestinal activity, gut colonisation and immunological protection (Newburg and Walker, 2007; Moore *et al.*, 2011). Whilst the evidence is weak and requires further study (Bombell and McGuire, 2009), such structured approaches run counter to much mainstream breastfeeding advice and this needs to be taken into account when advising mothers on preterm breastfeeding to avoid confusion and mixed messages.

Influences on preterm infant feeding decisions

Superficially the choice of how best to feed a newborn infant might seem easy, i.e. *ad libitum* mother's breast milk from the breast. However, for the preterm infant this option is not always possible and alternative sources of milk and delivery modalities need to be sought. Data, where they exist, concerning the mode of oral feeding for those infants unable to suck effectively or when mothers are absent are controversial (Hay, 2008; McInnes *et al.*, 2010). The ways in which mothers of term infants choose to feed their infant and what influences these decisions is a subject of detailed research. It seems that mothers' previous experiences of infant feeding are important (Hoddinott *et al.*, 2012; Hughes, 2012) and fathers, grandmothers and health care professionals are also known to be influential (Dykes, 2006; Sweet and Darbyshire, 2009; McInnes *et al.*, 2010). Preterm birth complicates feeding decisions for both healthcare practitioners and mothers themselves. Additionally, those working within neonatal units are not immune from wider social norms and behaviours, and as such decisions about parental practices in neonatal units reflect these socio-cultural points of reference.

Despite the impetus to promote breast milk feeding in neonatal units, the effects of these initiatives upon rates of breastfeeding post hospital discharge are less clear, but it is known that breastfeeding continuation is lower in this group of mothers compared to mothers of term infants, and that many factors influence this (Pineda, 2011). One example of these factors, whilst not causally related, might be that the promotion and routine use of fortification of expressed breast milk in many neonatal units somewhat undermines the premise that breast milk is best for their infant. This tension could potentially undermine a mother's decisions to continue breastfeeding or providing breast milk. In addition, the emotional importance to parents of successful oral feeding (interpreted as no gavage feeds) and continued patterns of weight gain cannot be under stressed; many neonatal units use these as criteria for determining readiness for discharge home. This might be an additional influencing factor when mothers of preterm infants make and review their feeding choices.

Supporting feeding choices that nurture

Preterm newborns require a balance between ensuring sufficient nutrients to guarantee adequate growth and providing opportunities for parental intimacy to promote attachment. This interplay between physical and emotional nurturance can make positive contributions to long term neurodevelopmental outcomes and wellbeing. The quality of the early mother–infant relationship plays an important role in infant development. However, highly stressed mothers of sick and preterm infants are less able to engage in social interactions with their infants. In part this is also because preterm infants' behaviour repertoires are more limited and difficult to interpret (Als *et al.*, 2005). Teaching parents about their infant's behaviour can help to sensitise them to their infant's needs (Westrup, 2007; Appleton, 2011).

The aims of preterm nutrition seek to confer advantages for the infant, the mother and wider public health concerns (Box 3.1); breastfeeding addresses many of these aims. It can also provide opportunities for mothers to learn about their infant's behavioural cues. Mothers of preterm infants who want to breastfeed face additional difficulties compared to mothers in other postnatal settings (Demirci *et al.*, 2012). For example, mothers whose infants are admitted to a neonatal unit experience additional emotional upheavals for which they are often unprepared (Wigert *et al.*, 2006; Aagaard and Hall, 2008). Mothers are often ill themselves, in physical pain and separated from their infants for periods of time and by distance. This makes unrestricted contact and opportunities for breastfeeding problematic. Furthermore, for some infants, oral feeding may be medically contraindicated, or they may be unable to tolerate the required volumes of milk to ensure nutritional

adequacy. Some initially lack the ability to coordinate sucking, swallowing and breathing simultaneously – behaviours which are essential for successful oral feeding.

At first inspection much of the attention given to preterm nutrition in practice and research is seemingly concerned with biomedical dimensions and promoting growth. However, focusing solely upon the nutritional benefits of breast milk ignores other dimensions of breastfeeding and nurturance (Flacking *et al.*, 2006). The act of breastfeeding (compared to bottle feeding) is associated with positive psychological effects in mothers and can reduce stress experiences (Buckley and Charles, 2006). Interventions to promote breastfeeding and breast milk feeding might offer the opportunity to reduce mothers' stress experiences following preterm birth and also help them regain a sense of control over events. As one mother recalled:

> Whilst my baby was on the neonatal unit, a lot of things were out of my control, but expressing enabled me to feel that I was doing something re-ally important for my baby and gave me a 'purpose' in those difficult early days. (Bliss, 2008, p. 2)

Why mothers stop breastfeeding and what helps them to continue

Numerous factors contribute towards mothers deciding to discontinue breastfeeding and milk expression. Some relate to personal choice, but others include lack of self-confidence, support and guidance, and neonatal unit practices. Mothers of infants born at term who begin and continue to breastfeed for longer tend to be older, married and have higher educational attainment and family income than mothers who do not breastfeed or stop earlier (Callen and Pinelli, 2004). However, the exact interrelationships of these associations are complex (Scott *et al.*, 2006). Studies of mothers of preterm infants report similar associations and complexities (Flacking *et al.*, 2007).

One study of mothers' infant feeding experiences reported that a common feature of mothers' accounts of their experiences of breastfeeding was the conflict they saw between the idealised aspirations espoused in official guidelines and the everyday realities of feeding. When faced with breastfeeding difficulties, many mothers placed greater emphasis on addressing immediate family wellbeing rather than more nebulous longer-term health benefits, suggesting that shorter-term incremental targets personalised for individual women might be more beneficial than more global targets (Hoddinott *et al.*, 2012). This could have important implications for how feeding advice is conveyed to mothers of preterm infants.

A UK survey of mothers of preterm infants reported that 70% of mothers found the experience of breast milk expression to be positive; other mothers were either indifferent or found it distressing (Bliss, 2008). In the same survey 62% of mothers also breastfed and most felt encouraged to do so, although a small number of mothers (5% of respondents) reported feeling pressurised to stop breastfeeding and use bottles (containing formula or expressed breast milk), either because of breastfeeding difficulties or to expedite discharge from hospital (Bliss, 2008). Indeed, the support mothers receive is highly influential on whether they establish breastfeeding (Demirci *et al.*, 2012). The everyday values and attitudes of neonatal nurses can affect breastfeeding patterns (McInnes *et al.*, 2010; Nyqvist *et al.*, 2012). Staff behaviours can lead to mothers receiving conflicting advice and varying amounts of practical and emotional support (McInnes *et al.*, 2010). This can over time lead to diminished milk supplies and mothers abandoning breastfeeding (Bliss, 2008).

The opportunity to extend the benefits of breastfeeding for preterm infants and their mothers to earlier ages post birth could have a significant impact upon preterm outcomes. Contrary to long established assumptions, there is an evidence base beginning to emerge that suggests that breastfeeding can be initiated much earlier than previously thought; with sufficient competence developed to establish exclusive breastfeeding between 32 and 38 weeks' gestation (Nyqvist, 2008). Kangaroo care (skin–skin contact) is known to be supportive of mothers' breastfeeding, reduce depressive symptoms and provide opportunity to establish emotional closeness (Riikka Korjaa *et al.*, 2008; Flacking *et al.*, 2011, 2012; Bigelow *et al.*, 2012). Howell and Graham (2011), however, revealed some inconsistencies in how staff provided this intervention. Younger mothers (16–27 years), when asked if they had as much kangaroo care with their infants as they wanted, reported markedly less satisfaction than older mothers (Howell and Graham, 2011). The reasons behind this finding are unclear and require further study, but it illustrates that there is some way to go before all neonatal units routinely apply best evidence. Ensuring that interventions like skin–skin contact are more widely used could also provide preterm infants with opportunities to develop and demonstrate their feeding competence and might improve breastfeeding prevalence. Assessment tools like the preterm infant breastfeeding behaviour scale (PIBBS: Nyqvist, 2008) could provide healthcare professionals and mothers with information about infant readiness to breastfeed.

The results from UK surveys of parental experience around infant feeding present a somewhat mixed picture. Some neonatal units are more consistent in the advice and support they give mothers about feeding, but others are less coherent and seemingly prioritise ensuring dietary intake quantification. This can leave mothers feeling confused and unsupported. Clearly, raising awareness, auditing and addressing shortfalls in practice can help to improve the standards of feeding support. However, McInnes and colleagues' (2010) conclusion that entrenched and sometimes contradictory cultural attitudes towards infant feeding prevail will also need addressing to ensure a rebalancing between physical and emotional nurturance.

In general, parents on neonatal units feel more supported when they participate in a range of different individual and collective interventions (Brett *et al.*, 2011). Despite somewhat mixed grades of evidence, the feature in common throughout these interventions is the key role that effective, meaningful and timely communication and information plays. Providing practical tailored advice to mothers relevant to preterm feeding, such as that provided by Bliss (2012), is to be commended. In addition, training staff in how to apply and adapt interventions known to be successful in supporting mothers' lactation and breastfeeding (see McInnes and Chambers, 2008; Renfrew *et al.*, 2009) could ensure greater consistency of advice and maternal satisfaction. The recently announced expansion of the ten steps to successful breastfeeding into neonatal care areas, the 'baby-friendly hospital initiative – revised, updated and expanded' (Nyqvist, 2012), could help to support mothers and increase breastfeeding and breast milk provision in neonatal units.

Preterm diet and its relationship to outcomes and wellbeing

Healthy fetal development is a precondition for healthy postnatal life. The last trimester of pregnancy is an important period of rapid fetal growth and deposition of nutrient stores (Kovacs and Kronenberg, 1997). For example, during this time around 80% of bone mineralisation occurs (Williford *et al.*, 2008); therefore infants born preterm are somewhat compromised. Accordingly, the nutritional needs of the preterm infant differ markedly from those of the term infant.

Fetal and neonatal nutrition has profound implications for future growth, development and health (Streimish *et al.*, 2012). Indeed, deprivation of timely adequate nutrition, in terms of both calorific quality and nutritional quality (mix of nutrients), can have lifelong effects (Bartley *et al.*, 1994). A number of studies of infants born with growth restriction or who fail to grow adequately after preterm birth show that poor growth is associated with increased mortality and inferior outcomes (Ehrenkranz *et al.*, 2006; Fattal-Valevski *et al.*, 2009; Cosmi *et al.*, 2011; Morgan *et al.*, 2011a). Concern about the future implications of growth failure has led to a widely held view that promoting growth along similar trajectories to that seen *in utero* is a desirable aim of preterm nutrition management. In reality, despite nutritional advances, this target is seldom achieved at discharge from hospital. Many low birth weight infants show poor growth in a range of growth parameters, such as weight, length and head circumference (De Curtis and Rigo, 2012). Hay (2008) suggests that around 15–50% of preterm infants show growth restriction at birth and that this figure rises to 100% by term (corrected age) in some neonatal units. This extra-uterine growth restriction is more prevalent in infants with severe co-morbidities of prematurity such as chronic lung disease, necrotising enterocolitis, sepsis and intraventricular haemorrhage, so unpicking exact relationships between nutrition and outcomes can be complex.

Consequences of growth restriction

Intrauterine growth restriction is closely associated with maternal health in pregnancy and socioeconomic status. It affects fetal and neonatal mortality, morbidity and resultant low birth weight (Cosmi *et al.*, 2011). When compared to preterm low birth weight infants who are an appropriate weight for their gestation, preterm infants who are also growth restricted at birth (sometimes referred to as 'small for gestation age') have greater mortality (Sharma *et al.*, 2004). In addition, despite the slightly reduced risk of developing surfactant-deficient lung disease (respiratory distress syndrome), possibly due to intra-uterine physiological stress promoting lung maturation, they have an increased risk of developing chronic lung disease and stay longer in hospital after birth. In contrast, a longitudinal cohort study carried out in Australia of infants born at less than 28 weeks' gestation in the early 1990s without apparent neurological and sensory harm found no link between fetal growth restriction and neurodevelopmental status on a range of measures at the age of 8 years (corrected for prematurity) (Kan *et al.*, 2008). Furthermore, actual weight and catch-up weight gain in earlier childhood were unrelated to any outcome measures, but a smaller head circumference was generally associated with poorer neurodevelopmental outcome (Kan *et al.*, 2008).

Children born with low birth weight (and often preterm) are at increased risk of developing a number of diseases of important public health concern. Long-term epidemiological studies of the effects of fetal growth restriction and of subsequent neonatal and infancy catch-up nutrition and growth suggest a link with a number of diseases (Barker *et al.*, 2002). In humans low birth weight and small body size during infancy are consistently associated with later adult diseases, including coronary heart disease and type 2 diabetes (Langley-Evans, 2009), whereas neonatal and early infancy catch-up growth have been linked to obesity and cardiovascular mortality.

Epidemiological and animal studies suggest that the mechanisms behind these effects are related to intrauterine growth restriction and resultant low birth weight, which leads to a persistent remodelling of metabolism and physiology, sometimes referred to as nutritional programming (Lucas, 2005; Langley-Evans, 2009), that predisposes individuals for later disorders. Exact explanations of the mechanism through which these health effects operate are thought to include endothelial and renal dysfunction during fetal life (Cosmi *et al.*, 2011). However, it must be remembered that these disorders are multi-factorial and numerous environmental and lifestyle factors are known to be influential.

Management of intrauterine growth restriction infants is controversial (Cosmi *et al.*, 2011). On the one hand they have an increased incidence of perinatal mortality and morbidities which can extend into childhood and beyond, yet on the other over-nutrition is also associated with adverse adult outcomes. Some commentators suggest that the benefits of catch-up growth for preterm intrauterine growth restriction and low birth weight infants far outweigh theoretical co-morbidities, since many infants are exposed to moderating background variables whereas poor growth has definitive links with poorer neurological cognitive and developmental outcomes.

An early critical period?

The notion of a period during early neonatal life when previous nutritional inadequacies can be overcome is attractive given the potential for long-term health benefits and reducing the effects of prematurity and low birth weight on functional status. There is evidence from several sources to support the idea of a critical period for brain growth in the newborn period. In humans the time between 24 weeks' gestation and two years of age represents a period during which 90% of brain growth (in terms of volume) takes place (Embleton and Tinnion, 2009). Head circumference correlates closely with brain size (Cooke *et al.*, 1977; Isaacs *et al.*, 2010) and in studies of children born preterm head circumference correlates closely with measures of cognitive function (Gale *et al.*, 2004; Fattal-Valevski *et al.*, 2009). Cooke (2006) observes that this suggests that postnatal head growth is a key factor in later functional performance.

A series of reports from studies in the 1980s and 1990s carried out by Lucas and co-workers demonstrated that relatively short-term increases in nutrient provision can increase growth and improve developmental assessment outcomes in preterm infants (Lucas *et al.*, 1984, 1994, 1998). These findings add credence to the idea of a critical period in neonatal brain development in the early postnatal period. It seems there is potentially a unique opportunity during a short postnatal time to positively influence the growth of neurological tissues and affect long-term outcomes. However, despite the widespread acceptance of the desirability of promoting growth, particularly head growth, following preterm birth, little is known about what the optimal growth velocity is in this group of newborns and what the longer term consequences of this 'catch-up' growth might be. Cooke (2006) suggests that interventions that aim to improve IQ in children should focus upon reducing intrauterine growth restriction and improving later childhood growth whilst avoiding adiposity, whereas those aiming to enhance motor skills need to target interventions that prevent perinatal brain injury. Clearly both sets of outcomes are desirable and more detailed research is required on the lifelong effects of nutritional management decisions in this group of infants.

Optimising growth

After the first few weeks of lactation, biologically active components, milk protein levels and calories tend to decline (Bauer and Gerss, 2011; Mehta and Petrova, 2011; Hartmann *et al.*, 2012). It is widely acknowledged that the reduction in milk protein over time results in insufficient nutrients to ensure desired growth velocities and can result in suboptimal growth of preterms (Agostini *et al.*, 2010). Managing this fall-off in growth for infants on neonatal units has become a major focus of recent attention. Mothers of preterm infants show considerable variation in protein levels, both between different milk expressions and between different mothers (Jones *et al.*, 2012). This finding might represent true physiological variation or reflect the effects of different techniques of milk expression, and further research is required to explore this.

Longitudinal biochemical analysis of serial samples of preterm milk highlight that preterm milk is generally higher in all the major nutrient groups when compared to term breast milk, and these differences persist for around eight weeks after delivery (Bauer and Gerss, 2001). This relationship seems to be consistent regardless of whether mothers are initiating lactation, undergoing transitional lactations or producing mature milks. One interpretation of this is that whilst preterm breast milk is associated with slower growth, it might be physiologically primed to provide an enhanced nutrient profile during this early postnatal critical period and avoid later over-nutritional responses. Furthermore (and speculatively), given the evolutionary background of human milk it might be that the changes we see in preterm breast milk composition over time might be a developmental response rather than a problem *per se*. This interpretation would imply that our expectations of preterm postnatal growth trajectories are erroneous in some way and would require reconsideration.

Evidence from randomised controlled trials shows the benefits in terms of weight gain and neurodevelopment of using formula milks adjusted for preterm nutrition over term formulas (Lucas *et al.*, 1984, 1994). These specialist infant milks, intended to be used under medical supervision in hospital settings, have become a pervasive component of preterm infant nutrition and provide indispensable dietary options for situations when human milks are unavailable. Today few clinicians would countenance using term formula milk for hospitalised preterm infants. The situation is less clear post hospital discharge. Recent years have seen the emergence of specialist nutrient-enriched post-discharge formulas into the market. There is evidence that very low birth weight preterm infants (<1 kg) fed these milks can achieve improvement in growth parameters (Lucas *et al.*, 2001), although other trial results are inconsistent in demonstrating this relationship and any developmental advantage (Aimone *et al.*, 2009). Morgan *et al.* (2011a) suggest that this might be because infants fed *ad libitum* at home probably reduce their milk intake relative to the calorie density of the milk.

To summarise, evidence demonstrating the effects of early nutrition on development is complex. It seems likely that it is not somatic growth *per se* that is important, but rather head circumference, implying brain growth that moderates neurodevelopmental outcomes. In studies to date breastfeeding is consistently associated with better neurodevelopmental outcome and yet simultaneously with poorer weight gain than seen with preterm formula fed infants (Anderson *et al.*, 1999; Heiman and Schanler, 2007). This seemingly contradictory situation has been termed the 'apparent breastfeeding paradox' (Rozé *et al.*, 2012) to illustrate the tension that this situation generates for healthcare professionals and neonatal nutrition. However, numerous mainly non-nutritional, pathological and environmental factors interact over time, affecting causal interpretations. For example, mothers who breastfeed, particularly for extended periods of time, tend to have higher educational attainment and socioeconomic status. Applying advances in understanding of nutritional physiology to routine practice and matching their effects to outcomes in preterm infants is likely to be difficult.

Dietary supplementation and fortification

Micronutrients play a critical role in determining infant responses to macronutrient provision. As such, the addition of extra micro- and macronutrients to milk feeds have become an increasing focus of research for their role in optimising growth. Metabolic bone disease and poorer bone mineralisation is often seen in stable and rapidly growing preterm infants, especially those of less than 1 kg, leading to osteopenia and rickets despite dietary vitamin and mineral supplementation (Mitchell *et al.*, 2009). However, a review (Fewtrell, 2011) casts doubt on the desirability of striving to increase mineral intakes that match those seen *in utero*. Fewtrell (2011) argues that the large variations seen in neonatal mineral intake appear to have no detectable effect on adult bone density. Consequently, a targeted approach to individual infants who are showing clinical effects of deficit would be inherently better than global increases in mineral consumption. However, few data relate to very low birth weight infants and further research is required. Interestingly, despite the relatively low mineral content of breast milk (when compared with formula milks) breast milk feeding is associated with higher bone mass. This is likely to be due, at least in part, to the increased bioavailability of minerals in breast milk.

Dietary supplementation with long chain polyunsaturated fatty acids

One example of the complexity and debate concerning the formulation of infant milks, and one that illustrates some of the difficulties with applying understandings of breast milk composition and the global biological effects of breast milk on growth and cognitive outcomes, is the supplementation of infant formulae with long chain polyunsaturated fatty acids (LCPUFA). LCPUFAs are known to be key constituents of cell membranes, particularly neuronal, retinal and vascular tissues, but also have a number of other important biological functions including inflammatory response (Agostoni, 2005). Observations of breast milk composition show that it contains LCPUFAs, particularly docosahexaenoic acid (n-3 DHA) and arachidonic acid (n-6 AA). Newborn infants are able to syntheses small amounts of these from essential precursor fatty acids: linoleic (n-6 LA) and alpha-linolenic acid (n-3 ALA) (Fleith and Clandinin, 2005). Based on the observation that breast milk contains these compounds they have been added to term and preterm formula milks on the expectation that this would enhance cognitive outcomes (Kennedy *et al.*, 2010).

Numerous clinical trials using LCPUFAs from a variety of animal and plant sources have been carried out to evaluate the effectiveness of this dietary supplementation upon infant growth, sensory function and cognition. Whilst the evidence about the biological effects of LCPUFA supplementation of formulae from individual trials is mixed, combined meta-analyses and long-term follow-up of infants (term and preterm) consistently report no convincing effects on neurodevelopment or growth (Beyerlein *et al.*, 2010; Kennedy *et al.*, 2010; Schulzke *et al.*, 2011; Simmer *et al.*, 2011); though there may be some marginal effect for very low birth weight infants (Beyerlein *et al.*, 2010; Makrides *et al.*, 2011), particularly preterm girls, who show increased adiposity and blood pressure at the age of ten years (Kennedy *et al.*, 2010). However, this differential gender effect may have been affected by the onset of puberty (Kennedy *et al.*, 2010). Nonetheless, it requires careful consideration given the potential health consequences in later life of childhood overweight.

Breast milk fortifiers

The chemical composition of human milk varies considerably between women and in an individual mother, depending upon the time since birth, stage of individual breastfeed and how it is expressed from the breast. This decline in energy and protein level is hypothesised as an explanation for the observed growth differentials seen between breast milk and formula-fed preterm infants. Feeding preterm infants with unmodified breast milk results in delays in growth and nutrient deficiencies both during and after their hospital stay. Improved growth is seen using preterm and post-discharge formulas when compared to unmodified expressed breast milk-fed infants. However, this situation is less clear when fortified breast milk is the comparator. In order to achieve the desired postnatal growth rates breast milk needs to be consumed at high, often unattainable, volumes (Agostoni *et al.*, 2010) and consequently the breast milk intended for rapidly growing infants requires nutrient fortification. This can be achieved in several ways: some neonatal units use mixed feeding (mother's breast milk and preterm formula) and others adopt a strategy of breast milk fortification.

Montjaux-Régis *et al.* (2011) found that, for infants born at less than 32 weeks' gestation, mothers' own breast milk was superior (in terms of weight gain) when compared to donor human milk. This is not surprising, given that donor milk sources are usually pooled expressed milk from mature lactations and their composition might not match that seen in a mother's own breast milk, which is attuned to their infant's age and needs. In addition to the loss of biologically active components, nutrients are also lost during processing, which would make donor milk less nutritionally complete (Ewaschuk *et al.*, 2010). The loss of fat during storage and processing of breast milk and during tube feeding (due to adhesion of fat molecules to containers) may account for this difference in growth rates (Tacken *et al.*, 2009). In studies that have used fortified donor milk these growth differences seem to disappear (Colaizy *et al.*, 2012). In order to compensate for these losses and enhance the nutritional profile of breast milk, multi-component breast milk fortification is routine in most neonatal units and it reflects concern to compensate for the relatively slow growth seen in breast milk-fed infants.

Internationally there are a variety of powdered and liquid commercial multi-component breast milk fortifiers available. All contain varying amounts of protein, carbohydrate, calcium, phosphate, vitamins and trace elements; this can make comparisons difficult and data on the optimum composition of fortifier remains unconfirmed. In practice, powdered fortifiers are often preferred as they do not further dilute the breast milk when added. Although some concerns about the effects of increased osmolarity have been voiced, these seem to be clinically less worrisome in standard dilutions (Srinivasan *et al.*, 2004).

Systematic reviews suggest that breast milk fortification is associated with short-term improvements in weight gain and growth in length and head circumference (Kuschel and Harding, 2004). Debate about optimal fortification strategies, when to begin fortification and when to stop, what form of fortification and how it should be managed (global approaches versus individually tailored arrangements against agreed criterion such as blood and milk assays) continues.

Very few studies have been conducted looking at the use of fortification beyond discharge. A Cochrane review concluded that preterm infants fed with multinutrient fortified breast milk (compared with unfortified breast milk) following hospital discharge had increased growth rates during infancy, although the long-term effects of this regimen of feeding remain unclear (McCormick *et al.*, 2010b). This conclusion was based on one small trial involving 39 infants who received fortification of expressed breast milk at home for 12 weeks after discharge (O'Connor *et al.*, 2008). A follow-up study reported that these growth differences in weight, length, head circumference (in smaller infants) and bone mineralisation were still apparent at one year follow-up (Aimone *et al.*, 2009).

In summary, evidence concerning the use of nutrient-enriched feeds (human milk fortification and formula enrichment) is inconsistent and long-term studies of the effects of nutritional supplementation and fortification are lacking. Further work is required to understand which specific nutrient groups confer the most advantages to which subgroups of infants, and to determine the optimum timings and durations of supplementation and fortification. The benefits of breast milk and breastfeeding are not restricted to nutritional aspects, but include biological and psycho-social factors which are important in long-term health and development. Because of this, more productive (in terms of volume and milk 'quality') techniques and modalities of milk expression and storage and processing of expressed breast milk may be more attractive options to address the unique nutritional challenges of the preterm infant.

Box 3.2 Necrotising enterocolitis

Necrotising enterocolitis is a serious and potentially fatal disorder of the neonatal gut affecting survivors into childhood (Pike *et al.*, 2012). It primarily affects infants born preterm and is a significant cause of death and morbidity (Berrington *et al.*, 2012). The exact pathogenesis is multi-factorial and is not established, but a number of factors are implicated. Prematurity and low birth weight (especially very low birth weight: < 1.5 kg) are consistent features, but perinatal hypoxia and abnormal gut flora also feature (Lin and Stoll, 2006). Evidence from animal models suggests that an exaggerated and uncontrolled response to bacterial colonisation of the intestines could be an important factor (Cilieborg *et al.*, 2012). Most cases are sporadic and the incidence is inversely related to weight and gestation at birth. Population-based figures are hard to come by, but a crude incidence of 0.5–5 per 1,000 live births can be surmised from published reports (Linn and Stoll, 2006). Individual studies report greater variance over time and between neonatal units. Overall mortality is of the order of 15–30%, but can be a high as 50% in those who require emergency surgery (Lin and Stoll, 2006).

Necrotising enterocolitis is rare in infants who have never orally fed and feeding them with formula milk increases the risk of developing the condition (Lin and Stoll, 2006). Conversely, exclusive breast milk (especially fresh) feeding is known to be protective (Sullivan *et al.*, 2010). This protective effect is thought to arise from a number of mechanisms, including the presence of complex non-nutritional carbohydrates (oligosaccharides) in breast milk and inoculation of the newborn gastrointestinal tract with beneficial bacteria (Meinzen-Derr *et al.*, 2009).

The role of probiotics and prebiotics in preterm feeding

As more knowledge about the constituents and properties of human milk is uncovered, mechanistic explanations of the relationships between breast milk and better outcomes emerge. Two areas that are currently the subject of much research attention and clinical debate concern the inclusion of artificial sources of non-absorbable substances into infants' diets and intestinal inoculation with beneficial bacterial species to create a more balanced and beneficial gut bacterial flora. Research into the use of prebiotic and probiotic substances is attempting to establish an evidence base for interventions in preterm infants who are formula-fed to promote a gut microbiota that closely resembles that of exclusively breastfed infants and thereby confer protection against a range of serious disorders, in particular necrotising enterocolitis (see Box 3.2).

Prebiotics

In 1995 Gibson and Roberfroid introduced our modern understanding of the concept of prebiotics and defined it thus:

A prebiotic is a nondigestible food ingredient that beneficially affects the host by selectively stimulating the growth and/or activity of one or a limited number of bacteria in the colon, and thus improves host health. (Gibson and Roberfroid, 1995, pp. 1405–6).

This premise is based on several observations. Breast milk naturally contains substances that act as prebiotics, most notably complex carbohydrate compounds that have no direct nutritional role – i.e. oligosaccharides (Petherick, 2010). Also, breastfed infants' intestinal tracts tend to be colonised by a particular bacterial species mix from the *Lactobacillus* and *Bifidobacterium* genera. In formula-fed and preterm infants the gut flora is typically less diverse than that found in breastfed infants (Echarri *et al.*, 2011). It is the presence of numerous different prebiotic oligosaccharides in breast milk that is thought to selectively stimulate the proliferation of *Bifidobacterium* and *Lactobacillus* genera in the infant gut (Gibson and Roberfroid, 1995). These bacteria are also thought to be important in postnatal intestinal development and adaptive immunity (Moore *et al.*, 2011). Clinical trials have demonstrated that formula-fed infants who receive the prebiotic short chain galacto-oligosaccharide and long chain fructo-oligosaccharides in their diet are seen to tolerate this addition without ill effects (Costalos *et al.*, 2008; Modi *et al.*, 2010). Furthermore, stool analysis showed increased levels of *Bifidobacterium* and lower levels of the more harmful *Clostridium* and *Escherichia coli* bacteria (Costalos *et al.*, 2008). However, these interpretations should be treated with caution, as the long-term effects of these prebiotic factors are not known.

One area that has received research attention concerns the role of intestinal flora in possibly moderating allergy. Food allergy and intolerance has emerged as an important public health concern; it is know that *Bifidobacterium* interacts with immune regulatory cells, and this has led to the idea that early gut colonisation might have a role in later allergenic disease. However, a Cochrane review of seven studies concluded that there was 'insufficient evidence to recommend the addition of prebiotics to infant feeds for prevention of allergic disease or food reactions' (Osborn and Sinn, 2007, p. 2). Despite this conclusion and because of the potential benefits for infant health, several commercial formula milk manufacturers now add mixes of prebiotics to their products.

There is emerging evidence that prebiotics may increase feeding tolerance of preterm infants. A randomised controlled trial of 160 preterm infants (32 or less weeks' gestation) found a small but statistically significant increase in toleration of milk feeds in infants of less than 28 weeks' gestation in the group that received prebiotics. Modi *et al.* (2010) concluded that the addition of prebiotics might confer additional clinically important benefits for mixed fed (breast milk and formula) infants of less than 28 weeks' gestation.

Probiotics

Probiotics are defined as bacterial species (occasionally fungi) that confer a health benefit on their host organism (AlFaleh *et al.*, 2011). Probiotics in the gastrointestinal tract are the most studied and are thought to exert their health effects in number of ways. These include competitive exclusion of other bacteria, interactions with intestinal cell walls which reduce its gut permeability, and stimulation of infants' immune response, particularly secretory immunoglobulins (IgA) and cytokines (Mshvildadze and Neu, 2009). Healthy, breastfed, vaginally delivered, term infants are considered the 'gold standard' of intestinal microbiota. However, this view is rather more complex; Echarri *et al.* (2011) found that breastfed infants' intestinal microbiota vary with geography. It is unclear if this variation reflects local dietary or environmental background effects, but is nonetheless a complicating factor for those seeking to promote the inclusion of particular probiotic strains and mixes into an infant's diet.

Studies on the efficacy of probiotic administration have been somewhat inconclusive. Rougé *et al.* (2009) failed to demonstrate any clinical effect on promoting feeding tolerance in very low birth weight infants and the trial was stopped early, whereas probiotic supplementation has been shown to reduce gastrointestinal colonisation by fungal colonies (*Candida*) in low birth weight infants of less than 35 weeks gestation (Romeo *et al.*, 2001). However, the major focus of attention in preterm probiotic research is on the role of probiotics in reducing the incidence and severity of necrotising enterocolitis. A systemic review of five oral probiotic trials carried out prior to 2006 concluded that the existing data were insufficient to comment on the safety of probiotics use in clinical practice. Heterogeneity of probiotic formulations, dosages and timing of doses made synthesis inappropriate, but overall results were suggestive of a reduction in the incidence of necrotising enterocolitis (Barclay *et al.*, 2007). It has been suggested that the variation in necrotising enterocolitis seen between individual trials might reflect slight differences in clinical diagnosis and risk of necrotising enterocolitis and may reflect a changing epidemiology as the population of infants in neonatal units change or that advances in midwifery and obstetric practice affect the prevalence of risk factors (de la Hunt, 2006).

Evidence from recently updated meta-analyses (Deshpande *et al.*, 2011a,b; AlFaleh *et al.*, 2011) are unequivocal in their conclusions and suggest that probiotics can be protective for necrotising enterocolitis and that combinations of probiotics show the most promise. AlFaleh *et al.*'s (2011) described that results from individual trials were variable, but when taken together it may be concluded that:

> Enteral supplementation of probiotics prevents severe NEC and all causes of mortality in preterm infants. Our updated review of available evidence supports a change in practice. More studies are needed to assess efficacy in ELBW [extremely low birth weight] infants and assess the most effective formulation and dose to be utilized.' (AlFaleh *et al.*, 2011, p. 2).

In response, some clinicians have called for this therapy to become part of routine practice. Others have expressed more caution and, whilst no trial to date has reported any case of exogenous sepsis due to probiotic use, this is a vulnerable immunologically compromised population and longer term untoward outcomes might arise. Embleton *et al.* (2011) point to a lack of readily available quality controlled standard and reliable products outside of trial situations as the major limiting factor, rather than any scientific or safety concerns *per se*. In an attempt to provide some clear and cohesive principles for clinical practice, Deshpande *et al.* (2011a) have developed core evidence-based guidelines to inform clinicians on the practical aspects of probiotic use. Notwithstanding the many unanswered questions concerning routine implementation of probiotic use, these guidelines will help to optimise their introduction and highlight areas where further research is required to address gaps in knowledge.

Concluding remarks

High-quality neonatal care relies upon the development and application of high-quality evidence into practice. Considerable strides in our understanding of preterm nutrition and how best to meet them have transpired in recent years, but a comprehensive picture of what constitutes optimum nutritional management in this vulnerable group remains elusive. In part this situation has arisen because, as we increase our understanding of neonatal physiology and breast milk, the goals evolve and shift.

Ensuring optimum oral nutrition in the preterm infant remains a considerable intellectual and clinical challenge. In summarising these various and sometimes contradictory challenges in neonatal units it seems best to focus upon those variables that we can control and leave other confounders for later designs of intervention. With regard to nutritional priorities for preterm infants, Lucas articulates a widely held accord and states:

> while slow growth (below the intrauterine rate) has some benefit for later cardiovascular outcome, it risks under-nutrition and its adverse consequences, and has a profound and diverse effect on later cognition. Currently the balance of risks favours the brain and preterm infants should be fed with specialized product to support rapid growth.' (Lucas, 2005, p. S5).

The nature of this 'specialised product' remains moot. As more becomes known about the properties of preterm breast milk, the provision of breast milk substitutes in the form of specialist preterm commercial formula milks that mimic these properties becomes ever more complex. However, as Petherick (2007, p. 7) states 'no matter how much we tinker with the composition of formula milk it will always lack many of the trace constituents of human milk'. Interventions to increase the use of expressed breast milk and breastfeeding could help to optimise nutrition and realise a myriad of other benefits of an exclusive human milk diet for preterm infants. In recent years there has been a move away from considering nutritional management challenges as solely clinical or physiological and a return to a more nuanced consideration that incorporates social and nurturance dimensions. This perspective questions the utility of focusing upon technological responses to the oral feeding needs of preterm infants rather than those interventions that could promote greater use of mothers' own fresh breast milk. It is this conceptual shift that will undoubtedly provoke ongoing debate and a number of new issues to concern us in the future.

References

Aagaard, H. and Hall, E. O. C. (2008) Mothers' experiences of having a preterm infant in the neonatal care unit: a meta-synthesis. *Journal of Pediatric Nursing*, **23**(3), e26–36.

Aggett, P. J., Agostoni, C., Axelsson, I. *et al.* (2006) Feeding preterm infants after hospital discharge: a commentary by the ESPGHAN committee on nutrition. *Journal of Pediatric Gastroenterology and Nutrition*, **42**, 596–603.

Agostoni, C. (2005) LC-PUFA content of human milk: is it always optimal? *Acta Paediatrica*, **94**, 1532–4.

Agostoni, C., Buonocore, G., Carnielli, V. P. *et al.* (2010) Enteral nutrient supply for preterm infants: commentary from the European Society for Paediatric Gastroenterology, Hepatology and Nutrition committee on nutrition. *Journal of Pediatric Gastroenterology and Nutrition*, **50**(1), 85–91.

Aimone, A., Rovet, J., Ward, W. *et al.* (2009) Growth and body composition of human milk-fed premature infants provided with extra energy and nutrients early after hospital discharge: 1-year follow-up. *Journal of Pediatric Gastroenterology and Nutrition*, **49**, 465–6.

AlFaleh, K. M., Anabrees, J., Bassler, D. and AlKharfi, T. (2011) Probiotics for prevention of necrotizing enterocolitis in preterm infants. *Cochrane Database of Systematic Reviews*, Issue 3. Art. No.: CD005496. doi: 10.1002/14651858.CD005496.pub3.

Als, H., Butler, S., Kosta, S. and McAnulty, G. (2005) The assessment of preterm infants' behavior (APIB): furthering the understanding and measurement of neurodevelopmental competence in preterm and full-term infants. *Mental Retardation and Developmental Disabilities Research Reviews*, **11**, 94–102.

Anderson, J. W., Johnstone, B. M. and Remley, D. T. (1999) Breast-feeding and cognitive development: a meta analysis. *American Journal of Clinical Nutrition*, **70**, 525–35.

Appleton, J. (2011) Newborn behavioural aspects. In: *Examination of the newborn* (ed. A. Lomax), pp. 201–17. Wiley Blackwell, Chichester.

Barclay, A. R., Stenson, B., Simpson, J. H., Weaver, L. T. and Wilson, D. C. (2007) Probiotics for necrotizing enterocolitis: a systematic review. *Journal of Pediatric Gastroenterology and Nutrition*, **45**, 569–76.

Barker, D. J. P., Eriksson, J. G., Forsén, T. and Osmond, C. (2002) Fetal origins of adult disease: strength of effects and biological basis. *International Journal of Epidemiology*, **31**, 1235–9.

Bartley, M., Power, C., Blane, D., Davey-Smith, G. and Shipley, M. (1994) Birth weight and later socioeconomic disadvantage: evidence from the 1958 British cohort study. *British Medical Journal*, **309**, 1457–9.

Bauer, J. and Gerss, J. (2011) Longitudinal analysis of macronutrients and minerals in human milk produced by mothers of preterm infants. *Clinical Nutrition*, **30**, 215–20.

Berrington, J. E., Hearn, R. I., Bythel, M., Wright, C. and Embleton, N. D. (2012) Deaths in preterm infants: changing pathology over 2 decades. *Journal of Pediatrics*, **160**, 49–53.

Beyerlein, A., Haddcrs-Algra, M., Kennedy, K. *et al.* (2010) Infant formula supplementation with long-chain polyunsaturated fatty acids has no effect on Bayley developmental scores at 18 months of age – IPD meta-analysis of 4 large clinical trials. *Journal of Pediatric Gastroenterology and Nutrition*, **50**(1), 79–84.

Bigelow, A., Power, M., MacLellan-Peters, J., Alex, M. and McDonald, C. (2012) Effect of mother/infant skin-to-skin contact on postpartum depressive symptoms and maternal physiological stress. *Journal of Obstetric, Gynaecological and Neonatal Nursing*, **41**, 369–82.

Bliss (2008) *Breastfeeding and Expressing for a Sick or Premature Baby: an Overview of 500 Women's Experiences*. Bliss, London.

Bliss (2012) *The Best Start: a Guide to Expressing and Breastfeeding Your Premature Baby*. Bliss, London.

Bombell, S. and McGuire, W. (2008) Delayed introduction of progressive enteral feeds to prevent necrotising enterocolitis in very low birth weight infants. *Cochrane Database of Systematic Reviews*, Issue 2. Art. No.: CD001970. doi: 10.1002/14651858. CD001970.pub2.

Bombell, S. and McGuire, W. (2009) Early trophic feeds for very low birth weight infants. *Cochrane Database of Systematic Reviews*. Issue 3, Art. No: CD000504. doi: 10.1002/14651858.CD000504.pub3.

Boyd, C. A., Quigley, M. A. and Brocklehurst, P. (2007) Donor breast milk versus infant formula for preterm infants: systematic review and meta-analysis. *Archives of Disease in Childhood Fetal and Neonatal Edition*, **92**, F169–75.

Brett, J., Staniszewska, S., Newburn, M., Jones, N. and Taylor, L. (2011) A systematic mapping review of effective interventions for communicating with, supporting and providing information to parents of preterm infants. *BMJ Open*, **2011**(1), e000023. doi:10.1136/bmjopen-2010-000023.

Buckley, K. M. and Charles, G. E. (2006) Benefits and challenges of transitioning preterm infants to at-breast feedings. *International Breastfeeding Journal*, **1**(13), doi: 10.1186/1746-4358-1-13.

Butte, N. F., Lopez-Alarcon, M. G. and Garza, C. (2002) *Nutrient Adequacy of Exclusive Breastfeeding for the Term Infant During the First Six Months of Life*. World Health Organization, Geneva.

Callen, J. and Pinelli, J. (2004) Incidence and duration of breastfeeding for term infants in Canada, United States, Europe, and Australia: a literature review. *Birth*, **31**(4), 285–92.

Cilieborg, M. S., Boye, M. and Sangild, P. T. (2012) Bacterial colonization and gut development in preterm neonates. *Early Human Development*, **88**, S41–9.

Claas, M. J., de Vries, L. S., Koopman, C. *et al*. (2011) Postnatal growth of preterm born children ≤ 750 g at birth. *Early Human Development*, **87**, 495–507.

Colaizy, T. T., Carlson, S. and Morriss, F. H. (2012) Growth in VLBW infants fed predominantly fortified maternal and donor milk diets: a retrospective cohort study. *BMC Pediatrics*, **12**(124), doi: 1186/1471-2431-12-124.

Cooke, R. W. I. (2006) Are there critical periods for brain growth in children born preterm? *Archives of Disease in Childhood Fetal and Neonatal Edition*, **91**, F17–20.

Cooke, R. W. I., Lucas, A., Yudkin, P. L. N. and Pryse-Davies, J. (1977) Head circumference as index of brain weight in the fetus and newborn. *Early Human Development*, **1/2**, 145–9.

Cosmi, E., Fanelli, T., Visentin, S., Trevisanuto, D. and Zanardo, V. (2011) Consequences in infants that were intrauterine growth restricted. *Journal of Pregnancy*, doi: 10.1155/2011/364381.

Costalos, C., Kapiki, A., Apostolou, M. and Papathoma, E. (2008) The effect of a prebiotic supplemented formula on growth and stool microbiology of term infants. *Early Human Development*, **84**, 45–9.

Crawley, H. and Westland, S. (2011) *Infant Milks in the UK*. The Caroline Walker Trust, Abbots Langley, Herts.

De Curtis, M. and Rigo, J. (2012) The nutrition of preterm infants. *Early Human Development*, **88**, S5–7.

de la Hunt, M. N. (2006) The acute abdomen in the newborn. *Seminars in Fetal & Neonatal Medicine*, **11**, 191–7.

Demirci, J. R., Happ, M. B., Bogen, D. L., Albrecht, S. A. and Cohen, S. M. (2012) Weighing worth against uncertain work: the interplay of exhaustion, ambiguity, hope and disappointment in mothers breastfeeding late preterm infants. *Maternal and Child Nutrition*, doi: 10.1111/j.1740-8709.2012.00463.x.

Department of Health (2010) *Birth to Five*. Department of Health, London.

Deshpande, G. C., Rao, S. C., Keil, A. D. and Patole, S. K. (2011a) Evidence-based guidelines for use of probiotics in preterm infants. *BMC Medicine*, **9**(92), www.biomedcentral.com/1747-7015/9/92.

Deshpande, G. C., Rao, S. C., Patole, S. K. and Bulsara, M. (2011b) Updated meta-analysis of probiotics for preventing necrotizing enterocolitis in preterm neonates. *Pediatrics*, **125**, 921–30.

Dykes, F. (2006) *Breastfeeding in Hospital: Mothers, Midwives and the Production Line.* Routledge, London.

Dykes, F. (2011) Twenty-five years of breast-feeding research in Midwifery. *Midwifery*, **27**, 8–14.

Echarri, P. P., Graciá, C. M., Berruezo, G. S. *et al.* (2011) Assessment of intestinal microbiota of full-term breast-fed infants from two different geographical locations. *Early Human Development*, **87**, 511–13.

Edmond, K. and Bahl, R. (2006) *Optimal Feeding of Low-birth-weight Infants: Technical Review.* World Health Organization, Geneva.

Ehrenkranz, R. A. (2007) Early, aggressive nutritional management for very low birth weight infants: what is the evidence? *Seminars in Perinatology*, **31**(2), 48–55.

Ehrenkranz, R. A., Dusick, A. M., Vohr, B. R. *et al.* (2006) Growth in the neonatal intensive care unit influence neurodevelopmental and growth outcomes of extremely low birth weight infants. *Pediatrics*, **117**, 1253–61.

Embleton, N. D. and Tinnion, R. (2009) Nutrition in preterm infants before and after hospital discharge. *Infant*, **5**(6), 174–8.

Embleton, N. D., Thwin, T., Kerr, J. and Cairns, P. (2011) Probiotics decrease the incidence of NEC and death: so why aren't we using them? *Infant*, **7**(1), 20–4.

Ewaschuk, J. B., Unger, S., O'Connor, D. L. *et al.* (2010) Effect of pasteurization on selected immune components of donated human breast milk. *Journal or Perinatology*, **31**, 593–8.

Fattal-Valevski, A., Toledano-Alhadef, H., Leitner, T., Geva, R., Eshel, R. and Harel, S. (2009) Growth patterns in children with intrauterine growth retardation and their correlation to neurocognitive development. *Journal of Child Neurology*, **24**(7), 846–51.

Flacking, R., Ewald, U., Hedberg Nyqvist, K. and Starrin, B. (2006) Trustful bonds: a key to 'becoming a mother' and to reciprocal breastfeeding. Stories of mothers of very preterm infants at a neonatal unit. *Social Science and Medicine*, **62**, 70–80.

Flacking, R., Nyqvist, K. H. and Ewald, U. (2007) Effects of socioeconomic status on breastfeeding duration in mothers of preterm and term infants. *European Journal of Public Health*, **17**(6), 579–84.

Flacking, R., Ewald, U. and Wallin, L. (2011) Positive effect of kangaroo mother care on long-term breastfeeding in very preterm infants. *Journal of Obstetric, Gynecological and Neonatal Nursing*, **40**, 190–7.

Flacking, R., Lehtonen, L., Thomson, G., Axelin, A., Ahlqvist, S., Hall Moran, V., Ewald, U. and Dykes, F. (2012) Closeness and separation in neonatal intensive care. *Acta Paediatrica*, doi: 10.1111/j.1651-2227.2012.02787.x

Fleith, M. and Clandinin, M. T. (2005) Dietary PUFA for preterm and term infants: review of clinical studies. *Critical Reviews in Food Science and Nutrition*, **45**, 205–29.

Fewtrell, M. (2011) Early nutritional predictors of long-term bone health in preterm infants. *Current Opinion in Clinical Nutrition and Metabolic Care*, **14**(3), 297–301.

Gale, C. R., O'Callaghan, F. J. O., Godfrey, K. M., Law, C. M. and Martyn, C. N. (2004) Critical periods of brain growth and cognitive function in children. *Brain*, **127**, 321–9.

Gibson, G. R. and Roberfroid, M. B. (1995) Dietary modulation of the human colonic microbiota: introducing the concept of prebiotics. *Journal of Nutrition*, **125**, 1401–2.

Hartmann, C., Doucet, S., Niclass, Y. *et al.* (2012) Human sweat odour conjugates in human milk, colostrums and amniotic fluid. *Food Chemistry*, **135**, 228–33.

Hay, W. H. (2008) Strategies for feeding the preterm infant. *Neonatology*, **94**(4), 245–54.

Heiman, H. and Schanler, R. J. (2007) Enteral nutrition for premature infants: the role of human milk. *Seminars in Fetal and Neonatal Medicine*, **12**, 23–34.

Hoddinott, P., Craig, L. C. A., Britten, J. and McInnes, R. M. (2012) A serial qualitative interview study of infant feeding experiences: idealism meets realism. *BMJ Open*, **2012**(2), e000504. doi: 10.1136/bmjopen-2011-000504.

Howell, E. and Graham, C. (2011) *Parents' Experiences of Neonatal Care: a Report on the Findings From a National Survey*. Picker Institute Europe, Oxford.

Hughes, A. J. (2012) Breastfeeding. In: *Perinatal mental health: a clinical guide*. (ed. C. R. Morton), pp. 459–72. MK Publishing, Keswick.

Isaacs, E. B., Fischl, B. R., Quinn, B. T., Chong, W. K., Gadin, D. G. and Lucas, A. (2010) Impact of breast milk on intelligence quotient, brain size and white matter development. *Pediatric Research*, **67**(4), 257–62.

Jones, E., Bell, S. and Shankar, S. (2012) An audit of preterm nutritional intake using a human milk analyser. *Infant*, **8**(2), 91–4.

Kan, E., Roberts, G., Anderson, P. J. and Doyle, L. W. (2008) The association of growth impairment with neurodevelopmental outcome at eight years of age in very preterm children. *Early Human Development*, **84**, 409–16.

Kashyap, S. (2007) Enteral intake for very low birth weight infants: what should the composition be? *Seminars in Perinatology*, **31**, 74–82.

Kennedy, K., Ross, S., Isaacs, E. B. *et al.* (2010) The 10 year follow-up of a randomised trial of long-chain polyunsaturated fatty acid supplementation in preterm infants: effects on growth and blood pressure. *Archives of Disease in Childhood*, **95**, 588–95.

Koletzko, B., Goulet, O., Hunt, J. *et al.* (2005) Guidelines on paediatric parenteral nutrition of the European Society of Paediatric Gastroenterology, Hepatology and Nutrition (ESPGHAN) and the European Society for Clinical Nutrition and Metabolism (ESPEN), supported by the European Society of Paediatric Research (ESPR). *Journal of Pediatric Gastroenterology and Nutrition*, **41**(Suppl. 2), S1–87.

Kovacs, C. S. and Kronenburg, H. M. (1997) Maternal–fetal calcium and bone metabolism during pregnancy, puerperium and lactation. *Endocrine Reviews*, **18**(6), 832–72.

Kramer, M. S. and Kakuma, R. (2002) *The Optimal Duration of Exclusive Breastfeeding: a Systematic Review*. World Health Organization, Geneva.

Krishnamurthy, S., Gupta, P., Debnath, S. and Gomber, S. (2009) Slow versus rapid enteral feeding advancement in preterm newborn infants 1000–1499 g: a randomized controlled trial. *Acta Pædiatrica*, **99**, 42–6.

Kuschel, C. A. and Harding, J. E. (2004) Multicomponent fortified human milk for promoting growth in preterm infants. *Cochrane Database of Systematic Reviews*, Issue 1. Art. No.: CD000343. doi:10.1002/14651858.CD000343.pub2.

Langley-Evans, S. C. (2009) Nutritional programming of disease: unravelling the evidence. *Journal of Anatomy*, **215**, 36–51.

Lin, P. W. and Stoll, B. J. (2006) Necrotising enterocolitis. *Lancet*, **368**, 1271–83.

Lucas, A. (2005) Long-term programming effects of early nutrition – implications for the preterm infant. *Journal of Perinatology*, **25**, S2–6.

Lucas, A., Gore, S. M., Cole, T. J. *et al.* (1984) Multicentre trial on feeding low birthweight infants: effects of diet on early growth. *Archives of Disease in Childhood*, **59**(8), 722–30.

Lucas, A., Morley, R., Cole, T. J., Lister, G. and Leeson-Payne, C. (1992) Breast milk and subsequent intelligence quotient in children born preterm. *Lancet*, **339**(8788), 261–4.

Lucas, A., Morley, R., Cole, T. J. and Gore, S. M. (1994) A randomised multicentre study of human milk versus formula and later development in preterm infants. *Archives of Disease in Childhood Fetal and Neonatal Edition*, **70**(2), F141–6.

Lucas, A., Morley, R. and Cole, T. J. (1998) Randomised trial of early diet in preterm babies and later intelligence quotient. *British Medical Journal*, **317**, 1481–7.

Lucas, A., Fewtrell, M. S., Morley, R. *et al.* (2001) Randomised trial of nutrient-enriched formula versus standard formula for post discharge preterm infants. *Pediatrics*, **108**, 703–11.

Makrides, M., Collins, C. T. and Gibson, R. A. (2011) Impact of fatty acid status on growth and neurobehavioural development in humans. *Maternal and Child Nutrition*, **7**(Suppl. 2), 80–8.

McCain, G. C. (2003) An evidence based guideline for introducing oral feeding to healthy preterm infants. *Neonatal Network*, **22**(5), 45–50.

McCormick, F. M., Tosh, K. and McGuire, W. (2010a) Ad libitum or demand/semi-demand feeding versus scheduled interval feeding for preterm infants. *Cochrane Database of Systematic Reviews*. Issue 2, Art. No: CD005255. doi: 10.1002/14651858.CD005255. pub3.

McCormick, F. M., Henderson, G., Fahey, T. and McGuire, W. (2010b) Multinutrient fortification of human breast milk for preterm infants following hospital discharge infants. *Cochrane Database of Systematic Reviews*. Issue 7, Art. No: CD004866. doi: 10.1002/14651858.CD004866.pub3.

McInnes, R. J. and Chambers, J. (2008) Infants admitted to neonatal units – interventions to improve breastfeeding outcomes: a systematic review. *Maternal and Child Nutrition*, **4**(4), 235–63.

McInnes, R. J., Shepherd, A. J., Cheyne, H. and Niven, C. (2010) Infant feeding in the neonatal unit. *Maternal and Child Nutrition*, **6**, 306–17.

Mehta, R. and Petrova, A. (2011) Biologically active breast milk proteins in association with very preterm delivery and stage of lactation. *Journal of Perinatology*, **31**, 58–62.

Meinzen-Derr, J., Poindexter, P., Wrage, L., Morrow, A. L., Stoll, B. and Donovan, E. F. (2009) Role of human milk in extremely low birth weight infants' risk of developing necrotizing enterocolitis or death. *Journal of Perinatology*, **29**, 57–62.

Mitchell, S. M., Rogers, S. P., Hicks, P. D., Hawthorne, K. M., Parker, B. R. and Abrams, S. A. (2009) High frequencies of elevated alkaline phosphatase activity and rickets exist in extremely low birth weight infants despite current nutritional support. *BMC Pediatrics*, **9**(47), doi: 10.1186/1471-2431/9/47.

Modi, N., Uthaya, S., Fell, J. and Kulinskaya, E. (2010) A randomized, double-blind, controlled trial of the effect of prebiotic oligosaccharides on enteral tolerance in preterm infants. *Pediatric Research*, **68**(5), 440–5.

Montjaux-Régis, N., Cristinin, C., Arnaud, C., Glorieux, I., Vanpee, M. and Casper, C. (2011) Improved growth of preterm infants receiving mother's own raw milk compared with pasteurized donor milk. *Acta Paediatrica*, **100**, 1548–54.

Moore, T. A., Hanson, C. K. and Anderson-Berry, A. (2011) Colonization of the gastrointestinal tract in neonates: a review. *Infant, Child and Adolescent Nutrition*, **3**, 291–5.

Morgan, C. (2011) Optimising parenteral nutrition for the very preterm infant. *Infant*, **7**(2), 42–6.

Morgan, J. A., Young, L., McCormick, F. M. and McGuire, W. (2011a) Promoting growth for preterm infants following hospital discharge. *Archives of Disease in Childhood Fetal and Neonatal Edition*, doi: 10.1136/adc.2009.170910.

Morgan, J., Young, L. and McGuire, W. (2011b) Slow advancement of enteral feed volumes to prevent necrotising enterocolitis in very low birth weight infants. *Cochrane Database of Systematic Reviews*, Issue 3. Art. No.: CD001241. doi: 10.1002/14651858. CD001241.pub3.

Mshvildadze, M. and Neu, J. (2009) Probiotics and prevention of necrotizing enterocolitis. *Early Human Development*, **85**, s71–4.

Neu, J. (2007) Gastrointestinal maturation and implications for infant feeding. *Early Human Development*, **83**, 767–75.

Newburg, D. S. and Walker, W. A. (2007) Protection of the neonate by the innate immune system of developing gut and of human milk. *Pediatric Research*, **61**(1), 2–8.

Nyqvist, K. H. (2008) Early attainment of breastfeeding competence in very preterm infants. *Acta Paediatrica*, **97**, 776–81.

Nyqvist, K. H., Haggkvist, A.-P., Hansen, M. N. *et al.* (2012) Expansion of the ten steps to successful breastfeeding into neonatal intensive care: expert group recommendations for three guiding principles. *Journal of Human Lactation*, **28**, 289–96.

O'Connor, D. L., Khan, S., Weishuhn, K. *et al.* (2008) Growth and nutrient intakes of human milk-fed preterm infants provided with extra energy and nutrients after hospital discharge. *Pediatrics*, **121**, 766–76.

Osborn, D. A. and Sinn, J. K. H. (2007) Prebiotics in infants for the prevention of allergic disease and food hypersensitivity. *Cochrane Database of Systematic Reviews*, Issue 4. Art. No.: CD006474. doi: 10.1002/14651858.CD006474.pub3.

Petherick, A. (2010) Mother's milk: a rich question. *Nature*, **468**, S5–7.

Pike, K., Brocklehurst, P., Jones, D., Kenyon, S., Salt, A., Taylor, D. and Marlow, N. (2012) Outcomes at 7 years for babies who developed neonatal necrotising enterocolitis: the ORACLE children study. *Archives of Disease in Childhood Fetal and Neonatal Edition*, **97**, F318–22.

Pineda, R. (2011) Direct breast-feeding in the neonatal intensive care unit: is it important? *Journal of Perinatology*, **31**, 540–5.

Premji, S. S. (1998) Ontogeny of the gastrointestinal system and its impact on feeding the preterm infant. *Neonatal Network*, **17**(2), 17–23.

Premji, S. S., Fenton, T. R. and Sauve, R. S. (2006) Higher versus lower protein intake in formula-fed low birth weight infants. *Cochrane Database of Systematic Reviews*. Issue 1, Art. No: CD003959. doi: 10.1002/14651858.CD003959.pub2.

Renfrew, M. J., Craig, D., Dyson, L. *et al.* (2009) Breastfeeding promotion for infants in neonatal units: a systematic review and economic analysis. *Health Technology Assessments*, **13**(40), I–XIV, 1–170.

Riikka Korjaa, R., Maunuc, J., Kirjavainene, J. *et al.* (2008) Mother–infant interaction is influenced by the amount of holding in preterm infants. *Early Human Development*, **84**, 257–67.

Romeo, M. G., Romeo, D. M., Trovato, L. *et al.* (2011) Role of probiotics in the prevention of the enteric colonization by Candida in preterm newborns: incidence of late-onset sepsis and neurological outcome. *Journal of Perinatology*, **31**, 63–9.

Rougé, C., Piloquet, H., Butel, M.-J. *et al.* (2009) Oral supplementation with probiotics in very-low-birth-weight preterm infants: a randomized, double-blind, placebo-controlled trial. *American Journal of Clinical Nutrition*, **89**, 1828–35.

Royal College of Nursing (2007) *Formula Feeds: RCN Guidance for Nurses Caring for Infants and Mothers*. RCN, London.

Rozé, J.-C., Darmaun, D., Boquien, C.-Y. *et al.* (2012) The apparent breastfeeding paradox in very preterm infants: relationship between breast feeding, early weight gain and neurodevelopment based on results from two cohorts, EPIPAGE and LIFT. *BMJ Open*, doi: 10.1136/ bmjopen-2012-000834.

Schanler, R. J., Lau, C., Hurst, N. M. and O'Brian Smith, E. (2005) Randomized trial of donor human milk versus preterm formula as substitutes for mothers' own milk in the feeding of extremely premature infants. *Pediatrics*, **116**, 400–6.

Schulzke, S. M., Patole, S. K. and Simmer, K. (2011) Longchain polyunsaturated fatty acid supplementation in preterm infants. *Cochrane Database of Systematic Reviews*, Issue 2. Art. No.: CD000375. doi: 10.1002/14651858.CD000375.pub4.

Scott, J. A., Binns, C. W., Oddy, W. H. and Graham, K. I. (2006) Predictors of breastfeeding duration: evidence from a cohort study. *Pediatrics*, **117**, e646–55.

Sharma, P., McKay, K., Rosenkrantz, T. S. and Hussain, N. (2004) Comparisons of mortality and pre discharge respiratory outcomes in small-for-gestational-age and appropriate-for-gestational-age premature infants. *BMC Pediatrics*, http://www.biomedcentral.com/1471/1-2431/4/9.

Simmer, K., Patole, S. K. and Rao, S. C. (2011) Longchain polyunsaturated fatty acid supplementation in infants born at term. *Cochrane Database of Systematic Reviews*, Issue 12. Art. No.: CD000376. doi: 10.1002/14651858.CD000376.pub3.

Streimish, I. G., Ehrenkranz, R. A., Allred, E. N. *et al.* (2012) Birth weight- and fetal weight-growth restriction: impact on neurodevelopment. *Early Human Development*, **88**, 765–71.

Srinivasan, L., Bokiniec, R., King, C., Weaver, G. and Edwards, A. D. (2004) Increased osmolarity of breast milk with therapeutic additives. *Archives of Disease in Childhood Fetal and Neonatal Edition*, **89**(4), F514–17.

Sullivan, S., Schanler, R. J., Kim, J. H. *et al.* (2010) An exclusive human milk-based diet is associated with a lower rate of necrotizing enterocolitis than a diet of human milk and bovine milk-based products. *Journal of Pediatrics*, **156**, 562–7.

Sweet, L. and Darbyshire, P. (2009) Fathers and breast feeding very-low-birthweight preterm babies. *Midwifery*, **25**, 540–53.

Tacken, K. J. M., Vogelsang, A., Van Lingen, R. A., Slootstra, J., Dikkeschei, B. D. and van Zoeren-Grobben, D. (2009) Loss of triglycerides and carotenoids in human milk after processing. *Archives of Disease in Childhood Fetal and Neonatal Edition*, **94**, F447–50.

Tsang, R., Uauy, R., Koletzko, B. and Zlotkin, S. (eds.) (2005) *Nutrition of the Preterm Infant. Scientific Basis and Practical Guidelines*, 2nd edn. Digital Educational Publishing, Cincinnati, OH.

Valentine, C. J. and Puthoff, T. D. (2007) Enhancing parenteral nutrition therapy for the neonate. *Nutrition in Clinical Practice*, **22**(2), 183–93.

Vlaardingerbroek, H., van Goudoever, J. B. and van den Akker, C. H. P. (2009) Initial nutritional management of the preterm infant. *Early Human Development*, **85**, 691–5.

Vohr, B. R., Poindexter, P., Dusick, A. M. *et al.* (2007) Persistent beneficial effects of breast milk ingested in the neonatal intensive care unit on outcomes of extremely low birth weight infants at 30 months of age. *Pediatrics*, **120**(4), e953–9.

Westrup, B. (2007) Newborn Individualized Developmental Care and Assessment Program (NIDCAP) – family-centered developmentally supportive care. *Early Human Development*, **83**, 443–9.

Wigert, H., Johansson, R., Berg, M. and Hellström, A. L. (2006) Mothers' experiences of having their newborn child in a neonatal intensive care unit. *Scandinavian Journal of Caring Science*, **20**, 35–41.

Williford, A. L., Pare, L. M. and Carlson, G. T. (2008) Bone mineral metabolism in the neonate: calcium, phosphorus, magnesium and alkaline phosphatase. *Neonatal Network*, **27**(1), 57–63.

World Health Organization (2003) *Global Strategy for Infant and Young Child Feeding*. World Health Organization, Geneva.

CHAPTER 4

Feeding the newborn baby: breast milk and breast milk substitutes

Sally Inch

Introduction

Mammary glands (after which the particular class of vertebrates to which humans belong are named) began their evolution some 120 million years ago, as specialised epidermal secretions started to develop nutritional and bacteriostatic functions. For the last 240,000 years milk production has proved a crucial factor in mammalian survival in a wide range of habitats.

Human breast milk (as with all other mammalian milks) is species-specific, adapted and optimised by the process of natural selection over 8,000 generations, which has included competitive interaction with viruses, bacteria and protozoans. Human milk thus has functions other than optimal nutrition for the human infant; it is a complex mixture of cells, membranes and molecules (Mitchie, 2001) (Table 4.1).

Historically, breast milk has been the only truly safe way of feeding human young, and it is still the case in many parts of the world that a baby who is not fed at the breast is at increased risk of dying. Less than 200 years ago most attempts to feed a human baby on anything other than breast milk and keep him or her alive were spectacularly unsuccessful, even in the relatively affluent West. For example, in 1829 the mortality rate at the Dublin foundling hospital was reportedly as high as 99.6% (Palmer, 1993, p. 143).

Historically, the need for a human child to receive human milk was not questioned, and in the great majority of cases it was the child's mother who provided the milk. However, in parts of some societies, another (lactating) woman would be paid to provide breast milk for a child who was not her own – a wet

Table 4.1 Constituents of human milk.

Component	Function – if known	
White blood cells	B cells	Aided by cytokines, B cells give rise to antibodies (IgA and IgM) targeted against specific microbes
	Macrophages	Kill bacteria and fungi outright in the infant's gut, produce lysosyme, prostaglandins, complement components and activate other components of the immune system
	Neutrophils	May act as phagocytes ingesting bacteria in the infant's digestive system
	T cells	Kill infected cells directly or send out chemical messages to mobilise other defences. They proliferate in the presence of organisms that cause serious illness in infants. They can also cross the gut mucosa intact and manufacture compounds that can strengthen the child's own immune system
Anti-infective factors	Antibodies of Secretory IgA class	Bind to microbes (and their toxins) in the infant's gut and thereby prevent them from adhering to (and passing through) the walls of the gut into the body's tissues
	B_{12} binding protein (haptocorrin) Folate binding protein	Reduces the amount of 'available' B_{12} and folate, which bacteria need in order to grow
	Bifidus factor	Promotes the growth of *Lactobacillus bifidus*, a harmless bacterium, in the infant's gut. Growth of such non-pathogenic bacteria helps to crowd out dangerous varieties
	Fatty acids	Disrupt membranes surrounding certain viruses and destroy them
	Lactoferrin	Binds to iron, a mineral many bacteria need to survive. Can also bind to a bacterial surface and cause cell death. Survives in and can pass through infant gut. Antiviral effect against CMV, HIV, Herpes simplex; antifungal against *Candida albicans*
	Lysosyme	Kills bacteria by disrupting their cell walls. Resists digestion to protect the gut. Concentrations in milk rise as lactation progresses – up to 2 yrs
	Complement	All 9 complement components are found in colostrum and mature milk. They collectively protect against respiratory and enteric infections.
	Lactoperoxidase	Transforms thiocyanate (part of saliva) into hypothiocyanate, which can kill gram positive and negative bacteria
	Fibronectin	Increases the microbial activity of macrophages; helps to repair tissues that have been damaged by immune reactions in the infant's gut

Table 4.1 (*continued*)

Component	Function – if known	
Glycoproteins	Mucins/lactadherin butyrophilin	Adhere to bacteria and viruses (e.g. rotavirus and *E. coli*) thus preventing them from attaching to mucosal surfaces
	Oligosaccharides	Bind to certain enteric and respiratory bacterial pathogens and their toxins thus preventing them from attaching to mucosal surfaces
	Glycosaminoglycans	Inhibit the binding of HIV gp120 to its host cell CD4 receptor, the first step in infection by the virus
Growth factors	Epidermal growth factor (EGF) Nerve growth factor (NGF) Insulin-like growth factor (IGF) Transforming growth factor (TGF)	Stimulate the infant's digestive tract to mature more quickly. Once the initially 'leaky' membranes lining the gut mature, infants become less vulnerable to micro-organisms Immunomodulatory function
Hormones	Thyroxine (T3, T4) Thyroid stimulating hormone (TSH) Thyrotropin releasing hormone (TSH)	Promote maturation of the newborn's intestine and development of intestinal host–defence mechanism
	Corticosteroids Adrenocorticotrophic hormone (ACTH) Luteinizing hormone releasing factor (LHRF) Gonadotropin releasing hormone (GnRH) Somatostatin	Response to stress in adult
	Insulin	Neonatal glycaemia
	Oxytocin	
	Prolactin	Enhanced development of B and T lymphocytes/ immunomodulatory and neuro-endocrine effects in later life
	B-casomorphin (opioid peptide)	Lowers response to pain, elevates mood
	Erythropoietin Calcitonin	Stimulates red blood cell synthesis
Anti-inflammatory agents and cytokines	Alpha I-antitrypsin, Alpha J-antichymotrypsin	May prevent the absorption of endogenous and bacterial proteases, thus contributing to the passive protection or extra intestinal organs such as the liver
	Interleukins	Homeostasis of the intestinal barrier and regulation of aberrant immune responses to pathogens. Some protect the breast itself
	Interferon (IFN-y)	Enhances anti-microbial activities of immune cells (lymphocytes)

Table 4.1 (continued)

Component	Function – if known	
	Tumour necrosis factor (TNF)	Anti-inflammatory function
	Prostaglandin E and F (PGE & F)	Cyto-protective
Digestive enzymes	Amylase (survives exposure to acid and pepsin in the stomach of young infants)	Its presence in milk significantly enhances carbohydrate digestion, as pancreatic amylase may be absent for the first 2–6 months of life
	Lipoprotein lipase	Aid gastric lipolysis – releasing free fatty acids and monoglycerides (from triglycerides), which have anti-protozoan/bacterial/viral activity
	Bile salt stimulated lipase	Aid gastric lipolysis – releasing free fatty acids and monoglycerides (from triglycerides), which have anti-protozoan/bacterial/viral activity

Data derived from: Garofalo and Goldman (1998), Hamosh (1999), Heitlinger *et al.* (1983), Lönnerdal (2003), Newman (1995), Peterson *et al.* (1998), Udall *et al.* (1985), Weaver (1997) and Xanthou (1998).

nurse. The status of the wet nurse varied according to the society, from that of someone with the ability to confer kinship to that of just another form of domestic servant. For centuries only wealthy women could afford to pay another woman to feed their child, and it was therefore regarded as a status symbol – though a double-edged one, as noblewomen were freed from lactation (and its contraceptive effect) only to find themselves repeatedly pregnant. This pattern is now being repeated in developing countries where breast milk substitutes have undermined breastfeeding, while artificial means of contraception have not kept pace.

With the advent of commercially available breast milk substitutes in the late nineteenth century, those who were less well off could afford the status symbol of not feeding their child themselves. Infant mortality was high at the time, so its association with the substance on which a child was fed from birth was not quickly made. Over time breast milk substitutes and delivery systems improved and the degree to which they were inferior to breast milk continued to be masked by the more obvious environmental factors that were associated with illness. It is only as research methods have improved that the effects of the differences between breast milk and commercial substitutes have become more apparent, and those making comparisons are able to document the disadvantages of formula milk feeding.

Some of these disadvantages, such as poorer cognitive development and visual acuity, increased weight gain, increased incidence of atopic disease, diabetes and necrotising enterocolitis, are probably due to compositional/nutritional differences between breast milk and breast milk substitutes (Heinig and Dewey, 1996); others, such as an increased incidence of gastro-intestinal illness, otitis media and respiratory and urinary tract infections, are likely to be due to the presence of immunological components in breast milk (Heinig and Dewey, 1996) that will always be absent from inert breast milk substitutes.

Furthermore, in biological terms the body of a pregnant woman is prepared, hormonally, for eventual lactation (with increased fat stores, calcium mobilisation etc.) and the body of a woman who has just given birth 'expects' to feed a baby. In evolutionary terms the breasts, ovaries and uterus were not intended to be exposed to the hormones of the menstrual cycle, particularly oestrogen, from menarche to menopause. The suspension of the menstrual cycle, which occurs during lactation, prevents more pregnancies worldwide than all other methods of contraception put together (Thapa *et al.*, 1988). It also reduces the exposure of the primary and secondary sexual organs and skeletal system to the effect of ovarian hormones (Collaborative Group on Hormonal Factors in Breast Cancer, 2002). Thus, for the parturient woman, *not* breastfeeding is associated with a higher incidence of breast and ovarian cancer, hip fracture and fertility (Heinig and Dewey, 1997).

It will, however, take more than an increased awareness of the real differences between breast milk and breast milk substitutes to reverse the cultural trend in the UK and other parts of the world where breastfeeding has been undermined. It also needs to be acknowledged that breastfeeding is a learned skill and that a woman's ability to learn has been reduced by the loss of those skills from what are now bottle feeding cultures. Health professionals will thus need to acquire the ability to teach the women in their care how to breastfeed effectively, before future generations can begin to be assured of their birthright – breast milk.

Composition and function of human milk

Popular nutritionists often focus on the need for protein in the human diet. This has led to the widely held view that the higher the protein content of the nation's food, the healthier the nation will be. Yet the human species, which has risen above all others largely by virtue of its brain size and capacity, has one of the lowest levels of protein in the milk produced to suckle the young. What is overlooked is that, whereas protein is qualitatively the most important feature in the structure of muscle, lipid (fat) is the most important in the brain and peripheral nervous system (Sinclair, 1992).

Human young are born immature by comparison with many other mammals and the brain grows rapidly after birth. The significant postnatal increase in brain weight is mainly due to the development of myelin, which consists of 70% structural lipid on a dry weight basis. Consequently, lipid factors will be important to postnatal development and evidence is growing that an incorrect lipid balance in milk (particularly in relation to long chain polyunsaturated fatty acids) may influence brain development (Farquharson *et al.*, 1992; Sinclair, 1992; Makrides *et al.*, 2011.) This section will therefore concentrate on the controversies and challenges that surround this particular aspect of infant nutrition.

Human milk has evolved to do far more than simply nourish the infant, and even substances that might be thought of as purely nutritional often have other functions as well. Water is the major constituent of human milk, closely followed by the disaccharide lactose. The lactose concentration of milk rises steeply as milk production begins and pulls water into the milk producing cells; thus lactose concentration is positively correlated with milk yield. In mature milk, lactose is present at an average concentration of 68 g/L and is one of the most stable constituents of human milk. Other sugars, present at much lower concentrations, include glucose, nucleotide sugars, glycolipids, glycoproteins and oligosaccharides. As well as providing energy, some of these also have anti-infective functions (Table 4.1).

The proteins in human milk (15.8 g/L in early secretions, slowly decreasing to 8–9 g/L as lactation becomes established, and largely unaffected by maternal diet) provide an important source of amino acids to rapidly growing breastfed infants. Many human milk proteins also play a role in facilitating the digestion and uptake of other nutrients in breast milk. Examples of such proteins are bile salt-stimulated lipase and amylase, which may aid lipid and starch digestion, and beta-casein, lactoferrin and haptocorrin, which may assist in the absorption of calcium, iron and vitamin B_{12}, respectively. Human milk proteins also exert numerous physiological activities benefiting breastfed infants in a variety of ways. These activities include enhancement of immune function, defence against pathogenic bacteria, viruses and yeasts, and development of the gut and its functions (Lönnerdal, 2003).

The fats in human milk provide about 50% of the total energy value (Picciano, 2001). The total lipid content rises more than three-fold from the colostrum up to the third month and then more slowly up to the 12th month (Agostoni *et al.*, 2001), providing a mean of 35–36 g/L for the first year of lactation (Mitoulas *et al.*, 2003). For an individual mother, the *amounts* of most fatty acids delivered to the infant over a 24-hour period and the fatty acid composition of milk and serum seems to change little during lactation and has been found to be similar in two consecutive lactations in the same woman (Mitoulas *et al.*, 2003). However, the *proportions* (g/100 g total fatty acids) of fatty acids have been found to differ significantly between mothers and over the first year of lactation (Mitoulas *et al.*, 2003).

Ninety eight per cent or more of the fat in human milk is in the form of triglycerides (0.5–1% occurs as phospholipid and 0.2–0.5% as sterols, of which cholesterol is the major one, ranging from 10–20 mg/100 ml milk). As well as being a source of energy, the breakdown products of fats (chiefly fatty acids) are essential to normal brain development, the structure and function of cell membranes, and prostaglandin synthesis (Sinclair, 1992). The 'released' fatty acids also have varying degrees of anti-infective function, in both human and non-human milk, and act by breaking down the cell walls of viruses, bacteria and protozoans. The presence of bile salt-stimulated lipase in human milk speeds up the breakdown (digestion) of triglycerides, (compared with fat in breast milk substitutes) and increases its anti-infective properties (Hamosh, 2001) (Table 4.1).

Over 100 different kinds of fatty acids have been identified in human milk, some saturated (46%) and some unsaturated (54%), of which some are monounsaturated (containing a single double bond in the molecule) and some polyunsaturated (containing two or more double bonds in the molecule). The molecules can be of different lengths, depending on the number of carbon atoms present in the chain. Two of these fatty acids (linolenic and linoleic acid) cannot be made in the human body and have to be obtained from the diet; they are thus referred to as *essential* fatty acids. However, in order to exert their full and specific biological effect, the molecules have to be desaturated and elongated to DHA (docosahexaenoic acid) and AA (arachidonic acid). These forms are also plentiful in breast milk and compensate for the rather slow conversion rates in the neonate at a time when the longer chain forms are needed quickly for the rapidly growing brain and retinal membranes.

The lack of AA and DHA in the diet of infants who were not breastfed has been shown to result in marked differences in the fatty acid profile of neonatal brains (Makrides *et al.*, 1994). There is also a demonstrable impact of not breastfeeding on visual acuity, cognitive function and even intelligence (Lucas *et al.*, 1992; Anderson *et al.*, 1999; Kramer *et al.*, 2008), which are thought to be related to the availability of these LCPUFAs (long chain polyunsaturated fatty acids) (Helland *et al.*, 2003). These observations, along with growing concerns about LCPUFA deficiency in the diet of both adults and children, have meant that this has been a major focus of research over the past two decades.

In the late 1980s, the lack of commercially purified sources of AA (an omega-6 series LCPUFA) led researchers to experiment with the nucleotide supplementation of breast milk substitutes in an attempt to speed the conversion of the parent fatty acids (Gil *et al.*, 1988; Pita *et al.*, 1988). Others worked on the ratio of the parent fatty acids to try and achieve the optimal conversion rates (Clark *et al.*, 1992). As purified sources became available, AA was added to breast milk substitutes by first one and then all of the major manufacturers over the course of the 1990s, although it was still questionable as to whether their mere addition would make any measurable difference to visual and cognitive function, even if changes could be demonstrated in plasma and red blood cell levels (Hamosh, 1998). Subsequently, some studies have shown a positive effect on visual acuity and cognitive function (Willatts *et al.*, 1998), while others have demonstrated a lack of effect on visual acuity and cognitive function in both term and preterm babies (Lucas *et al.*, 1999; Fewtrell *et al.*, 2002). Cochrane reviews suggest that any apparent functional benefits of the addition of LCPUFAs to breast milk substitutes are only temporary (Simmer and Patole, 2004; Simmer *et al.*, 2007).

Maternal diet and its relationship to fats in breast milk

Numerous studies have demonstrated that changes in the composition of external sources of fatty acids to the lactating mother (Jensen *et al.*, 2001), and/or cultural differences in dietary intake, are reflected in the fatty acid composition of breast milk samples, particularly monounsaturated, n-6, n-3 and *trans* fatty acids (Chen *et al.*, 1997; Hayat *et al.*, 1999; Smit *et al.*, 2002; Lauritzen and Carlson, 2011). The impact of these changes in composition, and what influences them, are considered below.

Medium chain fatty acids

Medium chain fatty acids (C6:0–C14:0) can be synthesised *de novo* in the mammary gland, as evidenced by the fact that medium chain fatty acids are higher in milk (8.36–21.37%) than in serum (1.59–9.6%) throughout lactation (Spear *et al.*, 1992). This ability of the breast to synthesise fats may, in part, explain the fact that total milk fat is less variable than composition in an individual woman.

Long chain (polyunsaturated) fatty acids

In a longitudinal study of 10 Italian mothers, Agostoni *et al.* (2001) found that the concentrations (mg/dL) of C20:4 and C22:6 remained stable from colostrum up to the 12th month of nursing, while their percentage levels were highest in colostrum and decreased afterwards in association with the increase in total fats. The C18:2n6 and C18:3n3 amounts progressively increased, following the trend of total fats. These data indicate that (providing the maternal diet does not change radically) the secretion of AA and DHA during lactation remains constant, in spite of changes in total fat and in the linoleic acid and alpha-linolenic acid contents of milk. Thus, provided that the baby is breastfed, his/her rapidly growing brain will have a constant and adequate supply of these LCPUFAs. As noted above, babies who are supplied only with the precursors of AA and DHA will be unable to convert them fast enough and this will be reflected in the different proportions of the different fatty acids that make up their brain tissue.

Hayat *et al.* (1999) analysed the milk of 19 fully breastfeeding Kuwaiti mothers and found that the content of LCPUFAs in human milk lipids did not correlate with their parent fatty acids, like linoleic and alpha-linolenic acids. However, the human milk LCPUFAs were related to the content of LCPUFAs in the maternal diet. Mothers reporting a high fish consumption showed significant amounts of C22:6 (DHA) omega-3 and C20:5 (EPA), omega-3 fatty acids (Hayat *et al.*, 1999). Earlier, Spear *et al.* (1992) had demonstrated that LCPUFAs (C20:1–C22:6) of the n-3 and n-6 series were higher in serum (6.76–12.53%) than in milk (1.57–4.42%).

Dietary supplements to increase LCPUFAs

In the UK, the low levels of omega-3 in the diet of the general population are currently a cause for concern (National Diet and Nutrition Survey, 2010) because of their relationship to neurological function and behaviour. Studies have shown that LCPUFA deficiencies or imbalances are associated with childhood developmental and psychiatric disorders including ADHD, dyslexia, dyspraxia and autistic spectrum disorders (Richardson, 2004; Richardson and Montgomery, 2005). Several researchers have investigated the effect of dietary supplements to increase the percentage of omega-3 derivatives obtained by the newborn and breastfeeding infant. Giving a DHA supplement (fish oil) to pregnant women was shown, in one small study, to have no effect on umbilical cord blood values of DHA. This suggests that, for dietary supplements to have no direct benefit, term infants must have accrued sufficient amounts of DHA while *in utero*, in spite of and/or at the expense of their mothers (Malcolm *et al.*, 2003). In another small study, giving the precursor (alpha-linolenic acid) to lactating women by supplementing their diet with flaxseed oil, did not increase the amounts of DHA in their milk (Francois *et al.*, 2003). Giving DHA supplements to breastfeeding mothers had previously been shown to increase the amount of DHA in their milk (Makrides *et al.*, 1996) and to have some effect on the rate of decrease as lactation progresses, but no effect was (later) found on either infant visual function or cognitive or behavioural development (Gibson *et al.*, 1997). This was possibly because of the 'saturable curvilinear nature of the relationship of breast milk DHA to infant plasma and erythrocyte phospholipid DHA' (Heird, 2001, p. 185) – 'enough' perhaps being 'as good as a feast'.

Trans *fatty acids*

Trans fatty acids are unsaturated fatty acids with at least a double *trans* configuration, resulting in a more rigid molecule, akin to a saturated fatty acid. These do appear naturally in dairy fat, but the relatively high levels found in Western diets, as opposed to Chinese or Mediterranean diets (Chen *et al.*, 1997), are probably due to high intakes of processed foods, which often use hydrogenated oils. In a study of 103 Canadian mothers with exclusively breastfed 2-month-old infants (Innis and King, 1999), the major dietary sources of *trans* fats were bakery products and breads (32%), snacks (14%), fast foods (11%) and margarines and shortenings (11%). This study found a wide range of *trans* fatty acid concentrations in the breast milk of these mothers, from 2.2% to 18.7% of total fatty acids, with a mean (± SEM) percentage of 7.1 ± 0.3%, which is almost twice the level (4%) currently set as the maximum permitted in the manufacture of breast milk substitutes (Infant Formula and Follow-on Formula (Amendment) Regulations, 1997).

In September 2003, a subgroup of the UK Scientific Advisory Committee on Nutrition (Maternal and Child Nutrition) recommended that the maximum permitted level of *trans* fats in formula be lowered further still to no more than 3% of total fatty acids (Scientific Advisory Committee on Nutrition, 2003). Furthermore, the fact that the breast milk levels were similar to those calculated for the diet suggested that the estimated value of 6.9 g *trans* fatty acids/day was a reasonable estimation of the *trans* fatty acid intake of the women in this study (Innis and King, 1999). Previous estimates of average daily intakes by adults in the USA, Canada, Europe and Australia based on food usage, food-frequency questionnaires, or duplicate portion analysis range from ~1–3 to 17 g/person (Hunter and Applewhite, 1991; Emken, 1995).

The (rising) levels of *trans* fatty acids in westernised diets are of concern because animal and *in vitro* studies are consistent with the hypothesis that *trans* fatty acids may interfere with the desaturation of 18:2n-6 by inhibiting the desaturase enzymes, thus slowing the conversion of C18:2n6 and C18:3n3 to C20:4n6 and C22:6n3 respectively (Sinclair, 1992; Koletzko, 1995). The study by Innis and King (1999) found a significant inverse relationship between milk concentrations of *trans* fats and 18:2n-6 and 18:3n-3, confirming the work of Chen *et al.* (1995).

Trans fatty acid consumption has implications in adult health for the development of hypertension, cardiac disease (Mozaffarian *et al.*, 2006) and some cancers (Hu *et al.*, 2011) and in infants for its potential impact on brain and retinal membrane development. Innis and King (1999) also showed a relation between the concentration of a specific *trans* fatty acid, conjugated linoleic acid (CLA),[1] in milk and in the plasma lipids of breast-fed infants. In contrast with other *trans* fatty acids, CLAs were found to be preferentially accumulated, by more than 2-fold, in the infants' plasma phospholipids rather than in triacylglycerols. More recently, a small randomised controlled trial of CLA supplements given to lactating women found that the fat content of their breast milk was significantly lower during the CLA treatment, as compared to the placebo treatment ($P < 0.05$). Data indicated no effect of treatment on milk output (Masters *et al.*, 2002). Whether CLAs have any direct physiological effects on breast-fed infants is not yet known.

Socio-economic status and fat consumption

The consumption of high levels of saturated fat and *trans* fatty acids and low levels of polyunsaturated fats are strongly linked to socio-economic status (although not in the same direction in all cultures/societies). International comparisons indicate a continuing, if narrowing, north–south gradient across Europe (European Food Information Council, 2012). In Ireland (Kelleher *et al.*, 2002), the Netherlands (Hulshof *et al.*, 2003), Australia (Turrell *et al.*, 2003), Finland (Laaksonen *et al.*, 2003) and Norway (Holmboe-Ottesen *et al.*, 2004), there is clear evidence of inverse social class gradients in intake of fruit and vegetables and dairy products and in reported patterns of healthy eating. Median carbohydrate and vitamin C intake levels are higher among socio-economic occupational groups 1 and 2 and mean saturated fat intake is lower. Conversely, in Greece and China (Trichopoulou *et al.*, 2002; Kim *et al.*, 2004 respectively) it is still the case that households of lower socio-economic occupational groups follow a healthier diet, in terms of greater availability of vegetable oils, fresh vegetables, legumes, fish and seafood.

In Italy, the relationship of socio-economic occupational group to healthier diet is in the process of changing, with most of the eating habits considered to be potentially harmful (high consumption of meat or fats and alcohol and low consumption of olive oil and fish) becoming more frequent in Northern than in Southern Italy. These habits were inversely correlated with educational level,

---

1   CLAs are positional and geometric isomers of 18:2n-6 (linoleic acid) that occur naturally as linoleic acid and are acted upon by bacteria in the stomachs of herbivores, such as cows. It is thus found in several foods, particularly dairy products and beef. It appears to have some biological activity (Watkins *et al.*, 1997; Li and Watkins, 1998). In animal studies it has been shown to alter bone formation rates, possibly as a result of its effect on prostaglandin E2 biosynthesis.

especially in the South (Vannoni *et al.*, 2003). In China, as socio-economic status improves, lifestyle becomes less healthy (Kim *et al.*, 2004). Thus concerns about dietary fat, health or lifestyle issues that alter food choices may impact not only on a mother's own health, but may also influence the quality of fatty acid nutrition of her breastfed infant.

It is timely that in the UK the Welfare Food Scheme, first established in 1940 and which provided tokens to families on low incomes that could be exchanged for liquid milk or breast milk substitutes, has been reformed in the shape of the Healthy Start Initiative (DH, 2002). Healthy Start, which was implemented in 2006, broadened the nutritional base of the scheme by allowing fruit and vegetables (as well as liquid milk or breast milk substitutes) to be obtained through the exchange of fixed value vouchers at a range of outlets, including local food co-ops and supermarkets (this was further amended in April 2011 to include frozen as well as fresh fruit and vegetables). It has meant that, in this respect at least, child health clinics no longer give a mixed message about their commitment to breastfeeding, as they are no longer the exchange point for vouchers for breast milk substitutes.

Substitutes for mother's own milk

This section will consider what was done in the past if a mother could not, or chose not to, feed her own baby. It will also chart the rise of commercial alternatives to breast milk.

Although, historically, the vast majority of women fed their own babies, wet nursing has been recorded since well before the common era. In many of the societies in which this happens now, including our own, it is an act of friendship and/or compassion and quite different from that of hiring another woman to feed the baby. In the past, although a wet nurse may have been hired to feed a baby whose mother had died, in many cases she was hired to demonstrate the mother's social standing in her community; a status symbol. Thus for some it became something to aspire to, even though it was evidently detrimental for the babies as they were more likely to succumb to diseases (Palmer, 2009).

Wet nursing also removed the contraceptive protection of breastfeeding – a combination of lactational amenorrhoea and (depending on the culture) sexual abstinence whilst breastfeeding. However, until the mass production of formula milks, wet nursing was, as it still is in many countries, the only viable alternative to the mother feeding her baby. During the 19th century, as the position of women in society changed and the workplace and home separated, a great many babies succumbed in the process of looking for artificial methods (dry nursing), which included direct suckling of animals, particularly goats, by the baby (Palmer, 2009).

The industrialised society provided both the necessity and the means for mass production of artificial food for babies. In the main these were based on cows' milk to which other ingredients were added (e.g. pea flour, wheat flour and bicarbonate of potash) and were offered for sale in liquid, condensed or powdered form. Such was the ignorance of the composition of human milk that these items were advertised as 'the perfect food' for infants (Palmer, 1993, p. 163). With a few notable exceptions, such as the child reared on beer who lived to be 70 years old (Still, 1931), the alarming mortality rates (usually from diarrhoea) amongst babies who were fed on these often bacteriologically contaminated substances seem to have given little pause for thought by the communities where this was common practice, such as areas of southern Germany and Finland in the 19th century, because the practice continued (Palmer, 2009).

As knowledge about the constituents of human milk and cows' milk increased in the late 19th and early 20th century, doctors devised recipes for imitating human milk, which they presented in the form of complex mathematical and chemical formulae, striving to make infant feeding 'scientific and exact' for each baby (Palmer, 1993, p. 175). Meanwhile, commercially prepared infant milks, available over the counter, reduced the necessity for a mother to visit (and thus pay) a doctor. The potential conflict between manufacturers and the medical profession was averted when the two formed an alliance in which mothers could buy formula milk in packages that bore no instructions for use other than to 'consult her doctor' before using the product. At the same time, new commercially prepared 'formulae' (such as Simulated Milk Adaptation) could be 'tested on unsuspecting babies in wards and hospitals' (Palmer, 1993, p. 176–7). The relationship between health professionals and the manufacturers of breast milk substitutes has a long, lucrative and ignoble history; one which ultimately can only be constrained by legislation.

Formula milks

The more that is known about the composition of breast milk, the harder it is to imitate. Similarly, the more that is known of the difference in health outcomes between breastfed and formula fed babies, the more important it becomes to regulate the composition and marketing of breast milk substitutes. This section will look at what legislation exists to safeguard infants who are fed breast milk substitutes and what still needs to be done.

The composition of breast milk substitutes in the UK is currently controlled by the Infant Formula and Follow-on Formula Regulations 1995 (UK) and its subsequent amendments. These regulations set out the permitted/prohibited sources of proteins, fats and carbohydrates and the permitted range for levels of specified amino acids, nucleotides, fatty acids, vitamins, major minerals and trace elements, as well as the total energy density of the formula, per 100 ml, when reconstituted.

In 1995 only cows' milk protein and soya protein isolates were listed for use (in the regulations above) in the manufacture of infant formulae. Nevertheless, a goats' milk formula, manufactured in New Zealand, has been sold in the UK since 1992. In 2002, at the request of the European Commission, the UK-based company submitted a dossier to the newly formed European Food Standards Agency, which in turn was asked to evaluate the data in order to give an opinion on the suitability of goats' milk protein as a source of protein in infant formulae and in follow-on formulae (Request No. EFSA-Q-2003-019). (This was with a view to amending the Commission Directive 91/321/EEC to include goats' milk protein as a suitable protein source.) Their finding, published in February 2004, was that 'the data submitted are insufficient to establish the suitability of goats' milk protein as a protein source for infant formula' (EFSA, 2004, executive summary). Meanwhile, in September 2003, the UK's Scientific Advisory Committee on Nutrition questioned the benefit of using any milk protein other than from cows, or any plant protein, including soya (Scientific Advisory Committee on Nutrition, 2003).

In January 2004 the Chief Medical Officer advised all doctors, via his on-line Update No.37 (http://www.dh.gov.uk/assetRoot/04/07/01/76/04070176.pdf), that soya-based infant formulas should not be used as the first choice for the management of infants with proven cows' milk sensitivity, lactose intolerance, galactokinase deficiency and galactosaemia. The main concern was that soya-based formulas' high phytoestrogen content could pose a risk to the long-term reproductive health of infants – according to a 2003 report from the Committee on Toxicity, an independent scientific committee that advises the UK Department of Health and other government agencies (although it can also provoke allergies, see below).

The Chief Medical Officer also quoted the advice from Scientific Advisory Committee on Nutrition, namely that there is no particular health benefit associated with the consumption of soya-based infant formula by infants who are healthy (no clinically diagnosed conditions) and no unique clinical condition that particularly requires the use of soya-based infant formulas. The Chief Medical Officer recommended that soya-based formulas should only be used in exceptional circumstances to ensure adequate nutrition. For example, they may be given to infants of vegan parents who are not breastfeeding or infants who find alternatives (such as amino acid formulae) unacceptable.

Guidance for parents on how to choose and use formula milks is now available from both UNICEF-BFI (2010a) and the Department of Health (2011); and for health professionals from UNICEF-BFI (2010b) and the Caroline Walker Trust (Infant Milks in the UK, 2011).

Adverse reactions to 'foreign' proteins

The response to the well-documented inability of some babies (2–7.5% of the population; Adler and Warner, 1991; Host *et al.*, 1999) to tolerate cows' milk-based formula has given rise to the development of hydrolysed protein formulae, as well as those based on amino acid mixtures. Even extensively hydrolysed products can sometimes cause a child with cows' milk allergy to respond adversely; evidence that only amino acid-based products can truly be regarded as non-allergenic. It follows that the 'HA' (hypoallergenic) formula milks introduced in the UK in August 2002, that are only partially hydrolysed, should not be fed to infants with a known milk allergy despite their claim to be 'hypoallergenic'. These milks were the subject of legal action in the USA in 1988 when several allergic babies suffered from anaphylactic shock as a result of their use. As a result the company was obliged to drop the 'HA' claim (Baby Milk Action, 2002a).

In July 2002, the response of the UK Minister of Health to concerns about the use of such claims for this product in the UK was that it would not be placed on shelves and would only be available from pharmacies through special order. The packaging would also carry a warning that the product was *not* for use for babies with cows' milk allergy. Appropriately modified soya and goats' milk formulas are also both currently marketed in the UK and elsewhere as suitable for children suffering from or at risk of cows' milk allergy. They are advocated for this purpose in writings and internet resources directed at a lay audience. Unfortunately, not only has clinically significant cross-allergenicity between cows' and goats' milk has been noted (Bellioni-Businco *et al.*, 1999), but at least one life-threatening cross-reaction has also been reported (Pessler and Nejat, 2004).

Although the incidence of documented allergic responses to soya is lower than that to cows' milk (0.5–1.1%) (American Academy of Pediatrics, 1998), it is not without hazard. Two large double-blind, placebo-controlled studies of infants with atopic dermatitis documented that soy positivity was demonstrated in 4–5% of children (Sampson, 1988; Businco *et al.*, 1992). In addition, up to 60% of infants with cows' milk protein-induced enterocolitis will be equally sensitive to soy protein (Eastham, 1989; Burks *et al.*, 1994; Whitington and Gibson, 1997). Much of this information is reflected in the advice available to the general public on the Food Standards Agency website (http://www.food.gov.uk/), and yet at the time of writing (December 2012) all the formulae discussed above were still available for the general public to purchase without prescription.

Other problems with formula milks

Although they may have come a long way since the mid-19th century and Liebig's 'perfect infant food' – made from wheat flour, cows' milk, malt flour, pea flour and bicarbonate of potash (Palmer, 1993, p. 163) – the fact remains, and will always remain, that breast milk substitutes can only ever imitate the substances in breast milk if:

- they are identifiable,
- the technology exists to synthesise them, and
- it is economic to synthesise them.

Although minimum and maximum permitted levels of named ingredients for formula milks for infants are laid down by statute, the recommendations for the upper and lower limits of nutrients are often based on limited data, data from adults or data from other species (Walker, 1993). Researchers are increasingly questioning precisely what goes into breast milk substitutes and compositional recommendations are frequently revised (e.g. Scientific Advisory Committee on Nutrition, 2003).

The manufacturers themselves make over a hundred changes to the 'formula' every year (Messenger, 1994). It follows, therefore, that all infants who consumed the breast milk substitutes prior to the change or addition, must have received food deficient in the substances newly defined as being necessary for optimal growth and development. Furthermore, the mere addition of a substance to the mixture does not necessarily mean that it will be available to the infant that consumes it. The ability of the baby to make use of the substance may depend on the form in which it is presented. For example, iron is only present in breast milk substitutes as an inorganic salt, of which only 10% can be absorbed; whereas in breast milk it is bound to a carrier protein, lactoferrin, making 70% of the iron 'available' for use (Akre, 1989; Williams, 1993). Indeed, the addition of one substance may cause another to fail to be utilised and the baby may end up with a deficiency. For example, if too much linoleic acid is added, alpha-linolenic metabolism may be inhibited (Farquharson *et al.*, 1992).

Clinical trials with bovine lactoferrin added to infant formula have not shown any enhancing effect on iron absorption or iron status (Fairweather-Tait *et al.*, 1987; Chierici *et al.*, 1992), which may be because bovine lactoferrin does not bind to the human lactoferrin receptor (Davidson and Lönnerdal, 1988). It is also possible that a positive effect of lactoferrin is found only when it is present in breast milk; when added to infant formula other constituents of the formula may interfere with iron utilisation from lactoferrin. It is also likely that the form in which lactoferrin is added to formula (dry blended or dissolved), and the subsequent processing of the formula (by heat treating), affects the ultimate activity of lactoferrin when fed to infants (Lönnerdal, 2003).

It goes without saying that something that began as cows' milk or soya beans can contain nothing that is species-specific to humans. It can also contain none of the living cells, enzymes, growth factors, hormones, or anti-infective factors listed in Table 4.1; not even those of bovine origin. The manufacturing process reduces the starting material to an inert, dry, powder.

Processing errors

As with all processed foods, there is the potential for inadvertent excesses or deficiencies during the manufacturing process. For example, in 2004 the Chinese news agency Xinhua reported that an inquiry had revealed that 45 sub-standard milk powders, produced by 141 factories, were on sale in one Chinese city. Police in Anhui province subsequently detained five wholesalers of fake formula milk. Around 200 babies in Anhui alone were fed formula of little nutritional value and the whole episode caused the worst cases of malnutrition Chinese doctors had seen in 20 years, according to the media reports (RCM, 2004). In the same year a German manufacturer was reported to be paying at least £8.7 million in compensation to Israeli families whose infants died or suffered developmental damage after they were fed a milk substitute lacking the B vitamin thiamin. Three babies died in 2003 after being fed the soy-based formula and 13 other infants were harmed by drinking the product.

Deliberate contamination of infant milk with melamine (which was added to the milk powder to make it appear to have a higher protein content) caused kidney stones and kidney damage in at least 300,000 babies in the People's Republic of China in 2008. Six of these babies subsequently died. Despite bans on exports from China to East Africa after the melamine scandal, 6% of all samples tested and 11% of international brand named products revealed melamine concentrations of up to 5.5 mg/kg in milk powder sampled in Dar es Salaam, the centre of international trade in East Africa: twice the tolerable daily intake suggested (Schoder, 2010).

There is also the danger of accidental contamination. Documented cases include contamination with inadvertent additions of aluminum, iodine and halogenated hydrocarbons, as well as contamination due to interaction between the can and its contents, particularly with regard to lead and plasticisers (Walker, 1993; Minchin, 2001). In May 1996, UK newspapers alerted the public to the fact that nine of the brands of baby milk on current sale were contaminated with phthalates – man-made chemicals that are used as a plastic softeners or solvents and which have been linked with cancer and a lowering of sperm count (British Medical Association, 1996).

Bacterial contamination also appears to be a widespread problem. A 1988 analysis of 141 powdered human milk substitutes obtained from 35 different countries, found bacterial organisms in 52.5% of the products evaluated. The species most frequently isolated included *Enterobacter agglomerans, Enterobacter cloacae, Enterobacter sakazakii* (now known as *Cronobacter sakazakii*), and *Klebsiella pneumoniae* (Forsythe, 2005). Although in none of these products was the level of contamination higher than the maximum limit recommended by the Food and Agricultural Organization of the United Nations, it highlights the fact that powdered infant formula is not sterile; and one major formula manufacturer has recently stated that current manufacturing processes are not sufficient to remove all contamination (IBFAN, 2002). As if to underline this point, the death (from meningitis) in 2002 of a 5-day-old Belgian baby who received contaminated formula whilst in hospital, received widespread media coverage. The baby was born healthy, but was fed with dried infant formula from a batch which was contaminated with *C. sakazakii*, which was the cause of the meningitis (Baby Milk Action, 2002b).

These concerns led to the European Food Safety Authority's Scientific Panel on Biological Hazards to issue new guidance in relation to the microbiological risks of infant and follow-on formulas (European Food Safety Authority, 2004). In 2006, the UK Food Safety Agency (FSA) and Department of Health changed their recommendations in relation to their reconstitution. Since February 2006, those making up feeds from powder are advised to make each feed just before it is needed, using water that has boiled and cooled to 70 °C, adding the powder, allowing the milk to cool and giving the feed straight away. Parents are advised that any remaining milk should be discarded after 2 hours.

Errors during preparation

The potential for error does not end with the manufacture of the breast milk substitutes. Those who buy it may use it inappropriately. This is most apparent where the purchaser cannot read the instructions on the tin or packet, either because they are illiterate or the instructions are in the wrong language. The cost of the breast milk substitutes may sometimes result in it being over-diluted to make it go further (RCM, 2003). In the more affluent West, feeds are often made up with too much powder for a given amount of water. Sometimes this is deliberate, when an extra scoop is added supposedly to 'satisfy' the baby, but more commonly it is a result of inaccuracies in either the measuring scoop or the fact that the instructions to either level it off or pack it down differ from brand to brand (RCM, 2003). All powdered formula available in the UK is now reconstituted using one scoop (provided with the powder) to 30 ml of water. Clear instructions about the volumes of powder and water are also printed on the container. Nevertheless, over- and under-concentration of formula may still occur.

The problem of accidentally over-concentrated feeds, which can result in obesity, intestinal obstruction, hypernatremia and other metabolic stresses, might be overcome if manufacturers supplied only packets containing a standard amount of dry powder, or bottles/cartons of ready-to-feed mixture (Jeffs, 1989; Lucas *et al.*, 1999). However, although these are now readily available, the price is likely to deter mothers from using them exclusively in favour of the dried powder.

In 1988, 274 mothers (recruited from 19 clinics in two areas of Australia, one predominantly middle class, one working class) who were bottle feeding their infants aged from 1 to 9 months, were interviewed by researchers (Lilburne *et al.*, 1988). Particular attention was paid to mixing technique and storage of reconstituted formula. Following the interview, a sample of milk from a previously prepared bottle was taken to measure osmolarity and to count the number of bacterial colonies. Errors in reconstituting the formulas, compared with the manufacturer's instructions, were made by 100 (30%) mothers. In 52 cases these were potentially serious errors, usually erring on the side of preparing an over-concentrated formula. This finding from the interviews was confirmed by osmolarity analysis of 34 milk samples. Twenty-two per cent of samples collected grew potential pathogens.

This study was one of five included in the systematic review of formula feed preparation conducted by Renfrew *et al.* in 2003. All found errors in reconstitution, with a tendency to over-concentrate feeds, although under-concentration also occurred. The review concluded that there was a paucity of evidence available to inform the proper use of breast milk substitutes and a large array of different preparations for sale in the UK. Given the impact that incorrect reconstitution of formula feeds can have on the health of large numbers of babies, the reviewers felt that there was an important and urgent need to examine ways of minimising the risks of feed preparation.

One way of doing this might be to ensure that all women who intend to bottle feed, and who begin doing so in hospital (in the UK, currently 19% of all those who give birth; Health and Social Care Information Centre, 2012), have the opportunity to make up feeds using what they will use when they go home. In reality this means that they would need to bring their own equipment into hospital with them. It would also mean that the 'ready to feed' formula, currently in use in many UK hospitals, would need to be withdrawn from general use. This runs counter to the current infection control ethos of removing risk from the hospital setting by means of pre-packed and single use 'equipment'. But perhaps this risk needs to be balanced against the evidence that there is a social class gradient in both the prevalence of bottle feeding and the risk of gastro-enteritis associated with bottle feeding; which compared with breastfed babies is 3.5 times higher in social class 1, and 10 times higher in social class 5 (Forsyth, 2004, personal communication; data from Howie *et al.*, 1990). This suggests that it is not only what is in the bottle that increases the risk, but the bottle itself in terms of its cleanliness. Denying women who are bottle feeding in hospital the opportunity to make up feeds and clean equipment under 'supervision' may run the risk of increasing the incidence of gastro-enteritis in their babies after they leave hospital. The 2010 Infant Feeding Survey revealed that just under half of mothers had not followed all three key recommendations for preparing formula: i.e. only making one feed at a time; making feeds within 30 minutes of the water boiling; and adding the water to the bottle before the powder (Health and Social Care Information Centre, 2012). Enabling women who elect to bottle feed from birth to make up feeds with their own baby milk powder and their own equipment while they are in hospital will, of course, have no impact on the much greater number who begin breastfeeding in hospital and then partially or wholly bottle feed days or weeks later (77% by 6 weeks according to the 2010 Infant Feeding Survey).

A leaflet entitled 'Preparing a bottle feed using baby milk powder' is available to mothers to anyone as a single A4 sheet of instructions (in English and other languages). It can be downloaded, free of charge, from the UNICEF UK Baby Friendly Initiative website. A similar companion leaflet 'Sterilisation of baby feeding equipment' is also available. These leaflets are independently produced and health facilities can 'customise' them with their own logo if they wish. The Department of Health in England also produce a free illustrated booklet with similar advice (2012, available at: https://www.gov.uk/government/publications/start4life-updated-guide-to-bottle-feeding).

It is generally assumed in the UK that boiled tap water will be free from bacterial contamination and any harmful chemicals, but from time to time this is shown not to be the case. In some areas of the UK, mothers who are feeding their babies on formula milk have to be provided with a separate supply of water (or are advised to boil the water for 10 minutes) because water from the tap has become contaminated (Hansard, 1989, House of Commons Hansard Debates for 28 February 1989). If bottled water is used, a still, non-mineralised variety suitable for babies must be chosen and it should be boiled as usual. Softened water is usually unsuitable.

Milk delivery

A breastfed baby who (temporarily) needs to be given his/her mother's milk by some other means than directly from the breast can be given the milk from a cup, spoon, dropper, syringe, bottle and teat, or via a naso-gastric tube. For a baby who is to be formula fed from birth, however, a bottle and teat is the predominant means of delivering the formula milk, certainly in the UK. Feeding bottles should meet the UK standard – made of food grade plastic with relatively smooth interiors. Crevices and grooves in a bottle may make cleaning difficult. Patterned or decorated bottles may make it less easy to see if the bottle is clean. Concern has been expressed in the past about the nitrosamine content of rubber teats and in some countries mothers have been urged to boil the teat several times with fresh water before using (Michie and Gilmour, 2001). Silicone teats are now widely available but these have been known to split and need to be checked regularly for signs of damage. It is often easier for the baby to use a simple soft long teat than industry labelled orthodontic teats (Kassing, 2002). Despite manufacturers' advertising claims, no bottle teat is like a breast. A bottle teat occupies only the oral cavity, whereas the teat formed from the breast and nipple is sucked up into the baby's palate, encouraging the eustachian tube to open properly (Thompson, 1994). The observed increase in the incidence of otitis media amongst bottle-fed babies may thus have a mechanical component as well as an immunological one.

Although a teat and bottle is the system most widely used by mothers to feed formula milk to their babies (as it 'mimics' the sucking and swallowing that the baby does at the breast) many health professionals have been sold the notion that feeding from a bottle and a teat is so different and so damaging to a baby's ability to breastfeed that they go to great lengths (in the place where they have influence/control – the hospital) to avoid exposing the breastfed baby to either. A study conducted in an un-named UK hospital found that staff used cups, syringes, droppers, tubes and fingers to give supplements to babies, without any evidence that these methods conferred any benefit (or did no harm) (Cloherty *et al.*, 2005). Furthermore they appeared to pay more attention to the route of, rather than the need for, supplemental feeds for breastfed babies. This is particularly unfortunate in view of strong evidence that such supplements are themselves the biggest single predictor of early cessation of breastfeeding.

A baby is 'programmed' to feed from a breast and these innate skills should be used when bottle-feeding. The baby's lips should be touched to elicit a gape and the teat should follow the line of the baby's tongue, so that the baby uses the teat effectively. The bottle should be held horizontal to the ground, tilted just enough to ensure that the baby is taking milk, not air, through the teat. (See also http://www.unicef.org.uk/BabyFriendly/Resources/Resources-for-parents/A-guide-to-infant-formula-for-parents-who-are-bottle-feeding/) This will allow the baby some control of his/her intake and may reduce the tendency to overfeed (Li *et al.*, 2010).

The manufacture and use of breast milk substitutes

The environmental impact of the manufacture and use of breast milk substitutes, on the current scale, is hugely negative. The cows graze on land that could be used for agriculture, are fed other foods that could have been fed to humans (soya, molasses), which is itself grown on land that may have been cleared forest, using fertilisers that pollute rivers and ground water. Cows produce 20% of the global emissions of methane, the second most important 'greenhouse' gas, and ammonia from their excrement further pollutes soil and water and contributes to acid rain (Radford, 1991).

The cows' milk has to be transported (using fuel), heat-treated (using fuel), spray dried at high temperatures (more fuel) and added to an assortment of factory-produced ingredients (yet more fuel). It is packed into containers for transport to the consumer (even more fuel). Packaging and labelling requires tin, aluminium, plastic, foil and paper or card. Large amounts of water, fuel and synthetic materials are involved in feeding the product to infants. Post-consumer, most of these items then make their way into landfill (leachate and water pollution) or incinerators (air pollution, including dioxins and PCBs) (Radford, 1991).

The use of breast milk substitutes contributes to government debt in developing countries, increased ill health in all countries and malnutrition and death (mostly from diarrhoea) in many. It drains healthcare budgets where these exist and family budgets everywhere. It contributes to the ill health of mothers worldwide through increased risk of cancer, osteoporosis and the loss of the (child spacing) contraceptive effect of lactation (Radford, 1991).

On its current scale, it exists primarily to make money for the 25 or so companies world wide involved in the production either of the substitutes or the means of delivery (bottles and teats). Millions of pounds are spent each year on advertising these products by any legal means (if not prohibited this could be directly to potential consumers or through the healthcare system).

The International Code on the Marketing of Breast Milk Substitutes

In 1974, the consequences of the marketing practices of the leading breast milk substitute manufacturer on the health of mothers and babies in developing countries was published by War on Want (Muller, 1974; see also: Action for corporate accountability 1973–1994). The furore that followed (including a failed libel suit by the company) resulted in an international boycott in 1977, triggering a US senate Committee of Inquiry (CIIR, 1993). This led, four years later, to the adoption of the International Code for the Marketing of Breastmilk Substitutes by the World Health Assembly. This Code was, and still is, designed to protect breastfeeding, rather than to prohibit bottle feeding. Its main points follow.

For products within its scope, the International Code bans:

- Advertising
- Free samples (unless for the purpose of professional evaluation or research)
- Contact between company representatives and pregnant women or mothers of infants and young children
- Promotion through healthcare facilities (e.g. no posters, no brand names on pens or writing pads, no leaflets for mothers)
- Gifts to health workers or mothers
- Labels which have pictures of babies or pictures or text which idealise the use of infant formula

And the Code requires that:

- Labels are in the appropriate language for the country and contain stipulated warnings and messages
- Stipulated warnings and messages appear in educational materials relating to infant feeding, whether written, audio or visual
- Information given to health professionals is limited to matters that are factual and scientific

Free supplies

Free supplies of products covered by the Code are banned 'in any part of the health care system' (International Baby Food Action Network, 2005) by resolution WHA 47.5, which was passed in 1986, when it became clear that companies were using some of their advertising budget to provide these. The international boycott was lifted in 1984 when the company publicly agreed to abide by the Code, and reinstated in 1988 when it became apparent that it was not. Currently Code compliance of all manufacturers is monitored internationally by IBFAN.

Every three years, IBFAN publishes a report on compliance with the International Code of Marketing of Breastmilk Substitutes and relevant World Health Assembly Resolutions. Their 2010 report, *Breaking the Rules, Stretching the Rules, 2010* (IBFAN, 2010), discussed each of the eleven (formula manufacturing) companies under different Code themes. It also highlighted the predominant marketing trends over the period 2007–2010:

- **Health facilities are still the preferred avenue for companies to reach mothers and babies**. This is especially so in facilities which are not baby friendly. Prescription pads with images of infant formula are widely used in the Middle East and 'many private clinics and hospitals still receive secret donations of free formula' (IBFAN, 2010, Executive Summary, p. 2).
- **New branding: 'premiumisation'**. Several companies brand their products as 'Gold' or 'Premium', suggesting superiority over other products and commanding higher prices. It also suggests some equity with breastfeeding, often referred to as 'the gold standard'.
- **Digital and direct marketing**. Online branding by formula companies is now prolific, costing less than print advertising. Companies have established 'mother and baby clubs' so that when mothers join the company will maintain their interest and build brand loyalty through a combination of gifts such as product samples, baby records and photo books.
- **Engaging mothers to promote products online to other mothers**. Social marketing, through blogging, tweeting and so on, are new marketing strategies that are being used by companies to offer mothers incentives in order to disseminate positive messages about a product or brand. It has been reported that companies recruit mothers to post messages about their products on parenting blogs, message forums and online parenting groups.
- **Claims about the health benefits of formula**. Companies use complex scientific terms, such as prebiotics, bifidus, lutein, DHA, AA, Optipro, LCPUFA, lactoferrin and Omega-3, 'to impress and confuse at the same time' (IBFAN, 2010, Executive Summary, p. 3). Products are idealised by claiming that these additives enhance the immune system, improve eyesight, reduce the risk of allergy and so on. Such claims, however, remain unsubstantiated and devalue breastfeeding and home-prepared family foods. Companies are challenging the conclusions of the European Food Safety Authority (EFSA) which disqualify the vast majority of claims submitted for approval. Synthetic DHA is now added to 90% of US formula.
- **Sponsorship and conflicts of interest**. Four national paediatric associations still endorse formula products, although the International Pediatric

Association is addressing the need to restrict the promotional activities of sponsors at meetings. It is against the law in India to sponsor meetings of health professionals.

■ **Evidence from Europe**. The scope of the European Directive (which forms the basis of most laws in the EU) is narrower than the International Code and is therefore too weak to adequately protect breastfeeding. Although most EU Member States have adopted the WHO recommendations for exclusive breastfeeding to 6 months, companies routinely promote complementary foods from 4 months.

According to Baby Milk Action, the organisation based in Cambridge UK which campaigns against the unethical marketing of baby milks, awareness of the impact of inappropriate commercial sponsorship is growing. In September 2004 they reported that in May 2004 the Breakthrough Breast Cancer Charity refused £1 million from Nestlé (Baby Milk Action, 2004). The 8th Nordic Conference on Nutrition organised by the Norwegian Nutrition Society, held in Tonsberg, Norway in June 2004, decided not to apply to Nestlé for financial support (Baby Milk Action, 2004). In the UK, the organisers of the 12th International Conference of the International Society for Research in Human Milk and Lactation (ISRHML) held in Queens' College Cambridge, UK, in September 2004, decided not to accept funding from the baby food industry – as it had done in previous years (Baby Milk Action, 2004).

Together with UNICEF, Baby Milk Action and IBFAN (its partner in the global network) have been urging the refusal of such sponsorship because it creates conflicts of interest and opportunities for undue influence. However, in the UK, where the International Code is only partially incorporated into the Infant Formula and Follow-on Formula Regulations (DH, 1995) (first passed in 1995, with subsequent amendments), companies are allowed to advertise infant formulae in publications specialising in baby care and distributed through the healthcare system, in scientific publications and for the purposes of trade prior to the retail stage. It also means that hospitals can accept funding for new facilities, such as the new hearing testing room set up in one London hospital in 1995 which carried a large sign over the door bearing the company's name. In the year following the opening of this room, sales in the local clinic of this company's milk increased by 560% (Baby Milk Action, 1997).

It took the Royal College of Midwives, despite (1) their avowed commitment in their 2004 position statement (No. 5) to both breastfeeding and the International Code (RCM, 2004); (2) their acknowledgement that part of the rapid decline in the breastfeeding duration from birth to six months was due to the 'aggressive marketing of breast milk substitutes'; and (3) their recommendation that training (in healthcare facilities) 'should be provided by employers without the involvement, sponsorship or provision of promotional materials by manufacturers of formula milk'; until 2010, under the leadership of a new General Secretary, Cathy Warwick, to stop accepting money from formula manufacturers to fund (amongst other things) their professional journal, which is sent to every member and associate member of the RCM.

While formula manufacturers are permitted to sponsor health workers' education by advertising in their professional journals and providing healthcare facilities with 'educational' material advertising their products, health professionals are likely to continue to believe the manufacturers' slogan that 'you can't get any closer to mothers' milk' (Becker, 1992, pp. 137–42). They will therefore have little incentive to acquire the knowledge and skills necessary to help women breastfeed successfully.

At the moment the only 'defence' against the commercial exploitation of the weaknesses of the UK law is the requirement, by the UNICEF UK Baby Friendly Hospital Initiative (part of the Global WHO/UNICEF Initiative), that as well as fully implementing the Ten Steps To Successful Breastfeeding (as set out in the joint WHO/UNICEF booklet 'Protecting, Promoting and Supporting Breast-feeding', 1989) hospitals who wish to obtain the Baby Friendly Award must fully comply with all elements of the International Code. Until the UK law is brought into full alignment with the International Code, breastfeeding will continue to be undermined by those whose commercial interest is served by seeing breastfeeding fail.

Human milk banks: another substitute for mothers' own milk

The current (international) system of collecting and freezing human milk from screened donors is an extension of the much older service of wet nursing. Instead of feeding the baby directly at another mother's breast, the mother with milk to spare collects it and sends it to her local milk bank, where it can be used for any baby, including those too small or too sick to suckle directly. Milk donors are screened for blood-borne diseases such as hepatitis and HIV, and in some parts of the world the milk is then given fresh to the babies that need it. In the UK, the milk is pasteurised before it is re-frozen and stored prior to use. In the late 1970s and early 1980s there were over 60 human milk banks in the UK. Most of them closed in the late 1980s, driven both by the fear of HIV transmission and the rising popularity of preterm formulas. By the early 1990s there were only six milk banks left in the UK.

Slowly this number has risen, encouraged by research which demonstrated the effectiveness of pasteurisation as a means of destroying HIV (Eglin and Wilkinson, 1987) and the importance of human milk in the prevention of necrotising enterocolitis (Lucas and Cole, 1990). The total number of milk banks in the UK in 2012 stands at 18. The most pressing need in the UK is not for donors, but for more milk banks and/or a system for transporting milk to geographical areas where it is needed.

In the National Breastfeeding Week of 1998 (sponsored by the Department of Health from 1993–2010), the UK Human Milk Banking Association (UKAMB) was launched and spearheaded by the oldest UK milk bank at Queen Charlotte's and Chelsea Hospital. Its purpose was to make human milk more readily available to preterm infants by setting up a milk bank next to work and to encourage and support the setting up of new milk banks. One of its first tasks was to update the British Paediatric Association Guidelines for Human Milk banks, first published in 1994 (2nd edn 1999, 3rd edn 2003) which provided a template for those wishing to set up new milk banks. In February 2010 this function was superseded by the publication of NICE Clinical Guideline 93 'Donor breast milk banks: the operation of donor milk bank services'.

Choosing not to breastfeed

Although knowledge of the benefits of breastfeeding is important, it would be naive to think that all women need is enough information and every baby would be breastfed. There may be evidence that a proportion of women who feed their babies with formula milk are unaware of the differences in health outcomes, but there is also evidence to suggest that many women choose to bottle feed knowing that breast milk is best for their baby (Hoddinott, 1998; Andrew and Harvey 2011), for 'while it is "known" that breastfeeding is better, our society is not structured to facilitate that choice' (Retsinas, 1987, p. 129). Nor is it truly a choice for many women. They may give a reason for their decision (e.g. 'embarrassing', 'partner would not like it', 'returning to work very soon'), but in fact the 'decision' is often neither rational nor made at a specific point in time (Hoddinott, 1998). Indeed, 31% of the UK population persistently formula feed (or use mixed feeding) from birth (Health and Social Care Information Centre, 2012) because of social adherence to culturally acquired patterns of feeding behaviour (Bilson and Dykes, 2009).

The characteristics of such women are well known from past research, particularly successive quinquennial Infant Feeding Reports; they are predominantly young, poorly educated and in the lower socio-economic occupational groups (e.g. < 18 years of age, left school at 16, never worked). However, there are important variations within different ethnic groups and many women with these characteristics may well start by breastfeeding (as opposed to never breastfeeding), or mix feed from birth (Thomas and Avery, 1997; Choudhry and Wallace, 2012). Data from randomised controlled trials may be lacking, but given the biology of breast milk and the evidence from cohort studies (Howie *et al.*, 1990; Kelly, 2004; Quigley *et al.*, 2007), some breast milk is better for the infant than none.

The best predictor of whether a woman will commence breastfeeding is if she has breastfed before. It is therefore hugely important to encourage and help mothers to feed their first baby, as this is likely to affect the way that they feed subsequent babies. Another predictor of breastfeeding behaviour is socio-economic status. The Infant Feeding Report for 2010 demonstrated that the gap between those who breastfeed in the highest and lowest occupation groups has narrowed in recent years. The report noted an increase in breastfeeding rates among all socio-economic groups, but the largest increase occurred among mothers in routine and manual occupations, with UK breastfeeding rates among these mothers increasing from 65% in 2005 to 74% in 2010 (Health and Social Care Information Centre, 2012). If the support infrastructure is missing, no amount of breastfeeding promotion is going to improve the health inequalities between the higher and lower social classes.

Women are more likely to do what they have done (or seen) before, as predicted by the theory of planned behaviour (Ajzen, 1991) – unfortunately many women have fed another woman's baby by bottle. However, actually seeing a baby being breastfed can strongly influence the decision to breastfeed, both positively and negatively, depending on the context (Hoddinott and Pill, 1999). This finding may be of particular relevance in the context of women from lower socio-economic groups, for whom theoretical knowledge may have less power than embodied knowledge. It has therefore been suggested that women intending to breastfeed might benefit from an antenatal 'apprenticeship' with a known breastfeeding mother. Peer group support can influence both the initiation and the continuation of breastfeeding (Fairbank, 2000), and introducing pregnant women to other mothers with young babies, as is often done as part of parent education classes, may be helpful (further discussion of breastfeeding peer support groups can be found in Chapter 6 in this book).

Changes are also needed in the social environment, such as greater provision for breastfeeding outside the home (e.g. in shopping centres and restaurants) and the implementation of housing programmes which eliminate overcrowding and thus the necessity for young mothers to share accommodation with other relatives (McIntosh, 1985; Dyson *et al.*, 2010). Feeding in public may be a huge issue for women in lower socio-economic occupational groups. 'Public' has to be defined in terms of the woman's individual life – if she is living with her parents she is always 'in public', and breastfeeding in public may be seen as inviting unwelcome sexual voyeurism (Renfrew, 2004; Dyson *et al.*, 2010). (See Chapter 7 of this book for a discourse analysis of online discussion fora and imagery relating to breastfeeding in public.) Focus groups of such women discuss breastfeeding in terms of its disadvantages – formula feeding is seen to have few disadvantages (Renfrew, 2004). Changing the socially accepted norm for a particular peer group, as with smoking and drink/driving, will happen only slowly, and then only when women's perceived lack of social support and/or the requirement to be separated from their children have been addressed with better help with breastfeeding, expressing, working arrangements and maternity leave.

If the decision to formula feed (or not) is heavily constrained by social circumstances, it is not surprising that the part played by health professionals in assisting a mother to choose is probably not very great (Hoddinott, 1998), but in so far as the professional has an influence, it should be positive and unequivocal (Crawford, 1992, Freed *et al.*, 1995). Given the powerful effect of breastfeeding to ameliorate some of the health outcomes associated with poverty (breastfed babies in social class 5 have health outcomes equivalent to or better than formula fed babies in social class 1, Forsyth, 2004) – mothers and babies deserve no less.

References

Adler, B. R. and Warner, J. O. (1991) *Food Intolerance in Children*. Royal College of General Practitioners Members Reference Book, pp. 497–502.

Agostoni, C., Marangoni, F., Lammardo, A. M., Galli, C., Giovannini, M. and Riva, F. (2001) Long-chain polyunsaturated fatty acid concentrations in human hindmilk are constant throughout twelve months of lactation. *Advances in Experimental Medicine and Biology*, **501**, 157–61.

Ajzen, I. (1991) The theory of planned behavior. *Organizational Behavior and Human Decision Processes*, **50**, 179–211.

Akre, J. (ed.) (1989) *WHO Bulletin Supplement Vol. 67. Infant Feeding – The Physiological Basis*. Chapter 2 – Lactation, p. 23.

American Academy Of Pediatrics: Committee on Nutrition (1998) Soy Protein-based Formulas: Recommendations for Use in Infant Feeding. *Pediatrics*, **101**, 148–53.

Anderson, J. W., Johnstone, B. M. and Remley, D. T. (1999) Breastfeeding and cognitive development: a meta-analysis. *American Journal of Clinical Nutrition*, **70**, 525–35.

Andrew, N. and Harvey, K. (2011), Infant feeding choices: experience, self-identity and lifestyle. *Maternal & Child Nutrition*, **7**, 48–60.

Baby Milk Action (1997) *Sponsorship is Advertising*. Available at: http://www.babymilkaction.org/pages/uklaw.html#7 (accessed 17 December 2012).

Baby Milk Action (2002a) *Nestlé Formula in UK – Is it Legal?* Update Issue 31 July. Available at: http://www.babymilkaction.org/update/update31.html (accessed 17 December 2012).

Baby Milk Action (2002b) *Belgian Baby Death*. Available at: http://babymilkaction.org/update/update31.html (accessed 17 December 2012).

Baby Milk Action (2004) *International Conference Says No to Baby Food Industry Sponsorship*. Press release 10 September. Available at: http://www.babymilkaction.org/press/press10sept04.html (accessed 17 December 2012).

Becker, G. (1992) Breastfeeding knowledge of hospital staff in rural maternity units in Ireland. *Journal of Human Lactation*, **8**, 137–142.

Bellioni-Businco, B., Paganelli, R., Lucenti, P., Giampietro, P. G., Perborn, H. and Businco, L. (1999) Allergenicity of goat's milk in children with cow's milk allergy. *Journal of Allergy and Clinical Immunology*, **103**, 1191–14.

Bilson, A. and Dykes, F. (2009) A bio-cultural basis for protecting, promoting and supporting breastfeeding. In: *Infant and Young Child Feeding: Challenges to implementing a Global Strategy* (eds. F. Dykes and V. Hall Moran). Wiley-Blackwell, Oxford.

British Medical Journal (1996) Editorial: Declining sperm counts. *British Medical Journal*, **312**, 457.

Burks, A. W., Casteel, H. B., Fiedorek, S. C., Williams, L. W. and Pumphrey, C. L. (1994) Prospective oral food challenge study of two soybean protein isolates in patients with possible milk or soy protein enterocolitis. *Pediatric Allergy and Immunology*, **5**, 40–5.

Businco, L., Bruno, G., Giampietro, P. G. and Cantani, A. (1992) Allergenicity and nutritional adequacy of soy protein formulas. *Journal of Pediatrics*, **121**, S21–S28.

Catholic Institute for International Relations (1993) *Baby Milk: Destruction of a World Resource*. Catholic Institute for International Relations, London.

Chen, Z.-Y., Pelletier, G., Hollywood, R. and Ratnayke, W. M. N. (1995) *Trans* fatty acid isomers in Canadian human milk. *Lipids*, **30**, 15–21.

Chen, Z.-Y., Kwan, K. Y., Tong, K. K., Ratnayake, W. M., Li, H. Q. and Leung, S. S. (1997) Breast milk fatty acid composition: a comparative study between Hong Kong and Chongqing Chinese. *Lipids*, **32**, 1061–7.

Chierici, R., Sawatzki, G., Tamisari, L., Volpato, S. and Vigi, V. (1992) Supplementation of an adapted formula with bovine lactoferrin. 2. Effects on serum iron, ferritin and zinc levels. *Acta Paediatrica*, **81**, 475–9.

Choudhry, K. and Wallace, L. M. (2012), 'Breast is not always best': South Asian women's experiences of infant feeding in the UK within an acculturation framework. *Maternal & Child Nutrition*, **8**, 72–87.

Clark, K. J., Makrides, M., Neumann, M. A. and Gibson, R. A. (1992) Determination of the optimal linoleic acid to alpha-linolenic acid ratio in infant formula. *Journal of Pediatrics*, **120**, S151–8.

Cloherty, M., Alexander, J., Holloway, I., Galvin, K. and Inch, S. (2005) The cup-versus-bottle debate: a theme from an ethnographic study of the supplementation of breastfed infants in hospital in the United Kingdom. *Journal of Human Lactation*, **21**, 151–62.

Collaborative Group on Hormonal Factors in Breast Cancer (2002) Breast cancer and breastfeeding: collaborative reanalysis of individual data from 47 epidemiological studies in 30 countries, including 50 302 women with breast cancer and 96 973 women without the disease. *Lancet*, **360**, 187–95.

Crawford, J. (1992) Understanding our own breastfeeding experiences. *JBI Newsletter*, No. 4, June, 1–2.

Davidson, L. A. and Lönnerdal, B. (1988) Specific binding of lactoferrin to brush border membrane: ontogeny and effect of glycan chain. *American Journal of Physiology*, **254**, G580–5.

Department of Health (1995) *The Infant Formula and Follow-on Formula Regulations 1995*. Statutory Instrument 1995 No. 77. HMSO, London.

Department of Health (2002) *Healthy Start: Proposals for Reform of the Welfare System*. DH, London. Available at: http://www.dh.gov.uk/assetRoot/04/10/25/09/04102509.pdf.

Department of Health (2011) *Guide to Bottle Feeding*. Available at: http://www.dh.gov.uk/en/Publicationsandstatistics/Publications/PublicationsPolicyAndGuidance/DH_124525.

Dewey, K. (1998) Growth characteristics of breastfed compared to formula fed infants. *Biology of the Neonate: Foetal and Neonatal Research*, **74**, 94–106.

Dyson, L., Green, J. M., Renfrew, M. J. *et al.* (2010) Factors influencing the infant feeding decision for socioeconomically deprived pregnant teenagers: the moral dimension. *Birth*, **37**, 141–9.

Eastham, E. J. (1989) Soy protein allergy. In: *Food Intolerance in Infancy: Allergology, Immunology, and Gastroenterology* (ed. R. N. Hamburger), pp. 223–36. Carnation Nutrition Education Series, Vol 1. Raven Press, New York.

Eglin, R. P. and Wilkinson, A. R. (1987) HIV infection and pasteurisation of breast milk. *Lancet*, **i**, 1093.

Emken, E. A. (1995) *Trans* fatty acids and coronary heart disease risk: physiochemical properties, intake, and metabolism. *American Journal of Clinical Nutrition*, **62**(Suppl.), 659S–669S.

European Food Safety Authority (2004a) Opinion of the Scientific Panel on Dietetic Products, Nutrition and Allergies on a request from the Commission relating to the evaluation of goats' milk protein as a protein source for infant formulae and follow-on formulae (Request N° EFSA-Q-2003-019). *EFSA Journal*, **30**, 1–15.

European Food Safety Authority (2004b) Opinion of the Scientific Panel on Biological Hazards (BIOHAZ) related to the microbiological risks in infant formulae and follow-on formulae. Available at: http://www.efsa.europa.eu/EFSA/efsa_locale-1178620753812_1178620777466.htm

European Food Information Council (2012) Fruit and vegetable consumption in Europe – do Europeans get enough? Available at: http://www.eufic.org/article/en/expid/Fruit-vegetable-consumption-Europe/.

Fairbank, L., Woolridge, M. J., Renfrew, M. J., O'Meara, S., Sowden, A., Lister-Sharp, D. and Mather, L. (2000) *Effective Health Care: Promoting the Initiation of Breastfeeding*. NHS Centre for Reviews and Dissemination/University of York.

Fairweather-Tait, S. J., Balmer, S. E., Scott, P. H. and Ninski, M. J. (1987) Lactoferrin and iron absorption in newborn infants. *Pediatric Research*, **22**, 651–4.

Farquharson, J., Cockburn, F., Patrick, W. A., Jamieson, E. C. and Logan, R. W. (1992) Infant cerebral cortex phospholipid fatty-acid composition and diet. *Lancet*, **340**(8823), 810–13.

Fewtrell, M. S., Morley, R., Abbott, R. A., Singhal, A., Isaacs, E. B., Stephenson, T., Mac-Fadyen, U. and Lucas, A. (2002) Double-blind, randomized trial of long-chain poly-unsaturated fatty acid supplementation in formula fed to preterm infants. *Pediatrics*, **110**, 73–82.

Forsyth, S. (2004) *Influence of Infant Feeding Practice on Health Inequalities During Childhood.* Presented at the UNICEF-UK Baby Friendly Annual Conference, November 2004. Available at: http://www.babyfriendly.org.uk/pdfs/04programe.pdf.

Forsythe, S. J. (2005) *Enterobacter sakazakii* and other bacteria in powdered infant milk formula. *Maternal & Child Nutrition*, **1**, 44–50.

Francois, C. A., Connor, S. L., Bolewicz, L. C. and Connor, W. E. (2003) Supplementing lactating women with flaxseed oil does not increase docosahexaenoic acid in their milk. *American Journal of Clinical Nutrition*, **77**(1), 226–33.

Freed, G. L., Clark, S. J., Sorenson, J., Lohr, J. A., Cefalo, R. and Curtis, P. (1995) National assessment of physicians' breastfeeding knowledge and experience. *Journal of the American Medical Association*, **273**, 472–6.

Garofalo, R. P. and Goldman, A. S. (1998) Cytokines, chemokines and colony stimulating factors in human milk: the 1997 update. *Biology of the Neonate: Foetal and Neonatal Research*, **74**(2), 134–43.

Gibson, R. A., Neumann, M. A. and Makrides, M. (1997) Effect of increasing breast milk docosahexaenoic acid on plasma and erythrocyte phospholipid fatty acids and neural indices of exclusively breast fed infants. *European Journal of Clinical Nutrition*, **51**(9), 578–84.

Gil, A., Lozano, E., De-Lucchi, C., Maldonado, J., Molina, J. A. and Pita, M. (1988) Changes in the fatty acid profiles of plasma lipid fractions induced by dietary nucleotides in infants born at term. *European Journal of Clinical Nutrition*, **42**, 473–481.

Givens, D. I. and Gibbs, R. A. (2006), Very long chain n-3 polyunsaturated fatty acids in the food chain in the UK and the potential of animal-derived foods to increase intake. *Nutrition Bulletin*, **31**, 104–10.

Glew, R. H., Huang, Y. S., Vander Jagt, T. A., Chuang, L. T., Bhatt, S. K., Magnussen, M. A. and Vander Jagt, D. J. (2001) Fatty acid composition of the milk lipids of Nepalese women: correlation between fatty acid composition of serum phospholipids and melting point. *Prostaglandins, Leukotrienes and Essential Fatty Acids*, **65**(3), 147–56.

Halpin, T. C., Byrne, W. J. and Ament, M. E. (1977) Colitis, persistent diarrhoea, and soy protein intolerance. *Journal of Pediatrics*, **91**, 404–7.

Hamosh, M. (1998) Protective functions of proteins and lipids in human milk. *Biology of the Neonate: Foetal and Neonatal Research*, **74**(2), 163–77.

Hamosh, M. (1999) *Breastfeeding: Unravelling the Mysteries of Mothers' Milk.* Available at: http://www.medscape.com/viewarticle/408813.

Hamosh, M. and Salem, N. (1998) Long chain polyunsaturated fatty acids. *Biology of the Neonate: Foetal and Neonatal Research*, **74**(2), 106–121.

Hayat, L., al-Sughayer, M. A. and Afzal, M. (1999) Fatty acid composition of human milk in Kuwaiti mothers. *Comparative Biochemistry and Physiology B: Biochemical and Molecular Biology*, **124**(3), 261–7.

Health and Social Care Information Centre, IFF Research (2012) *Infant Feeding Survey 2010.* Information Centre for Health and Social Care: London.

Heinig, M. J. and Dewey, K. G. (1996) Health advantages of breast feeding for infants: a critical review. *Nutrition Research Review*, **9**, 89–110.

Heinig, M. J. and Dewey, K. G. (1997) Health effects of breast feeding for mothers: a critical review. *Nutrition Research Review*, **10**, 35–56.

Heird, W. C. (2001) The role of polyunsaturated fatty acids in term and preterm infants and breastfeeding mothers. In: *Breastfeeding, Part 1. Pediatric Clinics of North America*, Vol. 48, No. 1. WB Saunders, Philadelphia.

Heitlinger, L. A., Lee, P. C., Dillon, W. P. and Lebenthal, E. (1983) Mammary amylase: a possible alternate pathway of carbohydrate digestion in infancy. *Pediatric Research*, **17**(1), 15–18.

Helland, I. B., Smith, L., Saarem, K., Saugstad, O. D. and Drevon, C. A. (2003) Maternal supplementation with very-long-chain n-3 fatty acids during pregnancy and lactation augments children's IQ at 4 years of age. *Pediatrics*, **111**(1), e39–e44.

Hernell, O. and Lönnerdal, B. (2002) Iron status of infants fed low iron formula: no effect of added bovine lactoferrin or nucleotides. *American Journal of Clinical Nutrition*, **76**, 858–64.

Hoddinott, P. (1998) Why don't some women want to breastfeed and how might we change their attitudes? *Unpublished MPhil. Thesis*, p. 62–5. University of Wales College of Medicine, Cardiff.

Hoddinott, P. and Pill, R. (1999) Qualitative study of decisions about infant feeding among women in east end of London. *British Medical Journal*, **318**(7175), 30–4.

Holmboe-Ottesen, G., Wandel, M. and Mosdol, A. (2004) Social inequality and diet. *Tidsskrift for den Norske Laegeforen*, **124**(11), 1526–8.

Host, A., Koletzko, B., Dreborg, S., Muraro, A., Wahn, U., Aggett, P., *et al.* (1999) Dietary products used in infants for treatment and prevention of food allergy. Joint statement of the European Society for Paediatric Allergology and Clinical Immunology (ESPACI) Committee on Hypoallergenic Formulas and the European Society for Paediatric Gastroenterology, Hepatology and Nutrition (ESPGHAN) Committee on Nutrition. *Archives of Diseases in Childhood*, **81**(1), 80–4.

House of Commons Hansard Debates for 28 February 1989. Available at: http://www.parliament.the-stationery-office.co.uk/.

Howie, P. W., Forsyth, J. S. and Ogston, S. A. (1990) Protective effect of breast feeding against infection. *British Medical Journal*, **300**, 11–16.

Hu, J., La Vecchia, C., de Groh, M., Negri, E., Morrison, H. and Mery, L. (2011) Dietary transfatty acids and cancer risk. *European Journal of Cancer Prevention*, **20**(6), 530–8.

Hulshof, K. F., Brussaard, J. H., Kruizinga, A. G., Telman, J. and Lowik, M. R. (2003) Socio-economic status, dietary intake and 10 y trends: the Dutch National Food Consumption Survey. *European Journal of Clinical Nutrition*, **57**(1), 128–37.

Hunter, J. E. and Applewhite, T. H. (1991) Reassessment of *trans* fatty acid availability in the US diet. *American Journal of Clinical Nutrition*, **54**, 363–9.

IBFAN (2002) *How Safe Are Infant Formulas? The Death of a One-week Old Formula-fed Baby in Belgium.* Available at: http://www.ibfan.org/english/news/press/press10may02.html (accessed 30 September 2005).

IBFAN (2005) *The International Code of Marketing of Breastmilk Substitutes.* Available at: http://www.ibfan.org/english/resource/who/fullcode.html (accessed 30 September 2005).

IBFAN (2010) *Breaking the Rules, Stretching the Rules 2010.* Available at: http://www.ibfan.org/news-2010-1224.html (accessed 25 March 2010).

Infant Milks in the UK (2011). Available from: http://www.cwt.org.uk/.

Innis, S. M., King, D. J. (1999) *Trans* fatty acids in human milk are inversely associated with concentrations of essential *all-cis* n-6 and n-3 fatty acids and determine *trans*, but not n-6 and n-3, fatty acids in plasma lipids of breast-fed infants. *American Journal of Clinical Nutrition,* **70**(3), 383–90.

Jeffs, S. G. (1989) Hazards of scoop measurements in infant feeding. *Journal of the Royal College of General Practitioners,* **39**, 113.

Jenkins, H. R., Pincott, J. R., Soothill, J. F., Milla, P. J. and Harries, J. T. (1984) Food allergy: the major cause of infantile colitis. *Archives of Disease in Childhood,* **59**, 326–9.

Jensen, R. G., Lammi-Keefe, C. J., MacBurney, M. and Wijendran, V. (2001) Parenteral infusion of a lactating woman with intralipid: changes in milk and plasma fatty acids. *Advances in Experimental Medicine and Biology,* **501**, 163–8.

Kassing, D. (2002) Bottle-feeding as a tool to reinforce breastfeeding. *Journal of Human Lactation,* **18**(1), 56–60.

Kelleher, C., Friel, S., Nolan, G. and Forbes, B. (2002) Effect of social variation on the Irish diet. *Proceedings of the Nutrition Society,* **61**(4), 527–36.

Kelly, M. (2004) *How the Baby Friendly Initiative makes a difference – Case studies (Northgate Medical Centre).* Paper presented at the annual UNICEF-UK Baby Friendly Conference: Reducing inequalities in breastfeeding: evidence and support for success. Clyde Auditorium, Scottish Exhibition and Conference Centre, Glasgow, 10–11 November 2004.

Kennedy, K. I. (1989) Concensus statement on the use of breastfeeding as a family planning method. *Contraception,* **39**(5), 477–96.

Kim, S., Symons, M. and Popkin, B. M. (2004). Contrasting socioeconomic profiles related to healthier lifestyles in China and the United States. *American Journal of Epidemiology,* **159**(2), 184–91.

Koletzko, B. (1995) Potential adverse effects of *trans* fatty acids in infants and children. *European Journal of Medical Research,* **1**, 123–5.

Kramer, M. S., Aboud, F., Mironova, E., Vanilovich, I., Platt, R. W., Matush, L., *et al.* (2008) Breastfeeding and child cognitive development: new evidence from a large randomized trial. Promotion of Breastfeeding Intervention Trial (PROBIT) Study Group. *Archives of General Psychiatry,* **65**(5), 578–84.

Laaksonen, M., Prattala, R., Helasoja, V., Uutela, A. and Lahelma, E. (2003) Income and health behaviours. Evidence from monitoring surveys among Finnish adults. *Journal of Epidemiology & Community Health,* **57**(9), 711–17.

Lauritzen, L. and Carlson, S. E. (2011) Maternal fatty acid status during pregnancy and lactation and relation to newborn and infant status. *Maternal and Child Nutrition,* **7**(Suppl. 2), 41–58.

Li, Y. and Watkins, B. A. (1998) Conjugated linoleic acids alter bone fatty acid composition and reduce *ex vivo* prostaglandin E2 biosynthesis in rats fed n-6 or n-3 fatty acids. *Lipids,* **33**(4), 417–25.

Li, R., Fein, S. B. and Grummer-Strawn, L. M. (2010) Do infants fed from bottles lack self-regulation of milk intake compared with directly breastfed infants? *Pediatrics*, **125**(6), e1386–e1393.

Lilburne, A. M., Oates, R. K., Thompson, S. and Tong, L. (1988) Infant feeding in Sydney: a survey of mothers who bottle feed. *Australian Paediatric Journal*, **24**(1), 49–54.

Lönnerdal, B. (2003) *American Journal of Clinical Nutrition*, **77**(6), 1537S–1543S.

Lucas, A. and Cole, T. J. (1990) Breast milk and neonatal necrotising enterocolitis. *Lancet*, **336**, 1519–23.

Lucas, A., Morley, R., Cole, T. J., Lister, G. and Leeson-Payne, C. (1992) Breast milk and subsequent intelligence quotients in children born pre-term. *Lancet*, **339**, 261–4.

Lucas, A., Stafford, M. and Morley, R. (1999) Efficacy and safety of LU-PUFA supplementation of infant formula milk: a randomised trial. *Lancet*, **354**, 1948–54.

Malcolm, C. A., McCulloch, D. L., Montgomery, C., Shepherd, A. and Weaver, L. T. (2003) Maternal docosahexaenoic acid supplementation during pregnancy and visual evoked potential development in term infants: a double blind, prospective, randomised trial. *Archives of Disease in Childhood*, **88**(5), F383–90.

MacFadyen, U. and Lucas, A. (2002) Double-blind, randomized trial of long-chain polyunsaturated fatty acid supplementation in formula fed to preterm infants. *Pediatrics*, **110**, 73–82.

Makrides, M., Neumann, M. A. and Byard, R. W. (1994) Fatty acid composition of brain, retina and erythrocytes in breastfed and formula fed infants. *American Journal of Clinical Nutrition*, **60**, 189–94.

Makrides, M., Neumann, M. A. and Gibson, R. A. (1996) Effect of maternal docosahexaenoic acid (DHA) supplementation on breast milk composition. *European Journal of Clinical Nutrition*, **50**(6), 352–7.

Makrides, M., Collins, C. T. and Gibson, R. A. (2011), Impact of fatty acid status on growth and neurobehavioural development in humans. *Maternal & Child Nutrition*, **7**, 80–8.

Masters, N., McGuire, M. A., Beerman, K. A., Dasgupta, N. and McGuire, M. K. (2002) Maternal supplementation with CLA decreases milk fat in humans. *Lipids*, **37**(2), 133–8.

McDonald, P. J., Goldblum, R. M., Van Sickle, G. J. and Powell, G. K. (1984) Food protein-induced enterocolitis: altered antibody response to ingested antigen. *Pediatric Research*, **18**, 751–5.

McIntosh, J. (1985) Barriers to breastfeeding: choice of feeding method in a sample of working class primiparae. *Midwifery*, **1**, 213–24.

Messenger, H. (1994) Don't shoot the messenger. *Heath Visitor*, **67**(5), 171.

Michie, C. A. and Gilmour, J. (2001) Breast feeding and the risks of viral transmission. *Archives of Diseases in Childhood*, **84**(5), 381–2.

Minchin, M. (2001) *Towards Safer Artificial Feeding*. Alma Publications, Australia.

Mitoulas, L. R., Gurrin, L. C., Doherty, D. A., Sherriff, J. L. and Hartmann, P. E. (2003) Infant intake of fatty acids from human milk over the first year of lactation. *British Journal of Nutrition*, **90**(5), 979–86.

Mozaffarian, D., Katan, M. B., Ascherio, A., Stampfer, M. J. and Willett, W. C. (2006). *Trans* fatty acids and cardiovascular disease. *New England Journal of Medicine*, **354**(15), 1601–13.

Muller, M. (1974) *The Baby Killer*. War on Want, London.

National Diet and Nutrition Survey (2010) *Headline Results from Year 1 of the Rolling Programme (2008/2009)*. Food Standards Agency and Department of Health.

Newman, J. (1995) How breastmilk protects newborns. Scientific American, **273**(6), 76.

Palmer, G. (1993) *The Politics of Breastfeeding*. Rivers Oram Press, London.

Palmer, G. (2009) *The Politics of Breastfeeding: When Breasts are Bad for Business*, 3rd edn. Pinter & Martin, London.

Pessler, F. and Nejat, M. (2004) Anaphylactic reaction to goats' milk in a cows' milk-allergic infant. *Pediatric Allergy and Immunology*, **15**(2), 183–5.

Peterson, J. A., Patton, S. and Hamosh, M. (1998) Glycoproteins of the human milk fat globule in the protection of the breastfed infant against infections. *Biology of the Neonate: Foetal and Neonatal Research*, **74**(2), 143–63.

Picciano, M. F. (1998) Human milk: nutritional aspects of a dynamic food. *Biology of the Neonate: Foetal and Neonatal Research*, **74**(2), 84–94.

Picciano, M. F. (2001) Nutrient composition of human milk. *The Pediatric Clinics of North America*, **48**(1), 53–67.

Pita, M., Fernandez, M. R., De-Lucchi, C., Medina, A., Martinez-Valverde, A., Uauy, R. and Gil, A. (1988) Changes in the fatty acids pattern of red blood cell phospholipids in duced by type of milk, dietary nucleotide supplementation, and postnatal age in preterm infants. *Journal of Pediatrics, Gastroenterology and Nutrition*, **7**, 740–7.

Quigley, M. A., Kelly, Y. J. and Sacker, A. S. (2007) Breastfeeding and hospitalization for diarrheal and respiratory infection in the United Kingdom Millennium Cohort Study. *Pediatrics*, **119**, e837–e842.

Radford, A. (1991) *The Ecological Impact of Bottle Feeding*. Baby Milk Action, London. (Document first launched at XIII IOCU World Congress, Hong Kong, July 1991).

RCM (2003) *Successful Breastfeeding. A Handbook for Midwives*. Churchill Livingstone, London.

RCM (2004) *Position Statement No. 5*. Available at: http://www.rcm.org.uk/ (accessed 30 September 2005).

RCM Journal (2004) News and appointments. May, p. 3.

Renfrew, M. J., Ansell, P. and Macleod, K. L. (2003) Formula feed preparation: helping reduce the risks; a systematic review. *Archives of Disease in Childhood*, **88**(10), 855–8.

Renfrew, M. J. (2004) Breastfeeding: state of the art. Report of a meeting at the Forum on Maternity and the Newborn of the Royal Society of Medicine. *Midwives*, **7**(7), 306–9.

Retsinas, J. (1987) Nature versus technology: the breastfeeding decision. *Sociological Spectrum*, **7**, 121–9.

Richardson, A. J. (2004) Long-chain polyunsaturated fatty acids in childhood developmental and psychiatric disorders. *Lipids*, **39**(12), 1215–22.

Richardson, A. J. and Montgomery, P. (2005) The Oxford-Durham study: a randomized, controlled trial of dietary supplementation with fatty acids in children with developmental coordination disorder. *Pediatrics*, **115**(5), 1360–6.

Sampson, H. A. (1988) The role of food allergy and mediator release in atopic dermatitis. *Journal of Allergy and Clinical Immunology*, **81**, 635–45.

Schoder, D. (2010) Melamine milk powder and infant formula sold in East Africa. *Journal of Food Protection*, **73**(9), 1709–14.

Scientific Advisory Committee on Nutrition (2003) Minutes of the meetings are available at: http://www.sacn.gov.uk/meetings/subgroups/maternal/2003_09_29.html.

Simmer, K., Patole, S. and Rao, S. C. (2007). Longchain polyunsaturated fatty acid supplementation in infants born at term. *Cochrane Database of Systematic Reviews*, Issue 1. Art. No.: CD000376. doi: 10.1002/14651858. CD000376.pub2.

Sinclair, C. M. (1992) Fats in Human Milk. Topics in Breastfeeding, set IV. Lactation Resource Centre

Simmer, K. and Patole, S. (2004) Longchain polyunsaturated fatty acid supplementation in preterm infants (Cochrane Review). In: *The Cochrane Library*, Issue 2. John Wiley & Sons, Chichester.

Smit, E. N., Martini, I. A., Mulder, H., Boersma, E. R. and Muskiet, F. A. (2002) Estimated biological variation of the mature human milk fatty acid composition. *Prostaglandins, Leukotrienes and Essential Fatty Acids*, **66**(5–6), 549–55.

Spear, M. L., Hamosh, M., Bitman, J., Spear, M. L. and Wood, D. L.(1992) Milk and blood fatty acid composition during two lactations in the same woman. *American Journal of Clinical Nutrition*, **56**(1), 65–70.

Still, G. F. (1931) *The History of Paediatrics*, p. 305. Oxford University Press, London.

Thapa, S., Short, R. V. and Potts, M. (1988) Breastfeeding, birth spacing and their effects on child survival. *Nature*, **335**, 679–82.

Thomas, M. and Avery, V. (1997) *Infant Feeding in Asian Families*. The Stationery Office, London.

Thompson, A. (1994) *Doctor*, 27 October, p. 23.

Trichopoulou, A., Naska, A., Costacou, T. and the DAFNE III Group (2002) Disparities in food habits across Europe. *Proceedings of the Nutrition Society*, **61**(4), 553–8.

Turrell, G., Hewitt, B., Patterson, C. and Oldenburg, B. (2003) Measuring socio-economic position in dietary research: is choice of socio-economic indicator important? *Public Health Nutrition*, **6**(2), 191–200.

Udall, J. N., Dixon, M., Newman, A. P. *et al.* (1985) Liver disease in alpha-1-antitrypsin deficiency: a retrospective analysis of the influence of early breast vs. bottle-feeding. *Journal of the American Medical Association*, **253**, 2679.

UNICEF-BFI (2010a) *A Guide to Infant Formula for Parents Who Are Bottle Feeding*. Available at: http://www.unicef.org.uk/BabyFriendly/Resources/Resources-for-parents/A-guide-to-infant-formula-for-parents-who-are-bottle-feeding/

UNICEF-BFI (2010b) *A Health Professional's Guide to 'A Guide to Infant Formula for Parents Who Are Bottle Feeding'*. Available at: http://www.unicef.org.uk/Documents/Baby_Friendly/Leaflets/health_professionals_guide_infant_formula.pdf

Vannoni, F., Spadea, T., Frasca, G., Tumino, R., Demaria, M., Sacerdote, C., Panico, S., Celentano, E., Palli, D., Saieva, C., Pala, V., Sieri, S. and Costa, G. (2003) Association between social class and food consumption in the Italian EPIC population. *Tumori*, **89**(6), 669–78.

Villalpando, S. and Hamosh, M. (1998) Early and late effects of breastfeeding: does breastfeeding really matter? *Biology of the Neonate: Foetal and Neonatal Research*, **74**(2), 177–191.

Walker, M. (1993) A fresh look at the risks of artificial infant feeding. *Journal of Human Lactation*, **9**(2), 97–107.

Watkins, B. A., Shen, C. L., McMurtry, J. P., Xu, H., Bain, S. D., Allen, K. G. and Seifert, M. F. (1997) Dietary lipids after histomorphometry and concentrations of fatty acids and insulin-like growth factor in chick tibiotarsal bone. *Journal of Nutrition*, **127**(6), 1084–91.

Weaver, L. T. (1997) Digestive system development and failure. In: *Seminars in Neonatology – Necrotising enterocolitis* (eds. A. R. Wilkinson and P. K. H. Tam). WB Saunders, Philadelphia.

Whitington, P. F. and Gibson, R. (1977) Soy protein intolerance: four patients with concomitant cow's milk intolerance. *Pediatrics*, **59**, 730–2.

Willatts, P., Forsyth, J. S., Di Modugno, M. K., Varma, S. and Colvin, M. (1998) The effect of longchain polyunsaturated fatty acids in infant formula on problem solving at 10 months of age. *Lancet*, **352**, 688–91.

Williams, A. (1993) In: *Forfar and Arneil's Textbook of Paediatrics*, 4th edn (eds. A. G. M. Campbell and N. McIntosh), p. 372. Churchill Livingstone, London.

WHO/UNICEF (1989) *Protecting, Promoting and Supporting Breast-feeding: the Special Role of Maternity Services. A Joint WHO/UNICEF Statement*. WHO, Geneva.

Xanthou, M. (1998) Immune protection of human milk. *Biology of the Neonate: Foetal and Neonatal Research*, **74**(2), 121–34.

CHAPTER 5

Weighing it up: the reasons breastfeeding mothers weigh their babies

Magda Sachs

Introduction

Weight monitoring of babies is a well-established practice, embedded in the expectations of mothers and health staff in the UK. It is perhaps the activity most associated with baby clinic in the minds of new parents. Women take their babies to clinics for weighing frequently as part of their pattern of good mothering, and the recorded weight gain informs their understanding of breastfeeding efficacy.

In 2009 the Department of Health adopted a UK version of the World Health Organization's (UK-WHO) 0–5 growth standards for use in England (with the rest of the UK soon to follow) (Wright *et al.*, 2010). This growth chart included, as part of the instructions, recommendations about the frequency of weighing. This was repeated in information in the parent-held child health record, and states that, after monitoring to ensure that the baby has regained birth weight, the baby 'should be weighed *no more* than once a month before 6 months' (Royal College of Paediatrics and Child Health, Department of Health and World Health Organization, 2009).

At the time of publication of the UK-WHO growth chart, feedback from health staff and parents alike indicated that this recommended frequency was not current practice and there would be a challenge in trying to implement it. Staff perceived the offer of weighing in clinics as an inducement to mothers to attend, which would then offer the possibility of interactions to support maternal confidence in the care of her baby or suggestions as to how to improve that care. In order to encourage women to weigh their babies less frequently and for staff to feel comfortable to restructure contacts so they do not automatically involve weighing, it may be useful to understand the reasons women give for their weighing habits.

A doctoral study on the impact of routine weight monitoring on the feeding decisions of breastfeeding women gathered data which included the reasons that these mothers gave for how often they took their baby to be weighed (Sachs, 2005). These were analysed and grouped into themes and provide some illumination of the influences articulated by mothers when deciding how frequently to weigh their baby.

Background

In the UK, women are cared for at the time of birth by midwives and remain under midwifery care until they are discharged, usually at 10 days (unless there are complications). Health visitor teams then take over care, conducting an initial home visit to assess the baby and to identify the health needs of the mother and baby or wider family. At the initial home visit, the baby is weighed and thereafter women attend clinics to access care from health visiting staff. At clinic visits, babies are weighed and information or advice is sought and given.

Surveys indicate that a high percentage of parents give baby weighing as their reason for attending clinic (Biswas and Sands, 1984; Sefi and MacFarlane, 1985; Sharpe and Lowenthal, 1992). Visiting the clinic and having the baby weighed is an expected activity for new parents. Davies (2000, p. 201) remarks that 'it would take more than an Act of Parliament to stop it', while Daws (1985, p. 79) notes that:

> ...bringing the baby to be weighed is the focus for the baby clinic. Parents can visit with no other ostensible reason than to weigh the baby. This alone validates the visit while enabling the mother or father to make use of a contact with the health visitor.

This observed pattern of behaviour stems from the historical development of preventative community child care and baby clinics. Weaver (2010, p. 51) describes how, from the start of the 20th century, the development of monitoring the growth of all babies in order to identify those who would benefit from intervention resulted in clinics in which 'weighing was a precondition of admittance'. The development and adoption of growth charts, alongside weighing balances and scales, defined the experience of supporting mothers and families to care for their infants. The most recent UK survey to report on frequency of clinic attendance showed that, when their baby was four or five months old, 9% of women went to clinic weekly, with a further 34% attending once a fortnight

(Hamlyn *et al.*, 2002). It is likely that frequency of attendance is greater at earlier ages. This attendance is likely to be almost identical to weighing frequency.

Parents and staff may scrutinise the baby's weights and change feeding and care in response. However, weight monitoring is not a screening procedure (Hall, 2000), and children who show a sustained decline through two centile spaces 'only constitute a high risk group who would merit closer investigation, rather than a definite diagnostic group' (Wright, 2000, p. 7). A 1998 meeting of paediatricians produced consensus guidelines based on clinical expertise recommending fewer weighing episodes, but paying more attention to these (Wright, 2000, p. 7; Hall, 2000). This has been included in guidance to professionals working in community child care (Hall and Elliman, 2003; Department of Health, 2009), and forms the basis for the recommended weighing frequency on the UK-WHO chart instructions (Wright *et al.*, 2010).

Weights are recorded on growth charts included in the parent-held child health record, introduced in 1991 and gradually adopted throughout the UK (Jackson, 1990; Owen, 1991). Prior to this, charts were generally held in clinic records and usually considered to be for professionals and not parents. Although now invited to join in looking at the chart, parents may not understand that plotted centiles require interpretation rather than any particular weight representing an actual danger to the baby (Sachs *et al.*, 2006a,b, 2011; Ben-Joseph *et al.*, 2007, 2009; Woolford *et al.*, 2007; Laraway *et al.*, 2009).

Approval of the growth pattern may be expressed by health visitors when weight conforms to the centiles, implying that fluctuations off the line are of concern (Dykes and Williams, 1999; Olin Lauritzen and Sachs, 2001; Sachs *et al.*, 2006b). Breastfeeding women, in particular, may use patterns of weight change as a measure of feeding success. Over-frequent weighing and misunderstanding about the importance of minor fluctuations of recorded weight may lead to changes to feeding style. This could involve supplementing breastfeeding with infant formula milk or solid foods rather than fine-tuning the physical attachment and positioning during breastfeeding or increasing breastfeeding frequency. In many cases, the concern is unwarranted and mothers may experience unnecessary anxiety and evolve a general distrust of the efficacy of breastfeeding and their ability to nourish their baby (Sachs *et al.*, 2006b; Redsell *et al.*, 2010).

Fulford (2001, p. 386) describes the feelings of dissatisfaction of health visitors with drop-in clinics which are 'rushed', where 'often babies were just weighed' without time for 'meaningful consultation'. Prior to the introduction of the UK-WHO charts there was no universal training guide on growth monitoring for community practitioners, and differences in interpretation could be found between different individual members of staff (Shaw-Flach, 2003; Tappin *et al.*, 2006; Wright *et al.*, 2011). Health visiting staff may not have received adequate pre-registration training in skills to support breastfeeding women (Tappin *et al.*, 2006). They may be wary of being too pro-breastfeeding as they wish to preserve an on-going relationship with the mothers in their care (Shaw-Flach, 2003; Sachs *et al.*, 2006b), and their understanding of the outcomes of breastfeeding and infant formula feeding on infant health are continually challenged and shaped by influences from the infant formula industry (Dykes *et al.*, 2012).

The reasons mothers give for why they weigh their babies

In this study I employed an ethnographic approach, including conducting participant observation. There were two phases of fieldwork. In the first phase I attended routine weekly sessions in a child health clinic in a town in the northwest of England. As well as observing interactions between health visitors and women coming to have their babies weighed, short interviews were conducted with nine breastfeeding mothers, and longer, private interviews with each of the four health visitors working in the clinic. I attended 14 sessions of the breastfeeding support group held at the clinic, during which 17 women participated. Both first- and second-time mothers were included and some women were giving both breast and infant formula feeds.

Field notes and taped interviews were transcribed and written up as soon as practical. Data from phase one were preliminarily analysed to inform interviews in phase two. In the second phase, I recruited 14 women through an information sheet distributed by the health visitors in the clinic. The aim was to conduct the first interview as soon as possible after the mother's first contact with the health visitor (at around 10–14 days), arrange a second interview when the baby was around three months old and a third at six months. Telephone contact was maintained between interviews, so that if the mother stopped breastfeeding the next interview could be arranged soon after this happened. If a woman ceased to breastfeed at all by the second interview, this was the last one conducted. Interviews were arranged in women's homes at times convenient to them. Altogether in phase two, 35 interviews of 40–90 minutes were conducted; I transcribed all tapes myself.

Consent was sought and received from the Local Research Ethics Committee. Throughout, care was taken that women in the clinic consented to my presence and, before arranging each interview in the second phase, that women were still willing to be included. Two women initially agreed to take part but withdrew from the study before a meeting took place. None of the women who were interviewed initially declined subsequent interviews. Pseudonyms are used in the presentation of data.

All data were analysed using a grounded theory approach with initial 'open' coding in phase one. These codes were then used to re-analyse all data to deepen analysis and investigate the properties and dimensions of each code (Strauss and Corbin, 2002). I did not initially intend to examine the reasons why women weighed their babies, but this category emerged during the data analysis phase. No previous study had been found which explored the reasons women give for taking their babies to be weighed: it appears to be assumed that each weighing encounter is undertaken for the same reasons. All comments which identified influences on the decision whether to take the baby to be weighed were included in the analysis, resulting in the categories presented here.

A study which included more women, and, crucially, women who were not breastfeeding, might discover further reasons for the frequency with which women have their babies weighed. It is also possible that the changes in information given to parents in the parent-held child health record from 2009 about weighing frequency may have resulted in differences in weighing habits. Although this study was conducted between 2001 and 2003, further research has yet to be conducted in this area. This analysis therefore offers a preliminary framework for understanding weighing frequency.

Findings

The women in this study had their babies weighed more frequently than recommended, in line with national findings (Hamlyn *et al.*, 2002). The analysis of reasons they gave uncovered a range of issues which impacted on their decisions. A single weighing episode could be undertaken (or delayed) for several different reasons, and a similar stated reason could lead to different women adopting dissimilar actions in response. By examining how women explained what influenced their decisions and actions on weighing frequency, some of the underlying needs which weighing met for them can be suggested.

Six themes were identified in the statements women made about attending clinic and having their baby weighed. Each theme included two aspects, one which provides rationales for increasing the frequency of weighing, and one which provides a 'reverse rationale', i.e. increasing the interval between weighing episodes. A brief description of these themed categories is provided in Tables 5.1 and 5.2.

Table 5.1 Reasons given for weighing or weighing frequency.

Medical weighing	Mother or baby ill
	Part of medical follow-up for previous problem
	Weight at immunisation appointments [set weighing times]
	Consistency of scales for best medical information
Portal weighing	Mother wishes to ask a question of health visitor unrelated to the weight of the baby
	Going to clinic for social reasons
	Going to breastfeeding support group/massage class
	Weight at immunisations – may seem to mother she needs to weigh as part of this
Recreational weighing	Going to breastfeeding support/baby massage group, weighing scales there so weight taken
	'Curiosity'
Accountability weighing	To report to family, friends
	Confidence to continue breastfeeding in face of suggestions to give a bottle of infant formula milk
	See baby is getting 'enough'
Keepsake weighing	To have a full record plotted on the chart, for visual impact
Grocer's weighing	To see whether products (nappy wraps, slings), which give a weight range for use, are suitable for the baby – or to forecast future suitability

Two other important aspects of weighing frequency were that the frequency for each mother–baby pair declined with time (although for many, weekly weighing continued until they returned to work at about six months), and that women with second babies tended to weigh less frequently, compared both to mothers with first babies and, reportedly, than they had done with their own first babies.

Reasons to weigh

Medical and reverse medical weighing
An important clinical rationale for routine weighing is to detect a problem, as one health visitor stated:

> Occasionally you get a baby with a medical condition…. We have certainly had several babies who haven't been diagnosed at birth, who've had serious heart conditions, and the fact of the matter is that they were apparently feeding quite well, but they hadn't put on weight.

Table 5.2 Reasons given for not weighing or decreasing weighing frequency.

Reverse medical	Want to see overall trend, not fluctuations
Reverse accountability	Embarrassment because gains are large
	Mother understands baby behaviour is normal, not due to lack of milk, therefore weighing not seen as appropriate reassurance
	Can see the baby is growing
Reverse portal	Clinic offers poor quality encounter
	Feel weighing can become too much of a focus
Reverse recreational	Baby finds it stressful being undressed
	Getting to the clinic is difficult
	Difficult to find time to go to clinic
	Hard to go if back at work
Reverse keepsake	Weighing less frequently means each gain is larger
	Feel weighing can become too much of a focus
Reverse grocer's weighing	No reverse grocer's weighing was identified for women in this study

In these circumstances women may also attend specialist paediatric clinics where the weighing frequency will be set by professionals. Such weighing should not be categorised as routine, but be seen as part of more specific monitoring or assessment for such babies. A few women in this study reported instances in which their babies were subject to medical scrutiny resulting from earlier problems. Zoë's baby had lost 12 ounces (340 grams) at the first health visitor weighing. She reported:

> She's also had follow up visits at the hospital from the jaundice, so she's been weighed then.

The mother of a formula-fed baby with a medical condition came to the clinic weekly, including one occasion when she attended even though she had been to the hospital the previous day with her baby. This suggests that an increase in weighing frequency due to a medical condition could sometimes lead to prolonged changes in weighing frequency: this mother was not interviewed as she was not breastfeeding.

Sometimes when babies were unwell women attended the clinic in order to have them weighed. Kerri attended with her husband; their daughter, now also eating some solid foods as well as breastfeeding, had only taken breast milk that morning and they were concerned. As well as examining and weighing her, the health visitor explained how to tell if she was dehydrated. At her next visit Kerri said that the baby had started behaving like her usual self later the same day. The weight was probably less important than the examination and discussion on this occasion, as this was the first day of illness. The inclusion of the father in this case appeared to mark the concern of the parents.

Weight fluctuations might be explained retrospectively as due to minor illness. Linda's baby had only gained a little and she explained: 'he weren't so good last week... he is all bunged up, he couldn't feed properly'. Rosemary believed that the only time her daughter had not gained weight was after she had been ill:

> She had a bit of a dip there [on the chart] when... she was poorly, she had a bit of a cold, she was quite sickly as well.

Mothers' illnesses might also be a consideration. Una explained:

> This week, with me being ill, 'cos I had sickness and diarrhoea, I'd like to check that he's still OK. He does feel a lot heavier... so I think he has [gained weight], but I'd like to have it confirmed because I've been a bit off.

Olivia suffered from a debilitating condition after the birth of her first son, and had relied on regular visits from her health visitor, which included weekly weighing. With her current baby, she had only had a few weight measurements done and said:

> ...my husband said I am more relaxed this time 'cos I don't have the same health issues for myself.

Women did not usually differentiate between times they went to the clinic for immunisations and had the baby weighed (which correspond to the suggested times for routine weights) and other occasions. At times, in the breastfeeding group, women who usually had their babies weighed there might mention that they had been for an immunisation (to their own GP practice), had the baby weighed, and did not need to weigh again. In one instance the health visitor reinforced this, saying: 'It's up to you about weighing, but if he has to go to the doctor tomorrow [for immunisation], he'll be weighed there'. However, when the health visitor left the room, this mother proceeded to weigh her baby. She had previously explained that her family would typically phone after her regular day for clinic visiting to find out about the baby's weight.

Sarah mentioned the effect of different scales on the accuracy of recorded weights:

I had her done at the breastfeeding group and she seemed to have put a lot of weight on and the following week, at the baby massage [held in a different clinic], they were offering to weigh her, so I had her done there and she put about an ounce and a half on, so clearly different-scales syndrome... I thought 'ohhh, this is a minefield... different scales and they're obviously not calibrated the same'.

Sarah was herself a health visitor and might be more aware than most mothers of the possibility that scales vary. She weighed her baby on the scales she had from work for the first four months, but these were 'repossessed' (as she put it) for use by another health visitor, leaving her to use clinic scales. Although her professional knowledge caused her to want to use the same scale, she did not conform to the weighing frequency suggested in the medical literature.

Tessa, who had made a deliberate decision not to have her baby weighed, explained this in terms of not being caught up in minor fluctuations, suggesting that a better assessment could be obtained by less frequent weighing:

Because it's a bit like, if, when people go on diets, they're not supposed to weigh themselves too often. You know, wait until you might get a result.

Women articulated the rationale for weighing to monitor the impact of illness on growth (although their timescale may have been too short to accurately do this) and showed that they understood some of the technical issues, such as different equipment and the impact of minor fluctuations in the short term. These statements meant that this set of reasons for weighing frequency most closely matched reasons for the consensus recommendations stated in professional literature.

Portal and reverse portal weighing

This type of weighing appeared to happen as a matter of course when women entered the door, even when they had another aim for coming to the clinic. The clinic was physically laid out reflecting the assumption that the baby would be weighed before other discussions took place: a mother entering would be ushered to take her baby's clothes off and asked for her parent-held child health record as she came in. As Olivia remarked: 'in the baby clinic it is just that that is how you talk to the health visitor – over the baby while he is being weighed'. Women attending the clinic for a social outing, or attending groups or classes might also weigh 'while I am here'. Olwen reported this from the breastfeeding group: 'everybody tends to weigh them every week'. Jayne remarked:

I think that made it easy for me – to take Oliver to the [breastfeeding] group and just get him weighed there. If I had just taken him to the clinic I don't think I would have gone as often.

At the time of her second interview, Una was taking her son to be weighed every two weeks. At the third interview (when the baby was 6 months), she was weighing him weekly at baby massage class: ''cos we're there and he's stripped off and ready, you might as well'. It seemed that being in the clinic with scales to hand had increased weighing frequency.

One health visitor felt that weighing in the breastfeeding group was positive:

Because the scales are not the focus… they can use them if they want to. And it's up to the mums to do it… I mean when I've been in, I've never weighed them. But mums have come and just gone ahead and used the scales if I've done the group… and in a way that's better.

Another mother (Olwen), however, described the atmosphere in the breastfeeding group in quite a negative fashion:

Everybody always asked 'Oh how much have they put on this week?' It was like a sort of friendly 'oo good' or 'oh, don't worry, they'll make up for it next week'. It was more like a slimming club. You know, like where someone loses 'well done' and if you don't 'well never mind, I'm sure next week'. It was like that really, but the opposite way.

To some extent having scales at groups and classes might be used to manage uninviting clinics. However by leaving it up to women whether to weigh or not, health visitors were not taking responsibility for informing women about the recommended frequency of weighing. They might also miss hearing about a weight change and not be able to help the mother interpret it in the context of normal growth.

Weighing as part of the 'ticket price' for gaining admittance to the clinic was shown when Olivia took her son to see the health visitor about eczema and found that the baby was weighed almost before she could say anything. Tessa described one of the few times she had her daughter weighed:

That was a bit of an accident – 'cos I was going to drop off some stuff for NCT and it was absolutely accidentally on a Wednesday… I was early and the midwives weren't there yet, so I saw I could be first, I wouldn't have to wait, so I did [have her weighed].

In this case, walking through the clinic doors triggered an unintended weighing episode.

One health visitor noted that mothers might use weighing as an acceptable excuse for asking about other concerns:

I think they use the weighing after a while as an excuse for other things….
They come and they have them weighed and say 'well while I'm here'…
they're not actually ringing, mithering me. They just happen to be in clinic and you've said 'how are you' so then they can you know, express their
concerns, 'well actually…'.

It was interesting that the use of weighing to instigate a contact with the health visitor was not mentioned by mothers in this study, although this was stated by parents in consultations about the draft UK-WHO growth charts (Sachs *et al.*, 2011).

The unchallenged expectation that the baby will always be weighed at a clinic visit adds to the frequency of weighing.

Recreational and reverse recreational weighing

Women valued frequent weighing, but it often seemed to be a routine act with little quality interpretation. Weighing as an act of passing through the portal was in many instances entwined with the category of recreational weighing. This was manifest in the aspect expressed above of doing it along with all the others because it was the thing to do.

Often mothers gave curiosity as their motive. Nadine said: 'I just sort of not had him done for a bit so I thought I'd see how he was doing'. Bethany remarked; 'I'm just curious, me. It's like having her measured and everything, I just like to know what she's up to'. This rather devalues weight measurement as a medical test, and increases the focus on short-term fluctuations rather than longer-term trends, which might offer a better gauge of the baby's health.

Another aspect of this was speculation on the weight within families, with some mothers mentioning that they had a bet with their partner, or that other relatives would phone to ask the weight. This was related to weighing accountability, but also appeared to be a way of expressing interest. Una reported:

Everyone was very interested in the birth weight. Work's had a sweepstake…
they didn't ring up to see if it was a boy or a girl, just what it weighed.

As in this example, such attention might actually sideline the baby, and also the mother and her feelings, by concentrating simply on a number. As one health visitor described:

I don't always necessarily think they [people who ask] give a monkey's what the baby weighs.... You know it's a conversation piece rather than for any actual beneficial reason.

Wendy, who had not had her baby weighed after the first health visitor visit, said: 'I think having her weighed, it's just novelty value, isn't it, really, 'oh she's put on another... few pounds'.

Things which made clinic visits unappealing, such as difficulties in getting there or parking, crowded clinics or hurried encounters, might lead to less frequent weighing, since women went only when they had specific appointments (Sharpe and Lowenthal, 1992). Sarah, herself a health visitor, said:

I think if the clinic... was better I probably would go more often, but it's cattle market city down there... there are three different health visitors talking to three different mums, with three different babies crying, and you can't concentrate on what you're being asked, let alone have a conversation.

The experience of the baby might also impact. Nadine reported: 'He doesn't like being weighed.... It's being in the pan, he's too big. He's hanging over the edge'.

Keepsake and reverse keepsake weighing

This type of weighing was the result of a desire for the end product of a well-filled-in chart. Marie said: 'that's the main reason I like to get them weighed, is because I think that is such a nice keepsake', and Rachel, when asked what she would say to a (hypothetical) pregnant friend about regular weighing replied 'I would explain that if you didn't have them weighed often enough, you wouldn't see the curve that I've got'. One mother came to clinic, requesting her daughter be weighed, 'because she is six months old today', so she wanted a weight for the record. Tessa had charts for both daughters – one chart was frequently completed, the other had only two points plotted, giving a very different look, which she commented on.

Alex mentioned a visual reason not to weigh so frequently:

I don't really see a big difference when you go every week.... It's just a couple of ounces. Whereas if I leave it to every other week, I may see the big difference.

This appeared to be related to more immediate gratification (seeing a big gain) than to the production of a keepsake, but might produce a keepsake in the form of an anecdote: 'and she gained *x* amount in *x* weeks!'.

Jayne and Kelly each mentioned that they had their own infant weight records, which their mothers had given them, indicating that this form of keepsake may be longstanding.

Olivia, who had not often weighed her baby, talked about the importance of her older son's parent-held child health record:

> With Jacob, the red book went everywhere and there were lots of notes from everyone... it had been a significant part of bringing Jacob up.

But it appeared to be what was written that she valued, not the chart, as she noted in response to a question:

> It was more the notes.... It was a good record to look back on. In David's there is nothing, just a few weights.

Perhaps the keepsake value of the parent-held child health record could be preserved even if weights were less frequently recorded while other parts of the book are well filled-in.

Grocer's and reverse grocer's weighing

Two women gave examples of this reason for weighing their breastfed baby. Tessa said:

> These nappy wrappers that I use were saying up to 11 pounds and they were getting very small and I was thinking 'I wonder if she's about to need to go into the next size?'.

This explanation signals the ubiquitous expectation that mothers in our society will know the weight of their babies and can use this for other purposes. Rachel talked of a similar incident in which she forecast the weight of her baby to the time of a planned holiday:

> We've got one of these slings... we bought it with the intention of being able to use it at the airport... the girl in the shop said to us 'the problem with this one is that it only goes up to a certain pounds, and some babies at the age of one are this heavy and others aren't'... I had a brainwave and I said 'I'll look at the chart because if I follow the line, it will tell me how heavy she'll be!'.

Lucas *et al.* (2006) reviewed published accounts of lay views of size and growth, and noted that parents may use clothing as a way of assessing whether their baby is of average size, with the potential that attained size could be a way of assessing parenting competence.

During the early decades of the 20th century, mothers were recommended to conduct test weighing – weighing the baby before and after every feed. Liddiard (1933) suggested hiring scales or borrowing from tradesmen over a weekend, so grocer's scales may literally have been used (see also *Lancet*, 1957). A contrast to this 'grocer-like' way of approaching baby care was noted by Abel (1986, p. 45), who conducted interviews in Tamil Nadu to try to understand why local mothers avoided regular baby weighing. The women felt 'that weighing is related to the sale of goods […] they do not want to sell their children'. This suggests that our conceptions of infant growth almost as a commodity are grounded in specific cultural understandings. This may be fostered by the widespread use of infant formula. When breastfeeding, a baby given access to the breast can regulate her or his own intake (Woolridge, 1995a,b), but formula-feeding mothers are instructed to judge the amount to give by the baby's weight: this has been the basis of calculations since the late 19th century (Wickes, 1952, 1953). Many of the women in this study who were breastfeeding also used formula. Some had used it for previous babies. It may be that decades of artificial feeding have entwined infant weighing and household shopping in their – and our – consciousness.

Although explicit resistance to grocer's weighing was not voiced by any of the women in this study. Wendy, who weighed infrequently, did turn the concept on its head, remarking: 'I haven't had her weighed [recently], I haven't got a clue, but she's in nappies to fit 18 to 40 pounds'. Those who weighed regularly might also mention this alternative way of seeing growth. Una mentioned: 'you can see as his clothes get tight'.

Accountability and reverse accountability weighing

This is the aspect of infant weight gain most often noted in discussions with breastfeeding women (Behague, 1993; Dykes and Williams, 1999; Murphy, 1999; Mahon-Daly and Andrews, 2002; Redsell *et al.*, 2010). Parents rear their children to be new members of their society, and each cultural group has norms of child-rearing which it seeks to enforce – through custom, law and 'informal techniques of social control' (Spradley, 1980, p. 152). Members of society have an interest in how infants are raised and parents and carers are accountable.

During the process of eliciting staff feedback on weight monitoring when creating the UK-WHO growth charts, a constant concern was expressed about the chart as the legal record which might be required to be presented, ultimately, in court (Wright *et al.*, 2011). In this sense both parents and staff are accountable for their care and attention to the charted weight.

By having recorded baby weights, particularly if these conform to the centiles on the chart, UK mothers demonstrate that they are caring adequately for the physical need for infant growth. Even where the recorded weight is of some concern, mothers can demonstrate proper concern for monitoring growth by collecting the record (Olin Lauritzen and Sachs, 2001). All parents are expected to feel accountable, but the widespread lack of trust in the adequacy of breastfeeding may make the feeling particularly acute for breastfeeding mothers.

Health visitors were asked if they thought that breastfeeding women were more concerned with weighing than women who were bottle feeding and gave mixed views:

I think, particularly breastfed babies, it's the only way that mums can gauge if babies are gaining weight and if they're feeding successfully.... It's a way of showing the mums that their babies are thriving, and they've no other way of seeing it other than weight.

Lots of women who are bottle feeding also do, because they are also wanting... the same feedback from the weight gain that the baby's doing fine.

Breastfeeding women in the clinic and in interviews stressed their desire to have their baby weighed in order to assure themselves that the baby was growing on their milk. In an early visit to the clinic Linda said: 'I like to see the weight every fortnight because with breastfeeding you can't tell how they are doing'. Val noted:

Knowing that I was doing me job, really, that it was working. Yeah, it gives you a good sort of indication, if they are putting on weight. 'Cos that's what I was worrying more than anything, is he getting enough off me and is he gaining weight?

Weight was important as something to report to other members of the family who are not often present at clinic sessions and for whom this may be a way of asking for and receiving information about the baby.

My sister asked a few times whether we'd had her weighed yet... so I could tell her that she put on eight ounces. She was quite shocked really, 'cos she thought that was quite a lot. (Wendy)

Isla, who had weighed her baby at the breastfeeding group even though she was due to attend to have her son immunised the next day when he would be weighed, reported: 'people are ringing up to see how big he is'.

Tessa had decided not to weigh routinely, but still felt the pressure of accountability, saying: 'we were doing a bit of a family tour, and I wanted to know what the weight gain was because they would all ask'. It was not just families, but the wider social circle who was interested. Jayne reported: 'everyone at my husband's work wanted to know how much he weighed'.

When the weight was not as good as hoped for, there could be pressure on the mother to change how she was feeding the baby:

> When she wasn't gaining weight my mother-in-law was doing her best 'put her on the bottle, put her on the bottle'. (Hannah)

Even when the weight was going well, family comments could show a lack of faith in the ability of breast milk to sustain a baby:

> I've had comments from the in-laws, like… when she's put a reasonable amount on, 'oh, you must have some good stuff then'. As if it's like impossible, like that you could possibly feed your own baby and it would grow. (Sarah)

> They just think he's a big elephant. My grandma keeps saying 'what are you feeding him on?', 'just breast milk', 'are you sure? What are you putting in it?'. (Una)

Health visitors were aware of the influence of families:

> The generation that we're in now, their parents were bottlefed…. And umm, they say 'that child's starving, give it a bottle', or 'it's unsettled, a bottle will help it sleep'.

> It would unfortunately seem that that is a bigger battle for… working-class women, basically. They seem to be more likely, anecdotally, to have a partner, or a family member, a matriarchal figure, who will be there in the background, saying 'well I think if you gave a bottle, it would be better'.

Pressure could come from the mother's own concern for the baby and focus on weight:

> My mum and everyone they are fine and they are very supportive, none of them have said to give him a bottle. It's me. I don't want him to suffer because of how I am feeding him. (Suze)

Tessa remarked; 'it's the only thing you can ask about a baby', but as babies got older, weight might be less of a focus:

Mum [baby's grandmother] does still ask 'is she putting weight on?' but perhaps not as often... I think the novelty's gone off it... (Rachel)

However, it might be mothers' preoccupation with weight, as reinforced by the clinic, that encouraged families and others to concentrate on this aspect of baby development. Zoë said she was asked to report the weight to her mum and when asked if other friends and family enquired about the weight, she replied: 'I don't know whether they ask, but they get told!'.

The urge to weigh to make sure the baby was gaining enough could act in reverse in two different ways. Olwen, whose baby grew quickly, said, 'I didn't dare weigh her at clinic, 'cos they'd say: 'oh Cora's a biggie'. She might have been uncomfortable at having attention on her daughter's 'good' performance or this might have been concern at the possibility that the baby was getting too big – a worry Zoë mentioned.

Olivia and Wendy both felt that one reason they weighed infrequently was that they could tell that their babies were getting bigger: 'I tend to just to tell by looking at her, really' (Wendy).

Moving between reasons for weighing

Women did not give one reason for all weighing visits, or even only one reason for each clinic visit. For example, Zoë described intense medical weighing while she and her baby were in hospital for early neonatal weight loss, and explained how she subsequently set the frequency:

I go see my mum once a month – I try and get her weighed just before I go... so I've got a reasonable tale to tell her. And... I think that's a reasonable amount really, just so I know that she's making the right progress.... My main concern is she doesn't like you taking her clothes off, and putting her clothes on, particularly sleeves and things... all I'm doing really is going down there, taking her clothes off, putting her on the scales, and putting them back on... I don't feel that the information that I'm getting is that important, to make her that stressed really. I mean I do think it's important that we know go every now and again. But I don't want to go every week, because it's too much for her.

Zoë cites her need to account to her mother, which helps set the timing; the stress of the visit for the baby, a reason for not weighing, categorised as reverse recreational; an absence of other reasons to go to the clinic, characterised as reverse portal; and finally notes the information is not that important at this stage – a reverse medical reason for attending.

Implications for practice

Weight change in the early weeks is a physical indicator of health and the establishment of effective feeding, and parents and staff both wish to monitor and interpret this. As babies grow there continues to be a need to chart this physical process. However, in the UK, attention to this may dominate and even exclude other measures of development and wellbeing. In a culture where breastfeeding is perceived as a rather chancy method of infant feeding, perhaps it is inevitable that breastfeeding women in particular focus on weight gain and interpret their baby's wellbeing though this measure (Sachs *et al.*, 2006b).

During the development of the UK-WHO growth charts, information in the parent-held child health record for parents was written and explicit guidance given on weighing frequency, using recommendations already in place. Information was included on understanding centile position, how weight gain will roughly track along (rather than absolutely follow) a centile, and temporary weight loss during short illnesses. No reports are available which examine whether this information has altered weighing frequency in practice or parental understanding of infant growth and development.

Weighing is often assumed to be a beneficial, or at least benign, activity. Women, however, may find that a weighing encounter raises concerns about their baby even when infant growth is following a normal pattern (Sachs *et al.*, 2006b). At the least, this can cause unwarranted worry, but it could also lead to inappropriate changes in feeding, such as introducing infant formula milk supplements to breastfed babies, increasing the number of infant formula milk feeds or adding additional powder to infant formula feeds for non-breastfed babies, premature introduction of solid foods, or overusing calorie-rich foods. However, it may be that general discussion of the dangers of overweight and obesity are changing perceptions that pursuing the maximum growth of babies is desirable and healthy (Lucas *et al.*, 2006).

The training of staff, using the materials developed by the UK-WHO Growth Chart group (Royal College of Paediatrics and Child Health, 2009; Department of Health, 2009) is intended to help them interpret weight measures with parents in clinics. Since the time of the study reported here, health visiting staff are increasingly likely to undertake training on breastfeeding management as part of a wider move to ensure that community services meet the requirements of the UNICEF Baby Friendly in the Community programme. In training modelled on UNICEF guidelines, the main causes of inadequate growth in breastfed babies are given as a lack of efficient attachment of the baby to the breast, impeding adequate milk transfer, and infrequent feeding, perhaps through externally imposed routines, or because the mother is insufficiently tuned-in to infant feeding cues (UNICEF UK Baby Friendly Initiative, 2008).

The examination of the motivations that women give for weighing their babies allows the possibility that some of their identified needs could be satisfied in other ways. In doing this, attention to the wider physical development of the baby as well as emotional and relational development of both mother and baby may be enhanced.

The physical and social organisation of child health clinics, which appear to assume weighing as the first action when parents enter the clinic, could be altered. The layout may often mean that the weighing scales are visible as soon as parents enter, with seating arranged so that parents can prepare their baby as they wait to speak to the health visiting staff. Simple changes such as putting scales in a less obvious place and structuring encounters so that weighing is not presumed might lessen the assumption that to access the clinic, the baby must be weighed as he or she comes through the portal. Fulford (2001) reports on how health visitors addressed this in one area by changing from drop-in clinics to a system of booked appointments. Arranging group sessions where scales are not on view is another issue which deserves consideration. However, staff will also need to consider how they speak to parents so as not to assume that attendance at clinic is for the purpose of weighing the baby.

It is important to ensure that parents value interactions with staff and seek input, so that staff can monitor infant wellbeing, offer support and information on early parenting, including feeding, and reinforce a number of public health messages in the teachable moment of new parenthood. This study identifies that parents particularly value the keepsake aspect of their parent-held child health record. At the time that the UK-WHO charts were inserted into the parent-held child health record, revised pictures in the section on child development were included (Helen Bedford, personal communication). These could feature more in discussions between parents and staff and parents encouraged to enter information on the development abilities of their baby.

Tchibindat *et al.* (2004) conducted interviews with women and health workers in the Republic of Congo and discovered that women in that cultural context preferred to focus on broader developmental milestones rather than weight for evaluating the progress of their babies. It may be that giving attention to recording such milestones could help parents, families and health staff take a more holistic view of infant progress and lessen the attention on the completed chart and the recreational aspects of weighing. A weight chart from the mid-20th century (Liddiard, 1946) incorporated developmental milestones, and an experiment of conducting a 'non-weighing session' at a baby clinic taught mothers 'to observe small changes in wellbeing, happiness, energy, and temper of the baby and to accept these as part of the wide variations in normal progress' (*Lancet*, 1957, p. 1273). Perhaps this approach could be revived.

One health visitor in the study introduced a note of caution:

> Mums say 'he should be sitting by six months and should be crawling by eight months' and they're on the phone to you saying there is a problem. They're sure something is wrong, but it doesn't work like that.

The simple substitution of measurement from weight to development may not lessen frequent reliance on an external, quantitative yardstick and could become another issue for families to worry over. Care would be required to avoid this.

In this study, it was clear that family members, work colleagues and others focus on the weight of the baby as the measure of wellbeing and success of maternal care. Mothers therefore feel they need to report on weights as they are accountable for the baby's wellbeing. Work with mothers attending clinic needs to be widened to include whole communities.

Overall, infant health and wellbeing could benefit from a change in the assumption that health is easily measured through physical weight gain, and that weight increases will happen in a linear, mechanical way due to feeding and care – the grocer-like approach. Current policy recommendations emphasise the importance of early intervention and support to build infant social and emotional capacity in order to ensure lifelong wellbeing and achievement (Gerhardt, 2004; Allen, 2011; C4EO, 2011). Breastfeeding is part of the support system for infant emotional and social development, and fosters the ability of the baby to form relationships, but such outcomes are less easily measured and monitored than weight gain.

Developing parents' abilities to develop and support their relationship with their baby is a primary aim of postnatal care. The impulses which bring women into contact with health care staff in order to reassure themselves that their infant is growing are important to understand and to address in a way which fosters the developing relationship. Outcomes can be enriched if an understanding of wellbeing wider than physical growth is involved.

The inclusion of information on the recommended frequency of weighing in the parent-held child health record may help to clarify medical reasons for weighing babies. In order to succeed in helping parents understand how they can monitor wider aspects of infant development, it could be useful to ensure that needs for keepsakes and meeting their accountability to the wider community can be met. These changes may then lessen the assumption that weighing babies is a recreational activity; if this is accompanied by an increase in attending to emotional development it may result in improved outcomes for infants and families.

References

Abel, R. (1986) Traditional beliefs against weighing children regularly. *Tropical Doctor*, **16**, 45–6.

Allen, G. (2011) *Early Intervention: The Next Steps. An Independent Report to Her Majesty's Government*. Available at: http://www.dwp.gov.uk/docs/early-intervention-next-steps.pdf (accessed 10 July 2012).

Behague, D. (1993) Growth monitoring and the promotion of breastfeeding. *Social Science and Medicine*, **37**, 1565–78.

Ben-Joseph, E. P., Dowshen, S. A. and Izenberg, N. (2007) Public understanding of growth charts: a review of the literature. *Patient Education and Counseling*, **65**, 288–95.

Ben-Joseph, E. P., Dowshen, S. A. and Izenberg, N. (2009) Do parents understand growth charts? A national web-based survey. *Pediatrics*, **124**, 1100–9.

Biswas, B. and Sands, C. (1984) Mothers' reasons for attending a child health clinic. *Health Visitor*, **57**, 41–2.

Bolling, K., Grant, C., Hamlyn, B. and Thornton, A. (2007) *Infant Feeding Survey 2005*. The Information Centre, London.

C4EO (2001) *Grasping the Nettle: Early Intervention for Children, Families and Communities*. Available at: http://www.c4eo.org.uk/themes/earlyintervention/files/early_intervention_grasping_the_nettle_full_report.pdf (accessed 10 July 2012).

Davies, D. P. (2000) Commentary. *Archives of Disease in Childhood*, **82**, 200–1.

Daws, D. (1985) Standing next to the weighing scales. *Journal of Child Psychotherapy*, **11**, 77–85.

Department of Health (2009) *Using the New UK-World Health Organization 0–4 Years Growth Charts: Information for Healthcare Professionals About the Use and Interpretation of Growth Charts*. Available at: http://www.dh.gov.uk/en/Publicationsandstatistics/Publications/PublicationsPolicyAndGuidance/DH_127423 (accessed 5 March 2012).

Dykes, F. and Williams, C. (1999) Falling by the wayside: a phenomenological exploration of perceived breast-milk inadequacy in lactating women. *Midwifery*, **15**, 232–46.

Dykes, F., Richardson-Foster, H., Crossland, N. and Thomson, G. (2012) 'Dancing on a thin line': evaluation of an infant feeding information team to implement the WHO code of marketing of breast-milk substitutes. *Midwifery*, **28**(6), 765–71.

Fulford, S. (2001) The quality agenda: reviewing traditional 'baby clinics'. *Community Practitioner*, **74**, 386–7.

Gerhard, S. (2004) *Why Love Matters: How Affection Shapes a Baby's Brain*. Routledge, Hove.

Hall, D. M. B. (2000) Growth monitoring. *Archives of Disease in Childhood*, **82**, 10–15.

Hall, D. M. B. and Elliman, D. (2003) *Health for All Children*, 4th edn. Oxford University Press, Oxford.

Hamlyn, B., Brooker, S., Olienikova, K. and Woods, S. (2002) *Infant Feeding 2000*. The Stationery Office, London.

Jackson, K. (1990) To have and to hold. *Health Visitor*, **63**, 221–2.

Lancet (1957) On not weighing the baby (comment). *Lancet*, **270**, 1273.

Laraway, K. A., Birch, L. L., Shaffer, M. L. and Paul, I. M. (2010) Parent perception of healthy infant and toddler growth. *Clinical Pediatrics*, **49**(4), 343–9.

Liddiard, M. (1933) *The Mothercraft Manual or the Expectant and Nursing Mother and Baby's First Two Years*, 8th edn. J & A Churchill, London.

Liddiard, M. (1946) *The Mothercraft Manual or the Expectant and Nursing Mother and Baby's First Two Years*, 10th edn. J & A Churchill, London.

Lucas, P. J., Arai, L., Baird, J., Kleijnen, J., Law, C. M. and Roberts, H. M. (2006) A systematic review of lay views about infant size and growth. *Archives of Disease in Childhood*, **92**(2), 120–7.

Mahon-Daly, P. and Andrews, G. J. (2002) Liminality and breastfeeding: women negotiating space and two bodies. *Health and Place*, **8**, 61–76.

Murphy, E. (1999) 'Breast is best': infant feeding decisions and maternal deviance. *Sociology of Health and Illness*, **21**, 187–208.

Olin Lauritzen, S. and Sachs, L. (2001) Normality, risk and the future: implicit communication of threat in health surveillance. *Sociology of Health and Illness*, **23**, 497–516.

Owen, M. (1991) Child Health Record sets new standards. *Midwife Health Visitor & Community Nurse*, **27**, 103–5.

Royal College of Paediatrics and Child Health (2009) UK-WHO Growth Charts. Available at: http://www.rcpch.ac.uk/Research/UK-WHO-Growth-Charts (accessed 5 March 2012).

Royal College of Paediatrics and Child Health, Department of Health, World Health Organization (2009) *UK-WHO Growth Charts, Nought to Four Years*. Royal College of Paediatrics and Child Health, London.

Redsell, S. A., Atkinson, P., Nathan, D., Siriwardena, A. N., Swift, J. A. and Glazebrook, C. (2010) Parents' beliefs about appropriate infant size, growth and feeding behaviour: implications for the prevention of childhood obesity. *BMC Public Health*, **10**, 711.

Sachs, M. (2005) Following the Line: an ethnographic study of the influence of routine baby weighing on breastfeeding women in a town in the northwest of England. *Unpublished PhD Thesis*, University of Central Lancashire.

Sachs, M., Dykes, F. and Carter, B. (2006a) Weight monitoring of breastfed babies in the UK – interpreting, explaining and intervening. *Maternal and Child Nutrition*, **2**, 3–18.

Sachs, M., Dykes, F. and Carter, B. (2006b) Feeding by numbers: an ethnographic study of how breastfeeding women understand their babies' weight charts. *International Breastfeeding Journal*, **1**, 29.

Sachs, M., Sharp, L., Bedford, H. and Wright, C. M. (2011) 'Now I understand': consulting parents on chart design and parental information for the UK-WHO child growth charts. *Child: Care, Health and Development*, **38**, 435–40.

Sefi, S. and MacFarlane, A. (1985) Child health clinics: why mothers attend. *Health Visitor*, **58**, 129–30.

Sharpe, H. and Lowenthal, D. (1992) Reasons for attending GP or health authority clinics. *Health Visitor*, **65**, 349–51.

Shaw-Flach, A. (2003) Health visitors' experiences of working with breastfeeding women – a phenomenological study. *Unpublished MSc Thesis*, University of Cambridge.

Spradley, J. P. (1980) *Participant Observation.* Harcourt, Brace, Jovanovitch, Fort Worth.

Strauss, A. and Corbin, J. (2002) *Basics of Qualitative Research.* Sage Publications, Thousand Oaks.

Tappin, D., Britten, J., Broadfoot, M. and McInnes, R. (2006) The effect of health visitors on breastfeeding in Glasgow. *International Breastfeeding Journal*, **1**, 11.

Tchibindat, F., Martin-Prevel, Y., Kolsteren, P., Marie, B. and Delpeuch, F. (2004) Bringing together viewpoints of mothers and health workers to enhance monitoring and promotion of growth and development of children: a case study from the Republic of Congo. *Journal of Health and Population Nutrition*, **22**, 59–67.

UNICEF UK Baby Friendly Initiative (2008) *Three-day Course in Breastfeeding Management.* UNICEF, London.

Wickes, I. G. (1952) Rate of gain and satiety in early infancy. *Archives of Disease in Childhood*, **140**, 449–56.

Wickes, I. G. (1953) A history of infant feeding: part IV – nineteenth century continued. *Archives of Disease in Childhood*, **28**, 416–22.

Weaver, L. T. (2010) In the balance: weighing babies and the birth of the infant welfare clinic. *Bulletin of the History of Medicine*, **84**, 30–57.

Woolford, S. J., Clark, S. J., Lumeng, J. C. *et al.* (2007) Maternal perspectives on growth and nutrition counseling provided at preschool well-child visits. *Journal of the National Medical Association*, **99**, 153–8.

Woolridge, M. W. (1995a) Baby-controlled breastfeeding: biocultural implications. In: *Breastfeeding: Biocultural Perspectives* (eds. P. Stuart-Macadam and K. Dettwyler), pp. 217–42. Aldine de Gruyter, New York.

Woolridge, M. W. (1995b) Breastfeeding: physiology into practice. In: *Nutrition in Child Health: Proceedings of Conference Jointly Organised by the Royal College of Physicians of London and the British Paediatric Association* (ed. D. P. Davies), pp. 13–31. RCPL Press, London.

Wright, C. M. (2000) Identification and management of failure to thrive: a community perspective. *Archives of Disease in Childhood*, **82**, 5–9.

Wright, C. M., Williams, A. F., Elliman, D., Bedford, H., Birks, E., Butler, G., Sachs, M., Moy, R. J. and Cole, T. J. (2010) Using the new UK-WHO growth charts. *British Medical Journal*, **340**, 647–50.

Wright, C. M., Sachs, M., Short, J., Sharp, L., Cameron, K. and Moy, R. J. (2011) Designing new UK-WHO growth charts: implications for health staff use and understanding of charts and growth monitoring. *Maternal and Child Nutrition*, **8**, 371–9.

CHAPTER 6

Issues of expertise: health professionals' views of a breastfeeding peer support service

Nicola Crossland and Gill Thomson

Introduction

The UK currently has one of the lowest breastfeeding rates in Europe. Although 81% of mothers initiate breastfeeding, this rate drops to 34% of women providing 'any' breast milk at six months (Health and Social Care Information Centre, 2012). The proportion of women initiating and sustaining breastfeeding in the UK is also substantially lower within socially deprived communities (Health and Social Care Information Centre, 2012). Breastfeeding promotes the short- and long-term health of mothers and babies (Hoddinott *et al.*, 2008), and infant feeding is internationally recognised as a public health issue (WHO, 2000, 2003). Furthermore, whilst there is strong policy support for breastfeeding in the UK (Department of Health, 2004a,b; Department for Education and Skills, 2004) a recent review of 33 countries indicated that only six have a written national policy on infant and young child feeding (World Breastfeeding Trends Initiative, 2010).

Breastfeeding peer support is viewed as an important means to improve breastfeeding rates. While different variations of peer support exist, we adopt the definition provided by Dennis (2003, p. 329):

> The provision of emotional, appraisal, and informational assistance by a created social network member who possesses experiential knowledge of a specific behaviour or stressor and similar characteristics as the target population.

Peer supporters are often members of the local community who have breastfed their own children and who serve as positive role models for women with regard to breastfeeding (McInnes *et al.*, 2000; Anderson and Grant, 2001; Alexander *et al.*, 2003; Dykes, 2003, 2005a; Kirkham *et al.*, 2006; Curtis *et al.*, 2007, Thomson *et al.*, 2012). Women with good social support, such as positive role models who accept breastfeeding as normal or supportive familial networks, breastfeed for longer than those who do not (Ekstrom *et al.*, 2003; Greene *et al.*, 2003; Grassley and Eschiti, 2008; Hoddinott *et al.*, 2010). The World Health Organization recommends implementation of breastfeeding peer support projects (WHO, 2003), and in the UK, the Department of Health and the National Institute for Health and Clinical Excellence (NICE) recommend, as a priority, the implementation of sustainable peer support programmes (Department of Health, 2002; NICE, 2008a,b), supported by breastfeeding peer support commissioning guidelines (NICE, 2008b; Department of Health, 2009). In the UK breastfeeding peer support programmes are increasingly being established within NHS maternity services, where breastfeeding peer supporters work alongside health professionals in hospital and community settings.

To date, the evidence concerning the impact and efficacy of peer support on breastfeeding rates (e.g. initiation, duration and continuation) is inconsistent. A systematic review and meta-regression of randomised controlled trials undertaken by Jolly *et al.* (2012) identified that while peer support interventions had a significantly greater effect on any and exclusive breastfeeding in low- or middle-income countries, this effect was not identified in high-income countries, particularly within the UK. This meta-analysis also revealed that while the 'intensity' of peer support provision (e.g. more than five contacts) and when support was only delivered postnatally positively influenced breastfeeding rates, these influences were not identified for exclusive breastfeeding rates. In a review of the evidence, Hoddinott *et al.* (2011) identify nine UK-based trials undertaken since 2000 that have not significantly improved breastfeeding rates, highlighting how these studies contrast with the positive outcomes on breastfeeding initiation and/or duration identified within a review of international studies (Chung *et al.*, 2008) or an earlier synthesis undertaken by Britton *et al.* (2007). Hoddinott *et al*'s review suggests that the discrepancies and inefficacy of these trials' results may be attributed to the wide heterogeneity in the design of the studies in terms of timing, amount, intensity, duration and consistency of intervention components; how, where, when and by whom the intervention was delivered; how the intervention was offered, i.e. reactive or proactive; how the intervention influences and is supported by existing care provision; contamination effects across the trial arm;

variation in the recruitment/inclusion criteria; wider contextual issues (e.g. BFI accreditation) in the local area; and outcome measurements used. For example, trials where workers made contact early in the postnatal period have demonstrated greater evidence of effect (Chapman *et al.*, 2004; Anderson *et al.*, 2005) compared to those where little contact occurred in the first week (Graffy *et al.*, 2004).

Most qualitative studies of breastfeeding peer support have focused on the experiences and perceptions of the breastfeeding mothers receiving the support services (Scott and Mostyn, 2003; Ingram *et al.*, 2005; Hoddinott *et al.*, 2006; Hegney *et al.*, 2008; Meier *et al.*, 2007; Wade *et al.*, 2009; Nor *et al.*, 2009; Nankunda *et al.*, 2010; Rossman *et al.* 2011; Thomson *et al.*, 2012). Findings from these studies indicate that women value peer supporters as mothers with similar experiences who can relate to their own situation, and in some cases, women establish emotional closeness with peer supporters, some comparing the relationship to a family relationship, or that of a friend or a role model (Scott and Mostyn, 2003; Hoddinott *et al.*, 2006; Meier *et al.*, 2007; Hegney *et al.*, 2008; Nankunda *et al.*, 2010; Rossman *et al.* 2011; Thomson *et al.*, 2012). However, some studies describe less positive perspectives, with some women reporting feeling that the peer supporter was too old to be a peer to them, or simply that she was a stranger to them (Wade *et al.*, 2009; Nankunda *et al.*, 2010) and, in one study, uptake of one-to-one support was low because mothers felt it would intrude on their privacy, and because they anticipated that peer support would be pressurising (Hoddinott *et al.*, 2006). Similarly, Nor *et al.* (2009) found that some women were afraid and suspicious of peer support and gave false information in order to avoid being contacted by peer supporters. More commonly, though, studies have found that women appreciated the increased social interaction and encouragement they gained from peer support (Scott and Mostyn, 2003; Hoddinott *et al.*, 2006; Meier *et al.*, 2007; Nankunda *et al.*, 2010).

Qualitative studies have found that women perceive peer supporters to have more time than health professionals to spend with them (Scott and Mostyn, 2003; Nankunda *et al.*, 2010; Thomson *et al.*, 2012). Findings suggest also that women appreciate receiving information about breastfeeding in a familiar language and form, and value the opportunity to assess information for themselves and decide whether it was relevant to their situation (Nankunda *et al.*, 2010), as well as appreciating the opportunity to ask questions (Martens, 2002; Rossman *et al.*, 2011). The communication and relational skills of the peer supporter are crucial to this information-giving role: as Nor and colleagues (2009) demonstrated in their study of infant feeding peer support in an area of high HIV prevalence, where peer supporters attempted to advise women without acknowledging their existing knowledge and experience, their information was seen by women as irrelevant, and this limited the extent to which peer supporters could counsel women.

Breastfeeding peer support has been shown to influence other areas of mothers' lives in addition to infant feeding. For example, Wade and colleagues (2009) found that peer support improved women's mental health, increased their self-esteem and confidence, and promoted feelings of wellbeing and competence. Women reported paying more attention to their own diet and having an increased interest in healthy eating (Wade *et al.*, 2009). In the study by Nor *et al.* (2009) discussed above, peer support offered women the chance to talk to someone about their HIV status, which they felt they could not discuss with anyone else, thus lessening their sense of isolation.

To date very few qualitative studies have investigated the experiences of health professionals in working alongside breastfeeding peer supporters (e.g. Raine 2003; Curtis *et al.*, 2007; Rossman *et al.*, 2012). As noted by Dykes (2005a) in her analysis of the implications of implementing breastfeeding peer support programmes, positive health professional engagement with such schemes is critical to their success. In an evaluation of a breastfeeding peer support intervention, Raine (2003) reported on the perspectives of six health professionals (midwives and health visitors) and six peer supporters. She found that acceptance among health professionals of the programme was variable and it took time to achieve, and argued for ongoing reinforcement to health professionals of the benefits of peer support. Curtis and colleagues, in their qualitative study of a UK-based breastfeeding peer support programme, describe both the benefits of this programme for health professionals and the tensions and ambiguities that arose (Curtis *et al.*, 2007). They conducted focus groups with nine health professionals (midwives and health visitors) and seven peer supporters, and found themes of 'benefits of working with peer support scheme', which included the supporting themes of 'easing the workload' and 'learning from volunteers and developing new ways of working', and the theme of 'constraints on enabling working relationships', which comprised the supporting themes 'invisible boundaries', 'gatekeeping by health professionals', 'working with versus working for health professionals'. They found that health professionals were able to significantly affect peer supporters' access to breastfeeding women and consequently, their effectiveness. Finally, Rossman and colleagues (2012) approached the issue of health professionals' perspectives of breastfeeding peer support through an analysis of breastfeeding peer support within the neonatal intensive care environment. The peer supporters in this study were mothers who had previously had a baby in the same neonatal intensive care unit, and who were given training specific to this highly specialised environment.

This study reported a largely positive response from health professionals, who felt that peer support fulfilled a specific need within the unit, lessened their workload, and enhanced the quality of care given to families. Very few episodes of friction were reported between the professionals and peer supporters in this study.

In this chapter we discuss findings from an evaluation of the implementation of a breastfeeding peer support programme in a maternity service in the northwest of England. As part of this study, we explored health professionals' views and experiences of working alongside breastfeeding peer supporters. A recurrent issue to emerge from the consultations related to how the peer supporters were perceived, or not, to be 'experts' in breastfeeding support. In this chapter, we discuss the health professionals' perceptions of the breastfeeding peer supporters 'expertise', in relation to how they deliver care to women, and the implications of this on their own professional practice.

After outlining the context of the study and methods of the evaluation, we provide a brief theoretical consideration of the notion of 'expertise'. This is followed by a thematic interpretation of the health professionals' attitudes towards the perceived 'expert' status of the peer supporters, together with the associated facilitators and tensions of integrating a breastfeeding peer support service in practice.

Evaluation of a breastfeeding peer support programme

In May 2009, a maternity trust in the north-west of England commissioned one of the UK's national breastfeeding organisations to provide a comprehensive model of breastfeeding peer support service across the perinatal period. This programme aimed to provide an additional tier of breastfeeding support and to increase initiation and breastfeeding duration rates (at 6–8 weeks postnatal). During the service evaluation period (2009–2011), this peer support service was being delivered by nine paid peer supporters, all of whom worked on a part-time basis. Three peer supporters provided breastfeeding support antenatally or on the hospital postnatal wards, four provided breastfeeding support in the community, and two were employed in a coordinator capacity. The service was also supported by volunteer peer supporters. All the peer supporters delivering this service were local mothers who had breastfed their child(ren), and who had accessed accredited training via a six- or 12-week training course. Most of the paid supporters had also accessed/completed a 12-month-long training programme. The peer support programme provided the following services.

Antenatal provision involved two levels of breastfeeding workshops. The first breastfeeding workshop was targeted to pregnant women post-24 weeks' gestation. The second workshop targeted women who were post-30 weeks' gestation. Women and a partner/friend/family member are invited to attend these workshops. Both sessions covered information detailed within the 'Ten Steps to Successful Breastfeeding' (WHO/UNICEF, 1989), and the second workshop specifically targeted the difficulties that women may face in the early postnatal period, such as nipple pain, together with strategies and coping mechanisms to overcome these issues.

The *hospital service* provided bedside breastfeeding information and practical and emotional support daily (morning, afternoon and early evening periods) on the maternity postnatal wards and, where appropriate (following requests or referrals), on the neonatal unit and paediatric ward. The peer supporters worked on rotation to ensure that at least one paid supporter was working each day/shift, supported by volunteer peer supporters where possible.

The *community service* was developed based on the NICE Commissioning Guidelines (2008b). Women were automatically referred in via the hospital peer supporters and contacted within 48 hours of discharge. These women were then offered up to eight weeks of breastfeeding support delivered via home visits, telephone calls, text message or meetings at community locations or events (e.g. breastfeeding groups). This part of the service generally operated on a case-load basis (e.g. the woman was assigned to one of the four community peer supporters); with support provided by another member of the team if the nominated supporter was unavailable.

Referral mechanisms and promotional materials were also in place, so that health and community professionals could direct women to the service or for women to self-refer. The service was open to any breastfeeding woman with a baby younger than eight weeks residing within the geographical area. The community peer supporters also coordinated breastfeeding support groups at local children's centres, and produced breastfeeding information display boards at the community centres in the locality. Peer supporters were also expected to encourage and/or accompany women they were supporting to local breastfeeding support groups to promote access to ongoing support after discharge from the service.

The MAINN unit at the University of Central Lancashire undertook an in-depth evaluation of this breastfeeding peer support service over a two-year period (March 2009–February 2011), funded by the local Primary Care Trust (first year) and the breastfeeding organisation (second year). The project was reviewed by the National Research Ethics Committee and received ethics approval by the relevant University Faculty of Health Research Committee and the Research and Design Unit at the maternity trust. This project was an action-based study involving consultations with service users (*n* = 47); health professionals (*n* = 40; comprising community and hospital based midwifery staff (*n* = 26), health visiting staff (*n* = 10), neonatal staff (*n* = 4)); and peer supporters (*n* = 19). Focus groups and interviews were undertaken to explore participants' attitudes, experiences and perceptions of the service as well as the impact of this service on breastfeeding continuation. Analysis was undertaken using the thematic network analysis model by Attride-Stirling (2001) to form basic, organising and global themes, supported by the MAXQDA qualitative software package. An analysis of women's experiences of the service has been published elsewhere (Thomson *et al.* 2012).

What is an expert?

The *New Shorter Oxford English Dictionary* defines 'expertise' as 'expert opinion or knowledge; know how, skill or expertness in something', and defines an 'expert' as '(1) experienced (in); having experience (of); (2) Trained by practice or experience; skilled, skilful (at, in, with); or (3) Tried, proved by experience' (Brown, 1993). These definitions highlight the importance of experience and practical knowledge in gaining expertise, and allude to the idea that theoretical knowledge alone is not sufficient to become 'expert'.

Researchers exploring the notion of expertise have variously focused on this element of practice and experience. For example, Ericsson (1996) proposed that expertise in a particular skill is gained through accumulating a large number of hours of deliberate practice, while Hatano and Inagki (1986) discuss 'adaptive expertise', that is, the ability of the expert to adapt his or her theoretical knowledge to novel situations. Schön's (1983) concept of the 'Reflective Practitioner', which has been widely used in discussing professional development in healthcare, emphasises 'reflection in action', where the practitioner is attentive to his or her own feelings and the phenomena they encounter, and 'reflection on action', that is, deliberation after the fact: both types of reflection help to build expertise.

Dreyfus and Dreyfus (1980) present a model of skill acquisition in which the novice progresses through five stages of competency to reach expert status, by which point his or her depth of experience allows an intuitive understanding which no longer relies on rules. This model of skill acquisition provides the basis for one of the most influential models of expertise within the nursing field, developed by Benner (2001). Benner interviewed nurses at varying stages from 'novice' to 'expert' based on their length of practice, and found that as nurses move from being novices to becoming experts, they become less reliant on abstract or theoretical knowledge to inform their decisions; rather, they increasingly start to depend on the wealth of their experience and intuitive knowledge to guide their care (Benner, 2001). An interpretive phenomenological study has also explored the nature of intrapartum midwifery expertise (Simpson and Downe, 2010). This study uncovered three domains of expert midwifery practice: 'physiological expertise', 'technical expertise' and 'integrated expertise'.

While these studies provide useful insights into what constitutes an expert, they do not assess the more contentious aspects of who is perceived to be the 'expert', nor the problems that can emerge when different 'experts' compete for authoritative status. As stated by Turner, expertise can be 'treated as a kind of possession which privileges its possessors with powers that the people cannot successfully control, and cannot acquire and share in' (Turner, 2001, p. 123). Expert status must be conferred: by society or institutions, by other experts, but also by non-experts who must acknowledge the validity of the expert's knowledge even though they do not possess this knowledge themselves (Koppl, 2010). When different groups of experts compete for primacy, the outcome may depend on the type of knowledge that is in dispute (Berger and Luckmann, 1967, p. 136). Where expertise has practical relevance, its validity can be asserted empirically, whereas competition between highly abstract bodies of knowledge cannot be settled in this way, being either continually contested or settled socially by being accepted by the dominant social group (Berger and Luckmann, 1967, p. 137).

Findings

During this evaluation a number of global themes emerged in relation to the 'hope' that peer supporters provided to women (Thomson *et al.*, 2012), and the difficulties that peer supporters faced as they moved into more 'professionalised' roles (Aiken and Thomson, 2013). In this chapter we present the global theme entitled 'Issues of expertise'. There are four underpinning organising themes (and their associated basic themes): (1) 'mother-to-mother care', which describes the attributes and practices of an effective breastfeeding supporter; (2) 'theoretical and practical knowledge', which discusses how health professionals benefited from or disputed the expert status of the peer supporters; (3) 'deterring and complementing service delivery', which relates to the consequences of the peer supporters' expertise, in terms of benefits for service users and increased job satisfaction for themselves, and concerns about the potential for peer support to diminish the professional role; and (4) 'gatekeeping', which encapsulates how health professionals sought to control both access and information, in order to protect their role and define standards of practice. An overview of the organising and basic themes is depicted in Figure 6.1.

Whilst no papers have specifically considered the expert status or nature of breastfeeding peer supporters, in our interpretations we have reflected on the

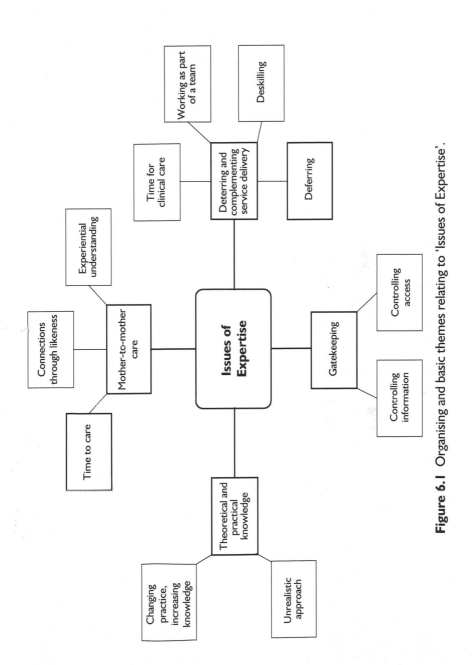

Figure 6.1 Organising and basic themes relating to 'Issues of Expertise'.

theoretical considerations of expertise to contextualise the points being made. Each of the themes and sub-themes are now described and discussed, contextualised by a selection of the participants' quotes. Pseudonyms have been used to protect the participants' identities.

Mother-to-mother care

The 'mother-to-mother' theme relates to the actual attributes of the peer supporters' expertise: how the peer supporters could deliver a level of 'expert practice' which health professionals sometimes perceived that they themselves could not. The sub-themes discussed relate to 'time to care', 'connections through likeness' and 'experiential understanding'. This theme highlights how the nature of the health professional–mother relationship, some of the health professionals' lack of direct experience of breastfeeding, and the inherent constraints of professional practice often inhibited them from incorporating the attributes of mother-to-mother support into their own practice.

Time to care

Having enough time – to lessen anxiety and stress and encourage women to relax, to build a rapport, to observe a feed and offer practical suggestions – is repeatedly emphasised in the literature as a fundamental element of effective breastfeeding support (Dykes, 2005b; Schmied *et al.*, 2011). Health professionals commented on the peer supporters' capacity to spend sufficient time with women, and valued the better service they saw women receiving as a result:

> When I see the peer supporters working they are not rushed at all. The women are made to feel – I am here for as long as you need me. That is how it should be. (Rachel, Midwifery).

Peer supporters were perceived to have time to spend with women due to the nature of their role, and the fact that they were not subject to the same time pressures and competing demands that the health professionals were faced with. The peer supporters were able to demonstrate this capacity through their style of engagement, which subsequently facilitated a more fruitful dialogue with women:

> Women are very perceptive and they do know when people are busy and they don't ask questions and they will just say 'Yes everything is fine' and I am sure that there are times when some people actually ask closed questions as opposed to giving the woman time to tell them how they feel. When you have got the mother-to-mother they have got the time and nobody is saying to them 'Why did you not do all these visits?' which

sometimes happens within the profession that one person manages to do 12 visits where someone else only does six, and 'only' is the operative word that is used. (Suzanne, Midwifery).

Connections through likeness

Many health professionals believed that the non-clinical status of the peer supporters was the key to their ability to build a connection with women. The fact that peer supporters worked outside of professional rule-bound remits, did not wear a clinical uniform and provided support and care as a woman with shared experiences, meant that the peer supporters and mothers were on a more equal footing. As with having 'time to care', this connection encouraged open dialogues for women to discuss their concerns with the peer supporters:

Because they are mums and because they have breastfed themselves I think they have got that special rapport and they can relate to them. Whereas we are in a uniform, they are a little bit more casual, isn't it, and the women probably voice concerns to them that they probably don't voice to us. I don't know why, but I think that is a possibility. (Rachel, Midwifery).

In specialised environments such as the neonatal unit, health professionals were cognisant of the likelihood of being seen as authority figures and recognised that their role involved a degree of '*watching*' the mother and her infant. They were aware that this could be a barrier to women's willingness to be '*honest*' about their difficulties, which could then impede their ability to provide effective breastfeeding support:

I think sometimes they tell us that they want to breastfeed and maybe they don't or they tell us what they think we want to hear, so maybe they are a bit more open and honest with them about 'oh I'm really struggling', or 'I'm not sure if I want to do this'. I don't know, maybe they think that we are, especially if the baby is in Intensive Care, they feel a bit watched and a bit judged, because we are there, we are watching them bath the babies, watching them do every feed, so maybe they just like the non-clinical side of it. (Siobhan, Neonatal).

Experiential understanding

Some health professionals viewed their own lack of personal experience of breastfeeding as a disadvantage which undermined both their confidence in their ability to support breastfeeding and their sense of their credibility as an expert from the perspective of the women they were supporting:

> ...they obviously like to hear that this is a mum that has breastfed and done it. Has got the experience. I have not got any children and sometimes they say 'have you got kids' and you go 'No'. Then you think. Just the plain simple fact that they have had their own babies and fed their own babies. Who am I to tell somebody how to breastfeed. Sometimes I think that does happen that they don't want to listen to you as you have never been there. (Siobhan, Neonatal).

The first-hand experience of the peer supporters could therefore be perceived to be a more authentic form of knowledge – '*what it is really like*' – than advice given by health professionals. In this view, the status of the health professional as an authority figure, rather than as an equal, paradoxically delegitimises them as experts in the eyes of the women: their professional knowledge is seen as theoretical and less relevant:

> I think if you have got mother-to-mother doing that then they see each other as equals and I think that is better in many ways than us health professionals telling them what is best. I think it just seeps in through little cracks. Like a drip, drip. (Suzanne, Midwifery).

Theoretical and practical knowledge

This theme concerns how the health professionals described both advancing their own theoretical and practical knowledge through their association with the peer supporters, and also questioning the validity of the peer supporters' knowledge and skills. These two opposing perspectives are illustrated by the sub-themes of 'changing practice, increasing knowledge' and 'unrealistic approach'.

Changing practice, increasing knowledge

In several interviews, health professionals recognised the peer supporters' capabilities in supporting women to breastfeed, and some adopted elements of the peer supporters' approach within their professional practice. Others described using the peer supporters' knowledge and experience as a resource to further their own professional development.

For example, a recurring issue discussed in the interviews was the contrast between the peer supporters' 'hands off' approach, whereby peer supporters aided women without physically touching them, and the tendency of some health professionals to use 'hands on' techniques to assist infants to attach to the mother's breast. In the following quote a midwifery professional alludes to this cultural difference as she describes how her practice had changed in response to her experience of working with and observing peer supporters' practice:

> I think some staff have still got a way to go with the hands off thing and you know I am being honest with you I was not always hands off, but I am now definitely. (Katie, Midwifery).

On one occasion, a health professional described something resembling a mentorship relationship from a peer supporter, where she had sought validation of, and further information to enhance, the care she had given a mother:

> When I said 'this is what I said', she [peer supporter] said 'that is great' and I asked her if [there was] anything else I should have said – so I used her as a resource – but she gave more concrete support and reinforced what I had already said and gave her [the mother] confidence to carry on. (Hillary, Health Visiting).

These insights thereby reflect Schön's (1983) concepts of 'reflection in action' and 'reflection on action' in terms of how the guidance and reassurance provided by the peer supporters helped to develop the health professional's skills and capacity to deliver effective breastfeeding support.

Unrealistic approach

While the peer supporters' skills were recognised, a few health professionals expressed doubts or scepticism about the validity or value of the peer support service. The programme was implemented in an area with low breastfeeding rates and a strong bottle-feeding culture. The proactive breastfeeding support offered by the peer supporters was sometimes perceived by health professionals to be problematic, as *'women don't like it'*. Further, health professionals did not always believe that the peer supporters' skills and knowledge were appropriate or sufficient to provide effective breastfeeding support.

At times, it was suggested that the peer supporters' 'hands off' approach was *'unrealistic'* and that it could not achieve the aim of getting a baby onto the mother's breast because it was not direct enough:

> Sometimes women just want you to just help them.... I'll probably get shot for saying it, but sometimes they want you to be a little bit hands on, they want you to guide their hands, they want you to show them, rather than just say, keep on with the skin to skin and see what happens, which

you know, is all well and good but at the end of the day if your baby has not fed for days, that's not going to get the job done. (Midwifery focus group).

The health professionals' traditional approach was perceived to be more appropriate as it was considered to be adaptive to circumstance, while the peer supporters' adherence to a 'hands off' approach was seen to be inflexible. In the following quote, a health professional relates a story told to her by a mother who had received breastfeeding support from the peer support service:

Interestingly enough she [the mother] said, 'none of them stood next to me', I think she was very conscious of this hands off, standing back approach, and she said that the only one who made any sense was an older midwife who said, 'I shouldn't be doing this' but then proceeded to put the bed down, did this, that and the other, and she said the baby latched on. But perhaps for her that was the right approach. (Health visitor focus group).

Here, length of experience is invoked as an indicator of expert status – '*an older midwife*' was the '*only one who made sense*' – and this traditional wisdom is held up in contrast to the '*hands off*' approach of the peer supporters, which in this characterisation is portrayed as '*standing back*'; that is, creating distance between the woman and supporter. Also, the actions of the 'older midwife' taking a traditional approach are described as transgressive – something she '*shouldn't be doing*' – furthering the implication of the peer supporters' approach as rule-bound. This belief is quite distinct from the views described in the 'mother-to-mother support' theme, in which the peer supporters' approach is seen as the more appropriate and effective one. Indeed, in this this occasion, the professionals perceive themselves to have 'adaptive expertise' (Hatano and Inagki, 1986), a status not endowed to the prescribed peer supporters' approach.

At times the appropriateness of the peer supporters' expertise was questioned, particularly in relation to specialised areas of practice, such as within the neonatal unit. Although the peer support service offered general interpersonal and breastfeeding support, there were concerns that the suggestions they offered were not realistic for this setting:

I think she [peer supporter] told the lady to express eight times a day. Normally we tell the ladies to express every three to four hours, so I suppose there is new advice out that they are giving the mums on the ward, but I suppose when you have got a premature baby that stress is kind of tenfold…. I don't think it is always practical to get the lady to be expressing eight times a day, it is quite a lot. (Shona, Neonatal).

Complementing and deterring service delivery

This theme relates to how the peer support programme was seen to have a positive impact on service provision by delivering an additional service which complemented and enhanced existing maternity care. However, health professionals were also aware of the potential to become deskilled as breastfeeding support increasingly became viewed as the province of the peer supporters. Health professionals' confidence in their own competence also became undermined by perceptions of the peer supporters as breastfeeding experts, leading to staff deferring responsibility to the peer supporters for breastfeeding support. Similar findings have been reported in other studies examining the relationship between health professionals and breastfeeding peer supporters (Raine, 2003; Curtis *et al.* 2007). The sub-themes discussed in this section relate to 'time for clinical care', 'working as part of a team', 'deskilling' and 'deferring'.

Time for clinical care

For many health professionals, the presence of the peer supporters on the maternity ward meant that they felt freed to carry out other, clinical, aspects of their role, and they were particularly aware of the need to divide their time between several women:

> Some midwives do like to give the care themselves, but there comes a point when you are caring for somebody, but you can't stand with that lady for two hours, you have got seven other ladies with different needs, unfortunately you cannot give two hours of your time. (Emma, Midwifery).

Being able to share responsibility for breastfeeding support served to relieve the frustration felt by some health professionals about their lack of capacity to deliver the standard of care they wished to:

> …you are running round and you feel you get to the end of your shift and you feel that you have failed that particular person because you have not been able to help her. Whereas if the peer supporters are on you know that they have had some input for the breastfeeders. You don't feel quite that you have not managed to get to them and failed in some way. I used to go home and think 'I really wanted to do this' and you can only do so much in a day and things prioritise. (Caroline, Midwifery).

Working as part of a team

For the most part, the peer supporters were seen as a complementary service, providing another layer of support for women. Health professionals often described the peer supporters as equals who were '*part of the team*', making no distinction in terms of hierarchy or status, but rather seeing the distinction only in terms of the type of service offered. By characterising the peer support role as a distinct, complementary service, health professionals avoided any implication that the peer supporters' expertise detracted from their own role:

> They are just here as part of the team absolutely. They are treated as part of the team. They are all very friendly and we are friendly with them. Just like normal colleagues, but they offer a different service to us. (Katie, Midwifery).

Having a shared, explicit, factual knowledge was seen as a key factor in putting peer supporters and health professionals on a level playing field, and it was acknowledged that expertise was not necessarily predicted by professional status or qualifications:

> …in terms of who is the expert I think we can all have the same knowledge whether you have got professional qualifications behind you or whether you are voluntary, as long as we have all got that same up-to-date current knowledge then in that degree we are all experts on breastfeeding. I don't think you need a health qualification behind you. (Maria, Health Visiting).

For some health professionals, working with the peer supporters improved their job satisfaction through the recognition that women were able to receive a better service:

> …it makes the midwives feel, I would suggest, it certainly makes me feel, that it is a much better service for women (Suzanne, Midwifery).

Deskilling

While the peer supporters' help in caring for women was welcomed, at the same time there was concern that their presence limited the experience that health professionals could gain in supporting breastfeeding women. It was observed that maintaining expertise requires regular practice, and that knowledge that was not regularly used would be lost:

> I think if you are not using your skills regularly it is very easy then. My brain only holds so much and if I don't need to have that information I don't have it.

That is just the state of my brain at the moment. I think the risk is that because they are doing such a good job then we almost delegate all of that responsibility to the peer supporters, which is I think is a huge risk and I don't know how we keep that balance. (Erica, Health Visiting).

A number of the health professionals felt that some areas of their expertise were in particular danger of becoming diminished. The rapport and partnership necessary for providing breastfeeding support, which is a key characteristic of the peer supporters' mother-to-mother approach, is also an important feature of midwifery care generally, and it was felt that this aspect of the role was being eroded by an increasing emphasis on clinical tasks. The presence on the maternity ward of a specialist whose work emphasised this feature of care was seen to exacerbate this erosion:

...some health professionals do not like peer supporters as it is making them feel bad at their job.... Peer supporters can go in, and give advice from a hands-off perspective – they bring the caring, emotional and affectionate role into midwifery. It makes you question what you are doing, and why you are doing it – you feel you are failing women as you cannot provide the care that they need. Some feel these positions are taking away the 'juicy' bits of their role. Midwives are given more and more jobs to do, medical and clinical checks, so we are missing out all the time. Some don't like the new role – we cannot get a rapport with women. (Laura, Midwifery).

Deferring

The perception of the peer supporters as breastfeeding 'experts' led some health professionals to defer responsibility for breastfeeding support to them:

They walk on this ward and someone says we've got an expert coming in now and she will be able to help you. She will answer all your questions and don't worry. We have said it all to them before. If you need any additional support I will get her to come in and have a chat with you. If you think of anything just ask her when she comes in. (Beth, Midwifery).

As discussed in the theme 'changing practice, increasing knowledge', several of the health professionals used their association with the peer supporters to develop their expertise. However, in some cases the introduction of this 'expert' service appeared to lead health professionals to minimise their own skills and knowledge, with some expressing reluctance in offering comprehensive breastfeeding support:

I pick up little bits and pieces so we can keep the mums going until the breastfeeding supporters get here, but I would not sit down and give them a lot of advice myself, because I am not qualified to do so. (Katie, Midwifery).

These insights indicate that comparing themselves with the peer supporters, whom they perceived to be the 'experts', could lead even experienced health professionals to doubt their ability to support women:

I think a lot of health visitors are aware of their limitations and knowledge of certain skills and I think are very happy therefore to pass that on – let the peer supporter do it – and therein lies the risk. The risk is I don't feel confident to do it, they have got more knowledge, they are better skilled at doing that, that is all they do therefore they are the best person to do it, therefore, I can stop.... Somebody has asked me a question and I have thought do I know that and I know I do know and I do know that I know how to, but for a split second I think I wish there were somebody here who could do this, because they will do it miles better than me (Erica, Health Visiting).

While health professionals acknowledged, and were concerned about, the risk of deskilling and the associated tendency toward deferring responsibility, participants largely did not know how this risk could be mitigated.

Gatekeeping

This theme reflected health professionals' wish to enforce role boundaries and standards of practice. Gatekeeping by health professionals in response to breastfeeding peer support has also been described in other studies (Raine 2003; Curtis *et al.*, 2007). At times, overt gatekeeping occurred where health professionals prevented the peer supporters from seeing women due to perceptions of their legitimacy. This theme also describes how health professionals' anxieties about the 'expert' status of the peer supporters generated a desire to control or limit their activities. The two sub-themes discussed are 'controlling access' and 'controlling information'.

Controlling access

Some health professionals admitted that they did not often refer women to the peer supporters. Their comments suggested that if they could not resolve the women's problems, then the peer supporters would be unlikely to do so:

Sometimes we do, it has been known, but we don't call them very often I must admit. We tend to have runs really. I think really we do manage quite well really. If we really can't get them to breastfeed then there are major problems. Perhaps breastfeeding buddies aren't going to get over the problems if we can't. (Ellen, Neonatal).

Health professionals sometimes expressed reservations about the degree of access that peer supporters were '*entitled to*'. Permission to see women in a health care context is typically only allowed to a controlled group of people – qualified health professionals – and so anxieties existed around extending this licence to non-professionals:

I know the peer supporters are in the hospital and they come out to the community, but I am not sure who is actually entitled to see the ladies. (Sophie, Midwifery).

In institutional settings such a maternity ward, status and legitimacy can be enforced partly by the use of symbols – what Berger and Luckmann (1967, p. 105) refer to as prestige symbols. The peer supporters' legitimacy on the ward was demonstrated symbolically with an ID badge and a distinctive T-shirt. While practice has subsequently changed in this area, at the time of undertaking the evaluation, the peer supporters' access, both to the ward, and to women was circumscribed, with health professionals acting as gatekeepers:

They go onto the ward, they have got IDs, they have got a hospital ID badge, which states that they are a volunteer, but like me they cannot access the ward, it does not allow them to open the doors, so they have to be let in to the wards and then they will go to a member of staff and say I am such a body, a peer supporter, which is evident now, they have got their own T-shirts, and ask for information about breastfeeding mums and if there is anybody that they should not approach on the ward. (Isobel, Midwifery).

At times, the presence of the peer supporters was viewed with ambivalence. Some health professionals, while acknowledging the value of additional breastfeeding support, expressed a desire for more surveillance of – and perhaps a desire for more control over – the peer supporters' activities:

Well I personally think that it is a very good thing they are doing, but I would like to know what they said and where they are up to. (Caroline, Midwifery).

To an extent this desire for surveillance reflects Berger and Luckman's 'double problem of legitimation' (Berger and Luckmann, 1967, p. 105). The 'insider' status of the health professionals must be delineated and defended against 'outsiders', but once 'outsiders' are admitted to 'insider' status – such as when peer supporters are given access to women on the maternity ward or in the community, which would otherwise be the realm of health professionals – these new insiders must be kept within the fold and kept adherent to its tenets.

Controlling information

Anxieties relating to access also surfaced with regard to information-giving. A number of the health professionals were concerned about whether the peer supporters were providing appropriate information, and regretted being unable to observe their practice. This participant noted that she was also unable to scrutinise her professional colleagues' practice, but this appeared to induce less anxiety:

> I think that needs addressing, but I don't know how they feel about it, because I have never listened in to what they say to the women, because I never have the time to do that. Maybe I would like to have gone in and stood at the back and listened to what they have to say. Not that I think they are going to be given any advice that I think they shouldn't have been given, but it would be nice to know what they are saying, but then again you don't know what your colleagues are saying do you? (Caroline, Midwifery).

There was concern that peer supporters may be giving women information that was not consistent with the information given by health professionals:

> …sometimes there is a bit of contention about who is doing what and maybe there are even they are saying slightly different things, which is important and a problem. (Sophie, Midwifery).

There were also questions about role boundaries and how far the peer supporters' expertise could be allowed to extend. In addition to visiting women one-to-one, the peer supporters also ran breastfeeding support groups. As these groups were typically attended by women later in the postnatal period, they sometimes included discussion on the introduction of complementary foods. This was considered by some health professionals to be outwith the peer supporters' sphere of expertise. As with breastfeeding information, there was particular concern over the consistency of information provided across the different services:

I know at the health visiting meeting when we had the peer supporters present, talking about them talking about baby led weaning [introduction of complementary foods] at one of the breastfeeding groups that they were holding and there were certain health visitors that were like, humph should they be giving that advice about baby led weaning and then they want clarification that the peer supporters are giving the same advice that we are giving and there was a lot of debate afterwards about is it not the health visitor's role to give weaning advice. (Maria, Health Visiting).

Implications for practice

In summary, our findings have illuminated how the peer supporters were perceived as 'experts' through their experiential and theoretical knowledge of breastfeeding, their capacity to spend sufficient time with women to support breastfeeding, and how being perceived as an equal enabled opportunities to develop more meaningful and trust-based relationships. These insights also identified the ways in which health professionals conceded expert status (as a breastfeeding supporter) to the peer supporters, while at other times the peer supporters' expertise was contested. Both the acknowledgement and questioning of expertise had consequences for health professionals' practice, and for service delivery. The inclusion of 'expert' breastfeeding peer support offers both benefits and challenges for health professionals. On one hand it was perceived to enhance and complement service delivery, and provide opportunities for skill and knowledge development, with a number of health professionals expressing a sense of relief and wellbeing due to women receiving '*a much better service*' since the integration of peer support provision. These insights support the findings of both Curtis and colleagues, who reported the themes of 'easing the workload' and 'learning from volunteers and developing new ways of working' (Curtis *et al.*, 2007), and Rossman *et al.* (2012), who describe how health professionals used peer supporters as a resource to 'lighten the nurse's load'. In Raine's (2003) study of breastfeeding peer support, 'street credibility' – the idea that the peer supporters' personal experiences give them credibility with women – also corresponds to our themes of 'experiential understanding' and 'connections through likeness'.

However, from a counter-perspective, the inclusion of this expertise within professional parameters has the potential to undermine health professionals' confidence and skills. Issues arose in terms of inconsistent practice between the health professionals and the peer supporters. Gatekeeping was also evident in terms of health professionals withholding the peer supporters' access to women; with several health professionals expressing concern about this expertise eroding professional practice. Likewise, Curtis *et al.* (2007) described 'invisible boundaries' and 'gatekeeping by professionals'. Our findings build on this notion, exploring further the themes of 'deskilling' and 'deferring' and elaborating on health professionals' reservations about peer support in the theme 'unrealistic approach'.

The breastfeeding peer support service described in this chapter was introduced as an 'additional' tier of support, and was not intended to be a replacement service. As peer supporters are only available over restricted periods, this has obvious implications for service provision. Furthermore, the time constraints on health professionals' capacity to support breastfeeding women indicated in this study are also well reported in the wider literature (Dykes, 2005b; Schmied *et al.*, 2009; Thomson *et al.*, 2012). While these findings emphasise the value and benefit of this service, in the current climate of economic adversity and lack of trial evidence to support the efficacy of breastfeeding peer support, there is no guarantee that peer services will be continued. Care therefore needs to be taken to ensure that health professionals are provided with suitable reassurance, support and skill development to ensure that the peer support service is sensitively and meaningfully integrated into practice.

Some suggestions for practice development in this area are detailed below.

First, clear communication and clarity about the role and remit of breastfeeding peer supporters needs to be emphasised and re-enforced during professional based forums (e.g. team meetings) to ensure that all staff are regularly offering and providing support to breastfeeding women.

Training and support to develop staff abilities and confidence in providing breastfeeding support needs to be provided on an ongoing basis. Skill based workshops could be provided in tandem with the peer supporters to ensure that all staff are competent in providing effective breastfeeding support.

During this study, differing opinions and practice concerning a 'hands on' approach were identified. The danger of 'manhandling' and 'objectifying' women's breasts, the implications of forcing an infant to feed, and women being treated as a passive recipient of care are key reasons as to why a 'hands on' approach should be avoided (Weimers *et al.*, 2006; Thomson *et al.*, 2012). This is not to suggest that 'touch' cannot be sensitive or helpful for successful attachment (Schmied *et al.*, 2009); however, health professionals need to respect women's personal boundaries in a perceptive and, if necessary a 'hands off' manner. This issue could be broached during skill based workshops, together with encouragement and practical skills to encourage a 'hands off' approach.

Inclusion of peer supporters within staff meetings and professional-based training opportunities (where appropriate) could help to break down any barriers between the groups; and encourage the benefits of 'team working' experienced by a number of participants in this study.

More formalised mentoring relationships could be forged between health professionals and peer supporters to include co-working, observing each other's practice and debriefing opportunities. This could enable positive working relationships to be formed, and skill and knowledge transfer and development. It could also provide the health professionals with reassurance about the types and form of support provided by the peer support service.

Peer supporters could also be allowed to observe and work alongside staff on the neonatal unit to advance their practice within such a specialised practice area. This would raise the profile of the service within the unit, develop the peer supporters' capabilities to provide breastfeeding support for mothers of preterm infants, and extend the peer support service within this population group.

Conclusion

In this chapter we have discussed one of the global themes to emerge from an evaluation into the implementation of a breastfeeding peer support programme. The overarching 'issues of expertise' theme has illuminated the different ways in which the peer supporters were perceived, or not, to be 'experts' in breastfeeding support, and the benefits and challenges of such on service delivery and professional practice. The integration of breastfeeding peer support within professional parameters of care can enhance and extend breastfeeding provision and skill development. However, suitable opportunities for co-working to encourage relationship formation, reassurance and knowledge transfer could ensure the service is sensitively and meaningfully integrated into practice.

References

Aiken, A. and Thomson, G. (2013) Professionalization of a breastfeeding peer support service: views and experiences of peer supporters. *Midwifery* **pii**, S0266-6138(13)00002-8.

Alexander, J., Anderson, T., Grant, M., Sanghera, J. and Jackson, D. (2003) An evaluation of a support group for breast-feeding women in Salisbury, UK. *Midwifery* **19**, 215–20.

Anderson, T. and Grant, M. (2001) The art of community-based breastfeeding support. The Blandford breastfeeding support group, incorporating the 'Blandford Bosom Buddies'. *MIDIRS Midwifery Digest*, **11**(Suppl. 1), 20–3.

Anderson, A. K., Damio, G., Young, S., Chapman, D.J. and Pérez-Escamilla, R. (2005) A randomized trial assessing the efficacy of peer counseling on exclusive breastfeeding in a predominantly Latina low-income community. *Archives of Pediatric and Adolescent Medicine*, **159**(9), 836–41.

Attride-Stirling, J. (2001) Thematic networks: an analytic tool for qualitative research. *Qualitative Research*, **1**, 385–405.

Benner, P. (2001) *From Novice to Expert in Clinical Nursing Practice: Commemorative Education*. Prentice Hall, New Jersey.

Berger, P. L. and Luckmann, T. (1967) *The Social Construction of Reality: A Treatise in the Sociology of Knowledge*. Penguin, Harmondsworth.

Britton, C., McCormick, F. M., Renfrew, M. J., Wade, A. and King, S. E. (2007) Support for breastfeeding mothers. *Cochrane Database of Systematic Reviews* Issue 1. Art. No.: CD001141.

Brown, L. (ed.) (1993) *The New Shorter Oxford English Dictionary on Historical Principles*, rev edn. Clarendon Press, Oxford.

Chapman, D. J., Damio, G., Young, S. and Pérez-Escamilla, R. (2004) Effectiveness of breastfeeding peer counseling in a low-income, predominantly Latina population: A randomized controlled trial. *Archives of Pediatric and Adolescent Medicine*, **158**(9), 897–902.

Chung, M., Ip, S., Yu, W. *et al.* (2008) *Interventions in Primary Care to Promote Breastfeeding: A Systematic Review*. Evidence Syntheses, No. 66. Agency for Healthcare Research and Quality (US): Rockville. Available at: http://www.ncbi.nlm.nih.gov/books/NBK35168/.

Curtis, P., Woodhill, R. and Stapleton, H. (2007) The peer-professional interface in a community-based, breast feeding peer-support project. *Midwifery*, **23**(2), 146–56.

Dennis, C.-L., Hodnett, E., Gallop, R. and Chalmers, B. (2002) The effect of peer support on breastfeeding duration among primiparous women: A randomized controlled trial. *Canadian Medical Association Journal*, **166**, 21–8.

Dennis, C.-L. (2003) Peer support within a health care context: a concept analysis. *International Journal of Nursing Studies*, **40**(3), 321–32.

Department for Education and Skills (2004) *Every Child Matters: Change for Children*. DH, London.

Department of Health (2002) *Improvement, Expansion and Reform: The Next Three Years Priorities and Planning Framework 2003–2006*. DH, London.

Department of Health (2004a). *National Service Framework for Children, Young People and Maternity Services*. DH, London.

Department of Health (2004b) *Choosing Health: Making Healthy Choices Easier*. DH, London.

Department of Health (2009) *Commissioning Local Breastfeeding Support Services*. DH, London.

Dreyfus, S. E. and Dreyfus, H. L. (1980) *A Five Stage-Model of the Mental Activities involved in Directed Skill Acquisition*. Storming Media. Available at: http://www.stormingmedia.us/15/1554/A155480.html (accessed 12 February, 2010).

Dykes, F. (2003) *Infant Feeding Initiative: A Report Evaluating the Breastfeeding Practice Projects 1999–2002*. DH, London.

Dykes, F (2005a) Government funded breastfeeding peer support projects: Implications for practice. *Maternal & Child Nutrition*, **1**, 21–31.

Dykes, F. (2005b) A critical ethnographic study of encounters between midwives and breast-feeding women in postnatal wards in England. *Midwifery*, **21**(3), 241–52.

Dyson, L., Renfrew, M., McFadden, A., McCormick, F., Herbert, G. and Thomas, J. (2006) *Effective Action Briefing on the Initiation and Duration of Breastfeeding*. National Institute for Clinical Excellence, London.

Ekstrom, A., Widstrom, A. and Nissen, E. (2003) Duration of breastfeeding in Swedish primiparous and multiparous women. *Journal of Human Lactation*, **19**, 172–8.

Ericsson, K. A. (1996) The acquisition of the expert performance: an introduction to some of the issues. In: *The Road to Excellence: The Acquisition of Expert Performance in the Arts and Sciences, Sports and Games* (ed. K. A. Ericsson), pp. 1–50. Erlbaum, Mahwah.

Graffy, J., Taylor, J., Williams, A. and Eldridge, S. (2004) Randomised controlled trial of support from volunteer counsellors for mothers considering breast feeding. *British Medical Journal*, **328**(7430), 26.

Grassley, J. and Eschiti, V. (2008) Grandmother breastfeeding support: what do mothers need and want? *Birth*, **35**(4), 329–35.

Greene, J., Stewart-Knox, B. and Wright, M. (2003). Feeding preferences and attitudes to breastfeeding and its promotion among teenagers in Northern Ireland. *Journal of Human Lactation*, **19**, 57–65.

Hatano, G. and Inagaki, K. (1986). Two courses of expertise. In: *Child Development and Education in Japan* (eds. H. Stevenson, H. Asuma and K. Hakauta), pp. 262–72. Freeman, San Francisco.

Health and Social Care Information Centre, IFF Research (2012) *Infant Feeding Survey 2010*. Information Centre for Health and Social Care, London.

Hegney, D., Fallon, T. and O'Brien, M. L. (2008) Against all odds: a retrospective case-controlled study of women who experienced extraordinary breastfeeding problems. *Journal of Clinical Nursing*, **17**, 1182–92.

Hoddinott, P., Chalmers, M. and Pill, R. (2006) One-to-one or group-based peer support for breastfeeding? Women's perceptions of a breastfeeding peer coaching intervention. *Birth-Issues in Perinatal Care*, **33**, 139–46.

Hoddinott, P. Tappin, D. and Wright, C. (2008) Breast feeding, *British Medical Journal*, **336**(7649), 881–7.

Hoddinott, P., Allan, K., Avenell, A. and Britten, J. (2010) Group interventions to improve health outcomes: a framework for their design and delivery. *BMC Public Health*, **10**, 800.

Hoddinott, P., Seyara, R. and Marais, D. (2011) Global evidence synthesis and UK idiosyncrasy: why have recent UK trials had no significant effects on breastfeeding rates? *Maternal and Child Nutrition*, **7**(3), 221–7.

Ingram, J. C., Rosser, J. and Jackson, D. (2005) Breastfeeding peer supporters and a community support group: evaluating their effectiveness. *Maternal and Child Nutrition*, **1**, 111–18.

Jolly, K., Ingram, L., Khan, K. S., Deeks, J. J., Freemantle, N. and MacArthur, C. (2012) Systematic review of peer support for breastfeeding continuation: metaregression analysis of the effect of setting, intensity, and timing. *British Medical Journal*, **344**, d8287.

Kirkham, M., Sherridan, A., Thornton, D. and Smale, M. (2006) 'Breastfriends' Doncaster: the story of our peer support project. In: *Maternal and Infant Nutrition & Nurture: Controversies and Challenges* (eds. V. Hall Moran and F. Dykes). Quay Books, London.

Koppl, R. (2010) The social construction of expertise. *Society*, **47**(3), 220–6.

McInnes, R. J., Love, J. G. and Stone, D. H. (2000) The Glasgow Infant Feeding Action Research Project: an evaluation of a community based intervention designed to increase the prevalence of breastfeeding in a socially disadvantaged urban area. *Journal of Public Health Medicine*, **22**(2), 138–43.

Meier, E. R., Olson, B. H., Benton, P., Eghtedary, K. and Song, W. O. (2007) A qualitative evaluation of a breastfeeding peer counselor program. *Journal of Human Lactation*, **23**, 262–8.

Nankunda, J., Tumwine, J. K., Nankabirwa, V. and Tylleskär, T. (2010) 'She would sit with me': mothers' experiences of individual peer support for exclusive breastfeeding in Uganda. *International Breastfeeding Journal*, **5**, 16.

NICE (2008a) *Clinical Guidance PH11; Improving the Nutrition of Pregnant and Breast-feeding Mothers and Children in Low-Income Households* (Revised July 2011). NICE/NHS, London.

NICE (2008b) *Implementing NICE Guidance Commissioning Guide a Peer-Support Programme for Women who Breastfeed.* UK NICE/NHS (available at Department of Health (2009) Commissioning Local Breastfeeding Support Services. DH, London).

Nor B., Zembe Y., Daniels K., Doherty T., Jackson D., Ahlberg, B. M. and Ekstrom, E. (2009) 'Peer but not peer': Considering the context of infant feeding peer counseling in a high HIV prevalence area. *Journal of Human Lactation*, **25**, 427–34.

Raine, P. (2003) Promoting breast-feeding in a deprived area: the influence of a peer support initiative. *Health and Social Care in the Community*, **11**(6), 463–9.

Rossman, B., Engstrom, J. L., Meier, P. P., Vonderheid, S. C., Norr, K. F. and Hill, P. D. (2011). 'They've walked in my shoes': mothers of very low birth weight infants and their experiences with breastfeeding peer counselors in the neonatal intensive care unit. *Journal of Human Lactation*, **27**(1), 14–24.

Rossman, B., Engstrom, J. L. and Meier, P. P. (2012) Healthcare providers' perceptions of breastfeeding peer counselors in the neonatal intensive care unit. *Research in Nursing and Health*, **35**(5), 460–74.

Schmied, V., Beake, S., Sheehan, A., McCourt, C. and Dykes, F. (2009) A meta-synthesis of women's perceptions and experiences of breastfeeding support. *JBI Library of Systematic Reviews*, **7**, 583–614.

Schmied, V., Beake, S., Sheehan, A., McCourt, C. and Dykes, F. (2011) Women's perceptions and experiences of breastfeeding support: a metasynthesis. *Birth: Issues in Perinatal Care*, **38**(1), 49–60.

Schön, D. (1983). *The Reflective Practitioner. How Professionals Think in Action.* Temple Smith, London.

Scott, J. A. and Mostyn, T. (2003) Women's experiences of breastfeeding in a bottle-feeding culture. *Journal of Human Lactation*, **19**, 270–7.

Simpson, L. and Downe, S. (2010) Expertise in intrapartum maternity practice. In *Essential Midwifery Practice: Leadership, Expertise and Collaborative Working* (eds. S. Downe, S. Byrom and L. R. M. Simpson), pp. 102–25. Wiley-Blackwell, Oxford.

Thomson, G., Crossland, N. and Dykes, F. (2012) Giving me hope: women's reflections on a breastfeeding peer support service. *Maternal & Child Nutrition*, **8**(3), 340–53.

Turner, S. (2001) What is the problem with experts? *Social Studies of Science*, **31**(1), 123–49.

Tylleskär, T., Jackson, D., Meda N., Engebretsen, I. M., Chopra, M., Diallo, A. H. *et al.* (2011). Exclusive breastfeeding promotion by peer counsellors in sub-Saharan Africa (PROMISE-EBF): a cluster-randomised trial. *Lancet*, **378**, 420–7.

Wade, D., Haining, S. and Day, A. (2009). Breastfeeding peer support: are there additional benefits? *Community Practitioner: The Journal Of The Community Practitioners' & Health Visitors' Association*, **82**(12), 30–3.

Weimers, L., Svensson, K., Dumas, L., Navér, L. and Wahlberg, V. (2006) Hands-on approach during breastfeeding support in a neonatal intensive care unit: a qualitative study of Swedish mothers' experiences. *International Breastfeeding Journal*, **1**, 20.

WHO/UNICEF (1989) *Protecting, Promoting and Supporting Breastfeeding: The Special Role of Maternity Services.* WHO, Geneva.

WHO (2000) *Collaborative Study Team on the Role of Breastfeeding on the Prevention of Infant Mortality. Effect of Breastfeeding on Infant and Child Mortality Due to Infectious Disease in Less Developed Countries: a Pooled Analysis.* WHO, Geneva.

WHO (2003) *Global Strategy on Infant and Young Child Feeding.* WHO, Geneva.

World Breastfeeding Trends Initiative (2010) *The State of Breastfeeding in 33 Countries.* BPNI/IBFAN, Delhi.

CHAPTER 7

Discretion, availability, and the breastfeeding mother's responsibility: infant feeding discourse in action in online discussion and imagery

Katherine Ebisch-Burton

Introduction

Women's experiences of breastfeeding, particularly in public spaces, have been the subject of a great deal of discussion and research in recent years (e.g. Stearns, 1999; Schmied and Barclay, 1999; Sheeshka *et al.*, 2001; Acker, 2009; Spurles and Babineau, 2011). The development of online media as fora for public discourse provides us with a rich source of data on public discourse surrounding breastfeeding, boosted by the public visibility of the issue due to health campaigns and periodic publicity surrounding guidelines.

The methodology of this qualitative observational commentary involved reading public online discourse on breastfeeding in public essentially as text and taking an interpretative approach to that text. I examine this discourse in relation to three core terms: *availability*; *discretion/exhibition*; and *responsibility*. These terms are in part derived from the discourse itself here and in part drawn out of a series of categories of demands and ascriptions made to mothers who breastfeed in public. While the category of availability looks at breastfeeding in general and in terms of the woman's intimate relationships, the other categories focus specifically on discourse surrounding breastfeeding in public and perceptions and assumptions around public breastfeeding.

The circular nature of much online discussion, as well as its juxtaposition of sweeping, generalising statements with individual experiences, provides ideal ground to observe this aspect of infant feeding discourse in action. Examining the interaction of first-hand perceptions with discursive commonplaces opens up to us the way in which the wider discourse influences the individual perception of the practice of breastfeeding from both the mother's and the observer's point of view. I will also examine the symbolism of breastfeeding covers, an invention which has emerged with the rise of public breastfeeding as a consciously debated issue in discourse, and breastfeeding rooms and facilities.

The investigation focuses on the UK and Germany, as Western European cultures familiar to the author and where breastfeeding practices share substantial similarities.[1] Although all contributions to Internet discussion fora and news discussion sites I have cited took place in public fora, I have abbreviated names and posting pseudonyms.

The narrative of availability

Breastfeeding, particularly of the public variety, possesses and transmits a peculiarly double-edged symbolism: it is a selfless act of idealised motherhood, but is also, in Western societies, seen to represent the mother's radical identification with the idealised mothering role to the point at which the mother might be seen to remove herself into the exclusivity of the breastfeeding relationship. This contradiction and conflict appears to be currently particularly acute. One interpretation of the issue of availability in relation to breastfeeding in public might posit that the mother who breastfeeds in public demonstrates idealised motherhood, but she demonstrates it as unavailability, as desexualisation of a sexualised part of her anatomy and hence as a reassigning of her role, a removal from the sphere of (sexual) availability to men. A breastfeeding mother, then, is both exceptionally (and exclusively) available (to her child) and radically unavailable (to other contexts, specifically the sexual one with which an exposed breast is primarily connoted). While availability to the baby as a key tenet of attachment and 'continuum' parenting is positively connoted and may provide women with approval and a sense of doing the 'right' thing as a new mother, it frequently finds itself in a tension or opposition towards the availability to other concrete relationships and abstract roles which determine much of women's lives.

An image used in an NHS-sponsored campaign, Best Beginnings, which aims to encourage women to breastfeed and bears the NHS logo, shows the naked torso

---

1   Translations of German quotations are provided by the author.

of a slim, flat-stomached woman from the breasts to the top of the pubic area. A baby's hand rests on the breast on the left as we look at the image, while a man's hand, exerting some pressure, rests on the right breast, and a woman's hand lies over it, the fingers positioned between the fingers of the male hand.[2]

The image, as well as not using the word 'breastfeeding' until reference is made to a '*free* breastfeeding DVD' available from midwives in the third line of copy, does not actually show breastfeeding; it shows two gestures of claiming; the baby claims one breast and the partner – or rather the intimate relationship, symbolised by the woman's hand resting on the man's – claims the other. The image is not entirely symmetrical, and the size of the right breast as we look at it indicates the man's hand is exerting pressure on it. The woman herself is not featured; she is reduced to a section of her torso which fills the image. The breasts become, here, a function, detached from the personhood of their owner, indeed re-appropriated to other owners. At the same time, the claiming hands serve the practical purpose of censoring the nipples.

The image is accompanied by the following text, centred on the image directly underneath the breasts:

Bond with your baby. Bond with your man

and underneath, in smaller type:

You can give your baby the best start in life and still feel confident your breasts will put a smile on your man's face. Ask your midwife for your free breastfeeding dvd or visit www.bestbeginnings.info

The typographical features of the image require pointing out here; 'Bond' is capitalised both times, which acts as emphasis and prioritisation. The capitalisation, along with the typographical and grammatical division of 'Bond with your baby' and 'Bond with your man' into two separate statements, almost assigning one task to each breast, makes the work of 'bonding' as expressed in the text a matter of two halves as also reflected by the image: the mother belongs half to the baby and half to the man; she is required to split her loyalties, her work and her breasts. 'Bonding' becomes, here, the work of the mother and her breasts the requisite tools, with the mother's personhood excluded from both the image and the discourse of satisfying others' needs – which might seem incongruous considering the fact that the definition of 'bonding' might be summarised to be 'building an intimate relationship', which generally involves the interaction of personhood with

---

2   http://www.bestbeginnings.org.uk/Shop/bond-with-your-baby-bond-with-your-man-a3-poster (accessed 16 January 2013).

personhood. The further text, focusing on the baby's needs and then 'your man's', likewise contains no mention of the woman herself or of any needs she might have. The image was reproduced in an *Independent* newspaper story revolving around the poster campaign of which the image is a part, reinforcing the discourse of breasts-as-tools by referring to the breasts in the images as 'multi-tasking'.[3]

The image and text suggest to mothers-to-be that they need not renounce their sexual availability in order to breastfeed – that they can balance both forms of availability. Comment on public breastfeeding elsewhere, however, defines public breastfeeding rather as a violation of availability to the child. Commenting on an incident, reported in the online edition of the *Daily Mail*, in which a young breastfeeding mother shopping in a clothing store was allegedly asked to go to a changing room or leave the store to feed her child, a contributor writes:

> I would imagine breast feeding is something mothers treasure and feel they are building a bond with their babies but I don't see how you could bond with your baby looking for a size 14 hoody or whatever.[4]

Here, the commentator's implication is that public breastfeeding may actually be a matter of lacking availability to the child; this refers to a strand of discourse in which the seclusion positively connotated with breastfeeding is an iconic figure of mother–child 'bonding'. In fact, we may argue that the Best Beginnings advertisement might be reacting against this strand of discourse by presenting breastfeeding as not a matter of seclusion with the child or exclusivity, but quite the opposite. Clothes shopping is represented in this comment as withdrawing necessary attention from the child; perhaps there is a secondary implication in which a mother looking for clothes is attending to matters related to her availability to other female roles rather than to motherhood. The commentator, however, follows up this opinion seamlessly by continuing:

> I am totally pro-breast feeding but I do know that people may feel uncomfortable with things like this so why would you want to make someone feel that way.[5]

---

3   Image published on http://www.independent.co.uk/life-style/health-and-families/health-news/the-posters-that-celebrate-cool-multitasking-breasts-816224.html, 27 April 2008.

4   Retrieved in July 2012 from http://www.dailymail.co.uk/news/article-1315803/Primark-tells-breastfeeding-mother-Do-changing-room-out.html; posted by M on 29 July 2012.

5   *ibid.*

The issue, then, to the mind of this contributor, is also about the perceived feelings of those sharing the public space of the breastfeeding mother and child.

The narrative of discretion/exhibition

A great deal of discourse around breastfeeding in public circles around the question as to whether it is conducted 'discreetly'; if so, it may be permitted, accepted or defended. Discretion and exhibition become a dichotomous pairing, possibly the two ends of a spectrum, in relation to which women are positioned by the judgement of the beholder. In this context, the inevitable consequence of a lack of discretion is an excess of exhibition, of a desire for attention specifically to sexualised areas of the body, with motherhood figured as a sort of respectable veneer for such desire for exhibition.

The following comment was left on the *Daily Mail* website in response to a report detailing an incident in which a visitor to Hampton Court Palace was told to go to the 'mother and baby room' to breastfeed her six-month-old, an incident which attracted some media attention at the time. The comment is cited almost in full, minus a potentially identifying detail, as it unites many of the strands of discourse around public breastfeeding we are analysing:

> I am the least prudish person on the planet [...] but quite frankly I find it irritating that women hang their breasts out in public and viewing a palace is not the place to do that. What is wrong with going into a little place to discreetly feed your baby. We all did! There are still some things in life that should be carried out with some decorum and this is one of them. So many women think they were the only ones that ever gave birth; most of us did and did not feel the need to walk around public places with our boobs hanging out. There is a time and place for everything! Either plan your trips around feeding times, or wait until the child is old enough or find a changing room. I hope she does not put her child on a potty in a stateroom!'[6]

The commentator takes up and echoes several refrains of the discussion: the implication that there is a 'time and a place' is one; we note that the commentator suggests the breastfeeding mother should go to a 'little place', implying closeness and seclusion, in implicit contrast to the 'big' or 'wide' setting of public space. Another, particularly striking discursive strand, echoed at other points in the discussion, is a sense of distaste at the woman's supposed or construed pride in

---

6   http://www.dailymail.co.uk/news/article-358785/Mother-told-breast-best-palace.html. Posted by MF. (Comments have since been removed from the site.)

having become a mother, an apparent need to show off or (as another participant, AS, puts it) 'attention seek'.[7] AS adds:

> She [the woman at the centre of the story] might be a 21st century mother, and used to exhibiting herself in public, but generally it is disliked and frowned upon by others.[8]

The definition of the '21st century mother', then, as implied here, is one who pushes herself forward inappropriately, 'exhibiting' herself to the sight of others rather than avoiding being seen. The connotations of 'exhibit[ing]' are at least potentially sexual, carrying echoes of 'exhibitionism'. MF's comment expresses disapproval of what she perceives as a sense of specialness felt by breastfeeding mothers, as being the 'only ones that ever gave birth', which she relates to a 'need' to expose parts of the self which are usually considered sexual and kept out of sight; in other words, a woman must believe herself special to some degree in order to violate the edict to discretion.

The contributor C claims that 'breastfeeding in public smacks of arrogance: 'I want to do this, so the rest of you can put up with it', and S, the first to comment on the story, wishes that:

> [...] campaigners for breastfeeding in public would get over themselves. If a mother is so concerned about doing what's right for her baby – then stay at home and be a proper mother instead of dragging your tiny off spring around the supermarket, public house or stately home to feed. If you have to venture out – then please spare us. Given it is an emotive subject – why thrust your flesh on complete strangers?[9]

This comment is particularly enlightening in that it implies that a woman with a (small) baby who is outside the domestic sphere – even engaged in domestically connoted activities such as supermarket shopping – is not being a 'proper mother'. Linguistically, the part of the sentence with the conjunction 'and' ('stay at home and be a proper mother') is not saying [list of imperatives: first, stay at home; second, be a proper mother], but rather [stay at home] as synonymous to, or substitutable for, [be a proper mother]. The use of the relatively rarely seen, particularly in colloquial conversation, full form of 'public house' instead of 'pub' might imply a register of indignation in which the speaker is denoting herself as 'proper' in contrast to the spoken-about.

---

7 *ibid.*; comment by AS.

8 *ibid.*

9 *ibid.*

The comment combines two strands of anti-breastfeeding discourse: the accusation of bad-mothering, here conceived of as the woman taking a full part in public life as if she were not a mother, and the accusation of 'thrust[ing her] flesh' on others, essentially an accusation of (violent) sexual exhibitionism. This might be seen as potentially encompassing the accusation, most frequently heard in relation to 'extended' breastfeeding, of a mother breastfeeding 'for herself' rather than for her child. The end point of this particular trajectory is suspicion of the woman claiming and embodying her sense of self, rather than her sense of being for others.

This discourse is echoed in German sources. In a discussion on the large women's forum Brigitte.de, which generally serves an educated demographic, the contributor P comments that members of the '*Stillfraktion*' ('the breastfeeding faction', i.e. a term carrying connotations of politics and antagonism) need not be surprised if they receive negative attention for feeding in public:

> *Da solche öffentlichen Stiller gerne an der Gesellschaft teilnehmen möchten wie vor der Geburt müssen sie also auch mit der Ansprache umgehen können.*[10]

In other words, the woman, by virtue of breastfeeding in a public place, is putting herself out there, exposing herself in more ways than one; she becomes open to challenge in an analogous way to that in which apologists for sexual assault imagine a skimpily dressed or inebriated woman becomes open to sexual aggression. The comment 'stay at home and be a proper mother' above connects directly to the observation from P that those who breastfeed in public are embodying an implicitly unreasonable demand to 'take part in society just like before the birth'; in other words, as we have examined in our discussion of availability above, the social behaviour of a 'proper mother', changes once she has become a mother; she withdraws from 'society'.

The word '*Stiller*' is the masculine form of the noun derived from the verb '*stillen*', to breastfeed. The feminine form would be '*Stillerinnen*', from the singular feminine '*Stillerin*', with the '-in' ending to denote feminine gender. In fact, neither form is widely used; much as in English, a 'breastfeeder' is referred to as a '*Stillende*', a 'breastfeeding [person]'. By using the effectively non-existent form, in the masculine, the contributor is artificially emphasising the agency and deliberate action of a woman who feeds in public, and denying her femininity: she

---

10 http://www.brigitte.de/foren/showthread.html?t=83917&highlight=stillen. 'Seeing as these public breastfeeders want to take part in society just like before the birth, they should be able to cope with being challenged on it.'

is not in fact a woman, as such immodesty and wanting to 'take part in society just like before the birth' does not befit one. In the same thread, L makes much the same argument, effectively denying the publicly breastfeeding woman the right to personal, intimate space:

> *Es trifft eine Mutter nicht unvorbereitet, sie kennt die Hungerzeiten des Babys. Wenn sie also Orte aufsucht, wo eine Intimität kaum möglich ist, wünscht sie auch keine Intimität; wäre jetzt meine Schlussfolgerung.*[11]

The idea that the baby's 'hunger times' are always or even largely predictable analogises breastfeeding to artificial feeding, while the remainder of the comment assumes that a mother who did not wish to expose herself to potentially negative public comment would plan her movements in such a way as to be behind closed doors at these times, leading to the contrary argument that not planning her movements, primarily with the needs of third parties in mind, thus renders a publicly breastfeeding woman a legitimate target of intrusion on her personal space. Her breasts, whatever the reality of the degree of exposure, become denoted as on show and therefore as public property in the same way as breasts exposed for aesthetic-sexual purposes, and her failure to anticipate the needs of others is seen as invalidating her right to be free of harassment.

In a discussion on a *Telegraph* online article entitled 'The nightmare of breast feeding in public', a contributor uses markedly sexual language with aggressive overtones to describe a woman whose breastfeeding practice he felt to fall into the category of exhibition:

> Like it or not, in our culture, breasts are sexual – feeding a baby or not. I saw a young girl breastfeeding her baby quite openly outside a very busy pub – and every guy in the place was riveted to her tits. I would not care to expose myself to such scrutiny but clearly the girl was enjoying the attention.[12]

---

11 *ibid.*: 'It doesn't come out of the blue, [the mother] knows when her baby's going to be hungry. I conclude from this that if she goes to places where she won't have any privacy, she doesn't want any privacy.' We note that the title of the thread is '*Stillen in der Öffentlichkeit – Normal oder Affront?*' ('Breastfeeding in public – normal or an affront?') The title was added by a moderator establishing a separate thread for an off-topic breastfeeding discussion begun in another thread – in other words, a person ostensibly disinterested in the topic has made the casual assessment that breastfeeding in public could be an 'affront'.

12 Retrieved on 8 July 2012 from http://www.telegraph.co.uk/comment/personal-view/3559591/The-nightmare-of-breast-feeding-in-public.html#disqus_thread; posted 18 June 2008 by W.

The comment makes clear references to the discourse of sexualised unashamedness in the woman and its effect on her availability to the sexual gaze: she breastfeeds 'openly', her baby effectively disappears and her 'tits' (strongly sexualised language) become the focus of attention, attention she is defined as 'enjoying'.

The issue of exposure, seemingly inescapably integral to the practice of breastfeeding in public, whether it be an actual or a symbolic exposure, appears frequently to be the crux of the practice's acceptability among supporters and detractors alike. A Mumsnet thread on a breastfeeding sit-in at a café in protest at a mother having been told she would have to sit in the corner if she wanted to breastfeed, and later allegedly verbally abused by a member of the café's staff, revolves around the question of whether this form of protest was justified or a good idea. The thread's original poster suggests that such a form of protest is counter-productive:

> Overall we all want breastfeeding to become so acceptable that incidents
> like the one that happened in the cafe don't happen, and making such an
> issue out of it won't achieve that.[13]

Here, as the perspective of the commentator is clearly pro-breastfeeding as a practice, her criticism might be seen to be of the protest's rejection of discretion as the key value required of a mother breastfeeding in public. Returning to MF's comment on the Hampton Court incident cited earlier, we note that MF assures her readers that she is 'the least prudish person on the planet', yet believes that some things should be carried out with 'decorum'. In other words, she rhetorically positions herself within a norm in terms of thinking, refutes any suggestion that her dislike of public breastfeeding relates to prudishness – which label alone associates breastfeeding with the potential for the sexual gaze – and yet maintains socially accepted boundaries of 'decorum' which public breastfeeding, as constructed in this discourse, violates.

MF concludes her comment by hoping the mother in question would not put her child 'on a potty in a stateroom'. The defence of breastfeeding as a natural practice that frequently enters such discussions becomes employed against it by refiguring it as – precisely because it is 'natural' – offensive and base; the contributor CO comments on the Hampton Court story thus:

---

13 Retrieved in July 2012 from http://www.mumsnet.com/Talk/breast_and_bottle_
feeding/1515280-Anyone-else-think-feeding-protests-are-freakshows; posted by B on
11 July 2012.

Of course breastfeeding is a natural thing which most of us do from the day we are born – but so are urinating and defecating. We have spent thousands of years developing the little 'niceties' which we call civilisation but people are all too ready to go backwards these days.[14]

Breastfeeding is thus figured as the act of the uncivilised, of a person who does not have complete control over herself, as, indeed, in this comment by SH:

> I think that the Palace staff were probably also embarrassed to have to ask her to stop it. Breastfeeding is natural but in a civilised society we have made provisions for women to feed in private – that's where she should have been breastfeeding.[15]

The phrase 'stop it' is associated with unwanted, usually immature behaviour, often on the part of children; the breastfeeding woman here becomes equivalent to a child who has to be told by the 'staff' – those given authority to control the space in question – not to touch the exhibits, yet who should know better. In a similar vein, a poster on the Mumsnet thread referenced above suggests that what is needed to make public breastfeeding socially acceptable is the visibility of:

> more 'normal looking' everyday people BF [breastfeeding] and being respectful and mature about it.[16]

We might surmise that 'respectful and mature' essentially equals discreet; there is an implicit converse association here of non-discreet breastfeeding with immaturity. A user of the large German parenting community eltern.de, calling herself 'Privatstillende' ('private breastfeeder'), makes the following comment in a discussion on parents' views of breastfeeding in public:

> *Die einzelnen Male, an denen ich mein Kind 'außer Haus' gestillt habe, wurde ich zwar nie blöd angesprochen oder angekuckt, dennoch war es mir immer ZUTIEFST unangenehm, meine Brust in der Öffentlichkeit auch nur für Sekunden zu entblößen. Ganz ehrlich, diesen Vergleich mit dem öffentlichen Urinieren habe ich auch schon bemüht, immerhin geht es beim einen wie beim anderen um eine Bedürfniserfüllung, die man gut und gerne in den eigenen vier Wänden oder zumindest außer-*

---

14 http://www.dailymail.co.uk/news/article-358785/Mother-told-breast-best-palace.html.
15 *ibid.*
16 Retrieved on 30 July 2012 from http://www.mumsnet.com/Talk/breast_and_bottle_ feeding/1515280-Anyone-else-think-feeding-protests-are-freakshows?pg=2, posted by A on 11 July 2012.

halb des Blickfeldes anderer Leute erledigen kann. Kein Behördengang, kein Einkauf, kein Spaziergang an der frischen Luft lassen sich nicht so planen, dass frau ihr Kind nicht zu Hause (oder zumindest abgeschieden) stillen könnte.[17]

The commentator is at pains to stress that the occasions in which she fed in public were rare and that she was always extremely uncomfortable during these occasions; if a woman cannot confine herself to home, she argues, they should 'at least' (she uses this word, '*zumindest*', twice) ensure they remain 'secluded' ('*abgeschieden*'), or out of others' sight. As her posting name (see footnote 17) suggests, '*Privatstillende*' identifies positively with the project of discretion and implicitly sets herself apart from the non-private breastfeeders. A male contributor, M, posting on breastfeeding.co.uk on a discussion on breastfeeding in public, also makes the demand that women:

be considerate of others [sic] feelings and plan a little better when it comes to going out with their babies, so that you don't have to make yourself and others deal with the issue.[18]

He continues:

Buy a breast pump. Carry the breast milk with you when you know that you will be in public.[19]

For a commentator on the clothing store story, avoiding breastfeeding in public is a matter of 'basic time management'; the mother, therefore, who finds herself

---

17 Retrieved on 30 July 2012 from http://www.eltern.de/baby/0-3-monate/umfrage-oef-fentlich-stillen.html?no_breadcrumb=1&no_tagcloud=1&no_contentBoxRelated=1; posted by 'Privatstillende' on 21 June 2012: 'The few times I fed outside the home, I never experienced people making stupid comments to me or looking at me, but I always felt DEEPLY uncomfortable exposing my breasts in public even only for a few seconds. To be completely honest, I've made this comparison with urinating in public before; after all, both the one and the other are about fulfilling a need, and both can certainly be done in your own home or at least out of sight of other people. There's no visit to a public office, no shopping trip, no walk which a woman can't plan in such a way as to ensure she can feed her child at home, or at least in a secluded place.' (I have made an exception from the practice of anonymising abbreviation of pseudonyms for this post, due to the relevance of the pseudonym chosen to the strength of feeling expressed in the content, and the fact that the posting name itself is not identifying).

18 Retrieved in July 2012 from http://www.breastfeeding.co.uk/index.php?option=com_content&view=article&id=535&limitstart=8

19 *ibid.*

in the position of feeding her baby in public is badly organised.[20] On the Mumsnet thread referenced above, a mother speaks thus of her experience of breastfeeding in public:

> When I first started bfing in public I felt so awkward and ashamed but over time I got over it [...] I wasn't going to stop going out! Now I'm a seasoned bfer but there are certain places where I can feel people staring and there's an atmosphere when I feed, even though I am very careful to ensure I am discreet and out of sight.[21]

This mother, after an initial phase of shame, rejects the idea of being as well organised as the contributor M demands for the benefit of others; nevertheless, even as a 'seasoned' public breastfeeder, a term resonant of having overcome challenges, she notes 'an atmosphere' which forms around her despite her attempts to fulfil the demand of discretion. Her presence in public feeding might be interpreted as her breaking the social contract of the organised mother whose focus is on the feelings of others.

Obviously, not all mothers who breastfeed in public are exposed to negative reactions. Many mothers who have not encountered negative reactions, when they report their experience in public contexts, often refer to being lucky or fortunate, as K reports on breastfeeding.co.uk:

> I've been very fortunate in that I've never had anyone complain or even behave in a disapproving manner.[22]

Another, anonymous contributor to the same discussion wonders about the reason why she has not received negative responses:

> I don't know whether I just don't notice if people are disapproving, or whether I look too scary to approach.[23]

The implication of this comment is that there is, effectively by default, a sense of disapproval around breastfeeding in public and that if this disapproval does not

---

20 Retrieved in July 2012 from http://www.dailymail.co.uk/news/article-1315803/Primark-tells-breastfeeding-mother-Do-changing-room-out.html; posted by R on 29 September 2010.

21 Retrieved on 30 July 2012 from http://www.mumsnet.com/Talk/breast_and_bottle_feeding/1515280-Anyone-else-think-feeding-protests-are-freakshows?pg=2; posted by GM on 11 July 2012.

22 Retrieved in July 2012 from http://www.breastfeeding.co.uk/index.php?option=com_content&view=article&id=535&limitstart=8.

23 *ibid.*

become explicit, the mother must either be failing to pick it up or the other must be restraining it.

The narrative of responsibility

The discursive negotiation of breastfeeding which takes place in public transforms it to some degree into a public matter, forging relationships of responsibility between the mother and those around her; it can at times appear as if the mother–baby relationship itself is entirely secondary or subordinate in the network of relationships initiated by the act of public breastfeeding. It seems from women's contributions to public discussion on breastfeeding in public that this sense of responsibility is clearly felt and assumed by breastfeeding mothers. In the eltern.de discussion referenced above, a mother comments that:

> *ich stille auch diskret (hab immer einen schal und eine mullwindel dabei), denn a) möchte ich niemanden in verlegenheit bringen, b) möchte ich mich vor fremden blicken und blöden sprüchen schützen und c) möchte ich meinem kind eine ruhige umgebung schaffen ohne zuviel ablenkung.*[24]

The hierarchy of her reasons is striking; top priority, in terms of the order in which she names her reasons, is given to not wishing to upset uninvolved others, while her own protection from the consequences of creating such upset comes second and shielding her child from presumed distractions comes third. In the same discussion, a poster self-identifying as male refers to the 'lack of respect' shown by breastfeeding mothers who *'ihre Brüste hemmungslos in Cafes auf den Tisch legen'*.[25] Strands of this discourse would indeed suggest that the responsibility of the breastfeeding mother to avoid impinging on, disturbing or offending those around her appears to relate particularly to men. A Mumsnet thread calling for posters to contribute their 'trickiest breastfeeding scenarios' described several incidents of breastfeeding in proximity to, or while engaging with, men, with

---

24 Retrieved on 30 July 2012 from http://www.eltern.de/baby/0-3-monate/umfrage-oef-fentlich-stillen.html?no_breadcrumb=1&no_tagcloud=1&no_contentBoxRelated=; posted by P on 28 March 2012: 'I also feed discreetly (I've always got a scarf and a muslin with me), because a) I don't want to embarrass anybody, b) I want to protect myself from strangers looking at me and people saying stupid things, and c) I want my child to have a calm, peaceful environment without too many distractions'.
25 Retrieved on 30 July 2012 from *ibid.*; posted by S38 on 8 June 2011: '[these mothers] put their breasts on the table in cafés without the slightest inhibition'.

two expressions of sympathy for the men in question, pitying them as 'poor'.[26] A contributor to another thread recounts how

> when I had to feed on the train I was surrounded by young men and it was crowded. They didn't have the option to go anywhere else if the sight offended them. So I did cover up and I'm sure they thought I was just cuddling my baby.[27]

Her assumption of responsibility for potential offence caused to the 'young men' leads to her hope that her act of feeding might have been interpreted as a socially acceptable mother–child interaction.

A father quoted in a *Daily Mail* online article discussing male partners' feelings on 'extended', or what the article refers to as 'extreme', breastfeeding says of his wife feeding their two-year-old elder son:

> I hate it when he lifts up his mum's top and bra so he can feed. To me, it's a massive invasion of personal space.[28]

Here, a third party to the interaction of the breastfeeding dyad registers an 'invasion of personal space' upon witnessing the act; whose space, he does not specify, meaning the comment can be read in two ways. If the 'space' he refers to is the mother's, his sense of intrusion on her behalf indicates that he feels her to be to a degree intimately intruded upon, in her two-year-old's asking for milk. If he is referring to his own 'space', this discourse revolves essentially around the conflict dramatised in the Best Beginnings image discussed above: ownership of the breasts as objects or tools.

In the Brigitte.de thread referenced earlier (see footnote 10), a contributor, M, effectively accuses a publicly breastfeeding woman of active violation of the personal space – indeed, the fundamental rights – of others:

> *was bitte ist denn so schlimm an der Forderung, wenn es schon öffentlich machen muss, es so diskret wie eben möglich zu tun und sich so verhalten, dass es möglichst wenige Leute sehen […] Es gibt da nunmal den Paragraphen im grundgesetz, dass die eigene freiheit aufhört, wo die der*

---

26 Retrieved in July 2012 from http://www.mumsnet.com/Talk/breast_and_bottle_feeding/1526008-Boob-on-tube-what-are-ur-trickiest-breast-feeding-scenarios; posted by TZ on 26 July 2012, and GD on 25 July 2012.

27 http://www.mumsnet.com/Talk/1364/518120; posted by B3.

28 *Daily Mail* online, 'How does a man cope when his wife won't stop breast feeding?', published 11 July 2012, retrieved in July 2012 from http://www.dailymail.co.uk/femail/article-2172282/Breastfeeding-How-does-man-cope-wife-wont-stop.html.

anderen anfängt und das ist eben durchaus auch der Fall, wenn andere nur peinlich berührt oder irritiert sind.[29]

Thus the publicly breastfeeding mother is cast as a violator of fundamental human rights; the '*Grundgesetz*' ('Basic Law') is the German constitution. M's long post contains two references to the criminal offence '*Erregung öffentlichen Ärgernisses*', whose content is described in the German penal code as publicly performing sexual acts and by this deliberately or consciously causing offence.[30] M continues:

Da stellt sich mir dann schon die Frage, was die stillende Dame denn so unbedingt demonstrieren und präsentieren möchte[31]

The use of '*Dame*' ('lady') – which in contemporary usage in German frequently has an ironic meaning, particularly when used with reference to younger women – and the effectively rhetorical question as to what this 'lady', by breastfeeding in public, wishes to 'demonstrate' and 'present' seeks to depict the woman who breastfeeds in public as using the feeding of her child to expose and flaunt a part of her sexuality. She presents her unavailability in public and in so doing draws attention to herself; she rejects the imperative to retreat to a closed and marginal space; she is as present as a mother in the act of public breastfeeding as her child is present, demonstrating a reciprocal relationship, rather than effectively disappearing behind her child. As noted, a common element of discussions on public breastfeeding involves the alignment of breastfeeding, whose 'naturalness'

---

29 http://www.brigitte.de/foren/showthread.html?t=83917&highlight=stillen: 'could someone please tell me what's so terrible about requiring [the noun '*Forderung*' is in fact more usually rendered as a 'demand'] [the breastfeeding mother] to do it as discreetly as possible, if she has to do it in public at all, and to make sure that as few people as possible see it? [...] After all, there is the paragraph in the Basic Law saying that your own freedom ends where that of others begins, and that is absolutely the case if others are so much as slightly ruffled or made to feel uncomfortable [by a mother breastfeeding in public]'. The 'paragraph' she refers to is the first part of Article 2 of the German Basic Law, which functions as a constitution; it guarantees every person 'the right to free development of his personality insofar as he does not violate the rights of others or offend against the constitutional order or the moral law.' (English translation of the *Grundgesetz* at http://www.bundestag.de/interakt/infomat/fremdsprachiges_material/downloads/ggEn_download.pdf).

30 The full German text of this article of the penal code is at http://dejure.org/gesetze/StGB/183a.html.

31 It does make me wonder what the breastfeeding lady is so desperate to demonstrate and present.

cannot be denied, with equally 'natural' but culturally private or offensive practices, particularly going to the toilet. This, however, is not the focus of our attention when we examine the comment N leaves on a Mumsnet thread:

> But why would you NOT be discreet if you can? When you use a public loo you have a choice. You can close the door and do what you have to do in private or leave it open and let everyone see/watch. Obviously the first option gives both parties some dignity. So it makes sense to choose it.[32]

She contrasts the women who afford the other 'part[y] some dignity' with those 'out to shock and upset and offend' by making the choice to reject discretion.[33] The phrase 'both parties', a somewhat legally flavoured term, defines outsiders who are present at the time of a public act of feeding as 'parties' to the breastfeeding relationship, thus implicitly endowing them with rights in the matter. The 'dignity' of everyone around her becomes the breastfeeding mother's responsibility, and a refusal to take responsibility for others' dignity in this way is read as a deliberate, antagonising attempt to 'shock and upset and offend', which implies that the nature of breast exposure for feeding purposes itself is shocking, upsetting and offensive. In relation to the Hampton Court incident discussed earlier, a spokeswoman for the organisation running the palace is cited in an online local news report as commenting that:

> [w]e have many visitors of all ages and nationalities who find women breast-feeding either offensive or a welcome distraction to their visit. The mother-and-baby room is the only area of the palace where we can guarantee privacy.[34]

The two parts of this statement are incongruous. The first sentence concerns itself with the feelings of others who may be offended or titillated (assuming that the statement did intend to refer to a 'welcome distraction'), locating responsibility with the breastfeeding mother. Conversely, the second sentence refers to a need to 'guarantee privacy', which one might assume would be for the benefit of the breastfeeding mother, yet this intent is belied by the previous sentence, which focuses on the needs of the observing parties to the breastfeeding-in-public relationship.

---

32 http://www.mumsnet.com/Talk/breast_and_bottle_feeding/a518120-im-getting-so-sick-of-being-told-bf-in-public#10525781; posted on 23 April 2008.

33 *ibid.*

34 Letter from Historic Royal Palaces, quoted in http://www.surreycomet.co.uk/news/619158.breast_is_best_mums_hit_out_at_palace_coverup_policy/.

The coverage of the Hampton Court incident on the *Daily Mail*'s website precedes the story with this call for discussion contributions: 'Should mothers be allowed to breastfeed in public places? Add your opinion by clicking on the link at the bottom of the page'.[35] Thus the anonymous online community is given, at least rhetorically, the power to 'allow' or deny breastfeeding women the privilege of feeding in public. The negotiation of public space, for mothers who wish or need to breastfeed in public, frequently revolves around the search for what one might term spaces of permission, where being 'allowed' to breastfeed is explicit and hence they have a chance of feeling comfortable. A Mumsnet poster, discussing the increasing practice for restaurants and businesses to put up signs indicating they are breastfeeding-friendly, relates to her mother-in-law discussing where they could go with her young baby for lunch, asking 'do they have the sign that allows it?'[36] The converse of this interpretation of the breastfeeding-friendly sign is that its absence implies a prohibition, and the implication of this in turn is that prohibition is the usual state of affairs and permission requires an explicit statement. Theoretically private spaces, too, often find the woman taking responsibility for the feelings of others by seeking permission to breastfeed. In the eltern.de discussion, a mother, reporting that she had found breastfeeding in public '*teils notwendig, aber immer unangenehm*' ('sometimes necessary, but always unpleasant') and a matter for the '*Notfall*' ('emergency'), explained how she had: '*Freunde und Verwandte immer gefragt ob ich in deren Gegenwart stillen kann oder ob ich rausgehen soll. Das war für mich kein Problem und ersparte peinliche Momente.*'[37]

Here, the negotiation of public space passes the rights to the other and the responsibility to the mother; the act of negotiation, however, also protects the mother from anticipated potential criticism and judgement. A comment in the Hampton Court discussion suggests that '[d]iscretion should be utmost [sic] in mothers' thoughts when feeding their babies'; in this view, the primary party to the breastfeeding relationship, the party whose needs count most, is the potential

---

35 http://www.dailymail.co.uk/news/article-358785/Mother-told-breast-best-palace.html.

36 Retrieved in July 2012 from http://www.mumsnet.com/Talk/breast_and_bottle_feeding/1515280-Anyone-else-think-feeding-protests-are-freakshows?pg=3; posted by E on 12 July 2012.

37 Retrieved on 30 July 2012 from http://www.eltern.de/baby/0-3-monate/umfrage-oeffentlich-stillen.html?no_breadcrumb=1&no_tagcloud=1&no_contentBoxRelated=1&cpage=3; posted by K on 22 November 2009: '[I] always asked friends and relatives whether I could feed in their presence or whether they wanted me to leave the room. It wasn't a problem for me, and saved embarrassing moments.'

observer. The same commentator continues, widening the theme of distaste for the visual representation of maternity:

> On a slightly different aspect, I personally do not like the trend of expect-ant mothers parading their bulges to all and sundry. Yes it is obvious they are pregnant but we do not need it shoved in our faces – there is nothing attractive about stretch marks or bulging tummy buttons.[38]

Once again, the mother who appears to be unduly seeking attention by her state is condemned, particularly because the pregnant state is viewed as not 'attractive'; as with breastfeeding, obvious pregnancy carries a connotation of sexual unavailability and therefore has no place in a public realm in which women are required to appear as both potentially available and pleasing. B, cited above in a Mumsnet discussion, continues in the same post:

> You catch more flies with honey than vinegar. So why go out of your way to irritate the people you want to PERSUADE that bf is the natural way to feed?[39]

Here, the poster ascribes all responsibility for avoiding offence (the possibility of which she assumes as a given) to the breastfeeding woman, who becomes a representative not only of herself but of public breastfeeding, required to 'persuade' others of its legitimacy. Breastfeeding thus becomes something along the lines of an unpalatable fact or a new lifestyle choice which needs to be made acceptable, and as such the reputation of all breastfeeding mothers stands and falls with the discreet behaviour of each. As the practice of breastfeeding is on trial in the cultural-discursive arena, so do all those who practise it in public go on trial as its advocates. In the *Telegraph* discussion referenced above, a contributor speaks in a similar vein by suggesting that:

> the 'behaviour' of the in your face earth mothers who spend all day en-gaging in their foul couldn't give a damn attitude towards ot[h]er peoples' sensibilities [...] sets back the cause of the sensible mother seeking to feed her baby.[40]

---

38 http://www.dailymail.co.uk/news/article-358785/Mother-told-breast-best-palace.html; posted by AT.

39 http://www.mumsnet.com/Talk/1364/518120.

40 Retrieved on 08 July 2012 from http://www.telegraph.co.uk/comment/personal-view/3559591/The-nightmare-of-breast-feeding-in-public.html#disqus_thread; posted on 18 June 2008.

'Sensible', equated here implicitly with 'discreet', is set against 'in your face'; again, it is what is assumed to be attention-seeking in the breastfeeding mother that draws the strongest condemnation. In this way, good/discreet breastfeeding mothers are discursively set against bad/shameful/exposing ones; it is a distinction that women themselves use. A local government representative in Berlin, asked in 2009 to move into a back row next time when feeding her baby in the local parliament's plenary room due to another parliamentarian's *'Schamgefühl'* (feeling of decorum, literally 'shame') having been injured, reported her feelings on the incident in an interview with the online edition of the *Süddeutsche Zeitung* newspaper:

Ich habe mich in dem Moment schon sehr geärgert. Ich gehöre nicht zu denen, die sich vollends entblößen, wenn sie ihr Kind stillen.[41]

The politician's juxtaposition of her self-image as a discreet practitioner of breastfeeding and her indignation at being asked to move to a less exposed place leaves room for a potential implication that such a request might have, in her view, been justified were she not to have been so discreet. The politician's utterance also creates a category of less-discreet mothers, whom – so runs the implication of the two-part statement – it might be justified to request to move or desist, and who would consequently not have the right to be 'cross' at having such a request made to them. Another dichotomy created in the discourse of acceptable versus unacceptable public breastfeeding revolves around the necessity or otherwise – as judged by the observing parties to the relationship of breastfeeding responsibility – of each act. TK, in what he possibly imagines is a spirited defence of the publicly breastfeeding mother in the course of a *Telegraph* website discussion, responds thus to negative comments:

no one breast feeds in public because she feels like it. People usually do it because an unplanned and urgent necessity has arisen like when you are stuck somewhere.[42]

The implication is that breastfeeding in public is an emergency act, in the context of which – as in all emergencies – general rules of behaviour and decorum may be put aside for the duration of the emergency. He adds:

41 Stefanie Winde, quoted in http://www.sueddeutsche.de/politik/berliner-abgeordneten-haus-platzverweis-fuer-stillende-mutter-1.460939; published 25 September 2009: 'I was pretty cross at that moment. I'm not one of those people who expose themselves completely when breastfeeding their child.'
42 http://www.telegraph.co.uk/news/yourview/1560285/Is-breast-feeding-always-best-for-mother-and-baby.html; post on 14 August 2007.

With a proper nursing bra and a certain amount of decorum you don't get to see anything anyway.[43]

Again the responsibility is on the woman to be 'proper[ly]' attired and exercise 'decorum'. Also interesting is the formulation 'you don't get to see anything', which wording carries the – almost certainly unintended – implication that 'seeing something' would be a (sexual) treat for the (presumably male) onlooker. Even a defence of breastfeeding in public, then, frames the action in sexual terms, permitting it in an 'emergency' only, excluding 'because she feels like it' as a legitimate reason and placing at the feet of the woman the responsibility for avoiding a sexual connotation with her act.

Demonstrative discretion: breastfeeding discretion products and the symbolism of the feeding room

The article on breastfeeding covers which appears on the US site InfoBarrel states:

Covers for breastfeeding exist primarily for social reasons, to relieve the mild discomfort strangers may feel near breastfeeding mothers. This is also often a benefit to mothers, who can't fully relax and enjoy the bonding experience with their baby if they feel others are watching or trying too hard not to watch. Because of this, nursing covers are marketed, simple cloth apron-like products that drape over baby and mother alike for added privacy.[44]

Breastfeeding covers, while most common in the USA, are emerging in the UK and elsewhere in Europe as a product whose chief use is for the mother to fulfil the responsibility set out above, to potential observers in a public breastfeeding scenario. One of the first covers, an American product, is now sold under the name of Bébé au Lait. The product website sets out its origins thus:

Bébé au Lait's first and best known product, its award-winning nursing cover, was born out of necessity when co-owner Claire Ekelund found nursing her infant daughter in public challenging.[45]

The 'challenge' referred to here is the negotiation of the potential shame of breastfeeding in public; the response to the challenge, originally named 'Hooter

---

43 *ibid.*
44 Retrieved in July 2012 from http://www.infobarrel.com/Discretion_Through_Covers_During_Breastfeeding; posted by TopicGuru on 7 April 2010.
45 http://www.bebeaulait.com/about-us/our-story, retrieved on 7 July 2012.

Hider', solves the problem by making public breastfeeding an act of what we might call demonstrative discretion.

We might describe the use of the Hooter Hider as performative discretion; the cover makes it glaringly obvious that the woman is breastfeeding, certainly to those who know what it is, while the act itself is removed from the image and replaced by a feminine, fashionable pattern which provides a signal of attractiveness, with a focus on outside appearance. Rather than the mother disappearing behind her child, as discussed above in terms of a socially approved concept of motherhood which public breastfeeding violates, the use of a breastfeeding scarf or cover renders the child invisible and leaves only the mother visible. In these terms, we might view the image as reflecting our observation above that the societal relationships of responsibility which the mother is viewed as creating by breastfeeding in public exist between mother and onlooker and exclude the child. The nursing cover signals to the outside world that the mother cares what others think of her in terms of her breastfeeding. However, the cover, as a signal of capitulation to demands for decorum and of the censorship of the breastfeeding act, demonstrates and performs mother–child exclusivity without the threat to the woman's availability represented by the visible breast. In a way, the Hooter Hider makes the breastfeeding woman all things to all people, or rather to all attitudes towards breastfeeding in public.

The name 'Hooter Hider' makes its purpose very clear; the current product name, Bébé au Lait, reminiscent of a café latte as well as punning on breastmilk, carries strong connotations of what has been widely termed the 'yummy mummy' lifestyle.[46] The choice of 'hooter' as the breast slang is almost certainly down to the rhythm and alliteration; we may, however, remark that 'hooter' (and the German equivalent '*Hupe*', both meaning 'car horn') carries the connotation of noise, of intrusiveness, of attracting attention. The breast as 'hooter' is an inevitable source of attention and needs hiding if it is required to be put on show.

An image included on the website of the UK product Mamascarf shows a woman sitting at an outdoor café table smiling down at a baby wrapped in, and almost completely concealed by, a black Mamascarf she is wearing.[47] In the colour

---

46 The website features 'nursing covers' under the Bébé au Lait and Hooter Hiders brands side by side, and states: 'Hooter Hiders would not be here today if not for the early, loyal fan following who called and wrote, "It will always be Hooter Hiders to us!" when the name was initially changed to Bébé au Lait in 2006 [...] For this reason, the beloved name was kept and today our fashion-forward nursing covers sell under two brand names.' (http://www.bebeaulait.com/brands/hooter-hiders, retrieved on 7 July 2012).

47 Image retrieved on 7 July 2012 from http://www.mamascarf.co.uk/wp-content/uploads/2012/05/mamascarf-4.jpg.

Breastfeeding scarf (above) and cover (right).

shown here, the scarf has the effect of a veil; it cuts across the predominantly light colours of the woman's clothing and colouring. Among the benefits listed under the initial product description are 'See your baby and maintain eye contact', 'Less distraction for your baby', 'Hidden pocket to store your breastpad' and 'Hides your post pregnancy tummy'. The removal of the child from the visual image of the breastfeeding mother is sold here as reinforcing and intensifying the mother–child dyad by placing a barrier between child and outside world. Read in analogy to the use of the term 'headscarf' as a religiously motivated head covering, a 'mamascarf' covers the 'mamas', the mammaries. Both the 'post pregnancy tummy' and its cause are excluded from the visual image; in terms of the evaluation of breastfeeding by others, the mother both nurtures in terms of removing her child from 'distraction' and adapts to the demand of responsibility when breastfeeding in public.

A further competitor product on the UK market bears the name 'Freedom Babe', with the website's welcome page announcing that 'As the name suggests, the covers give you the freedom to breastfeed anywhere!'[48] In this discourse, while internet users are rhetorically given the power to 'allow' a woman to breastfeed in public or not, a cover which visually censors breast and baby from view grants a mother her 'freedom' of movement.

The Freedom Babe product information lists among the features of the breastfeeding cover, a 'Semi-rigid neckline holds the cover away from the body

---

48 Retrieved on 8 July 2012 from http://www.freedombabe.co.uk/.

thus creating a secluded space for mum to maintain eye contact with baby.'[49] In this description, the product becomes a boundary, the demarcator of a '*secluded space*' which, it is implied, is required in order for the breastfeeding relationship to function – the mother and baby need to be set apart from the rest of the life taking place around them.

One version of the Freedom Babe declares explicitly 'Feeding in Progress', in large white capital letters on a cover that is otherwise completely black, with a touch of humour conveyed by the use of a drawing of a baby's smiling face to constitute the 'o' of 'Progress'.[50] The wording recalls notices on doors to prevent unauthorised entry when an activity which is not to be disturbed is going on; here, in striking monochrome, it both screens out the would-be onlooker and draws attention to the act of breastfeeding. In this way, it represents demonstrative decorum; the wearer veils and shrouds her feeding while stating and performing her identity as a breastfeeding mother. In terms of its visual impact, it might be compared to a 'Censored' sign across an explicit image; the cover, in this way, makes an explicit call to the imagination while claiming, in its property as a veil, to protect the modesty and 'discretion' of its object.

Breastfeeding rooms, whose proliferation is increasing, might be seen to represent an extension of the pretty, secluded but evident space provided by the breastfeeding cover. Feeding facilities are much sought after by breastfeeding mothers who would prefer to feed in privacy and comfort, particularly in the early weeks; they are also a symbol and synecdoche of the determining power of the observer or potential observer in the breastfeeding relationship. The website of major shopping complex the Trafford Centre advertises its 'main breast-feeding room', specially designed, as a 'calming and attractive environment [...] We hope to roll out these designer rooms in the future, to show our commitment to our youngest visitors.'[51] The shopping centre's 'Breastfeeding Policy', while evidently concerned with supporting both public and private (in feeding facilities) breastfeeding, makes repeated use of the word 'allow', including its directions to staff in case of receiving a complaint about another customer breastfeeding: 'Deal with the complaint appropriately by stating that it is company policy to allow

---

49 Retrieved on 8 July 2012 from http://www.freedombabe.co.uk/Breastfeeding-Cover-Apron/.

50 Image retrieved on 8 July 2012 from http://www.freedombabe.co.uk/store/product.php?id=18.

51 Retrieved in August 2012 from http://www.traffordcentre.co.uk/visitorinformation/family-facilities.

breastfeeding'.[52] In its certificate of achievement of the Trafford Breastfeeding Friendly Award, The Centre is listed as, among other points, doing the following: 'Allows mums the right to breastfeed in a general area' and 'Where possible allows mums the right to privacy in order to breastfeed (not a toilet)'.[53] While breastfeeding, in public or in private, is figured as a 'right', the right is framed in this language as one to be 'allowed', with the implicit corollary that it could, were 'company policy' different, be denied. The script for responses to complaints also means the complaining customers hear the language of breastfeeding being 'allowed', implying a potential for renegotiation of public space to exclude public breastfeeding, with the presence of the 'calming' designer feeding rooms potentially supporting such renegotiation; as in the case of the breastfeeding cover, the mother is given, at considerable care and expense, a 'facility' whose non-use puts her out of step with mothers who do use them and potentially makes her a legitimate target for unwanted attention.

The feeding room also appears, in some quarters, in the apparently dedicated space of the maternity ward. A participant in a discussion on giving birth in Germany on LEO, a forum for amateur and professional linguists, reports – in an entirely neutral tone – the existence, after the (clearly relatively recent) birth of her child, of an '*Extra Still-Raum wenn einem im eigenen Zimmer zuviel los war oder zuviel "Fremdbesuch" rumrannte*'.[54] In other words, even the intimate space of the maternity ward may become subject to negotiation of responsibilities and withdrawal from the space by the breastfeeding mother.

Concluding observations

The practice of breastfeeding, particularly in public spaces, appears to remain a flashpoint of public discourse with considerable symbolic value which translates into a concrete impact on those who do it. Specifically, the visibility of breastfeeding in the public space remains a profoundly controversial matter, with much debate revolving around its undisguised or uncensored visibility. As our observations have demonstrated, this discourse seeks to establish

---

52 Retrieved in August 2012 from http://www.traffordcentre.co.uk/visitorinformation/family-facilities/bffaward.

53 *ibid.*

54 http://dict.leo.org/forum/viewGeneraldiscussion.php?idThread=657904&idForum=&lp=ende&lang=de; post by S on 23 January 2009: 'a separate breastfeeding room for when there was too much going on in your own room or too many visitors belonging to other people about the place'. German hospitals generally provide rooms for their patients containing between two and four beds.

relationships of responsibility between the publicly breastfeeding mother and those around her in the public space, with the primary responsibility assigned to the former.

It is a debate to which there appears to be no easy resolution available. The key importance of 'discretion' and the potential for sanctions against breastfeeding mothers deemed to fall outside the category of the discreet, provides (potentially reversible) tolerance rather than freedom and security for mothers wishing or having to breastfeed in public. An observational reading of this discourse as text has shown that the complex interaction of the categories of discretion and exhibition with ideas of female availability and responsibility to and for those around her problematises the establishment and continuation of uncomplicated breastfeeding relationships, particularly where responsive or demand breastfeeding is practised. The implications of these observational findings for individual and public health, women's experience of breastfeeding and the discourse of motherhood in society require further and concerted study.

References

Acker, M. (2009) Breast is best... but not everywhere: Ambivalent sexism and attitudes toward private and public breastfeeding. *Sex roles*, **61**(7), 476–90.

Schmied, V. and Barclay, L. (1999) Connection and pleasure, disruption and distress: women's experience of breastfeeding. *Journal of Human Lactation*, **15**(4), 325–34.

Sheeshka, J., Potter, B., Norrie, E., Valaitis, R., Adams, G. and Kuczynski, L. (2001) Women's experiences breastfeeding in public places. *Journal of Human Lactation*, **17**(1), 31–8.

Spurles, P. K. and Babineau, J. (2011) A qualitative study of attitudes toward public breastfeeding among young Canadian men and women. *Journal of Human Lactation*, **27**(2), 131–7.

Stearns, C. A. (1999) Breastfeeding and the good maternal body. *Gender & Society*, **13**(3), 308–25.

Acknowledgements

The figures on p. 230 are reproduced by kind permission of Freedom Babe and Bébé au Lait.

News and comment websites:

Daily Telegraph: http://www.telegraph.co.uk/
Independent: http://www.independent.co.uk/
Daily Mail: http://www.dailymail.co.uk/
Süddeutsche Zeitung: http://www.sueddeutsche.de/
Surrey Comet: http://www.surreycomet.co.uk/

Discussion fora

Discussion on breastfeeding.co.uk: http://www.breastfeeding.co.uk
Brigitte magazine, online version: http://www.brigitte.de/foren

Eltern.de baby forum: http://www.eltern.de/baby/0-3-monate/
Forum of Munich-based language resource website Leo: http://dict.leo.org/forum/
Mumsnet: http://www.mumsnet.com/

Breastfeeding cover manufacturers
Bébé au Lait: http://www.bebeaulait.com/
Freedom Babe: http://www.freedombabe.co.uk/
Mamascarf: http://www.mamascarf.co.uk/

Other
InfoBarrel: http://www.infobarrel.com/
Trafford Centre: http://www.traffordcentre.co.uk/

CHAPTER 8

Balancing the risks and benefits of breastfeeding in the context of HIV

Tyra Gross and Alex Kojo Anderson

Introduction

Breast milk is recognized internationally as the optimal form of nutrition for infants (World Health Organization, 2003). There is extensive evidence of the benefits of breastfeeding for both the infant and the mother. For infants, breast milk improves cognitive function, protects against immune related diseases (e.g. coeliac disease), reduces risk of obesity and protects against diarrhoea morbidity and mortality (Owen *et al.*, 2005; Schack-Nielsen and Michaelsen, 2006; Lamberti *et al.*, 2011). Maternal benefits of breastfeeding include reduced risk for postpartum bleeding, postpartum depression, diabetes, hip fractures, and breast and ovarian cancers (Turck, 2007; Lamberti *et al.*, 2011). In the Global Strategy on Infant and Young Child Feeding, the World Health Organization (WHO) recommends that infants be exclusively breastfed until age six months for 'optimal growth, development and health' (World Health Organization, 2003, p. 8). From then on, WHO recommends introducing appropriate and nutritionally adequate complementary foods while breastfeeding continues until two years of age or older.

In 2010, 3.4 million children (under the age of 15 years) were reported to be living with HIV worldwide. An estimated 390,000 children were newly infected with the virus that same year (UNAIDS, 2011). Over 90% of these children live in sub-Saharan Africa, where about 3.1 million children are living with HIV. Southeast Asia has the second highest number of children living with the virus, with an estimated 160,000 children infected. Globally, there were also an estimated 250,000 child deaths due to AIDS in 2010, a 20% decrease from 2005 (UNAIDS, 2011).

Despite the known health benefits of breastfeeding, as well as the social and economic benefits, there is a debate on whether breastfeeding is best for all infants and whether or not the practice should be encouraged in the context of HIV (Chinkonde *et al.*, 2010; Koricho, *et al.*, 2010; Slater *et al.*, 2010) due to breastfeeding being one route of mother-to-child transmission of the virus. There is growing evidence, however, that exclusive breastfeeding (feeding the infant only breast milk without additional water, food or drink) is associated with a lower risk of HIV transmission than mixed feeding (breastfeeding and giving the infant additional food or drink) (Coovadia *et al.*, 2007; Kuhn *et al.*, 2007; Becquet *et al.*, 2008; World Health Organization, 2009a). Addressing the issue of breastfeeding as a mode of transmission of HIV is particularly challenging in developing countries where HIV is prevalent and breastfeeding is the norm and also critical for infant survival (Nor *et al.*, 2009; Bulterys *et al.*, 2010; Levy *et al.*, 2010; Slater *et al.*, 2010; Mepham *et al.*, 2011). The absence of breastfeeding is associated with very high infant mortality in developing countries (Nelson and Williams 2007; Jackson *et al.*, 2009) and infants not breastfed in these areas have as much as a six-fold risk of death due to illnesses attributed to malnutrition, pneumonia and diarrhoea (World Health Organization, 2009a).

It is now well established that HIV is transmitted throughout the duration of breastfeeding (Kuhn and Aldrovandi, 2010) and late postnatal transmission has been shown to account for as much as 42% of the total mother-to-child transmission of HIV (Breastfeeding and HIV International Transmission Study Group, 2004). Several maternal factors are known to increase the risk of HIV transmission through breast milk, including high plasma viral load, low CD4 count, breast pathology (including mastitis and abscesses), mode of infant feeding, and prolonged duration of breastfeeding (more than 6 months) (Semba *et al.*, 1999; John-Stewart, 2004). Most breastfeeding transmission occurs in countries where breastfeeding is a common practice or alternative feeding options are neither safe nor feasible (Nelson and Williams 2007). This therefore poses a challenge to the promotion and practice of breastfeeding. Thus guidelines for infant feeding in the context of HIV differ between developed and developing countries (Jackson *et al.*, 2009; Kuhn *et al.*, 2010).

Breastfeeding is reported to be safer in developing countries especially where HIV-infected mothers or HIV-exposed infants are provided with antiretroviral therapy to reduce the likelihood of HIV transmission (Peltier *et al.*, 2009; Homsy *et al.*, 2010; Mcintyre 2010; Saloojee and Cooper 2010; Kesho Bora Study Group and Devincenzi 2011). WHO updated its guidelines on HIV and infant feeding in November 2009 to reflect this evidence (World Health Organization, 2009a).

However, only 53% of pregnant women living with HIV and 35% of infants born to HIV-infected mothers are reported to receive antiretroviral therapy for preventing mother-to-child transmission of HIV in low- and middle-income countries (World Health Organization, 2010c). Since antiretroviral therapy may be lacking or not adhered to in certain areas of the developing world, other interventions that can reduce maternal transmission of HIV to the infant through breastfeeding are needed.

According to WHO, 'The dilemma has been to balance the risk of infants being exposed to HIV through breastfeeding with the risk of death from causes other than HIV if infants are not breastfed' (World Health Organization, 2009a, p. 2). In light of the revised HIV and infant feeding guidelines and the current debate, this chapter examines recent literature on breastfeeding and alternative infant feeding options for HIV-exposed mother–infant dyads in developed and developing countries. Specifically, this chapter will examine: (1) the infant feeding practices in developing countries where HIV is prevalent and (2) the influences on HIV-positive mothers' decision to breastfeed or not. The chapter also identifies gaps in the literature and scientific knowledge to inform future research.

Guidelines for infant feeding in the context of HIV

Previous WHO guidelines on HIV and infant feeding recommended exclusive breastfeeding as a safer infant feeding option than mixed feeding in the early postpartum period (World Health Organization, 2009a). Research on infant feeding in the context of HIV has expanded since then. Current evidence shows that providing antiretroviral therapy to mothers infected with HIV during pregnancy and lactation or their exposed infants can greatly reduce the risk of transmission of the virus through breastfeeding (World Health Organization, 2010a). Thus, WHO held a Guideline Development Group meeting in October 2009 to review the scientific evidence on HIV and infant feeding to update the previous guidelines. A set of comprehensive HIV and infant feeding guidelines developed from this meeting was published in 2010 (World Health Organization, 2010a) along with new guidelines on prevention of mother-to-child transmission through antiretroviral therapy (World Health Organization, 2009b). These guidelines are expected to influence the counselling and treatment services provided to HIV-infected mothers and their exposed infants by national health authorities (World Health Organization, 2009a).

The 2010 HIV and infant feeding guidelines differ in two major ways from the 2006 guidelines (World Health Organization, 2009a, 2010b), as illustrated in Table 8.1. Firstly, the 2010 guidelines emphasize the protective effect of

Table 8.1 Comparison of the 2006 and 2010 WHO HIV and infant feeding guidelines.

	2006 Guidelines	2010 Guidelines
Antiretroviral therapy	No recommendation provided	Mothers known to be HIV-infected should be provided with lifelong antiretroviral therapy or antiretroviral prophylaxis interventions to reduce HIV transmission through breastfeeding according to WHO recommendations
Infant feeding decision	The most appropriate infant feeding option for an HIV-infected mother should continue to depend on her individual circumstances, including her health status and the local situation, but should take greater consideration of the health services available and the counselling and support she is likely to receive	National health authorities should promote a single infant feeding practice as the standard of care: ■ breastfeed and receive antiretroviral interventions OR ■ avoid all breastfeeding, as the strategy that will most likely give infants the greatest chance of remaining HIV uninfected and alive While information about other practices should be made available to mothers, health services would principally support one approach
Duration of exclusive breastfeeding	Exclusive breastfeeding is recommended for HIV-infected mothers for the first six months of life unless replacement feeding is acceptable, feasible, affordable, sustainable and safe for them and their infants before that time At six months, if replacement feeding is still not acceptable, feasible, affordable, sustainable and safe, continuation of breastfeeding with additional complementary foods is recommended, while the mother and baby continue to be regularly assessed	Mothers known to be HIV-infected (and whose infants are HIV uninfected or of unknown HIV status) should exclusively breastfeed their infants for the first 6 months of life, introducing appropriate complementary foods thereafter, and continue breastfeeding for the first 12 months of life
Breastfeeding cessation	The optimal duration for the cessation process is not known, but for most women and babies a period of about two to three days up to two to three weeks would appear to be adequate, based on expert opinion and programmatic experience. All breastfeeding should stop once a nutritionally adequate and safe diet without breast milk can be provided	Mothers known to be HIV-infected who decide to stop breastfeeding at any time should stop gradually within one month Stopping breastfeeding abruptly is not advisable Breastfeeding should then only stop once a nutritionally adequate and safe diet without breast milk can be provided

Table 8.1 (*continued*)

	2006 Guidelines	2010 Guidelines
Replacement feeding	When replacement feeding is acceptable, feasible, affordable, sustainable and safe (AFASS), avoidance of all breastfeeding by HIV-infected mothers is recommended	Mothers known to be HIV-infected should only give commercial infant formula milk as a replacement feed to their HIV-uninfected infants or infants who are of unknown HIV status, when specific conditions are met

Note: Adapted from WHO HIV and Infant Feeding: New evidence and programmatic experience, 2006 and WHO HIV and Infant Feeding Guidelines, 2010

antiretroviral therapy provided during breastfeeding, which is reflected in the principles and recommendations. The previous set of guidelines was devised prior to concrete evidence on the effectiveness of antiretroviral therapy in minimizing transmission of HIV through breastfeeding. Secondly, where the 2006 guidelines emphasized individualized counselling for HIV-infected mothers to choose the appropriate infant feeding option considering their situation, the 2010 guidelines encourage national or sub-national health authorities to decide which infant feeding option will be promoted and sustained as the standard of care in their context: i.e. breastfeeding with antiretroviral therapy or complete avoidance of all breastfeeding (World Health Organization, 2009a, 2010a). Table 8.2 highlights the key principles of the 2010 HIV and infant feeding guidelines, while the key recommendations are summarized in the next section.

According to WHO 2010 guidelines, HIV-infected mothers should be provided with lifelong antiretroviral therapy to prevent the transmission of HIV

Table 8.2 HIV and infant feeding key principles.

1. Balancing HIV prevention with protection from other causes of child mortality

2. Integrating HIV interventions into maternal and child health services

3. Setting national or sub-national recommendations for infant feeding in the context of HIV

4. When antiretroviral drugs are not (immediately) available, breastfeeding may still provide infants born to HIV-infected mothers with a greater chance of HIV-free survival

5. Informing mothers known to be HIV-infected about infant feeding alternatives

6. Providing services to specifically support mothers to appropriately feed their infants

7. Avoiding harm to infant feeding practices in the general population

8. Advising mothers who are HIV uninfected or whose HIV status is unknown

9. Investing in improvements in infant feeding practices in the context of HIV

to the child through breastfeeding. They should also exclusively breastfeed their infants until six months of age. This guideline applies to all infants, whether infected or uninfected, and also infants of unknown HIV status. The 2010 guidelines also recommend exclusive breastfeeding if antiretroviral therapy is not immediately available, stating that 'mothers should be counseled to exclusively breastfeed in the first six months of life and continue breastfeeding thereafter unless environmental and social circumstances are safe for, and supportive of, replacement feeding' (World Health Organization, 2010a, p. 4). After the age of six months, complementary foods (such as other milks, foods or drinks) can be introduced into the infant's diet (World Health Organization, 2010a). Breastfeeding should be continued until the age of 12 months. The current WHO guidelines emphasize that breastfeeding should cease only if 'a nutritionally adequate and safe diet without breast milk can be provided' (World Health Organization, 2010a, p. 6). Also, the 2010 guidelines state that HIV-infected mothers should not abruptly stop breastfeeding, but wean (transition the infant from human breast milk to non-breast milk foods) gradually within a month. This particular recommendation in the 2010 HIV and infant feeding guidelines is in direct opposition to the 2006 guidelines, which emphasised abrupt weaning (transitioning the infant from human breast milk to non-breast milk foods) after exclusive breastfeeding. Another important addition to the 2010 guidelines is for mothers and infants who are on antiretroviral therapy to continue their therapy for an additional week after the cessation of breastfeeding (World Health Organization, 2010a).

Infants born to HIV-infected mothers should be provided with safe and adequate breastfeeding alternatives once breastfeeding ceases. Alternatives recommended for infants younger than age six months include commercial infant formula or expressed breast milk that is heat-treated (World Health Organization, 2010a). According to the 2010 guidelines, formula feeding should only be an option if specific conditions are met, with the most important being access to safe water and good sanitation, the ability to provide adequate formula for proper growth and development, and the ability to prepare it hygienically and frequently to decrease the potential risk of malnutrition and diarrhoea. Table 8.3 highlights all of the specific conditions mentioned by the 2010 WHO HIV and infant feeding guidelines that replace the AFASS (acceptable, feasible, affordable, sustainable and safe) criteria from the 2006 guidelines. Also mentioned in the 2010 guidelines is advice against the use of home-modified animal milk as a breast milk replacement (substitute) for infants less than six months of age (World Health Organization, 2010a).

Table 8.3 Conditions needed to formula feed safely.

Mothers known to be HIV-infected should only give commercial infant formula milk as a replacement feed to their HIV-uninfected infants or infants who are of unknown HIV status, when specific conditions are met:

(a) Safe water and sanitation are assured at the household level and in the community, and,

(b) The mother, or other caregiver can reliably provide sufficient infant formula milk to support normal growth and development of the infant; and,

(c) The mother or caregiver can prepare it cleanly and frequently enough so that it is safe and carries a low risk of diarrhea and malnutrition; and

(d) The mother or caregiver can, in the first six months, exclusively give infant formula milk; and

(e) The family is supportive of this practice; and

(f) The mother or caregiver can access health care that offers comprehensive child health services.

These descriptions are intended to give simpler and more explicit meaning to the concepts represented by AFASS (acceptable, feasible, affordable, sustainable and safe).

Note: Adapted from WHO HIV and Infant Feeding Guidelines, 2010

From the age of six months all infants need complementary foods. WHO recommends commercial infant formula if home conditions are satisfactory, or animal milk (boiled for infants younger than 12 months of age) (World Health Organization, 2010a). Suggested complementary foods can include milk-based feeds, other family or staple foods, or a combination of the two. Regardless of the type of food, nutritionally adequate complementary foods should be provided to infants at least four to five times daily. If infants are known to be HIV-infected, mothers are encouraged to follow the infant feeding recommendations for the general population, exclusive breastfeeding until the age of six months and continued breastfeeding with adequate and appropriate complementation until the age of two years or older (World Health Organization, 2010a).

Country recommendations on infant feeding in the context of HIV

As previously mentioned, the 2010 WHO HIV and infant feeding guidelines recommend national or sub-national health authorities to decide which infant feeding option to be encouraged and supported by their Maternal and Child Health Services (World Health Organization, 2010a). Currently, guidelines for HIV and infant feeding differ between developed and developing countries for a variety of reasons, including lack of resources, differences in context, infant mortality and health services. Although breastfeeding of infants in high-income countries offers health benefits compared to replacement feeding, in the context of HIV, the risks outweigh the benefits. This is due to the availability and accessibility of clean water, good sanitation and safe commercial infant formula (Avert, 2011). For example, the Centers for Disease Control and Prevention (CDC) recommends that HIV infected mothers in the USA avoid breastfeeding their infants, even if they are on antiretroviral therapy (Centers for Disease Control and Prevention, 2010). In the UK, the Department of Health also recommends avoidance of breastfeeding as part of an overall programme to reduce mother-to-child transmission of HIV (UK Chief Medical Officers' Expert Advisory Group on Aids (EAGA), 2004). Health officials in Australia also recommend complete avoidance of breastfeeding, since replacement feeding with infant formula milk is considered 'a safe practice in Australia, where safe water and good quality infant formula are readily available' (Department of Health, 2009, p. 9). Additionally, Canada also endorses the 2010 WHO recommendation of replacement feeding in the context of HIV in developed countries, noting that replacement feeding is not only safe but also culturally acceptable (Macdonald, 2006). HIV-positive mothers in developed countries may be charged with child endangerment if they choose to breastfeed despite national recommendations (Walls, 2010).

Developing countries bear a greater burden of HIV infection and mother-to-child transmission of the virus than their developed counterparts (UNAIDS, 2010). They also have fewer resources for prevention of mother-to-child transmission programmes, counselling and treatment of HIV-infected mothers and their children (Chopra *et al.*, 2009; Fadnes *et al.*, 2010). Therefore, infant feeding guidelines in the context of HIV in developing countries have been different from the recommendations for developed countries, as highlighted in the following examples. In South Africa, nutritional support is provided to all breastfeeding HIV-infected mothers and formula feeding HIV-infected mothers who are food insecure. Breastfeeding recommendations in the context of HIV for South Africa mirror those outlined by WHO. All mothers who are HIV-infected who choose to breastfeed their infants should exclusively breastfeed for six months, whether the mothers are on lifelong antiretroviral therapy or not (National Department of Health South Africa & South African National Aids Council, 2010). Next, complementary foods should be introduced, with breastfeeding continuing for the first 12 months of life. In Uganda, infant feeding guidelines encourage replacement feeding of HIV-exposed infants if the environment and situation meet the AFASS criteria outlined in the 2006 WHO guidelines. Otherwise, exclusive breastfeeding is encouraged for the first 6 months of age for HIV-exposed infants, unless adequate replacement feeding is available before that age (Republic of Uganda Ministry of Health, 2009). The infant feeding guidelines of India match those outlined by the 2010 WHO guidelines (Rajeshwari *et al.*, 2010). However, unmodified animal milk is offered as an option for infants under the age of six months, while wet-nursing by an HIV-negative woman and human milk banks are offered as alternative options to breastfeeding for HIV-exposed infants of all ages (Rajeshwari *et al.*, 2010). These examples illustrate the wide range of infant feeding guidelines in the context of HIV in developing countries.

Following the release of the 2010 HIV and infant feeding guidelines, several countries have revised their infant feeding guidelines in light of the evidence that antiretroviral therapy significantly reduces the likelihood of HIV transmission through breastfeeding. In the UK, the British HIV Association and Children's HIV Association (BHIVA/CHIVA) have updated their position statements on infant feeding in the context of HIV (Taylor, 2011). Although it is acknowledged that complete avoidance of breastfeeding is the best and safest option to prevent mother-to-child transmission for HIV-infected mothers in the UK, the current position statement explains that 'under exceptional circumstances, and after seeking expert professional advice on reducing the risk of transmission of HIV through breastfeeding, a highly informed and motivated mother might be assisted to breastfeed' (BHIVA/CHIVA, 2010, p. 2). HIV-infected mothers are becoming aware of the reports of the effectiveness of antiretroviral therapy in reducing mother-to-child transmission through breastfeeding and HIV-infected mothers who are natives of countries in sub-Saharan Africa where breastfeeding is the cultural norm are beginning to question the Department of Health's recommendation for replacement feeding (Morrison, 2011). In their position statement, the BHIVA/CHIVA states:

> In the very rare instances where a mother in the UK who is on effective HAART [highly active antiretroviral therapy] with a repeatedly undetectable viral load chooses to breastfeed, BHIVA/CHIVA concur with the advice from the UK Expert Advisory Group on AIDS (EAGA) (2004) and do not regard this as ground for automatic referral to child protection teams. Maternal HAART should be carefully monitored and continued until 1 week after all breastfeeding has ceased. Breastfeeding, except during the weaning period, should be exclusive and all breastfeeding, including that during the weaning period, should have been completed by the end of 6 months. (Taylor, 2011, p. 390).

Although the UK Department of Health recommends avoidance of breastfeeding in the context of HIV, it previously advised that HIV-infected mothers might be supported in their decision to breastfeed if they had sought expert advice and were highly informed on the risk of mother-to-child transmission of HIV (UK Chief Medical Officers' Expert Advisory Group on Aids, 2004). Currently, no reports are available from other developed countries reporting similar shifts in perspectives. Morrison *et al.* (2011) argue that the HIV and infant feeding guidelines in developed countries have been based on the assumptions that the risk of mother-to-child transmission of HIV from breastfeeding is high and that replacement feeding is a safer option. The researchers also argue that industrialised countries should rethink their HIV and infant feeding guidelines in lieu of recent science and support HIV-infected mothers' infant feeding decisions if and when conditions are appropriate.

One country that has had a major shift in infant feeding policies for HIV-infected mothers is South Africa. Because of the country's high prevalence of HIV, the South African government instituted a policy allowing HIV-infected mothers to receive free infant formula until the infant was six months of age in order to prevent transmission of HIV through breastfeeding (UNICEF, 2012). Doherty *et al.* (2011) encouraged the South African government to phase out its policies on providing free infant formula as part of prevention of mother-to-child transmission programmes. The authors noted that some HIV-infected mothers in South Africa were choosing replacement feeding even though they did not meet the conditions to formula feed safely, which could result in increased diarrhoea and infant mortality. The results of a WHO cost analysis favouring the provision of maternal or infant antiretroviral therapy combined with breastfeeding versus maternal antiretroviral therapy and free infant formula were highlighted (World Health Organization, 2010a). Poor infant feeding counselling was another limitation mentioned by the authors. Additionally, Doherty and colleagues (2011) cited research indicating that replacement feeding of HIV-exposed infants did not result in additional survival gain.

The South African Minister of Health announced in August 2011 that hospitals would no longer provide free infant formula for HIV-infected mothers in an effort to promote exclusive breastfeeding for all mothers (UNICEF, 2012). The main factors influencing this policy change, as previously presented by Doherty and colleagues, were the country's low exclusive breastfeeding rates and critical infant and child mortality rates in South Africa. Dr Anna Coutsoudis, a professor and expert on paediatric HIV in South Africa, noted that when the provision of free formula began over 10 years ago the primary concern was to prevent HIV transmission (UNICEF, 2012). However, an increased prevalence of diarrhoea and pneumonia, which also threaten infant and child survival, were seen as a result of increased formula use. Doherty *et al.* (2011, p. 65) believe that phasing out the free formula programme will encourage exclusive breastfeeding, with antiretroviral therapy 'as the default feeding option to HIV-positive women' in that country. Similarly, Kuhn (2012) applauds South Africa's infant feeding policy change for HIV-infecting mothers, adding that focus should be placed on providing antiretroviral therapy since formula feeding cannot prevent mother-to-child transmission of HIV during pregnancy.

Infant feeding practices in HIV-prevalent developing countries

WHO encourages exclusive breastfeeding for the first six months of life for all infants, including those born to HIV-infected mothers. Although exclusive breastfeeding is recommended during this time for optimal growth and development, reports indicate that most mothers worldwide are not adhering to this guideline (World Health Organization, 2010b; Hausman, 2011). Globally, an estimated 35% of infants less than six months of age are breastfed exclusively (World Health Organization, 2010b). In most developing countries, mothers traditionally practice mixed feeding (Desclaux and Alfieri, 2009; Jackson *et al.*, 2009; Hausman, 2011), defined as breastfeeding while feeding additional solid foods, liquids, and non-human milks, such as animal milk or infant formula (World Health Organization, 2008).

Mixed feeding increases transmission of HIV as 'it puts babies in contact with HIV at the same time that it disturbs their digestive system, making them susceptible to infection' (Hausman, 2011, p. 137). Contaminated fluids or foods may cause inflammation in the infant's gastrointestinal tract, making the infant more susceptible to infection of HIV from breast milk (Coutsoudis *et al.*, 1999; Wise, 2001; Maru *et al.*, 2009). Coutsoudis and colleagues (1999) examined transmission rates by different infant feeding methods at 3 months postpartum and found that mixed feeding carried a significantly higher risk of HIV transmission than exclusive breastfeeding. The estimated proportion of HIV-1 infected infants at 3 months was statistically significantly lower in exclusively breastfed children compared to children who were mixed fed (14.6% vs. 24.1%, $P = 0.03$). Additionally, the rate of HIV-1 infection was similar between children never breastfed and children who were mixed fed (0.85 [0.51–1.42]) (Coutsoudis *et al.*, 1999).

Exclusive breastfeeding versus alternative options

According to the 2003 South Africa Demographic Health Survey, exclusive breastfeeding is seldom practised by mothers in the country, with only 8% of infants under the age of six months exclusively breastfed (Department of Health *et al.*, 2007). Other reports indicate that complementary foods are introduced as early as the first to the sixth week of age (Ladzani *et al.*, 2011). A cross-sectional study that assessed the infant feeding choices of 815 HIV-infected women, with infants aged 3–6 months, receiving prevention of mother-to-child transmission services in Gert Sibande District, Mpumalanga, South Africa, showed that 51% of these women exclusively formula-fed their infants, compared to about 36% who exclusively breastfed while 12% practised mixed feeding (Ladzani *et al.*, 2011). As a result of the above mentioned findings, as well as concerns about high infant and child mortality rates, South Africa officially announced in August 2011 its plan to cease the distribution of free formula to HIV-infected mothers (UNICEF, 2012).

Rates of exclusive breastfeeding are higher in Zambia compared to South Africa, and have increased from 40% in 2002 to 67% in 2007 (Central Statistical Office *et al.*, 2009). In Lusaka, Zambia, a study that assessed the infant feeding choices of 811 mothers found that of the women infected with HIV, 26% never breastfed while 55% had ceased breastfeeding by 6 months postpartum (Chisenga *et al.*, 2011). In contrast, HIV-negative women and women of unknown HIV status continued breastfeeding for longer. The median age of breastfeeding cessation was 3 months, 15 months, and 14 months for HIV-infected women, HIV-negative women, and HIV-unknown women, respectively (Chisenga *et al.*, 2011). Findings from this particular study demonstrate that infant feeding practices of HIV-infected women in Zambia does not conform to WHO HIV and infant feeding guidelines.

Similar to infant feeding trends in Zambia, rates of exclusive breastfeeding in Tanzania have generally increased over the years, although it is still not widely practised. Only 41% of infants aged less than 6 months are exclusively breastfed (National Bureau of Statistics & ORC Macro, 2005). Additionally, complementary foods are introduced very early, with 32% of infants aged 2–3 months given complementary foods (National Bureau of Statistics & ORC Macro, 2005). Also, a cross-sectional study of infant feeding behaviors of 196 HIV-infected mothers, with children aged 6–10 months conducted in greater Dar es Salaam, Tanzania, found that although 95% of women initiated breastfeeding, the median duration of exclusive breastfeeding was only 3 months (Young *et al.*, 2010). According to the same study, rates of exclusive breastfeeding sharply declined between the age of 2 months (80%) and 4 months (34%). Corn-based porridge was reported as the most commonly used complementary food (95%) with 4 months of age being the median age of introduction. Like the previous study in Zambia (Chisenga *et al.*, 2011), findings indicate that HIV-infected mothers may need additional support and guidance in order to meet WHO guidelines for exclusive breastfeeding (Young *et al.*, 2010).

In addition to the three countries previously mentioned, India is another country with disparate rates of exclusive breastfeeding. Despite national recommendations for exclusive breastfeeding for the first six months of life, less than half of infants under the age of six months are exclusively breastfed (International Institute for Population Sciences & Macro International, 2007). Assessment of infant feeding choices of HIV-infected women enrolled in a prospective cohort study in rural Tamil Nadu, India, found that a third of the women used replacement feeding. Among the women who breastfed their infants, the median duration of breastfeeding was 3 months (Read *et al.*, 2010). The rate of exclusive breastfeeding was about 70% at one week after birth but declined sharply thereafter (Read *et al.*, 2010). Again, these findings indicate that HIV-infected mothers struggle to follow international guidelines for infant feeding.

Cessation of breastfeeding

According to the 2010 WHO HIV and infant feeding guidelines, 'Mothers known to be HIV-infected who decide to stop breastfeeding at any time should stop gradually within one month. Stopping breastfeeding abruptly is not advisable' (World Health Organization 2010a, p. 6). WHO considers this a strong recommendation, although the evidence supporting it is described as low quality. Since mixed feeding is a known risk factor for mother-to-child transmission of HIV, abrupt weaning was originally recommended to decrease infant exposure to the virus (Kuhn *et al.*, 2008). However, the observed association between early cessation of breastfeeding with increased morbidity and mortality in HIV-exposed infants informed the latest recommendation (Homsy *et al.*, 2010; Kindra *et al.*, 2012).

Several studies on abrupt weaning have been conducted in Zambia, where prolonged breastfeeding is the norm (Kuhn *et al.*, 2008, 2009, 2010; Fawzy *et al.*, 2011). A randomized controlled trial conducted in Lusaka, Zambia, which randomized HIV-infected mothers to wean abruptly at 4 months (intervention group) or to continue breastfeeding (control group) assessed the effect of early and abrupt weaning on postnatal mother-to-child transmission of HIV, and morbidity and mortality in HIV-exposed infants (Kuhn *et al.*, 2008). About 70% of the women in the intervention group weaned their infants early. In the intention-to-treat analysis, no significant difference was observed for HIV-free survival at age 24 months among infants born to HIV-infected women who weaned abruptly compared to infants born to HIV-infected women who continued breastfeeding past 4 months postpartum (68.4% vs 64.0% respectively; $P = 0.13$) (Kuhn *et al.*, 2008). Rates of transmission of HIV were similar among the intervention and control group (21.4% vs. 25.8% respectively; $P = 0.11$). Additionally, the mortality rates among uninfected children was not statistically different between the intervention and control groups (13.6% and 14.4% respectively; $P = 0.81$) (Kuhn *et al.*, 2008). Interestingly, children born to women with less advanced HIV disease had significantly poorer outcomes if their mothers weaned early compared to those who continued breastfeeding. The opposite effect was observed in children born to women with advanced HIV disease, who had significantly better outcomes if their mothers weaned early (Kuhn *et al.*, 2009). Kuhn *et al.* (2010) also examined the association between age of weaning and infant health and mortality of children born to HIV-infected mothers. Half of the cohort was randomised to wean abruptly at 4 months while the other half was randomised to continue breastfeeding. The effects of weaning in children aged 0–3 months, 4–5 months, 6–11 months and 12–18 months were compared with children who weaned at ages older than18 months (comparison group). Children weaned at 0–3 months had a 3.59-fold increase, weaning at 4–5 months had a 2.03-fold increase, weaning at 6–11 months had a 3.54-fold increase, and weaning at 12–18 months had a 4.22-fold increase in mortality compared to the comparison group (Kuhn *et al.*, 2010). Lastly, between the ages of 4 to 6 months, the likelihood of diarrhoea was 1.8 times greater in children weaned abruptly compared to children who were breastfed longer (Fawzy *et al.*, 2011).

Cultural, political and socio-biological determinants of infant feeding choices among HIV-infected mothers

Choosing a method of infant feeding can be difficult for HIV-infected mothers (Chisenga *et al.*, 2011). The primary reason that informs the choice of infant feeding in the context of HIV should be the desire to prevent transmission of the virus to the infant (Oladokun *et al.*, 2010) and to protect the life of the child. However, breastfeeding is embedded in 'biological, social, cultural, economic and political contexts, especially in developing countries' (Coutsoudis *et al.*, 2008, p. 210). In most developing countries where breastfeeding is the norm, mothers may face stigma if they choose replacement feeding, as formula feeding may suggest they are infected with HIV (Hausman, 2011). Quantitative research has found that higher socioeconomic status, regular maternal income, older maternal age, higher knowledge of HIV transmission, health worker advice and clean water supply are important determinants of formula feeding or intention to formula feed (Bland *et al.*, 2007; Njom Nlend *et al.*, 2007; Ladzani *et al.*, 2011). In contrast, lower socioeconomic status, low educational level, non-disclosure of HIV status and not meeting criteria for safe replacement feeding are associated with breastfeeding (Leroy *et al.*, 2007; Chisenga *et al.*, 2011). Evidence also indicates that other groups of HIV-infected mothers choose replacement feeding although they do not meet the criteria for safe replacement feeding (Bland *et al.*, 2007; Doherty *et al.*, 2007; Chisenga *et al.*, 2011; Kindra *et al.*, 2012). A prospective cohort study by Doherty and colleagues (2007) found that infants who are formula fed by mothers who do not meet the criteria for safe replacement feeding have the highest risk of HIV transmission and death. To better address the issue of HIV transmission through breastfeeding, more research is therefore needed to help understand the underlying factors that impact HIV-infected mothers' infant feeding choices, and to improve the impact of prevention of mother-to-child transmission programmes and services, especially in resource-limited areas (Hausman, 2011).

A multi-site qualitative study in Burkina Faso, Cambodia and Cameroon that examined HIV-infected mothers' infant feeding choices, also documented the determinants influencing their choice and the difficulties they encounter (Desclaux and Alfieri, 2009). The study included both observations in health facilities and interviews with HIV-infected mothers and health workers. In terms of infant feeding choices, health workers' counselling recommendations were found to be driven by economic aspects, while HIV-infected mothers were driven by social aspects. Several mothers were prescribed only one option of infant feeding by health workers. One mother from the study stated 'I was told it is forbidden to breastfeed' because health workers assumed patients at that particular Cambodian clinic could afford and practice safe replacement feeding (Desclaux and Alfieri, 2009, p. 823). Similar attitudes on replacement feeding were reported by a midwife in Cameroon, 'Breastfeeding is for mothers who do not have money. If the mother has money, she must give formula' (Desclaux and Alfieri, 2009, p. 824). Mothers perceived to be too poor to afford formula were therefore advised to exclusively breastfeed. Most mothers interviewed placed a high value on breastfeeding yet would have preferred replacement feeding to prevent HIV transmission to their infants if formula was provided at no cost.

Aside from concerns about infant health, mothers were driven to be perceived as good mothers. Several social factors were identified as influencing the choice of infant feeding, including cultural norms on infant feeding, HIV stigma and fathers' attitudes (Desclaux and Alfieri, 2009). This study was conducted under the previous WHO guidelines, when it was advised that HIV-infected mothers should receive individual counselling about the risks and benefits of the various infant feeding options. Mothers then had to decide which option best fit their situation. However, several reports mention occurrences of poor infant feeding counselling (Rea *et al.*, 2007; Saloojee and Cooper, 2010) or HIV-infected mothers inappropriately choosing formula feeding when they did not meet the AFASS criteria for replacement feeding (Bland *et al.*, 2007; Doherty *et al.*, 2007; Chisenga *et al.*, 2011; Kindra *et al.*, 2012). Due to this finding, and to prevent the health consequences that can result from inadequate replacement feeding, the 2010 WHO guidelines encourage national and sub-national health authorities to encourage one infant feeding option as standard care. This decision must take into account the local socioeconomic and cultural factors, prevalence of HIV in pregnant women, accessibility and quality of healthcare services, and determinants of maternal and child malnutrition and mortality (World Health Organization, 2010a).

Similar findings were found from interviews and focus groups conducted by Chisenga *et al.* (2011). Determinants of HIV-infected mothers' infant feeding choices in Zambia included: (1) cost of infant formula, (2) health workers' advice, (3) influence from relatives, (4) stigma and not disclosing HIV results and (5) difficulties of maintaining exclusive breastfeeding or replacement feeding. In addition, both mothers and nurses were found to be confused by the international HIV and infant feeding guidelines. Lastly, many HIV-infected mothers inappropriately chose replacement feeding without meeting the criteria (Chisenga *et al.*, 2011).

In Malawi, several qualitative studies have examined HIV-infected mothers' decisions on infant feeding (Levy *et al.*, 2010; Chinkonde *et al.*, 2010; Ostergaard and Bula, 2010). One ethnographic study included observations of prevention of mother-to-child transmission programmes, semi-structured interviews and focus groups with HIV-infected women and interviews with key informants (Levy *et al.*, 2010). Findings from this study were similar to other studies on determinants of infant feeding. Many women were confused about the reasons for exclusive breastfeeding. One HIV-infected woman shared in an interview, 'They just told me to exclusively breastfeed for six months, but they didn't tell me the reason why' (Levy *et al.*, 2010). Mothers also found early weaning challenging. 'We heard the advice that we should stop breastfeeding our babies at six months, and the message is in our ears. But I think that to stop breastfeeding the baby at six months is difficult', stated another woman in a focus group (Levy *et al.*, 2010). Stigma was also highlighted as an issue since it is culturally acceptable to breastfeed until an infant's third birthday (Levy *et al.*, 2010). A unique theme that emerged from this study by Levy *et al.* was the psychosocial burden of downloaded responsibility, meaning HIV-infected mothers struggled with worries about breastfeeding transmission and also struggled to afford replacement feeding after weaning. In one focus group, one woman described, 'We feel bad thinking that, as the baby is being breastfed, he or she can contract the virus in the process' (Levy *et al.*, 2010). Another woman added in the same focus group, 'I think there is unfairness because, if they know that the baby is to stop breast milk, then they should find us an alternative solution. Because, on our own, we can't manage' (Levy *et al.*, 2010).

Discussion

This chapter has discussed the revised 2010 WHO HIV and infant feeding guidelines and their implementation in developed and developing countries, infant feeding trends in HIV prevalent countries, and factors influencing HIV-infected mothers' decisions on infant feeding options. WHO recommends exclusive breastfeeding for the first six months of life for HIV-exposed infants, with gradual weaning, and introduction of complementary foods at six months of age. However, current evidence suggests that infant feeding practices of both the general population and HIV-infected mothers in developing countries do not meet these guidelines. Additionally, antiretroviral therapies are not readily available to all infected mothers or their infants. Mixed feeding and delayed weaning are cultural norms in several developing countries (National Bureau of Statistics and ORC Macro, 2005; International Institute for Population Sciences and Macro International, 2007; Central Statistical Office *et al.*, 2009; World Health Organization, 2010b; Hausman, 2011).

HIV-infected mothers face stigma, confusion about infant feeding recommendations, difficulties with exclusive breastfeeding or formula feeding, worry about transmitting the virus through breastfeeding, biased advice from health workers, and barriers to safe replacement feeding. Although the previous WHO guidelines provided much needed guidance for developing countries on infant feeding in the context of HIV, Downs and Cooper stated that these guidelines 'need[ed] to be strengthened through investments in high quality, widely available HIV counselling, support for choice of feeding, and exclusive breastfeeding for those HIV-infected mothers who opt to breastfeed' (Downs and Cooper, 2007, p. 37). The 2010 WHO HIV and infant feeding guidelines have reflected changes in the field of HIV, notably the effectiveness of antiretroviral therapy in reducing mother-to-child transmission of the virus, and also barriers in clinical practice, such as replacing the AFASS criteria with simpler wording. Studies describing the translation of the current WHO guidelines into national policies and clinical practice are lacking. One question is: are the 2010 WHO HIV and infant feeding guidelines realistic? In comparison to the previous guidelines, the answer is yes. However, only half of HIV-infected mothers worldwide are receiving their needed antiretroviral therapy and only over a third of HIV-exposed infants are. Given that the 2010 guidelines are based on the effectiveness of antiretroviral therapy, developing countries may still experience difficulty implementing the guidelines. Several disconnections are apparent in the literature. There is a disconnection between WHO recommendations and national policies, a disconnection between national policies and district health services, a disconnection between health workers' advice and HIV-infected mothers' decisions, and lastly, a disconnection between mothers' decisions and the best feeding option for their infants (Rea *et al.*, 2007; Chopra *et al.*, 2009; Sibeko *et al.*, 2009; Chinkonde *et al.*, 2010; Koricho *et al.*, 2010; Levy *et al.*, 2010; Nankunda *et al.*, 2010; Saloojee and Cooper, 2010; Chisenga *et al.*, 2011; Ladzani *et al.*, 2011).

Several studies have noted the difficulties in translating WHO HIV and infant feeding recommendations. Sibeko *et al.* (2009) reported, 'Translation of international infant feeding guidelines into national policies and ultimately into prevention of mother-to-child transmission programmes requires evidence-based tools that facilitate operational implementation of the recommendations' (p. 1988). Translating new HIV and infant feeding guidelines into practice is a process that requires political will, resources, support of local health workers and ongoing evaluation. Rapid assessments of HIV prevention policy in several countries have indicated that infant feeding was not a priority in prevention of mother-to-child transmission programmes and that policy makers and health workers were often confused by infant feeding guidelines in the context of HIV infection (Chopra *et al.*, 2009; Chinkonde *et al.*, 2010). Health workers, such as nurses and peer counsellors, are critical to implementing international and national guidelines through infant feeding counselling. However, studies indicate that infant feeding counselling is often done poorly (Rea *et al.*, 2007; Saloojee and Cooper, 2010). Health workers have expressed similar feelings as infected mothers regarding infant feeding options in the context of HIV and their fears and anxieties often reflect in their counseling (Koricho *et al.*, 2010). Other studies have reported that health workers have poor knowledge of mother-to-child transmission, outdated training and offer conflicting advice to HIV-infected mothers on infant feeding (Chopra and Rollins, 2008; Desclaux and Alfieri, 2009; Fadnes *et al.*, 2010).

Scaling up prevention of mother-to-child transmission interventions to expand services to infected mothers and their children should include standardised training for all health workers on infant feeding. Additionally, prevention of mother-to-child transmission services, including infant feeding counselling provided to HIV-infected mothers, need to be culturally appropriate and take into account the roles of partners and extended family in the decision making process (Nankunda *et al.*, 2010; Ladzani *et al.*, 2011).

A paucity of research exists regarding HIV-infected mothers' attitudes toward other breastfeeding options, such as wet-nursing, milk banks and heat-treatment. The current WHO guidelines only mention heat-treatment as a strategy (World Health Organization, 2010a), although the 2003 Global Strategy for Infant and Young Child Feeding discusses the other two options as alternatives in 'exceptional circumstances' (World Health Organization, 2003, p. 10). Wet-nursing was found to be a promising strategy in a study in Burkina Faso (Nacro *et al.*, 2010), while another study found wet-nursing, milk banks and heat-treated expressed milk as the least preferred infant feeding options for HIV-exposed infants in western Kenya (Wachira *et al.*, 2009). WHO recommends heat-treated breast milk as an interim strategy for HIV-infected mothers to reduce transmission of HIV through breastfeeding (World Health Organization, 2010a). Mbuya *et al.* (2010) found that expressing and heat treating breast milk was a feasible and sustainable strategy for HIV-exposed infants in rural Zimbabwe after cessation of direct breastfeeding. More research on the acceptability and feasibility of all three of these options in HIV prevalent countries is needed.

Limited published studies are available on HIV and infant feeding dilemmas in countries outside of sub-Saharan Africa. Although the HIV epidemic is greatest in this region of the world, HIV is an immense public health concern in other resource poor areas, such as the Caribbean, Latin America, and South and Southeast Asia. Findings in sub-Saharan Africa may not translate into appropriate policies in other settings with different cultural norms and beliefs regarding HIV and infant feeding.

WHO guidelines state that the research supporting the recommendations for weaning, timing of introduction of complementary foods, and criteria for safe replacement feeding are all based on low-quality evidence (World Health Organization, 2010a). Findings from qualitative studies indicate that HIV-infected mothers have concerns regarding these topics (De Paoli *et al.*, 2008; Lunney *et al.*, 2008; Levy *et al.*, 2010; Morgan *et al.*, 2010; Ostergaard and Bula, 2010). More research studies are needed to validate and support the current recommendations to inform mothers' decisions.

Conclusion

Evidence strongly supports exclusive breastfeeding for the first six months of life for HIV-exposed infants. In developing countries, HIV-infected mothers' infant feeding decisions differ from the new WHO HIV and infant feeding guidelines. Several factors influence their infant feeding choices, including stigma, influence of partners and extended family, conflicting advice from health workers, and barriers to replacement feeding. Although the benefits of breastfeeding appear to outweigh the risks associated with replacement feeding in the presence of HIV infection, mothers require additional support to achieve these recommendations. It is recommended that researchers and clinicians alike evaluate the feasibility of the 2010 WHO infant feeding and HIV guidelines in their own contexts, most importantly those in developing countries. WHO should continue to review the current HIV and infant feeding guidelines using experience from the field to update the guidelines to ensure that HIV-infected mothers can make the best feeding decisions for their infants, and to prevent transmission of HIV.

References

Avert (2011) *HIV and Breastfeeding*. Available at: http://www.avert.org/hiv-breastfeeding.htm (accessed 26 July 2011).

Becquet, R., Ekouevi, D. K., Menan, H., Amani-Bosse, C., Bequet, L., Viho, I. *et al.* (2008) Early mixed feeding and breastfeeding beyond 6 months increase the risk of postnatal HIV transmission: ANRS 1201/1202 Ditrame Plus, Abidjan, Cote d'Ivoire. *Preventive Medicine*, **47**, 27–33.

Bland, R. M., Rollins, N. C., Coovadia, H. M., Coutsoudis, A. and Newell, M. L. (2007) Infant feeding counselling for HIV-infected and uninfected women: appropriateness of choice and practice. *Bulletin of the World Health Organization*, **85**, 289–96.

Breastfeeding and HIV International Transmission Study Group (2004) Late postnatal transmission of HIV-1 in breast-fed children: an individual patient data meta-analysis. *Journal of Infectious Diseases*, **189**, 2154–66.

BHIVA/CHIVA Writing Group on Infant Feeding in the UK (2010) British HIV Association (BHIVA) and Children's HIV Association (CHIVA). *Position Statement on Infant Feeding in the UK*. Available at: http://www.bhiva.org/documents/Publications/Infant-Feeding10.pdf (accessed 15 January 2013).

Bulterys, M., Ellington, S. and Kourtis, A. P. (2010) HIV-1 and breastfeeding: biology of transmission and advances in prevention. *Clinical Perinatology*, **37**, 807–24, ix–x.

Centers for Disease Control and Prevention. (2010) *Breastfeeding: Diseases and Conditions: HIV and AIDS*. Available at: http://www.cdc.gov/breastfeeding/disease/hiv.htm (accessed 26 July 2011).

Central Statistical Office, Ministry of Health, Tropical Diseases Research Centre, University of Zambia & Macro International Inc. (2009) *Zambia Demographic and Health Survey 2007*. Calverton, Maryland, USA: CSO and Macro International Inc. Available at: http://www.measuredhs.com/pubs/pdf/FR211/FR211%5Brevised-05-12-2009%5D. pdf (accessed 26 July 2011).

Chinkonde, J. R., Sundby, J., De Paoli, M. and Thorsen, V. C. (2010) The difficulty with responding to policy changes for HIV and infant feeding in Malawi. *International Breastfeeding Journal*, **5**, 11.

Chisenga, M., Siame, J., Baisley, K., Kasonka, L. and Filteau, S. (2011) Determinants of infant feeding choices by Zambian mothers: a mixed quantitative and qualitative study. *Maternal and Child Nutrition*, **7**, 148–59.

Chopra, M., Doherty, T., Mehatru, S. and Tomlinson, M. (2009) Rapid assessment of infant feeding support to HIV-positive women accessing prevention of mother-to-child transmission services in Kenya, Malawi and Zambia. *Public Health Nutrition*, **12**, 2323–8.

Chopra, M. and Rollins, N. (2008) Infant feeding in the time of HIV: rapid assessment of infant feeding policy and programmes in four African countries scaling up prevention of mother to child transmission programmes. *Archives of Disease in Childhood*, **93**, 288–91.

Coovadia, H. M., Rollins, N. C., Bland, R. M., Little, K., Coutsoudis, A., Bennish, M. L. *et al.* (2007) Mother-to-child transmission of HIV-1 infection during exclusive breastfeeding in the first 6 months of life: an intervention cohort study. *Lancet*, **369**, 1107–16.

Coutsoudis, A., Pillay, K., Spooner, E., Kuhn, L. and Coovadia, H. M. (1999) Influence of infant-feeding patterns on early mother-to-child transmission of HIV-1 in Durban, South Africa: a prospective cohort study. *Lancet*, **354**, 471–6.

Coutsoudis, A., Coovadia, H. M. and Wilfert, C. M. (2008) HIV, infant feeding and more perils for poor people: new WHO guidelines encourage review of formula milk policies. *Bulletin of the World Health Organization*, **86**, 210–14.

De Paoli, M. M., Mkwanazi, N. B., Richter, L. M. and Rollins, N. (2008) Early cessation of breastfeeding to prevent postnatal transmission of HIV: a recommendation in need of guidance. *Acta Paediatrica*, **97**, 1663–8.

Department of Health (2009) *South Australian Perinatal Practice Guidelines*. Available at: http://www.health.sa.gov.au/PPG/Default.aspx?PageContentMode=1&tabid=228 (accessed 25 July 2012).

Department of Health, Medical Research Council & ORC Macro (2007) *South Africa Demographic and Health Survey 2003*. Pretoria: Department of Health. Available at: http://www.measuredhs.com/pubs/pdf/FR206/FR206.pdf.

Desclaux, A. and Alfieri, C. (2009) Counseling and choosing between infant-feeding options: overall limits and local interpretations by health care providers and women living with HIV in resource-poor countries (Burkina Faso, Cambodia, Cameroon). *Social Science & Medicine*, **69**, 821–9.

Doherty, T., Chopra, M., Jackson, D., Goga, A., Colvin, M. and Persson, L. A. (2007) Effectiveness of the WHO/UNICEF guidelines on infant feeding for HIV-positive women: results from a prospective cohort study in South Africa. *AIDS*, **21**, 1791–7.

Doherty, T., Sanders, D., Goga, A. and Jackson, D. (2011) Implications of the new WHO guidelines on HIV and infant feeding for child survival in South Africa. *Bulletin of the World Health Organization*, **89**, 62–7.

Downs, J. H. and Cooper, P. A. (2007) HIV and Lactation. *Annales Nestlé*, **65**, 29–38.

Fadnes, L. T., Engebretsen, I. M., Moland, K. M., Nankunda, J., Tumwine, J. K. and Tylleskar, T. (2010) Infant feeding counselling in Uganda in a changing environment with focus on the general population and HIV-positive mothers – a mixed method approach. *BMC Health Services Research*, **10**, 260.

Fawzy, A., Arpadi, S., Kankasa, C., Sinkala, M., Mwiya, M., Thea, D. M. *et al.* (2011) Early weaning increases diarrhea morbidity and mortality among uninfected children born to HIV-infected mothers in Zambia. *Journal of Infectious Diseases*, **203**, 1222–30.

Hausman, B. L. (2011) *Viral mothers: Breastfeeding in the Age of HIV/AIDS*. University of Michigan Press.

Homsy, J., Moore, D., Barasa, A., Were, W., Likicho, C., Waiswa, B. *et al.* (2010) Breast-feeding, mother-to-child HIV transmission, and mortality among infants born to HIV-Infected women on highly active antiretroviral therapy in rural Uganda. *Journal of Acquired Immune Deficiency Syndromes*, **53**, 28–35.

International Institute for Population Sciences & Macro International (2007) *National Family Health Survey (NFHS-3), 2005–06: India: Volume I*. Mumbai IIPS. Available at: http://www.measuredhs.com/pubs/pdf/FRIND3/10Chapter10.pdf.

Jackson, D. J., Goga, A. E., Doherty, T. and Chopra, M. (2009) An update on HIV and infant feeding issues in developed and developing countries. *Journal of Obstetric, Gynecologic, and Neonatal Nursing*, **38**, 219–29.

John-Stewart, G., Mbori-Ngacha, D., Ekpini, R., Jano!, E. N., Nkengasong, J., Read, J. S. *et al.* (2004) Breast-feeding and transmission of HIV-1. *Journal of Acquired Immune Deficiency Syndromes*, **35**, 196–202.

Kesho Bora Study Group and Devincenzi, I. (2011) Triple antiretroviral compared with zidovudine and single-dose nevirapine prophylaxis during pregnancy and breastfeeding for prevention of mother-to-child transmission of HIV-1 (Kesho Bora study): a randomised controlled trial. *Lancet Infectious Diseases*, **11**, 171–80.

Kindra, G., Coutsoudis, A., Esposito, F. and Esterhuizen, T. (2012) Breastfeeding in HIV exposed infants significantly improves child health: a prospective study. *Maternal and Child Health Journal*, **16**(3), 632–40.

Koricho, A. T., Moland, K. M. and Blystad, A. (2010) Poisonous milk and sinful mothers: the changing meaning of breastfeeding in the wake of the HIV epidemic in Addis Ababa, Ethiopia. *International Breastfeeding Journal*, **5**, 12.

Kuhn, L. (2012) Maternal and infant health is protected by antiretroviral drug strategies that preserve breastfeeding by HIV-positive women. *Southern African Journal of HIV Medicine*, **13**. Available at: http://www.sajhivmed.org.za/index.php/sajhivmed/article/view/820/661 (accessed 20 June 2012).

Kuhn, L. and Aldrovandi, G. (2010) Survival and health benefits of breastfeeding versus artificial feeding in infants of HIV-infected women: developing versus developed world. *Clinical Perinatology*, **37**, 843–62.

Kuhn, L., Sinkala, M., Kankasa, C., Semrau, K., Kasonde, P., Scott, N. *et al.* (2007) High uptake of exclusive breastfeeding and reduced early post-natal HIV transmission. *PLoS One*, **2**, e1363.

Kuhn, L., Aldrovandi, G. M., Sinkala, M., Kankasa, C., Semrau, K., Mwiya, M. *et al.* (2008) Effects of early, abrupt weaning on HIV-free survival of children in Zambia. *New England Journal of Medicine*, **359**, 130–41.

Kuhn, L., Aldrovandi, G. M., Sinkala, M., Kankasa, C., Semrau, K., Kasonde, P. *et al.* (2009) Differential effects of early weaning for HIV-free survival of children born to HIV-infected mothers by severity of maternal disease. *PLoS One*, **4**, e6059.

Kuhn, L., Sinkala, M., Semrau, K., Kankasa, C., Kasonde, P., Mwiya, M. *et al.* (2010) Elevations in mortality associated with weaning persist into the second year of life among uninfected children born to HIV-infected mothers. *Clinical Infectious Diseases*, **50**, 437–44.

Ladzani, R., Peltzer, K., Mlambo, M. G. and Phaweni, K. (2011) Infant-feeding practices and associated factors of HIV-positive mothers at Gert Sibande, South Africa. *Acta Paediatrica*, **100**, 538–42.

Lamberti, L. M., Walker, C. L. F., Noiman, A., Victora, C. and Black, R. E. (2011) Breastfeeding and the risk for diarrhea morbidity and mortality. *BMC Public Health*, **11**, S15.

Leroy, V., Sakarovitch, C., Viho, I., Becquet, R., Ekouevi, D. K., Bequet, L. *et al.* (2007) Acceptability of formula-feeding to prevent HIV postnatal transmission, Abidjan, Cote d'Ivoire: ANRS 1201/1202 Ditrame Plus Study. *Journal of Acquired Immune Deficiency Syndromes*, **44**, 77–86.

Levy, J. M., Webb, A. L. and Sellen, D. W. (2010) 'On our own, we can't manage': experiences with infant feeding recommendations among Malawian mothers living with HIV. *International Breastfeeding Journal*, **5**, 15.

Lunney, K. M., Jenkins, A. L., Tavengwa, N. V., Majo, F., Chidhanguro, D., Iliff, P. *et al.* (2008) HIV-positive poor women may stop breast-feeding early to protect their infants from HIV infection although available replacement diets are grossly inadequate. *Journal of Nutrition*, **138**, 351–7.

Macdonald, N. E., Canadian Paediatric Society, Infectious Diseases and Immunization Committee (2006) Maternal infectious diseases, antimicrobial therapy or immunizations: very few contraindications to breastfeeding. *Paediatric Child Health*, **11**, 489–91.

Maru, S., Datong, P., Selleng, D., Mang, E., Inyang, B., Ajene, A. *et al.* (2009) Social determinants of mixed feeding behavior among HIV-infected mothers in Jos, Nigeria *AIDS Care*, **21**, 1114–23.

Mcintyre, J. (2010) Use of antiretrovirals during pregnancy and breastfeeding in low-income and middle-income countries. *Current Opinion in HIV and AIDS*, **5**, 48–53.

Mepham, S. O., Bland, R. M. and Newell, M. L. (2011) Prevention of mother-to-child transmission of HIV in resource-rich and -poor settings. *British Journal of Gynecology*, **118**, 202–18.

Morgan, M. C., Masaba, R. O., Nyikuri, M. and Thomas, T. K. (2010) Factors affecting breastfeeding cessation after discontinuation of antiretroviral therapy to prevent mother-to-child transmission of HIV. *AIDS Care*, **22**, 866–73.

Morrison, P., Israel-Ballard, K. and Greiner, T. (2011) Informed choice in infant feeding decisions can be supported for HIV-infected women even in industrialized countries. *AIDS*, **25**, 1807–11.

Nacro, B., Barro, M., Gaudreault, S. and Dao, B. (2010) Prevention of mother to child transmission of HIV in Burkina Faso: breastfeeding and wet nursing. *Journal of Tropical Pediatrics*, **56**, 183–6.

Nankunda, J., Tylleskar, T., Ndeezi, G., Semiyaga, N. and Tumwine, J. K. (2010) Establishing individual peer counselling for exclusive breastfeeding in Uganda: implications for scaling-up. *Maternal and Child Nutrition,* **6**, 53–66.

National Bureau of Statistics & ORC Macro (2005) *Tanzania Demographic and Health Survey 2004–05.* National Bureau of Statistics & ORC Macro, Dar es Salaam. Available at: http://www.measuredhs.com/pubs/pdf/FR173/11Chapter11.pdf (accessed 26 July 2011).

National Department of Health South Africa & South African National Aids Council (2010) *Clinical Guidelines: PMTCT (Prevention of Mother-to-Child Transmission of HIV).* Pretoria.

Nelson, K. E. and Williams, C. M. (2007) *Infectious Disease Epidemiology: Theory and Practice.* Jones and Bartlett, Sudbury, MA.

Njom Nlend, A., Penda, I., Same Ekobo, C., Tene, G. and Tsague, L. (2007) Is exclusive artificial feeding feasible at 6 months post partum in Cameroon urban areas for HIV-exposed infants? *Journal of Tropical Pediatrics*, **53**, 438–9.

Nor, B., Zembe, Y., Daniels, K., Doherty, T., Jackson, D., Ahlberg, B. M. *et al.* (2009) 'Peer but not peer': considering the context of infant feeding peer counseling in a high HIV prevalence area. *Journal of Human Lactation*, **25**, 427–34.

Oladokun, R. E., Brown, B. J. and Osinusi, K. (2010) Infant-feeding pattern of HIV-positive women in a prevention of mother-to-child transmission (PMTCT) programme. *AIDS Care*, **22**, 1108–14.

Ostergaard, L. R. and Bula, A. (2010) 'They call our children "Nevirapine babies?"': A qualitative study about exclusive breastfeeding among HIV positive mothers in Malawi. *African Journal of Reproductive Health*, **14**, 213–22.

Owen, C. G., Martin, R. M., Whincup, P. H., Smith, G. D. and Cook, D. G. (2005) Effect of infant feeding on the risk of obesity across the life course: a quantitative review of published evidence. *Pediatrics*, **115**, 1367–77.

Peltier, C. A., Ndayisaba, G. F., Lepage, P., Van Griensven, J., Leroy, V., Pharm, C. O. *et al.* (2009) Breastfeeding with maternal antiretroviral therapy or formula feeding to prevent HIV postnatal mother-to-child transmission in Rwanda. *AIDS*, **23**, 2415–23.

Rajeshwari, K., Bang, A., Chaturvedi, P., Kumar, V., Yadav, B., Bharadva, K. *et al.* (2010) Infant and young child feeding guidelines: 2010. *Indian Pediatrics*, **47**, 995–1004.

Rea, M. F., Dos Santos, R. G. and Sanchez-Moreno, C. C. (2007) Quality of infant feeding counselling for HIV+ mothers in Brazil: challenges and achievements. *Acta Paediatrica*, **96**, 94–9.

Read, J. S., Samuel, N. M., Srijayanth, P., Dharmarajan, S., Van Hook, H. M., Jacob, M. *et al.* (2010) Infants of human immunodeficiency virus type 1-infected women in rural south India: feeding patterns and risk of mother-to-child transmission. *Pediatric Infectious Disease Journal*, **29**, 14–17.

Republic of Uganda Ministry of Health (2009) *Policy Guidelines on Infant and Young Child Feeding.* Available at: http://www.health.go.ug/nutrition/docs/IYCF_Guidelines.pdf (accessed 26 July 2011).

Saloojee, H. and Cooper, P. A. (2010) Feeding of infants of HIV-positive mothers. *Current Opinion in Clinical Nutrition & Metabolic Care*, **13**, 336–43.

Schack-Nielsen, L. and Michaelsen, K. F. (2006) Breast feeding future health. *Current Opinion in Clinical Nutrition & Metabolic Care*, **9**, 289–96.

Semba, R. D., Kumwenda, N., Hoover, D. R., Taha, T. E., Quinn, T. C., Mtimavalye, L. *et al*. (1999) Effect of breastfeeding and formula feeding on transmission of HIV-1: a randomized clinical trial. *Journal of Infectious Diseases*, **180**, 93–8.

Sibeko, L., Coutsoudis, A., Nzuza, S. and Gray-Donald, K. (2009) Mothers' infant feeding experiences: constraints and supports for optimal feeding in an HIV-impacted urban community in South Africa. *Public Health Nutrition*, **12**, 1983–90.

Slater, M., Stringer, E. M. and Stringer, J. S. (2010) Breastfeeding in HIV-positive women: what can be recommended? *Paediatric Drugs*, **12**, 1–9.

Taylor, G., Anderson, J., Clayden, P., Gazzard, B., Fortin, J., Kennedy, J., Lazarus, L. and Newell, M. (2011) British HIV Association and Children's HIV Association position statement on infant feeding in the UK 2011. *HIV Medicine*, **12**, 389–93.

Turck, D. (2007) Later effects of breastfeeding practice: the evidence. *Nestlé Nutrition Workshop Series: Pediatric Program*, **60**, 31–42.

UK Chief Medical Officers' Expert Advisory Group on Aids (EAGA) (2004) *HIV and Infant Feeding: Guidance from the UK Chief Medical Officers' Expert Advisory Group on AIDS*. Department of Health Publications, London. Available at: http://www.dh.gov. uk/prod_consum_dh/groups/dh_digitalassets/@dh/@en/documents/digitalasset/ dh_4089893.pdf (accessed 26 July 2011).

UNAIDS (2010) *Global Report: UNAIDS Report on the Global AIDS Epidemic 2010*. Available at: http://www.unaids.org/globalreport/documents/20101123_GlobalReport_ full_en.pdf (accessed 26 July 2011).

UNAIDS (2011) *Global HIV/AIDS Response: Epidemic Update and Health Sector Progress Towards Universal Access: Progress Report 2011*. Available at: http://www. unaids.org/en/media/unaids/contentassets/documents/unaidspublication/2011/JC2216_ WorldAIDSday_report_2011_en.pdf (accessed 25 July 2012).

UNICEF (2012) *In a Major Policy Shift, Mothers in South Africa Are Encouraged to Exclusively Breastfeed Instead of Using Formula*. Available at: http://www.unicef.org/ infobycountry/southafrica_62139.html (accessed 25 July 2012).

Wachira, J., Otieno-Nyunya, B., Ballidawa, J. and Braitstein, P. (2009) Assessment of knowledge, attitudes and practices of infant feeding in the context of HIV: a case study from western Kenya. *SAHARA Journal*, **6**, 120–6; quiz 127–33.

Walls, T., Palasanthiran, P., Studdert, J., Moran, K. and Ziegler, J. B. (2010) Breastfeeding in mothers with HIV. *Journal of Paediatrics and Child Health*, **46**, 349–52.

Wise, J. (2001) Breast feeding safer than mixed feeding for babies of HIV mothers. *British Medical Journal*, **322**, 511.

World Health Organization (2003) *Global Strategy for Infant and Young Child Feeding*. WHO, Geneva. Available at: http://whqlibdoc.who.int/publications/2003/9241562218. pdf (accessed 26 July 2011).

World Health Organization (2007) *HIV and Infant Feeding: New Evidence and Programmatic Experience*. WHO, Geneva.

World Health Organization (2008) *HIV Transmission Through Breastfeeding: a Review of Available Evidence: 2007 Update*. WHO, Geneva.

World Health Organization (2009a) *Key Messages. New WHO Recommendations: Infant Feeding in the Context of HIV*. Available at: http://www.who.int/hiv/pub/paediatric/infant_key_mess.pdf (accessed 26 July 2011).

World Health Organization (2009b) *Rapid Advice: Use of Antiretroviral Drugs for Treating Pregnant Women and Preventing HIV Infection in Infants*. WHO, Geneva. Available at: http://www.who.int/hiv/pub/mtct/rapid_advice_mtct.pdf (accessed 20 February 2010).

World Health Organization (2010a) *Guidelines on HIV and Infant Feeding 2010: Principles and Recommendations for Infant Feeding in the Context of HIV and a Summary of Evidence*. WHO, Geneva. Available at: http://whqlibdoc.who.int/publications/2010/9789241599535_eng.pdf (accessed 26 July 2011).

World Health Organization (2010b) *Infant and Young Child Feeding Fact Sheet*. Available at: http://www.who.int/mediacentre/factsheets/fs342/en/ (accessed 26 July 2011).

World Health Organization (2010c) *Towards Universal Access: Scaling Up Priority HIV/ AIDS Interventions in the Health Sector. Progress Report 2010*. WHO, Geneva. Available at: http://whqlibdoc.who.int/publications/2010/9789241599535_eng.pdf (accessed 26 July 2011).

Young, S. L., Israel-Ballard, K. A., Dantzer, E. A., Ngonyani, M. M., Nyambo, M. T., Ash, D. M. *et al.* (2010) Infant feeding practices among HIV-positive women in Dar es Salaam, Tanzania, indicate a need for more intensive infant feeding counselling. *Public Health Nutrition*, **13**, 2027–33.

CHAPTER 9

Baby-led weaning: a developmental approach to the introduction of complementary foods

Gill Rapley

Introduction to the second edition

Since the first edition of this book was published in 2006, baby-led weaning (BLW) has become a term familiar to the majority of health professionals working in the field of infant feeding in the UK. Most of its basic principles (notably the relevance of general motor development for the introduction of solid foods, the appropriateness of encouraging self-feeding as soon as the infant shows interest and the importance of shared family mealtimes) are reflected in the latest information produced by the various Departments of Health (e.g. DH, 2011) and the topic is discussed widely by parents, both one-to-one and via Internet forums. It is also known about, debated and implemented in many other countries. However, there remains a great deal of confusion about the evidence underpinning BLW and this, combined with the lack (so far) of much in the way of empirical evidence to support it, leads some people to question both the logic and the safety of this approach. For this reason the opportunity to re-examine the basis for the concept is welcome.

What is weaning?

Taken literally, the term *weaning* refers to the process by which an infant's total dependence on his mother for food (in the form of breast milk) is transformed into complete independence of any direct need for her, nutritionally speaking. This process begins when anything other than breast milk (solid or liquid) is introduced into the infant's diet, and ends with the last breastfeed of that child's life. In the UK, the nation whose practices form the focus of this chapter, the word 'weaning' is used in at least two ways: to signify the cessation of breastfeeding and, more commonly, to denote the introduction of foods other than either breast milk or infant formula. (It is worth noting here that, although the giving of supplementary drinks of water or juice to young breastfed infants is relatively common in the UK – 27% by four weeks, McAndrew *et al.*, 2012 – this is not generally acknowledged as being part of weaning.)

The World Health Organization (WHO) recommends exclusive breastfeeding for the first six months of a child's life (WHO/UNICEF, 2002). Accordingly, foods and drinks given before this age are defined as 'breast milk substitutes' (WHO, 1981) – sometimes also referred to as 'supplementary foods' – while those given from six months onwards are known as 'complementary foods' (WHO/UNICEF, 2002). Since this distinction is blurred when 'complementary' foods are introduced earlier than the recommended minimum age (thereby replacing, rather than adding to, the breast milk being consumed), these terms are not always helpful when studying the actual practices of parents. Further confusion arises from the use of the term 'solids' to refer to these foods, even though most are semi-solid in consistency. For the sake of clarity, the terms 'introduction of solid foods' and 'initiation of weaning' will be used throughout this chapter to describe the expansion of the predominantly breastfed infant's diet beyond breast milk alone, via semi-solid foods and/or those that require biting and chewing.

The move to the introduction of solid meals depends on the availability of suitable foods. Much of the existing research on weaning has been conducted in countries where either food is scarce or families do not have ready access to it. In this case, close supervision and management may be required to ensure that the child receives adequate nourishment (WHO, 2001). This has led some to question the wisdom of an approach that puts the infant in control. However, I will argue that, in the context of the western world at least, the granting of greater autonomy to the infant may be both appropriate and desirable.

For many years, researchers have sought to establish the optimal age for weaning to commence. From 1994 until 2003, the recommendation in the UK was that weaning foods should not be introduced before four months of age (DH, 1994). In May 2003, the official recommendation in England, Wales and Northern Ireland was changed to six months (DH, 2003), in line with WHO recommendations published the previous year (WHO/UNICEF, 2002). A similar move in Scotland followed a few years later. This change has come about, not only as a result of studies which have demonstrated the adequacy of breast milk for the first six months (e.g. Butte *et al.*, 2002; Kramer and Kakuma, 2002), but also because of the growing body of evidence of the detrimental effects, in terms of health and growth, of the early introduction of other foods (e.g. Howie *et al.*, 1990; Heinig and Dewey, 1996; Oddy *et al.*, 2003; Kramer *et al.*, 2004). At the same time, evidence has been collated showing that infants are not ready, in terms of their oral motor, gastro-intestinal and immunological abilities, to manage other foods before this age (Naylor, 2001). What has not been considered with the same degree of rigour is *how* this transition should be managed and who should initiate and control the process. Since the infant of six months behaves differently and has different abilities from those of the infant of four months, it makes sense to revise the information that parents receive about how to recognise an infant's readiness for other foods and how to introduce him to them in a way that takes this into account.

The concept of developmental readiness

Throughout a baby's first year many developmental milestones are achieved, but it is difficult to identify any whose timing is not initiated by the infant. Smiling, rolling over, sitting up, crawling – all may be stimulated by those around him but are ultimately controlled by the baby. A parent may hope that their son will walk before the child next door, and thus appear 'advanced', but they have no direct control over the matter. While they await the momentous event, however, they regularly provide him with opportunities to walk; he is being given just such an opportunity even at one day old, when his mother puts him on the floor 'to have a kick'. The only constraining factor is his own ability to coordinate the necessary muscles.

It is, of course, possible to delay a child's development by *not* providing the necessary opportunities, as has been explained in seminal work by Illingworth and Lister (1964) – a paper which has had enormous consequences for the practice of weaning and to which we shall return later. Provision of opportunity is therefore crucial to ensuring that an infant walks as soon as he is able, but it is his own development that limits how young he is when he takes his first step. Thus, it appears that, given the right environment, infants will develop new skills when they are ready – no earlier and no later.

This approach – of letting the infant indicate his readiness – appears to be applied consistently to all aspects of an infant's early development, with one significant exception: the introduction of solid foods. This chapter seeks to establish a rationale which allows us to see BLW as a logical, realistic and safe approach to this significant milestone of development.

The historical perspective

For most of the 20th century British infants have been subjected to the prevailing fashion with regard to the introduction of foods other than milk, with recommendations ranging from one to nine months after birth and beyond. Commercial interests have played a significant part in this variation by promoting a general down-playing of the importance of breastfeeding and an accompanying encouragement to replace breast milk with proprietary infant foods, including formula (Palmer, 2009, 2011).

For example, in 1934, the advice to mothers was that infants should not normally be given anything other than breast milk for the first eight months of life, at which point they should be started on an adapted cows' milk mixture (Liddiard, 1934). Parents were further cautioned that:

> for several months [after this] the milk mixture forms the chief part of baby's nourishment and must not be superseded by a large quantity of semi-solid starchy foods. (Liddiard, 1934, p. 41)

In 1956, Moncrieff, professor of child health at the University of London, advised that mixed feeding should commence at about five or six months of age (Moncrieff, 1956). The transition was to be a gradual process, taking one month to replace the first of the five (scheduled) breastfeeds with bone and vegetable soup, given by spoon. Weaning from the breast was to be completed by the age of nine months. The same procedure was recommended for infants fed with formula milk.

By the 1960s and 70s, the acceptable age for moving beyond a milk-only diet (whether breast or formula) had been reduced to three months, but there were suggestions that a more appropriate age would be between four and six months (MAFF, 1976). In 1994, the UK's Department of Health confirmed that weaning should be initiated between four and six months (DH, 1994), while the World Health Assembly recommended that weaning should begin at 'about six months' (WHA, 1994, cited in WHO, 1998).

Six years later, in 2000, it was clear that the Department of Health's advice was not being followed by all UK parents. Figures show that 24% of infants had received some solid foods (i.e. foods not liquid in origin) by the age of three months, rising to 85% by the age of four months. At six months of age, only 2% of British infants were being fed on milk alone (Hamlyn *et al.*, 2002). By 2005, when the recommended minimum age of introduction of complementary foods had been changed to six months, these figures had improved considerably, with only 10% of infants having received solid foods by three months and 50% by four months (Bolling *et al.*, 2007). By 2010, these figures were 5% and 30% respectively.

Even as the report of the Committee on Medical Aspects of Food and Nutrition Policy (COMA) (DH, 1994) was being published, writers such as Borresen (1995) were arguing in favour of a recommendation that foods other than breast milk should not be introduced before six months and, as the 21st century began, two key reviews – by Naylor and Morrow (2001) and Kramer and Kakuma (2002) – confirmed that there was sufficient evidence for exclusive breastfeeding to be recommended for the first six months. WHO and UNICEF accordingly published their Global Strategy, which stated that:

> To achieve optimal growth, development and health, infants should be exclusively breastfed for the first 6 months of life. Thereafter, to meet their evolving nutritional requirements, infants should begin to receive nutritionally adequate and safe complementary foods while breastfeeding continues for up to two years of age or beyond. (WHO/UNICEF, 2002, Section 3.1)

Since the coining of the term 'baby-led weaning' in 2002, interest in this approach to the introduction of solid foods has grown, gaining momentum in 2008 with the publication of the definitive book on the subject (Rapley and Murkett, 2008). Since then, various commentators and researchers have examined the phenomenon (Reeves, 2008; Wright *et al.*, 2010; Brown and Lee, 2011a,b,c; Rowan and Harris, 2012; Townsend and Pitchford, 2012) and information about it is spreading. What is worth noting, however, is that the practice of BLW is not new; anecdotal reports from parents show that it has been widely used for an indefinite amount of time, especially by experienced parents, who have the confidence to do what makes sense to them rather than doing things the 'proper' way. The only thing that is new is the name.

What prompts the move to solid feeding?

Mothers choose to initiate weaning for a variety of reasons (McCallion *et al.*, 1998; Anderson *et al.*, 2001; McDougall, 2003; Wright *et al.*, 2004). Many introduce solid foods because they are advised to do so, or believe they have been advised to do so, by health workers and child care manuals. It has been suggested that the information that mothers receive from health professionals can be ambiguous or inconsistent. McDougall (2003) sampled 108 mothers and found that, although 68% of mothers reported that they had received advice from a health visitor, only 10% were able to state correctly the currently recommended age for initiation of weaning.

Both Savage (1998) and Wright *et al.* (2004) found that the main reason given by mothers for introducing solids was the perception that their baby was hungry. A commonly accepted sign of hunger (among both mothers and health professionals) is the baby's 'return' to a pattern of waking at night. This implies an assumption that the baby will already be sleeping through the night on a regular basis, which is unlikely in a breastfed baby. In any event, there is no evidence to suggest that solid feeding is associated with longer periods of sleep (Heinig *et al.* 1993).

Another sign often interpreted as hunger, or as a readiness for tastes other than milk, is the baby's apparent fascination with watching his parents eating. However, logic suggests that it is likely to be the activity itself (i.e. the handling of food and eating utensils) which interests the baby, since what he sees his parents doing is not within his frame of reference as a means of satisfying hunger.

Health professionals have often suggested that solid foods should be started when an infant's rate of weight gain begins to lessen. Work by Dewey (1992, 1995) has shown that this happens naturally in breastfed infants from three months onwards and is not a sign of underfeeding nor any cause for concern. (This is reflected in the growth charts in use in the UK since 2009, which are based on the WHO charts published in 2006, and may mean that such advice is less commonly given nowadays.) By the same token, given what we now know about infants' digestive abilities (Walker, 2001), it is clear that infants who *are* in need of extra food would gain more from their mothers being given help to increase their breast milk supply (or, if this were not possible, from supplementation with donor breast milk or a suitable artificial formula), than from the introduction of other foods.

My own personal observations over twenty years of health visiting suggest that both mothers and health professionals vary, over time and between individuals, in the markers they use to identify infants' readiness for solid feeding. These range from simple body weight – commonly used prior to 1974 and cited variously as 12 lb or 15 lb – to a variety of behavioural signs thought, but not proven, to be related to hunger. Since infants' developmental progress and their actual need for other foods do not vary from year to year or from one professional to another, it is clear that at least some of these markers are fortuitous rather than accurate.

Breastfeeding as the start of the self-feeding continuum

Reid and Adamson (1998) point out that, although the infant's progress from milk to solid feeding is a continuous process, the majority of the literature dealing with the nutritional intake of infants treats milk feeding and solid feeding as two distinct stages. A study of the mechanics and features of breastfeeding shows that this method of feeding at least forms part of an ongoing continuum with more advanced feeding.

Breast milk is the ideal food for human infants. Not only does it contain everything needed for normal growth and development (Akre, 1991) but it varies from feed to feed. The flavour of breast milk changes with the mother's diet (Menella, 1994), so that the infant is introduced from birth to a variety of tastes and is thus prepared for the introduction of other foods. In addition, the breastfed infant can control the fat content of his feed through the amount of time spent at the breast and the frequency of feeding (Woolridge and Fisher, 1988). He is thus able to accommodate all his fluid needs independently of the remainder of his diet. This adaptability means that breastfeeding is ideal both as a preparation for, and for combining with, complementary feeding.

In order to milk the breast effectively, the infant has to take a substantial amount of breast tissue, as well as the nipple, into his mouth in a process known as attachment. Although the exact mechanism needed to milk the breast is unclear, there is general agreement that active jaw movements by the baby are required and that these are different from the mechanism used to feed from a bottle (Woolridge, 1986; Geddes *et al.*, 2008). It is likely that this use of the jaw is more closely related to the chewing movements required for the manipulation of solid foods than is the reliance on suction associated with bottle feeding.

Breastfeeding is self-feeding: it is not possible to achieve effective breastfeeding without the baby taking an active part in the process; the mother offers the opportunity and the baby feeds (or not). By contrast, it is possible to manoeuvre a bottle teat into a baby's mouth and, by moving it against the palate, to trigger the sucking reflex. Bottle feeding has also been shown to be associated with a greater degree of control by the mother than breastfeeding (Wright *et al.*, 1980). Thus the concept of feeding as something a mother does *to* her baby (i.e. with the baby in the passive role) would appear to be more closely related to bottle feeding than to breastfeeding. It follows that an approach to weaning which suggests that it is a natural, spontaneous progression on the *baby's* part, rather than something the mother imposes on the baby, fits neatly within the biological paradigm of breastfeeding.

There is evidence that breastfeeding mothers are more likely to follow BLW than those who formula feed (Brown and Lee, 2011a) and they are more likely to have a feeding style that is low in control (Brown and Lee, 2011b). Whether this is because this is the mother's pre-existing style, and that it is this that has helped her to sustain breastfeeding, or whether she has developed it as a result of her experience of how to make breastfeeding easier or more effective is not clear. Either way, it suggests that breastfeeding may be a good fit with BLW from the mother's point of view as well as the infant's. This does not mean that BLW is inappropriate or impossible for bottle-fed infants or their parents; merely that the nature of the transition, and their experience of it, may not be quite the same.

The timing of first solids – physical development

Breast milk is best delivered by the infant feeding directly from the breast. Indeed, the action of breastfeeding itself has been shown to convey health benefits (e.g. Neiva *et al.*, 2003; Peres *et al.*, 2007), indicating that it is the biological norm for the infant to gain nourishment in this way. The ability of the infant to cope with foods other than liquids relies on the development of the mouth and the alimentary tract. The infant gut at birth is not equipped to digest foods other than breast milk (or, to a lesser extent, infant formula). Instead, the ability to produce the necessary enzymes for the digestion of more complex foods is acquired over several months (Walker, 2001). The reflexes present in the mouth also change over time: at birth, a reflex tongue thrust is apparent, which begins to fade at about three months and is usually absent soon after four months. Between four and seven months the ability to 'munch' develops. This is followed, at between seven and twelve months, by the development of chewing movements, accompanied by the ability of the tongue to move laterally, so moving food to the cheek teeth. Adult-type rotary chewing movements are generally achieved soon after the first birthday (Naylor, 2001). Thus, the ability to manoeuvre food around the mouth and to bite and chew develops alongside the ability of the gut to produce the necessary enzymes for the digestion of complex foods.

Naylor and Morrow (2001) described a 'convergence of maturation', in terms of an infant's oral motor, digestive and immunological abilities, occurring at around six months of age. This, they claim, points to an overall developmental readiness for foods other than breast milk at this age. However, they did not consider the development of other skills relevant to feeding that might also form part of this convergence. Parkinson and Drewett (2001) studied feeding behaviour in the weaning period and suggested that an investigation of infants' other developing abilities was warranted:

> An obvious sequel to the present study would be to examine feeding be-
> haviour developmentally, and to relate it to other developmental changes
> such as those in… motor skills. (Parkinson and Drewett, 2001, p. 976)

Sheridan (1973) described the following sequence of infant behaviours. At birth, the rooting reflex enables the infant to locate the nipple and attach to the breast. At one month, his fingers – normally held closed – fan out when his arms are extended (a movement which may assist him to maintain his attachment at the breast). At around three months, the infant can wave his arms symmetrically and bring them together into the midline over his chest or chin. He watches the movements of his hands and is beginning to clasp and unclasp them. By six months he can sit with support and hold his head firmly erect. He fixates his gaze on small objects and stretches out both hands to grasp them. He uses his whole hand in a palmar grasp and takes everything to his mouth. Between six and twelve months, both the pincer grasp (using thumb and forefinger) and visual acuity develop to allow the infant to pick up progressively smaller objects. He also begins to release objects purposefully. He is thus able to transport small items to his mouth with increasing accuracy.

The sequence of events that Sheridan (1973) described is evident to anyone who observes infants and young children. Her work forms the basis of developmental surveillance to this day, and yet its fundamental importance to the initiation of weaning has been consistently overlooked. Indeed, we have sought to override and restrict infants' natural abilities with regard to feeding, presumably so that we could control the process according to the rules we have devised. Thus, while infants of eight to nine months, who have already demonstrated their ability to handle objects and transport them accurately to their mouth, are encouraged to feed themselves with their fingers, younger infants who are just beginning to develop these skills are rarely allowed to practise, except on toys.

By broadening our view to incorporate the work of observers such as Sheridan we can see that hand–eye coordination and fine motor development also appear to reach a certain level at around six months. It is not unreasonable to suggest that nature has designed the 'biologically-driven processes' (Naylor, 2001) necessary for the move away from exclusive breastfeeding to include the development of self-feeding skills. If so, this means that infants are fully equipped to make the transition to solid feeding unaided provided that, as with walking, they are given the necessary opportunities. It is, indeed, possible that infants have evolved never to need to be fed actively by another person, but rather are pre-programmed to move on to solid feeding gradually, unaided – beginning at around six months.

The presentation of weaning foods – spoon feeding and purées examined

Infants under six months old are not normally able to pick up food and get it to their mouth accurately, nor are they able to chew. If they are to have non-liquid foods it therefore follows that these will need to be puréed and fed to them by spoon. Spoon feeding has thus become the usual way for early solid foods to be given to infants, such that it is seen as an inherent part of the introduction of solid foods, rather than something related to the infant's abilities at the time of introduction. The predominance of references to spoon feeding in the literature on infant feeding reinforces the sense that feeding is something done to the infant by his mother, rather than something done by the infant for himself.

Our familiarity with spoon feeding in relation to infants may explain why, despite the move away from the very early introduction of solid foods, the advice given to British mothers about how weaning foods should be selected, prepared and presented has changed very little over the years, with purées and spoon feeding being the usual method of choice. This is at last beginning to change, with references to purées being replaced by a more vague allusion to 'soft' and mashed foods. However, while some leaflets for parents (e.g. NHS Health Scotland, 2010; DH, 2011) hint that finger foods may be appropriate from the outset (provided the baby is at least six months old), the illustrations accompanying the text continue to imply the use of spoons.

Many advocates of the early (i.e. before six months) introduction of solid foods maintain that there is a 'window of opportunity' during which infants will readily accept new foods and that this should be capitalised upon. Concern amongst health professionals about the consequences of missing the opportunity provided by this 'window' appear to stem from the paper by Illingworth and Lister (1964), who drew attention to the importance of the 'critical or sensitive period' in relation to the development of feeding skills.

Illingworth and Lister's work (1964) is based on the theory that there are critical periods for learning new skills; if the right stimuli are not provided at the right time, children will not achieve key developmental milestones. Thus, if they are not introduced to chewing at the appropriate stage of their development, they will not develop this skill. However, closer perusal of Illingworth and Lister's study (1964) reveals two key flaws in the extrapolation of their findings that has since taken place. Firstly, of the children they studied, only one was described as 'normal', while several were 'retarded' and others had anatomical problems such as oesophageal atresia. The 'normal' girl had, for reasons which are unclear, been fed exclusively on puréed foods until the age of two years.

Secondly, Illingworth and Lister did not study the children at the point when *semi*-solids were introduced; their evidence relates to solid foods, which require biting and chewing. Their contention was that 'if a baby is not given solid foods shortly after he has learned to chew, there may well be considerable difficulty in getting him to take solids later' (Illingworth and Lister, 1964, p. 843) and that 'the average age at which [chewing] develops is 6 months' (*op. cit.*, p. 847). This suggests that children need to be introduced to *food that requires chewing* soon after six months. It is only the assumption that such foods *must* be preceded by semi-solids – irrespective of the age at which they are introduced – that leads to the conclusion that 'solid' feeding should begin before six months. Interestingly, Stevenson and Allaire (1991) found no evidence to support the use of transitional foods, such as soft purées, in order to help infants progress, and noted that many cultures do not focus on such foods as a significant part of the weaning process.

More recent work by Northstone *et al.* (2001) found that infants who were introduced to lumpy foods after 10 months of age were significantly less likely to be eating family foods at 15 months. The reasons for late introduction of lumpy foods in each case were not made clear, and several possibilities exist. The figures do, however, point to a difficulty in making the *transition* from puréed foods to those of a more solid consistency. According to Gisel (1991), children utilise the easiest motor skills possible for any food, so if a child can manage a meal by sucking, it is likely that he will do so. If this is so, then the introduction of solid foods as purées at an age when the infant is capable of chewing – far from providing a means to 'bridge the gap between liquid and solid foods' (Reeves, 2008) – may in fact be a *hindrance* to the development of chewing skills.

Advocates of the early introduction of 'solids' point out that older infants who are not accustomed to spoon feeding will frequently turn their heads or use their hands to push away the spoon. This 'spoon refusal' is often interpreted as food refusal, and it appears to be at the root of most mealtime battles between toddlers and their parents. What is rarely acknowledged is that spoon feeding provides a means whereby (semi-)solid food can be inserted into the mouth of an infant too immature to achieve this for himself. Seen in this light, the response of the older infant to turn his head or push the spoon away can be interpreted as the reasonable actions of an individual who is sufficiently physically mature to make his wishes plain, while the 'acceptance' of the younger infant becomes simply evidence of his inability to resist.

The emphasis on the need to introduce spoon feeding when the infant is unlikely to show resistance appears to be based on the premise that acceptance by an infant of being fed in this manner is a necessary goal. Pridham (1990) makes this very clear: the ability to use the mouth to take food from a spoon is presented as one of four fundamental feeding skills and is expected to precede the skill of self-feeding – with either fingers or a spoon. Clearly, this is important only if the child is to be fed by someone else, since there is no evidence to suggest that a child who has not been spoon fed as an infant will have difficulty learning, eventually, to use a spoon to feed himself. Indeed, if this were the case, few children would ever manage to use forks!

Leaving aside a possibly genuine belief that infants require solid foods at an age when they are not capable of feeding themselves with them, the desire of adults to manage or control the feeding process could be a key reason (albeit unacknowledged) for the emphasis on spoon feeding. The use of a spoon achieves control in two important ways; it makes eating less messy (something which is not a matter of concern to most infants) and it allows the carer to dictate what is eaten, how much and how fast. Reeves (2008) states that 'purées are ideal for being able to introduce a known volume of food to the infant', implying that it is entirely desirable that the infant's ability to regulate his intake should be overridden (and ignoring the fact that even quite young children can, and do, spit out food once it has been put into their mouth). And yet there is no evidence that children need to be actively fed in this way in order to achieve good nutrition.

Controlling a child's eating is not without risk. Akre (1991) tells us that: 'once a mother assumes responsibility for the amount of food her child receives, overfeeding becomes a possibility' (Akre, 1991, p. 64). This is borne out by the work of Townsend and Pitchford (2012), who found that infants allowed to feed themselves from the outset had a lower body mass index (BMI) and a greater preference for healthy foods in the toddler years than those who were spoon-fed. Spoon feeding therefore has implications for the child's health as well as the development of his self-feeding abilities.

Managing lumps and eating safely

My experience as a health visitor suggests that the use of a spoon presents problems for many infants when they progress from purées to more textured foods and 'second-stage dinners', with gagging and spitting out of lumps commonly reported by mothers. A closer look at how infants learn to eat from a spoon offers an explanation: adults use different mechanisms when taking solid pieces of food from a spoon than when ingesting, for example, soup. When young infants are first given puréed foods on a spoon they use their existing oral skills to take the food, i.e. they suck (Wickendon, 2000). When a suck-type mechanism is used to empty a spoon, any lumps will tend to be transferred directly to the back of the throat, resulting in gagging and, potentially, choking. This risk is increased if the infant is in a semi-reclining position. By contrast, if the food is presented as a piece, and if the child uses his hands to control how much goes into his mouth, the risk of choking is less. This is because the development of early biting and chewing movements precedes the development of the ability to form a bolus of solid or semi-solid food and move it to the back of the mouth for swallowing (Naylor, 2001). Indeed, infants commonly 'lose' the first foods they bite off for themselves because they are unable to hold them in their mouth for chewing. Thus, far from making feeding safer, spoon feeding may in fact predispose to choking in young infants.

Anecdotal evidence suggests that gagging or retching, which is not the same as choking, is common in the early days of solid feeding in infants who are allowed to feed themselves. This is often alarming for parents and carers, but it is possible that it provides infants with an additional, built-in safety mechanism against choking. During infancy, the point on the tongue at which touch triggers the gag reflex moves progressively farther back (Naylor, 2001). Thus, the reflex is triggered very readily at six months, but less so at, say, nine months. The gag reflex operates to push forward food that has been insufficiently chewed, or which has been transferred to the back of the mouth without having been formed into a bolus for swallowing. Provided the infant is sitting upright or leaning forward, the reflex can normally be relied upon to propel the offending piece of food towards the front of the mouth, where it can be chewed further, or out of the mouth altogether.

This progressive change in sensitivity of the gag reflex allows an infant of six months to experiment with solid foods without risk to his airway, and to discover for himself how far back it is comfortable (and therefore safe) to push a piece of food, or how full it is reasonable to fill his mouth. Evidence from my own practice suggests that it is predominantly infants who have not been allowed to self-feed until they are eight or nine months or older (that is, until the gag reflex trigger point is approaching the posterior part of the tongue) who are inclined to overfill their mouths or to attempt to swallow without chewing. This suggests that delay in providing the opportunity for practice may itself invoke a greater risk with regard to choking. It is clear that well-designed studies are needed in order to investigate this further.

All these observations appear to cast doubt on the assumption that spoon feeding follows on – either naturally or logically – from breastfeeding and, therefore, on the appropriateness of its use in early solid feeding. And yet, although many authors have noted the importance of the environment and the behaviour of the care-giver in determining the acceptance of food by the infant (e.g. Southall and Schwartz, 2000; Parry and Jowett, 2001; Engle, 2002), none appear to have examined the significance of the feeding method itself.

Learning to chew

Infants do not 'learn' to chew, any more than they 'learn' to walk. Rather, they become able, through a process of maturation, to perform new movements.

According to Naylor (2001), sucking (as opposed to suckling) develops between six and nine months, together with 'a new type of swallow… which can be initiated without a preceding suckle' (Naylor, 2001, p. 23). Naylor further describes the development 'at or after six months' of the muscles of the tongue and mouth, which enables the infant to manipulate food that is more solid, in preparation for swallowing. This suggests that infants of this age are ready to deal with foods that require chewing.

Returning to the work of Illingworth and Lister (1964), we see that the key to encouraging the development of a new skill is to provide the opportunity for it to be practised. This would suggest that the best way for an infant to become skilled at chewing is to be given the opportunity to chew. If we further accept that he is not likely to choke as long as he is sitting upright and is allowed to take the food to his mouth himself, food would seem to be the best material for him to practise on. Firm foods are more likely to elicit chewing than viscous or puréed foods, whether or not the infant has any erupted molar teeth (Arvedson, 2000), and the provision of a variety of textures encourages the development of the various oral movements needed to cope with them (Wickendon, 2000). So the most appropriate way to encourage the development of chewing would seem to be to provide the infant with a selection of different foods with which to experiment.

Learning about food

Infants often appear to spit out food, and this is sometimes interpreted as food refusal. There are several probable reasons for this behaviour. One is the operation of the tongue thrust – an involuntary reflex action, present until around four months of age, which involves anything inserted into the mouth being spontaneously pushed forwards. This can be assumed to be an evolutionary feature designed specifically to prevent anything getting into the infant's mouth which he has not put there himself. Mothers who find difficulty in spoon feeding their three-month-old, and who later report that he has 'got used to the spoon' are merely observing the natural disappearance of the tongue thrust reflex.

Another possible reason for spitting out food is neophobia, the fear of new foods. This also manifests itself as a wish not to eat 'unseen' food and is thought to be an important survival mechanism with evolutionary advantage (Wickendon, 2000). Being able to see one's food may be an important part of ensuring one's safety. However, the reality for many infants is that they are prevented from seeing what is fed to them, so that they need to spit it out in order to be able to examine it. Feeling food with the fingers is an important experience, enabling learning about the relationships between the sight and feel of objects and their size, so the opportunity to handle food may assist the development of an integrated sensory system (Wickendon, 2000).

Denying infants the opportunity to link taste and texture with appearance may increase their reluctance to try anything new. It is no coincidence that a key element of the behavioural approach to helping children who refuse food is to allow the child the time and space to explore what he is being offered (Douglas, 2000) – an approach which gives him control over the situation and allows him to unlearn the fear he has developed.

Infants learn by mimicking adult behaviour (Jessel, 1990). Thus, the infant who avidly watches his parents eating is probably motivated to copy the activity, without necessarily being aware that it has anything to do with filling his stomach. It follows that the infant should be given the opportunity to handle food before he is expected to eat it. Allowing him to explore food, with his hands as well as his mouth, may fulfil his desire to join in with what he sees others doing, as well as enhancing his learning and skill development. Later, he will become skilled with cutlery through the same process of observation and imitation.

Infants who are enabled to handle food from an early age learn how to relate size, shape and texture, using their eyes and hands, with the experience of taste being added to the mix when they first manage to get a piece of food successfully into their mouth. At this point they also begin to equate the appearance of food and its feel on the skin with its feel in the mouth and its taste. They may begin to distinguish foods they like from those they dislike long before they are ready to swallow them. This developmental progression suggests that it is not hunger that motivates an infant to begin exploring solid foods but curiosity, and that, in fact, ingestion occurs as a fortuitous by-product of allowing a baby to follow his instincts to find out about the world. Of course, the infant's experience needs to make sense if it is to help him gain confidence. Most puréed food bears little resemblance to the same food in its whole form, especially where the constituents of a meal are blended together, so what the infant learns about an early meal is unlikely to help him to identify the same foods later unless the food is presented in a consistent format.

Self-feeding and developmental readiness

There are clearly persuasive arguments for an alternative approach to weaning, which allows the infant to be the decision-maker regarding the timing and pace of the transition to solid feeding, and which relies on his innate abilities to guide the process. My own small observational study (Rapley, 2003), carried out in 2001–2, investigated whether such an approach might work in practice. The results suggested that infants will, if given the opportunity, begin to reach out and grasp foods from around six months, and begin swallowing them soon after that. The likelihood of this being the case for most babies has been reinforced by Wright *et al.* (2010), who found that the majority of a cohort of over 600 infants first reached out for food before the age of seven months and that only 6% had not done so by eight months. Wright and her colleagues commented that some infants might have reached out sooner, had the opportunity been provided earlier, and concluded that BLW 'is probably feasible for a majority of infants' (p. 27). They added a caveat: that self-feeding alone could be nutritionally unsafe for infants with developmental delay. However, the study showed that the age of reaching out for food was linked to the infant's general development in relation to walking and talking, offering the possibility that those infants for whom this approach might not be suitable could be identified through their overall developmental achievements at six months.

It is becoming increasingly clear that giving solid foods to an infant who is too young to digest them has potentially serious consequences, but a key challenge in defining an age to initiate weaning (i.e. to introduce solid foods) for all children is how to allow for the fact that not all infants will be ready at exactly the same age. Alimentary, oral and immunological readiness are difficult to detect and, as infants get older, the differences between them in terms of development become more marked. For example, while most infants will smile between five and seven weeks of age – a difference of two weeks – the normal variation in age for walking is of the order of six months. This suggests that a one-size-fits-all approach to solid feeding is inappropriate, and is even more likely to be wide of the mark for some infants at six months than it is at four months. If, however, it is the case that hand–eye coordination and fine motor skills develop in parallel with the rest of the infant's abilities, perhaps it is possible to use them as indicators of readiness. It may be that exposing infants to the opportunity to handle food offers a way of ensuring that weaning begins at the optimal time for each individual baby. It also avoids the need to 'wean' infants twice – once on to purées and then again on to food with lumps.

The enjoyment of eating

In their study of one-year-olds, Young and Drewett (2000) found that 'food refusal is a common feature of eating behaviour in normal children at this age' (Young and Drewett, 2000, p. 171). This is surely a regrettable situation. Eating, at best, is about more than simply staving off hunger. It can be an immensely pleasurable experience, with the appearance, temperature, texture and flavour of the food and the sociability of eating with others all playing a part. For most adults, the idea of having all their meals spoon-fed to them, luke-warm, in homogenised format, at a pace decided by a carer, is the stuff of nightmares – of incapacity and old age. We appreciate being able to choose what to eat, when, how fast and how much. Why should this be any different for infants? Could it be that denying the very young the opportunity to make these sorts of choices has the potential to lead to serious consequences for their long-term relationship with food?

When each meal contains few contrasts in terms of texture and appearance, the only variable part of the feeding experience is the taste. It is therefore possible that, in such circumstances, the infant will pay more attention to taste than he would otherwise, and taste will play a greater part in determining what he will and won't accept. His parents may find that he will eat chocolate pudding with no problem but that they have to resort to games to distract him if they are to get him to eat anything else – tactics which, according to Carruth *et al.* (1998), may themselves lead to 'pickiness'. Occasionally, parents may even go so far as to pinch the infant's nose to force him to open his mouth. Experiences such as this, when observed through the infant's eyes, could explain the common anecdotal reports of infants who will eat a piece of apple but refuse to be fed with apple purée.

Where several foods are puréed together, as in, for example, a meal of chicken and vegetables, the infant has the option of accepting or refusing (if he is able) what is offered, but is given no opportunity to compare tastes or to blend them for himself. If he doesn't like a food whose flavour pervades each mouthful he will likely refuse every mouthful. Thus, because he is unable to work out – far less to tell his parents – that he does not like parsnip, they could be driven to conclude that he will not eat a roast chicken dinner.

A glance at the shelves of 'baby food' in any supermarket reveals how similar puréed meals can appear, even when they differ hugely in content. So, for the infant, yellow-orange mush may be a savoury 'Sunday lunch' one day and mango-flavoured the next – a fact that he may not discover until the spoon is in his mouth. (Smell may provide some clues, but not if he is being fed from a jar while his nostrils are being assailed with the smells of the rest of the family's meal cooking!). We should therefore not be surprised if he shows a reluctance to try new foods, or regularly spits out the first mouthful of each meal.

For practitioners who work with children who have food phobias, the starting point is almost always to 'give the control back to the child'; only then can real progress be made. The fact that this approach works raises the question 'what if control had never been taken away from the child in the first place?'. If newborn infants are capable of finding their mother's breast and, by six months, are able to feed themselves with solid foods, there seems no rationale for an approach to weaning which takes control away from them, only for it to be given back later. BLW may provide a means of avoiding at least some of the commonly seen fussiness and food fads of childhood, as well as the possibility of preventing more serious eating disorders.

Information for parents

Health professionals are rightly concerned about giving parents information about weaning that will lead to adequate nutrition for the infant. Some are understandably reluctant to encourage shared family meals and self-feeding in situations where the family diet is seen as unsuitable for a baby. And yet presumably at some point children growing up in these families will be encouraged to eat the same foods as their parents, by which time it may be too late to prevent them developing a preference for the foods they have seen the adults eating. The introduction of solid foods provides an opportunity for parents to reconsider their own eating habits; for some, the option to include their baby in their mealtimes may be the trigger they need to make changes that will have long-term implications for the whole family.

There is, however, a further obstacle for the health professional to overcome, and that is the language available for a discussion of solid feeding (Rapley, 2011). Many of the words and phrases commonly used to talk about weaning carry an underlying assumption that it is the adult who is in control of the feeding, such that they become meaningless when the baby is allowed to choose. Even the concept of 'starting solids' is different when the process is truly baby-led. The spoon-fed baby has the food inserted into his mouth (whether or not he wants it) and, because of its consistency and the way he takes the food from the spoon, he is obliged to swallow at least some of it. The baby who self-feeds, on the other hand, may spend days or even weeks exploring food before he even gets it to his mouth, and may not necessarily swallow any even then. At what point can he be said to have 'started solids'? To fully embrace BLW we need to move away from a need to know exactly when the first mouthful was swallowed and how much the baby has eaten, and focus instead on his interest in food and on providing him with role models for healthy eating.

The future

There are many things we still need to know about the feeding of young children. For example, can all infants be relied upon to choose a diet which will ensure adequate nutrition? And is a self-feeding approach as appropriate for bottle-fed infants, who have not been used to self-feeding and whose parents are used to a certain measure of control over feeding, as it is for breastfed infants?

Another area worthy of examination is the role of fluids other than milk in the diets of young children. Breastfeeding can continue to provide all the fluid a child needs for as long as the mother is happy to continue offering it, and yet there is a tendency among many parents and health professionals to persuade infants to switch to other drinks as part of the introduction of solid foods. Might the rush to introduce other fluids be a contributory factor in the risk of inadequate iron levels during the weaning period, as identified by a number of researchers (e.g. Butte *et al.*, 1987; Pisacane *et al.*, 1995; Griffin and Abrams, 2001; Domellof *et al.*, 2002)? Is it possible that research into the nature of the transition that babies would naturally make, given the opportunity, could change our perception of their requirements for additional vitamins and minerals?

We need to recognise that BLW isn't new. The signs are that infants have always known much of what science is only slowly establishing, namely that they are fully equipped to follow a path to family meals, without fuss and at the right time, in a way that will enhance both their development and their nutrition. Perhaps, if we listen to babies and trust their instincts, it will be they themselves who complain later, when asked to choose between chicken nuggets and sausage and chips on the children's menu of their parents' favourite restaurant!

References

Akre, J. (ed.) (1991) *Infant Feeding – The Physiological Basis*. WHO, Geneva.

Anderson, A. S., Guthrie, C. A., Alder, E. M., Forsyth, S., Howie, P. W. and Williams, F. L. (2001) Rattling the plate – reasons and rationales for early weaning. *Health Education Research: Theory and Practice*, **16**(4), 471–9.

Arvedsen J (2000) Evaluation of children with feeding and swallowing problems. *Language, Speech and Hearing Services in Schools*, **31**, 28–41.

Bolling, K., Grant, C., Hamlyn, B. and Thornton, A. (2007) *Infant Feeding Survey 2005*. The Information Centre, London.

Borresen, H. C. (1995) Rethinking current recommendations to introduce solid food between four and six months to exclusively breastfeeding infants. *Journal of Human Lactation*, **11**(3), 201–4.

Brown, A. and Lee, M. (2011a) A descriptive study investigating the use and nature of baby-led weaning in a UK sample of mothers. *Maternal & Child Nutrition*, **7**(1), 34–47.

Brown, A. and Lee, M. (2011b) Maternal control of child feeding during the weaning period: differences between mothers following a baby-led or standard weaning approach. *Maternal and Child Health Journal*, **15**(8), 1265–71.

Brown, A. and Lee, M. (2011c) Maternal child-feeding style during the weaning period: association with infant weight and maternal eating style. *Eating Behaviors*, **12**, 108–11.

Butte, N. F., Garza, C., Smith, E. O., Wills, C. and Nichols, B. L. (1987) Macro- and trace mineral intakes of exclusively breast-fed infants. *American Journal of Clinical Nutrition*, **45**, 42–7.

Butte, N. F., Lopez-Alarcon, M. G. and Garza, C. (2002) *Nutrient Adequacy of Exclusive Breastfeeding for the Term Infant During the First Six Months of Life*. WHO, Geneva.

Carruth, B. R., Skinner, J., Houck, K., Moran, J., Coletta, F. and Ott, D. (1998) The phenomenon of 'picky eater': a behavioral marker in eating patterns of toddlers. *Journal of the American College of Nutrition*, **17**(2), 180–6.

Department of Health (2003) National Breastfeeding Awareness Week press release, 12 May.

Department of Health (2011) *Introducing Solid Foods: Giving Your Baby a Better Start in Life*. Central Office of Information, London.

Department of Health Committee on the Medical Aspects of Food Policy (1994) *Weaning and the Weaning Diet* (Report on Health and Social Subjects No. 45). HMSO, London.

Dewey, K. G., Heinig, M. J., Nommsen, L. A., Peerson, J. M. and Lonnerdal, B. (1992) Growth of breast-fed and formula-fed infants from 0 to 18 months: The Darling Study. *Pediatrics*, **89**(6), 1035–41.

Dewey, K. G., Peerson, J. M., Brown, K. H., Krebs, N. F., Michaelsen, K. F., Persson, L. A., Salmenpera, L., Whitehead, R. G. and Yeung, D. L. (1995) Growth of breast-fed infants deviates from current reference data: a pooled analysis of US, Canadian, and European data sets. *Pediatrics*, **96**(3), 495–503.

Domellof, M., Lonnerdal, B., Abrams, S. A. and Hernell, O. (2002) Iron absorption in breast-fed infants: effects of age, iron status, iron supplements, and complementary foods. *American Journal of Clinical Nutrition*. **76**(1), 198–204.

Douglas, J. (2000) The management of selective eating in young children. In: *Feeding Problems in Children* (eds. A. Southall and A. Schwartz), pp. 141–52. Radcliffe Medical Press, Abingdon, Oxon.

Engle, P. L. (2002) Infant feeding styles: barriers and opportunities for good nutrition in India. *Nutrition Reviews*, **60**(s5), S109–S114.

Geddes, D. T., Kent, J. C., Mitoulas, L. R. and Hartmann, P. E. (2008) Tongue movement and intra-oral vacuum in breastfeeding infants. *Early Human Development*, **84**, 471–7.

Gisel, E. G. (1991) Effect of food texture on the development of chewing of children between six months and two years of age. *Developmental Medicine and Child Neurology*, **33**, 69–79.

Griffin, I. J. and Abrams, S. A. (2001) Iron and breastfeeding. *Pediatric Clinics of North America*, **48**(2), 401–13.

Hamlyn, B., Brooker, S., Oleinikova, K. and Wands, S. (2002) *Infant Feeding 2000*. The Stationery Office, London

Heinig, M. J. and Dewey, K. G. (1996) Health advantages of breastfeeding for infants: a critical review. *Nutrition Research Reviews*, **9**, 89–110.

Heinig, M. J., Nommsen, L. A., Peerson, J. M., Lonnerdal, B. and Dewey, K. G. (1993) Intake and growth of breast-fed and formula-fed infants in relation to the timing of introduction of complementary foods: the DARLING study. *Acta Paediatrica*, **82**(12), 999–1006.

Howie, P. W., Forsyth, J. S., Ogston, S. A., Clark, A. and Florey, C. D. (1990) Protective effect of breast feeding against infection. *British Medical Journal*, **300**, 11–16.

Illingworth, R. S. and Lister, J. (1964) The critical or sensitive period, with special reference to certain feeding problems in infants and children. *Journal of Pediatrics*, **65**(6), 839–48.

Jessel, C. (1990) *Birth to Three*. Bloomsbury Publishing Ltd, London.

Kramer, M. S. and Kakuma, R. (2002) Optimal duration of exclusive breastfeeding. *The Cochrane Database of Systematic Reviews* 2002, Issue 1. Art. No.: CD003517. doi: 10.1002/14651858.CD003517.

Kramer, M. S., Guo, T., Platt, R. W., Vanilovich, I., Sevkovskaya, Z., Dzikovich, I., Michaelsen, K. F. and Dewey, K. (2004) Feeding effects on growth during infancy. *Journal of Pediatrics*, **145**(5), 600–5.

Liddiard, M. (1934) In: *The Hygiene of Life and Safer Motherhood* (ed. W. A. Lane), pp. 38–42. British Books Ltd, London.

Ministry of Agriculture, Fisheries and Food (1976) *Manual of Nutrition*. HMSO, London.

McAndrew, F., Thompson, J., Fellows, L., Large, A., Speed, M. and Renfrew, M. J. (2012) *Infant Feeding Survey 2010*. Health and Social Care Information Centre, London.

McCallion, C. R., Scott, E. M. and Doherty, M. (1998) Influences on weaning practices. *Journal of Social and Administrative Pharmacy*, **15**(2), 117–24.

McDougall, P. (2003) Weaning: parents' perceptions and practices. *Community Practitioner*, **76**(1), 25–8.

Mennella, J. (1994) A medium for flavor experiences. *Journal of Human Lactation*, **11**(1), 39–45.

Moncrieff, A. (1956) *Infant Feeding*. W & J Mackay & Co. Ltd, Chatham.

Naylor, A. J. (2001) Infant oral motor development in relation to the duration of exclusive breastfeeding In: *Developmental Readiness of Normal Full Term Infants to Progress from Exclusive Breastfeeding to the Introduction of Complementary Foods: Reviews of the Relevant Literature Concerning Infant Immunologic, Gastrointestinal, Oral Motor and Maternal Reproductive and Lactational Development* (eds. A. J. Naylor and A. Morrow). Wellstart International and the LINKAGES Project Academy for Educational Development, Washington, DC.

Naylor, A. J. and Morrow, A. (eds.) (2001) *Developmental Readiness of Normal Full Term Infants to Progress from Exclusive Breastfeeding to the Introduction of Complementary Foods: Reviews of the Relevant Literature Concerning Infant Immunologic, Gastrointestinal, Oral Motor and Maternal Reproductive and Lactational Development*. Wellstart International and the LINKAGES Project Academy for Educational Development, Washington, DC.

Neiva, F. C., Cattoni, D. M., Ramos, J. L. and Issler, H. (2003) Early weaning: implications to oral motor development. *Jornal de Pediatria*, **79**(1), 7–12.

NHS Health Scotland (2010) *Fun First Foods: An Easy Guide to Introducing Solid Foods*. NHS Health Scotland, Edinburgh.

Northstone, K., Emmett, P., Nethersole, F. and ALSPAC Study Team (2001) The effect of age of introduction to lumpy solids on foods eaten and reported feeding difficulties at 6 and 15 months. *Journal of Human Nutrition and Dietetics*, **14**(1), 43–54.

Oddy, W. H., Sly, P. D., de Klerk, N. H., Landau, L. I., Kendall, G. E., Holt, P. G. and Stanley, F. J. (2003) Breast feeding and respiratory morbidity in infancy: a birth cohort study. *Archives of Disease in Childhood*, **88**, 224–8.

Palmer, G. (2009) *The Politics of Breastfeeding*, 3rd edn. Pinter & Martin, London.

Palmer, G. (2011) *Complementary Feeding: Nutrition, Culture and Politics*. Pinter & Martin, London.

Parkinson, K. N. and Drewett, R. F. (2001) Feeding behaviour in the weaning period. *Journal of Child Psychology and Psychiatry*, **42**(7), 971–8.

Parry, A. and Jowett, S. (2001) The origin of early feeding problems. *Community Practitioner*, **74**(4), 143–5.

Peres, K., Barros, A., Peres, M. and Victora, C. (2007) Effects of breastfeeding and sucking habits on malocclusion in a birth cohort study. *Rev Saúde Pública*, **41**(3), 343–50.

Pisacane, A., De Vizia, B., Valiante, A., Vaccaro, F., Russo, M., Grillo, G. and Giustardi, A. (1995) Iron status in breast-fed infants. *Journal of Pediatrics*, **127**, 429–31.

Pridham, K. F. (1990) Feeding behaviour of 6- to 12-month-old infants: assessment and sources of parental information. *Journal of Pediatrics*, **117**(2pt2), S174–80.

Rapley, G. (2003) Can babies initiate and direct the weaning process? *Unpublished MSc Thesis*. Interprofessional Health and Community Studies (Care of the Breastfeeding Mother and Child). Canterbury Christ Church University College, Kent.

Rapley, G. (2011) Talking about weaning. *Community Practitioner*, **84**(8), 40–1.

Rapley, G. and Murkett, T. (2008) *Baby-led Weaning: Helping Your Child to Love Good Food*. Vermilion, London.

Reeves, S. (2008) Baby-led weaning. *British Nutrition Foundation Nutrition Bulletin*, **33**, 108–10.

Reid, M. and Adamson, H. (1998) *Opportunities for and Barriers to Good Nutritional Health in Women of Child-bearing Age, Pregnant Women, Infants Under 1 and Children Aged 1 to 5*. Health Education Authority, London.

Rowan, H. and Harris, C. (2012) Baby-led weaning and the family diet. A pilot study. *Appetite*, **58**, 1046–9.

Savage, S. A. H., Reilly, J. J., Edwards, C. A. and Durnin, J. V. G. A. (1998) Weaning practice in the Glasgow longitudinal infant growth study. *Archives of Disease in Childhood*, **79**, 153–6.

Sheridan, M. (1973) *Children's Developmental Progress*. NFER Publishing Co. Ltd, Windsor.

Southall, A. and Schwartz, A. (eds.) (2000) *Feeding Problems in Children*. Radcliffe Medical Press, Abingdon.

Stevenson, R. D. and Allaire, J. H. (1991) The development of normal feeding and swallowing. *Pediatric Clinics of North America*, **38**(6), 1439–53.

Sullivan, S. A. and Birch, L. L. (1994) Infant dietary experience and acceptance of solid foods. *Pediatrics*, **93**(2), 271–7.

Townsend, E. and Pitchford, N. J. (2012) Baby knows best? The impact of weaning style on food preferences and body mass index in early childhood in a case-controlled sample. *BMJ Open* 2012;2:e000298 doi:10.1136/bmjopen-2011-000298.

Walker, W. A. (2001) Gastrointestinal development in relation to the duration of exclusive breastfeeding. In: *Developmental Readiness of Normal Full Term Infants to Progress from Exclusive Breastfeeding to the Introduction of Complementary Foods: Reviews of the Relevant Literature Concerning Infant Immunologic, Gastrointestinal, Oral Motor and Maternal Reproductive and Lactational Development* (eds. A. J. Naylor and A.

Morrow). Wellstart International and the LINKAGES Project Academy for Educational Development, Washington, DC.

Wickendon, M. (2000) The development and disruption of feeding skills: how speech and language therapists can help. In: *Feeding Problems in Children* (eds. A. Southall and A. Schwartz), pp. 3–23. Radcliffe Medical Press, Abingdon.

Woolridge, M. (1986) The 'anatomy' of infant sucking. *Midwifery*, **2**, 164–71.

Woolridge, M. and Fisher, C. (1988) 'Colic', overfeeding, and symptoms of lactose malabsorption in the breast-fed baby: a possible artefact of feed management? *Lancet*, **8605**, 382–4.

World Health Organization (1981) *International Code of Marketing of Breast-milk Substitutes*. WHO, Geneva.

World Health Organization (1998) *Complementary Feeding of Young Children in Developing Countries – A Review of Current Scientific Knowledge*. WHO, Geneva.

World Health Organization (2001) *Complementary Feeding: Report of the Global Consultation convened jointly by the Department of Child and Adolescent Health and Development and the Department of Nutrition for Health and Development*. WHO, Geneva.

World Health Organization/UNICEF (2002) *Global Strategy for Infant and Young Child Feeding*. WHO, Geneva.

Wright, P., Fawcett, J. and Crow, R. (1980) The development of differences in the feeding behaviour of bottle and breast fed human infants from birth to two months *Behavioural Processes*, **5**(1), 1–20.

Wright, C. M., Parkinson, K. N. and Drewett, R. F. (2004) Why are babies weaned early? Data from a prospective population based cohort study. *Archives of Disease in Childhood*, **89**, 813–16.

Wright, C. M., Cameron, K., Tsiaka, M. and Parkinson, K. N. (2010) Is baby-led weaning feasible? When do babies first reach out for and eat finger foods? *Maternal & Child Nutrition*, **7**(1), 27–33.

Young, B. and Drewett, R. (2000) Eating behaviour and its variability in 1-year-old children. *Appetite*, **35**, 171–7.

CHAPTER 10

Seafood and omega-3s for maternal and child mental health

Wendy Hunt and Alexandra McManus

Introduction

The World Health Organization (WHO) defines mental health as: 'a state of well-being in which the individual realizes his or her own abilities, can cope with the normal stresses of life, can work productively and fruitfully, and is able to make a contribution to his or her community' (WHO, 2001). This definition acknowledges mental health as being the foundation of wellbeing and also the interdependent nature of mental and physical health.

Mental ill health is an increasing burden of disease worldwide (WHO, 2008) and the focus of many health professionals on child health, including the gestational period, is aimed at preventing and reducing mental ill health. Mental health is multifactorial and encompasses genetic predispositions, environmental and individual biological, and physiological and social factors (Ramakrishnan, 2011). A nutritionally balanced and healthy diet is one biological factor which is necessary for both the physical and mental development of children (Tomlinson et al., 2009). There is strong evidence linking nutritional interventions with reductions in the incidence and prevalence of mental health disorders (Sanchez-Villegas et al., 2009; Hibbeln, 1998, 2002; Shannon, 2009; Cetin and Koletzko, 2008; Hibbeln et al., 2006a,b; Tomlinson et al., 2009; Noaghiul and Hibbeln, 2003; Richardson, 2006; Clayton et al., 2007).

The role of nutrition in cognitive development and child health has been the basis of many global campaigns aimed at preventing mental illness. UNICEF programmes, for example, have been designed to promote the use of iodised salt in developed and developing countries alike in order to reduce the known learning difficulties and mental and physical retardation that result from iodine deficiency in early childhood. It is estimated that 70% of the world's households now use iodised salt, and as a result 91 million newborns are protected from the adverse mental and physical health issues associated with iodine deficiency (UNICEF, 2011). Despite the resounding success of many interventions, WHO recognises that children who are disadvantaged socioeconomically or nutritionally are never able to catch up with well-nourished or affluent children (WHO, 2008).

In addition to the widely regarded role of a healthy diet in prevention of adverse mental health outcomes, in recent years the use of nutrition as a complementary therapy for many health concerns has also gained impetus. Investigations into nutritional therapy have been focused on both specific nutrients and on whole of diet or dietary pattern approaches.

One focus of intense interest is the health benefits associated with marine-sourced omega-3 long chain polyunsaturated fatty acids (n-3 LCPUFAs), which has followed observations first made in the 1950s. It was noted that Eskimos native to Greenland had a low incidence of heart disease despite having a diet high in oil (McManus *et al.*, 2010). Ensuing studies in the populations of Alaskan and Greenland Eskimos and Japanese populations revealed a relatively low incidence and morbidity associated with coronary heart disease (He *et al.*, 2004). More recently consumption of seafood and omega-3 fatty acids has been linked with positive health outcomes in infant development, dementia, Alzheimer's disease, platelet aggregation, cardiovascular disease, hypertension, hyperlipidaemia, inflammation and nutrition-related cancers (Ruxton and Derbyshire, 2009; McManus *et al.*, 2010). The association between seafood and marine-sourced omega-3 fatty acid consumption and child development and cognition is now widely accepted, with eminent experts advising that limiting seafood consumption during pregnancy may in fact be a risk factor for suboptimal neurodevelopment outcomes in children (Hibbeln *et al.*, 2007).

This chapter will discuss child and maternal mental health with emphasis on the role of maternal, gestational and childhood nutrition. Promising outcomes of research into mental health disorders and the positive role of seafood and marine sourced long-chain polyunsaturated omega-3 fatty acid consumption is reviewed.

Overview of mental health disorders and significance to children

Mental health disorders account for seven of the top 20 causes of moderate and severe disability worldwide (WHO, 2001). Notably, these seven are: depression; alcohol dependence and problem use; bipolar disorder; schizophrenia; Alzheimer's disease and other dementias; panic disorder; and drug dependence and problem use.

Of these mental health concerns, mood (affective) disorders are of the largest concern globally. Depression, classified within the fourth edition of the *Diagnostic and Statistical Manual of Mental Disorders* (DSM-IV) as a mood disorder, is the third most disabling condition worldwide, with global incidence estimated to be 151 million (Funk *et al.*, 2010). Further, depression is the single largest source of burden of disease in women in both developing and developed countries (WHO, 2008). The burden of disease from depression in low-income countries (3.2%) is in fact comparable to that of malaria (4%) (Funk *et al.*, 2010).

Mental health is of immense concern for high-income countries also. It is predicted that around 50% of Americans will meet the criteria for a DSM-IV disorder, including those disorders from the spectra of anxiety, mood, impulse control and substance-use disorders, at some time in their life (Kessler *et al.*, 2005). Based upon inherent study bias, this estimate is purported to be conservative. Similar levels of incidence are reported around the world. The 2007 Australian National Survey of Mental Health and Wellbeing, for instance, revealed that 45% of the 16 million respondents aged 16–85 years had experienced a mental health disorder within their lifetime; one in five people within the 12 months preceding the interview (Australian Bureau of Statistics, 2008). A further 10% of people reported suffering from a long-term mental or behavioural problem (Australian Bureau of Statistics, 2006). Anxiety and mood (affective) disorders were the most commonly reported. Mental health disorders accounted for 22.8% of the total burden of disability in the UK in 2008/09 and are estimated to cost the UK economy £105.2 billion each year (Department of Health, 2010). These figures equate to around 1 in 4 adults affected by mental health disorders annually, with the major disorders being depression, anxiety, schizophrenia and dementia.

The importance of investigating factors contributing to mental illness is highlighted by the prevalence of mental ill health even at an early age. A review conducted of 49 international studies reported an incidence of prevalence of mental health disorders in children and youth of 12%. Calculating the incidence of mental health disorders can be problematic and understated when it is based on those receiving professionals' assistance. Only a minority of children meeting mental disorder criteria are seen by health professionals (Sawyer *et al.*, 2001). Adequate data from developing countries can be confounded by concerns of even greater under-reporting and diagnosis than in developed countries.

The prevalence of mental health disorders in childhood, adolescence and into adulthood highlights the importance of implementing prevention and early treatment interventions focusing on youth (Kessler *et al.*, 2005). Analysis of the World Health Organization's World Mental Health Survey Initiative data led researchers to report that it may be profitable to begin public health interventions in childhood, especially given that people with early onset disorders frequently wait more than a decade before seeking treatment (Kessler *et al.*, 2007). Preclinical and clinical trials are needed to determine whether the severity or persistence of disorders is reduced with early intervention. Additionally, epidemiological research is required to determine whether early intervention impacts on long-term secondary prevention (Kessler *et al.*, 2007).

Co-morbidities associated with poor mental health in youth can have lifelong negative influences. Strong co-morbidity associations are identified with adverse developmental and health concerns, including poor educational achievements, substance misuse, violence and sexual health issues (Patel *et al.*, 2007). Additionally, discussion of the incidence of mental health disorders would be incomplete without considering suicide morbidity and mortality. Globally, 844,000 people die from suicide each year (Funk *et al.*, 2010). Suicide is identified as the primary cause of premature death in people suffering from mental illness, with 72% of people reporting suicide ideation also reporting a concurrent mental health disorder (Australian Institute of Health and Welfare, 2010).

The high prevalence of mental health disorders around the world, combined with trends of increasing incidence, highlights the importance of prevention strategies early in life.

Omega-3 fatty acids – what are they?

Lipids in the natural state are made up of aliphatic monocarboxylic acids which are commonly called fatty acids. Fatty acids are named in the same way as hydrocarbons, with designations reflecting the length of the carbon chain as well as the number and location of double bonds within the molecule (Nawar, 1985). The terminal carboxyl group is numbered carbon one in the carbon chain. When reference is made to an omega-numbered fatty acid however, the omega number refers to the carbon adjacent to the first double bond numbered from the methyl end of the fatty acid molecule.

Docosahexaenoic acid (22:6n-3) (DHA), for example, is a molecule with a backbone that is 22 carbon atoms in length, containing 6 double bonds with the first double bond occurring on carbon 3 from the methyl end of the molecule (McManus *et al.*, 2010). Figure 10.1 displays the three omega-3 fatty acids commonly found in food. DHA and eicosapentaenoic acid (EPA) are marine-sourced omega-3 fatty acids, while alpha-linoleic acid (ALA) is found in flaxseed and other non-

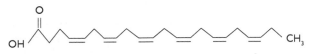

Docosahexaenoic acid (DHA) – 22:6n-3

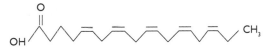

Eicosapentaenoic acid (EPA) – 20-5n-3

O
||
OH — CH₃

Alpha-linoleic acid (ALA) – 18:3n-3

Figure 10.1 Nomenclature of omega-3 fatty acids (McManus *et al.*, 2010).

marine foods. The marine-sourced omega-3 fatty acids, DHA and EPA, have been identified as the most biologically relevant long-chain polyunsaturated fatty acids for optimal mental health (Bodnar and Wisner, 2005).

Despite the structural similarity of omega-3 fatty acids, there are differences not only in their physiological function but also their metabolism (McManus *et al.*, 2010). ALA is categorised as an essential fatty acid in human diets, as humans do not possess the enzymes for its synthesis (Goyens *et al.*, 2006). In contrast, the human body is able to convert ALA into DHA or EPA through a processes of elongation and desaturation; the enzymes catalysing desaturation are thought to limit rates of conversion. Research has recently identified genetic variations in the Fatty Acid Desaturase 1 and 2 (FADS1 and FADS2) allelles that code for the desaturase enzyme responsible for fatty acid conversion. The investigators surmised that FADS may account for nearly one third of tissue polyunsaturated fatty acid and long-chain polyunsaturated fatty acid variability (Glaser *et al.*, 2011). Rates of conversion, however, continue to be debated among researchers, and as measurements provide only static insight into the dynamic system of fatty acid flux within plasma, careful interpretation of results is required (McManus *et al.*, 2010). Some experts quote up to 8% conversion of ALA to EPA, though conversion to DHA is limited (Goyens *et al.*, 2006).

In the study of omega-3 fatty acid metabolism, it is important to consider dietary intake of omega-6 fatty acids. As omega-3 fatty acids (n-3 LCPUFAs) contain a carbon–carbon double bond between the third and fourth carbons from the methyl end of the fatty acid molecule, omega-6 fatty acids (n-6 LCPUFAs) and omega-9 fatty acids (n-9 LCPUFAs) contain a double bond on the sixth and ninth carbons from the methyl end respectively. The balance of fatty acids within the diet is critical to biological status, as there is evidence of an antagonistic relationship between n-3 and n-6 LCPUFAs (Brenna *et al.*, 2009). This antagonistic relationship is significant because the major dietary n-6 LCPUFAs, linoleic acid (LA, 18:2n-6) and arachidonic acid (AA, 20:4n-6), occur naturally in seed oils and as a result are a significant component of the western type dietary pattern (McManus *et al.*, 2010). This fatty acid balance is vastly different from human diets in evolutionary terms.

As a result of interactions between the dietary fatty acids, the profile of dietary fatty acid intake is an important factor determining the effectiveness of EPA and DHA conversion. Increased tissue AA has been identified as a consequence of high dietary intakes of LA with concomitant reductions in tissue n-3 LCPUFA levels and associated alterations to the nervous system, including very low levels of DHA in the fatty acid composition of the brain, which is of particular concern during times of rapid brain development (Brenna *et al.*, 2009; Gibson *et al.*, 2011; Sanders *et al.*, 1984). Optimal EPA synthesis occurs in diets low in LA, and DHA synthesis has been noted to increase with consumption of in diets high in ALA (Goyens *et al.*, 2006). Researchers note, however, that DHA synthesis is 'extremely limited' and that a diet low in LA and high in ALA will not provide the significantly increased plasma DHA that could be obtained from a moderate intake of seafood or fish oils. As a result, seafood consumption remains the only demonstrable pathway to significantly increased DHA status; exchange of dietary LA for ALA in order to enhance fatty acid plasma profiles is recommended as a less effective option for individuals who do not consume seafood (Goyens *et al.*, 2006).

Seafood and mental health – more than omega-3s

While long-chain omega-3 polyunsaturated acids have received a great deal of attention in the public arena and scientific communities alike, seafood as a whole food provides health benefits beyond those that can be attributed to omega-3 fatty acids alone. There is emerging awareness of the health benefits associated with the nutritional components of seafood other than omega-3 fatty acids. One study has revealed that the health benefits, particularly in relation to brain function, may in fact be attributable to the selenium in fish consumed (Berr *et al.*, 2009).

Furthermore, the superior bioavailability of nutrients in seafood leads to the conclusion that seafood as a whole food is among the best dietary source of many nutrients. Seafood is a valuable source of lean protein, omega-3 fatty acids, iron, iodine, zinc, selenium, and vitamins A and D, as well as B group vitamins. With regard to cognitive and neurological development and mental health the nutrients of particular interest are iodine, selenium, vitamin B_{12} and zinc.

Iodine deficiency disorders are diverse and include debilitating mental and physical disorders (Li *et al.*, 2006). Iodine is essential for the effective functioning of the thyroid gland and thyroid hormone production and as such facilitates normal growth, metabolism, cell oxygen consumption and central nervous system development. Fish and seafood contain the highest levels of iodine found in commonly consumed foods in most diets, with shellfish containing the most abundant quantities (Gunnarsdottir *et al.*, 2010). Seafood as a part of a healthy diet will improve iodine status.

Selenium prevents cellular damage and is protective against oxidative stress (Weber *et al.*, 2008). Recent research has suggested that supplementation with selenium during pregnancy may in fact reduce the incidence of postpartum depresssion (Mokhber *et al.*, 2011). Other investigations have identified that a lower dietary intake of selenium is associated with an increased risk of depression. The researchers suggest that the role of selenium as a selenoprotein constituent, and as such important in redox homeostasis, is the likely mechanism for this relationship, particularly in the glutathione system (Pasco *et al.*, 2012). Further discussion of the antioxidant properties of selenium can be found in Chapter 1 of this book.

Vitamin B_{12} is important to DNA synthesis and also red blood cell and neurological function. Deficiency of vitamin B_{12} can be associated with megoblastic anemia, neurological disorders, myelopathy, memory impairment, dementia, depression and cerebrovascular disorders. Dietary intake of fish has been linked to significant improvements in plasma B_{12} status (Vogiatzoglou *et al.*, 2009).

Zinc plays a role in optimal growth and development and functioning of the immune system. Zinc deficiency may result in stunted growth, vulnerability to infection and poor pregnancy outcome (Ekweagwu *et al.*, 2008). As zinc binds to protein, seafoods, which are sources of both zinc and protein, optimise bioavailability of dietary zinc (Alloway, 2009). Oysters are known to be one of the richest natural sources of zinc.

The importance of seafood as a whole food, in addition to omega-3 LCPUFAs, cannot be underestimated. Seafood offers a range of nutrients that are frequently under-represented in habitual diets, including iodine, calcium, vitamin D, zinc and iron.

Fetal and infant neural and cognitive development

The fatty acids DHA, EPA and AA are essential to fetal and neonatal brain development and maturation (Shannon, 2009). These fatty acids accumulate expressly during the periods of rapid brain growth and development that occur in gestation and during the first year of life; fetal accretion of omega-3 fatty acids is notably high during the last trimester of pregnancy (Ramakrishnan *et al.*, 2009). In addition to cognitive and neurological development, DHA is an integral constituent of lipids of the retina; it is thought that DHA may comprise up to 50% of the outer segments of rods and cones (Stillwell and Wassall, 2003).

Higher maternal DHA consumption during pregnancy and lactation has been associated with improved infant neurodevelopmental outcomes (Cetin and Koletzko, 2008). Evidence exists for omega-3 fatty acid deficiency being associated with adverse outcomes, including intrauterine growth retardation; delayed or suboptimal depth perception; adverse neurodevelopmental measures; residual deficits in fine motor skills; speed of information processing in infants; and irreversible deficits in serotonin and dopamine release (Hibbeln *et al.*, 2007; Cetin and Koletzko, 2008). Further, lower omega-3 fatty acid intake during pregnancy has been demonstrated to predict lower verbal IQ scores in children at 8 years of age (Hibbeln *et al.*, 2007).

The European Commission, the World Association of Perinatal Medicine, the Early Nutrition Academy and the Child Health Foundation have supported recommendations, reached through expert consensus and based on systematic literature reviews, that pregnant women should aim at consuming 200 mg of DHA daily (Koletzko *et al.*, 2008).

The potential risks to fetal neural development associated with methyl mercury in seafood have been well publicised. With the exception of a few key species that can be easily avoided, the benefits of seafood consumption outweigh the potential risks to the general population including women of childbearing age (Mozaffarian and Rimm, 2006). Nutritional and associated neurodevelopmental benefits associated with seafood consumption during pregnancy (based on consumption of 340 g seafood per week) transcend the potential risk of exposure to trace contaminants in seafood (Hibbeln *et al.*, 2007). Research assessing maternal fish consumption and child development outcomes to nine years of age has been unable to support a hypothesis that a neurodevelopmental risk is presented to children through maternal consumption of ocean fish (Myers *et al.*, 2003). The Centers for Disease Control and Prevention provides public guidelines for the minimisation of any potential risk (Centers for Disease Control and Prevention, 2011). There are three levels of consumption recommended during pregnancy and for children under six years of age:

- 2–3 servings/week any fish or seafood except orange roughy, catfish, shark, or billfish (swordfish/broadbill/marlin) *or*
- 1 serving/week of orange roughy (seaperch) *or* catfish *then* no other fish that week or
- 1 serving/fortnight of shark (flake) *or* billfish *then* no other fish for that fortnight.

It should also be noted that a recommended child's serving is 75 g and an adult's is 150 g.

Fatty acid profiles in breast milk mirror the fatty acid composition of maternal plasma, which in turn is a reflection of maternal diet (Gibson *et al.*, 2011). It is clear that the lipids contained in breast milk and infant formula have important developmental outcomes for infants. In the first place, lipids are the major source of energy, supplying approximately half the caloric contribution of both breast milk and infant formula (Koletzko *et al.*, 2008). Secondly, DHA and AA are found in human milk, but traditionally have not been included in infant formula (Koletzko *et al.*, 2008). While breastfeeding should be supported, if mothers choose to use an infant formula it is important that the formula contains preformed DHA and AA; provision of precursor fatty acids without preformed DHA and AA will not allow infants to achieve the equivalent circulating levels of DHA and AA as those of breastfed infants (Koletzko *et al.*, 2008). This is particularly important for pre-term infants, who have an elevated risk of poor developmental and cognitive outcomes compared with full-term infants. It is recommended that DHA should comprise 0.2% of fatty acids but not exceed 0.5%, as the full evaluations of elevated intake are not yet complete (Koletzko *et al.*, 2008).

The evidence linking maternal supplementation of DHA to neurodevelopmental outcomes in her infant is limited, but one investigation that supplemented mothers' diets with 800 mg of DHA daily from 21 weeks gestation did not find any difference in language or cognitive development in toddlers aged 18 months (Makrides *et al.*, 2010). The results of this study may have implications for high levels of supplementation or simply reinforce the need for further research into the complex influence and combination of genetic variations in FADS genes, physiological interactions of dietary lipids consumed and other factors influencing the physiology and metabolism of omega-3 fatty acids. Variability in all factors influencing maternal and fetal DHA status and transfer requires further investigation (Lauritzen and Carlson, 2011). Expression of FADS allelles, for instance, has been identified as important in the transfer of DHA from maternal plasma to breast milk and correspondingly to altered responsiveness to supplementation with fish oil (Lauritzen and Carlson, 2011).

The drastic change in the lipid composition of Western diets over the last few decades has implications for pregnancy, lactation and infant health. A review of dietary changes notes that between 1944 and 1990, the LA of a mean Western diet consumed in the USA increased from 6% to 15% (Gibson *et al.*, 2011). The authors surmise that, along with changes in maternal diet, the nutrition of breast milk in 1980 is different from the nutrition of breast milk today. Further research is required to support an increase in omega-6 fatty acids, known for pro-inflammatory action, and the potential that elevated intakes may play a role in increasing the incidence of asthma and allergies. The influence of altered diet and a high balance of omega-6 fatty acids may also increase fat deposition in early life, contributing to overweight and obesity (Aihaud *et al.*, 2008).

Childhood mental health and cognitive development outcomes

The accretion of DHA in the neuron-rich grey matter of the brain is particularly important during the last trimester of pregnancy and the first year of infant life (Lauritzen and Carlson, 2011). Consumption of DHA is recommended to continue after the the introduction of solids and the first six months, although qualitative recommendations of optimal intakes are not yet available (Koletzko *et al.*, 2008). A lack of adequate nutrition during gestation and early childhood cannot be compensated for at a later stage of development. Animal studies carried out in non-human primates reveal that infants of mothers who were deficient in omega-3 fatty acids had impaired cognitive function and visual acuity which could not be reversed by later supplementation (Gibson *et al.*, 2011).

The role of long-chain polyunsaturated acid in the developing immune and central nervous systems and brain development can also have a long-term impact not only on health but on chronic illnesses (Lauritzen and Carlson, 2011). Observations of the benefits of DHA intake to preterm infants have led investigators concerned with growth-restricted infants to propose that DHA may in fact be neuroprotective for young children from disadvantaged or low-income backgrounds (Makrides *et al.*, 2011).

Early diet is purported to be important to mental health in childhood. The strongest evidence around omega-3 fatty acids is related to mood or impulsivity disorders (Richardson, 2006). Lower levels of red blood cell DHA are negatively correlated with clinician depression scores in children with juvenile bipolar disorder (Clayton *et al.*, 2008). The cause of altered lipid profiles is not clear. Red blood cell PUFA profiles have been related to dietary intake rather than disorder aetiology in some but not all research (Clayton *et al.*, 2008).

Red blood cell phospholipid profiles of children and adolescents with attention deficit hyperactivity disorder (ADHD) are lower in levels of DHA and total omega-3 fatty acids when compared to normal controls (Colter *et al.*, 2008). North American data reveal that ADHD could affect up to 13% of school-aged children. ADHD has high co-morbidity with conditions including oppositional defiance disorder, obsessive compulsive disorder and depression. In 60% of cases symptoms and difficulties are maintained into adulthood (Colter *et al.*, 2008) affecting social, educational and occupational functioning (Richardson, 2006).

In summary, research into the association of child and adolescent mental health and omega-3 polyunsaturated fatty acid profiles is emergent, and despite early encouraging results, a consensus has not yet been reached by the experts. Select researchers do not identify a likely benefit of n-3 LCPUFA supplementation for autism or bipolar disease (Clayton *et al.*, 2007), despite convincing epidemiological data (Hibbeln *et al.*, 2006b). Other researchers concur, citing limited evidence to support treatment of ADHD with n-3 LCPUFA supplements (Tomlinson *et al.*, 2009) and that certain benefit was not identified (Clayton *et al.*, 2007). Greater consensus is achieved in the field of depression, with a likely benefit of n-3 LCPUFA treatment identified for children and adolescents with unipolar depression (Clayton *et al.*, 2007).

Maternal mental health

Clear benefits for seafood consumption within a healthy diet have been demonstrated for maternal health. Pregnant and lactating women have greater nutritional requirements and as such may be at greater risk of nutrient deficiencies which may consequently increase their risk of depression (Bodnar and Wisner, 2005). As a public health concern, depression is consistently responsible for the greatest burden of disease in women across low-, middle- and high-income countries (World Health Organization, 2008). Estimates of the prevalence rates of antenatal and postpartum depression around the world range from 10–40% (Ramakrishnan, 2011). It is estimated that the global disease burden of postpartum depression potentially attributable to low levels of omega-3 polyunsaturated fatty acid deficiency is 65.5% (Hibbeln *et al.*, 2006b) based on analysis of the dietary data from 38 countries. Other disease burdens potentially attributed to omega-3 fatty acid deficiency are for homicide mortality (28.4%), postpartum depression (65.5%), major depression (98.5%) and bipolar depression (99.9%) (Hibbeln *et al.*, 2006b). These results do not imply a causal relationship for n-3 LCPUFA in bipolar depression for instance; rather, n-3 LCPUFA can reduce the risk of affective disorders (Noaghiul and Hibbeln, 2003) with the acknowledgement that a multitude of factors are contributory (Hibbeln *et al.*, 2006b). Population-based, cross-national epidemiological studies have demonstrated that seafood consumption can predict lifetime prevalence rates of bipolar disorders, including bipolar I disorder, bipolar II disorder and bipolar spectrum disorder (Noaghiul and Hibbeln, 2003). The authors identify an apparent vulnerability threshold of 50 lb seafood consumption per capita per annum.

Poor nutritional status with regard to energy or protein restrictions and iron deficiency are known to confound altered long-chain polyunsaturated fatty acid status (Lauritzen and Carlson, 2011). Adequate DHA concentration in breast milk has a strong negative correlation with postpartum depression rates (Hibbeln, 2002). The influence of diet on breast milk DHA is clear. Higher prevalence of postpartum depression has been observed in Brazilian women with an imbalance in omega-6 to omega-3 fatty acid intake during the first trimester of pregnancy (da Rocha and Kac, 2010).

The proposed mechanism for DHA in depressive disorders begins with decreased DHA concentrations in neural tissue; two pathways ensue (Ramakrishnan *et al.*, 2009). The first pathway is related to the role of DHA in membrane fluidity and structure and influences serotonin, norepinephrine and dopamine metabolism and signalling. The second pathway relates to the role of DHA in cytokine production influencing inflammatory response (Ramakrishnan *et al.*, 2009). Cross-national studies support recommendations that women of childbearing age should ingest at least 200 mg of DHA per day (Cetin and Koletzko, 2008).

Frequent fish and seafood consumption has been associated with a decreased risk of depression (Hibbeln, 1998). Seafood provides dietary omega-3 fatty acids and essential nutrients where nutritional status is commonly marginal, such as iodine, iron and other nutrients where deficiency has been linked to mental health. Nutrient deficiencies that have increased prevalence in depressed individuals include folic acid, vitamin B12, iron, zinc and selenium (Bodnar and Wisner, 2005). The greatest evidence, however, is consistently demonstrated with marine sourced long chain omega-3 fatty acids.

Pregnant women who have depression are likely to be less motivated to take care of themselves, thereby influencing pregnancy outcomes. Additionally, they may be less responsive to the care of their infant, who is almost completely dependent on the mother during the first year of life (Ramakrishnan, 2011). Despite the implications of antenatal and postnatal depression on infant health, there is a lack of large, well-designed studies of women in the postpartum period, with virtually no research carried out in developing countries where need is likely to be elevated. The burden of disease of antenatal and postpartum depression calls for investigations in this field.

Summary: nutritional interventions and mental health

Multinational epidemiological studies have overwhelmingly revealed links between fish, seafood, omega-3 fatty acid consumption and mental disorder prevalence. This relationship, however, requires a greater foundation of large clinically based trials and community-based prevention programmes. The role of seafood and omega-3 fatty acids in developmental nutrition and the influence of diet during gestation, early childhood and adolescence on the incidence reduction of lifelong mental health disorders in particular require consideration.

There is enormous potential for complementary therapies to reduce the burden of disease relating to mental health. Nutritional therapy, based upon robust scientific evidence and administered by qualified health professionals, is safe, easy to administer and inexpensive.

Dietary research that studies dietary patterns rather than single nutrients refers to the human diet as the whole being more than the sum of its parts (Van Horn, 2011). The research presented herewith includes studies based on seafood and omega-3 fatty acid consumption and status. The results of each field of investigation, however, are frequently parallel. Dietary patterns characterized by higher levels of EPA, DHA or seafood consumption may be indicative of healthful dietary patterns that provide health benefits that extend beyond the long-chain polyunsaturated omega-3 fatty acid content.

The study of a single nutrient, such as omega-3 fatty acids, needs to be considered within the context of the whole diet. While DHA and EPA may be among the nutritional factors that can decrease morbidity and suffering attributed to mental health disorders, the ratio of omega-3 to omega-6 fatty acids, especially within the Western diet, is critical. The omega-6 fatty acids, commonly found in seed and vegetable oils, are dissimilar to omega-3 fatty acids in physiological function. There is an antagonistic relationship between the omega-6 fatty acids and omega-3 fatty acids; reductions in omega-6 fatty acid consumption can reduce omega-3 requirements by as much as 90% (Hibbeln *et al.*, 2006b). This interaction is highlighted by a commonality of research outcomes confirming that depressed individuals demonstrate lower blood omega-3 fatty acid levels and a higher ratio of omega-6:omega-3 long-chain polyunsatured fatty acids (Bodnar and Wisner, 2005). Children and adolescents with ADHD display the same pattern of lower phospholipid omega-3 fatty acids and adverse omega-6:omega-3 fatty acid ratios (Colter *et al.*, 2008). The study of omega-3 fatty acids and health benefits reveals the strongest evidence to be associated with the marine-sourced omega-3 long chain polyunsatured fatty acids, EPA and DHA; other forms of omega-3 fatty acids are not physiologically equivalent (McManus *et al.*, 2010). These complex interactions may describe, in part, why discrete trials generate conflicting results.

As pertains to mental health and a Western dietary pattern, there are several nutrients that have a clear role in normal brain function, yet deficiency of these nutrients is commonly observed within the general population: i.e. omega-3 fatty acids, folic acid, vitamin B_{12}, antioxidants, selenium, iron and zinc (Bodnar and Wisner, 2005). Seafood in particular is a good source of lean protein and provides vitamins A and D, B group vitamins, iron, iodine, zinc and selenium in addition to omega-3 polyunsaturated fatty acids (Hostenkamp and Sorensen, 2009). While further research is required to investigate the influence of early childhood and lifelong nutrition on mental health, and the influence of early intervention on longevity and severity of mental disorders via community-based prevention trials (Ramakrishnan *et al.*, 2009), the emergent evidence is promising. There are clear benefits to health from the consumption of seafood and marine-sourced omega-3 fatty acids within a healthy diet, not only for mental health but for the prevention and management of several chronic conditions.

There is support for the relationship between major depressive disorders, essential fatty acid and folic acid status, and there is a strong possibility that these nutrients may be used to treat or augment treatment (Bodnar and Wisner, 2005). For example, research indicates that adequate omega-3 fatty acid intake in early development and into adulthood may prevent aggression and hostility (Hibbeln *et al.*, 2006a).

As no nutrient works in isolation, the value of seafood within a healthy diet cannot be understated. Inclusion of seafood within a healthy diet is an invaluable complementary treatment approach for mental health. The evidence indicates that nutritional therapy, in conjunction with current best practice treatments, has the potential to significantly impact the burden of disease attributable to mental health disorders.

References

Aihaud, G., Grimaldi, P. and Cunnane, S. C. (2008) An emerging risk factor for obesity: does disequilibrium of polyunsaturated fatty acid metabolism contribute to excessive adipose tissue development?. *British Journal of Nutrition*, **100**, 461–70.

Alloway, B. J. (2009) Soil factors associated with zinc deficiency in crops and humans. *Environmental Geochemical Health*, **31**, 537–48.

Australian Bureau of Statistics (2006) *National Health Survey: Summary of Results 2004–05*. Commonwealth of Australia.

Australian Bureau of Statistics (2008) *National Survey of Mental Health and Wellbeing: Summary of Results 2007*. Commonwealth of Australia.

Australian Institute of Health and Welfare (2010) *Mental Health Services in Australia 2007–08*. Commonwealth of Australia.

Berr, C., Akbaraly, T., Arnaud, J., Hininger, I., Roussel, A. M. and Barberger Gateau, P. (2009) Increased selenium intake in elderly high fish consumers may account for health benefits previously ascribed to omega-3 fatty acids. *Journal of Nutrition, Health and Aging*, **13**, 14–18.

Bodnar, L. M. and Wisner, K. L. (2005) Nutrition and depression: Implications for improving mental health among childbearing-aged women. *Biological Psychiatry*, **58**, 679–85.

Brenna, J. T., Salem Jr, N., Sinclair, A. J. and Cunnane, S. C. (2009) α-linoleic acid supplementation and conversion to n-3 long-chain polyunsaturated fatty acids in humans. *Prostaglandins, Leukotrienes and Essential Fatty Acids*, **80**, 85–91.

Centers for Disease Control and Prevention (2011) *National Report on Human Exposure to Environmental Chemicals*. CDC.

Cetin, I. and Koletzko, B. (2008) Long-chain omega-3 fatty acid supply in pregnancy and lactation. *Current Opinion in Clinical Nutrition and Metabolic Care*, **11**(3), 297–302.

Clayton, E. H., Hanstock, T. L., Garg, M. L. and Hazell, P. L. (2007) Long chain omega-3 polyunsaturated fatty acids in the treatment of psychiatric illnesses in children and adolescents. *Acta Neuropsychiatrica*, **19**, 92–103.

Clayton, E. H., Hanstock, T. L., Hirneth, S. J., Cable, C. J., Garg, M. L. and Hazell, P. l. (2008) Long-chain omega-3 polyunsaturated fatty acids in the blood of children and adolescents with juvenile bipolar disorder. *Lipids*, **43**, 1031–8.

Colter, A. L., Cutler, C. and Meckling, K. A. (2008) Fatty acid status and behavioural symptoms of Attention Deficit Hyperactivity Disorder in adolescents: a case-control study. *Nutrition Journal*, **7**, 1–11.

Da Rocha, C. M. M. and Kac, G. (2010) High dietary ratio of omega-6 to omega-3 polyunsaturated acids during pregnancy and prevalence of post-partum depression. *Maternal and Child Nutrition*, **8**, 36–48.

Department of Health (2010) *No Health Without Mental Health: a Cross-government Mental Health Outcomes Strategy for People of All Ages*. Department of Health, London.

Ekweagwu, E., Agwu, A. E. and Madukwe, E. (2008) The role of micronutrients in child health: a review of the literature. *African Journal of Biotechnology*, **7**, 3804–10.

Funk, M., Drew, N., Freeman, M. and Edwige, F. (2010) *Mental Health and Development: Targeting People with Mental Health Conditions as a Vulnerable Group*. World Health Organization, Geneva.

Gibson, R. A., Muhlhausler, B. and Makrides, M. (2011) Conversion of linoleic acid and alpha-linoleic acid to long-chain polyunsaturated fatty acids (LCPUFAs), with a focus on pregnancy, lactation and the first 2 years of life. *Maternal and Child Nutrition*, **7**, 17–26.

Glaser, C., Lattka, E., Rzehak, P., Steer, C. and Koletzko, B. (2011) Genetic variation in polyunsaturated fatty acid metabolism and its potential relevance for human development and health. *Maternal and Child Nutrition*, **7**, 27–40.

Goyens, P. L. L., Spilker, M. E., Zock, P. L., Katan, M. B. and Mensink, R. P. (2006) Conversion of a-linoleic acid in humans is influenced by the absolute amounts of a-linoleic acid and linoleic acid in the diet and not by their ratio. *American Journal of Clinical Nutrition*, **84**, 44–53.

Gunnarsdottir, I., Gunnarsdottir, B. E., Steingrimsdottir, L., Maage, A., Johannesson, A. J. and Thorsdottir, I. (2010) Iodine status of adolescent girls in a population changing from high fish to lower fish consumption. *European Journal of Clinical Nutrition*, Advance online publication (accessed 16 June 2010).

He, K., Song, Y., Daviglus, M. L., Liu, K., Van Horn, L., Dyer, A. R. and Greenland, P. (2004) Accumulated evidence on fish consumption and coronary heart disease mortality. *Circulation*, **109**, 2705–11.

Hibbeln, J. R. (1998) Fish consumption and major depression. *Lancet*, **351**, 1213.

Hibbeln, J. R. (2002) Seafood consumption, the DHA content of mother's milk and prevalence rates of postpartum depression: a cross-national, ecological analysis. *Journal of Affective Disorders*, **69**, 15–29.

Hibbeln, J., Ferguson, T. A. and Blasbalg, T. L. (2006a) Omega-3 fatty acid deficiencies in neurodevelopment, agression and autonomic dysregulation: opportunities for intervention. *International Review of Psychiatry*, **18**, 107–18.

Hibbeln, J. R., Nieminen, L. R. G., Blasbalg, T. L., Riggs, J. A. and Lands, W. E. M. (2006b) Healthy intakes of n-3 and n-6 fatty acids: estimations considering worldwide diversity. *American Journal of Clinical Nutrition*, **83S**, 1483S–93S.

Hibbeln, J. R., Davis, J. M., Steer, C., Emmett, P., Rogers, I., Williams, C. and Golding, J. (2007) Maternal seafood consumption in pregnancy and neurodevelopmental outcomes in childhood (ALSPAC study): an observational cohort study. *Lancet*, **369**, 578–85.

Hostenkamp, G. and Sorensen, J. (2009) Are fish eaters healthier and do they consumer less health-care resources? *Public Health Nutritionition*, **13**, 453–60.

Kessler, R. C., Angermeyer, M., Anthony, J. C., De Graaf, R., Demyttenaere, K., Gasquet, I., *et al.* (2007) Lifetime prevalence and age-of-onset distributions of mental disorders in the World Health Organization's World Mental Health Survey Initiative. *World Psychiatry*, **6**, 168–76.

Kessler, R. C., Berglund, P., Demler, O., Jin, R., Merikangas, K. R. and Walters, E. E. (2005) Lifetime prevalence and age-of-onset distributions of DSM-IV disorders in the National Comorbidity Survey replication. *Archives of General Psychiatry*, **62**, 593–602, 768.

Koletzko, B., Lien, E., Agostoni, C., Bohles, H., Campoy, C., Cetin, I., *et al.* (2008) The roles of long-chain polyunsaturated fatty acids in pregnancy, lactation and infancy: review of current knowledge and consensus recommendations. *Journal of Perinatal Medicine*, **36**, 5–14.

Lauritzen, L. and Carlson, S. E. (2011) Maternal fatty acid status during pregnancy and lactation and relation to newborn and infant status. *Maternal and Child Nutrition*, **7**, 41–58.

Li, M., Eastman, C. J., Waite, K. V., Ma, G., Zacharin, M. R., Topliss, D. J., *et al.* (2006) Are Australian children iodine deficient? Results of the Australian National Iodine Nutrition Study. *Medical Journal of Australia*, **184**, 165–9.

Makrides, M., Collins, C. T. and Gibson, R. A. (2011) Impact of fatty acid status on growth and neurobehavioural development in humans. *Maternal and Child Nutrition*, **7**, 80–8.

Makrides, M., Gibson, R. A., McPhee, A. J., Yelland, L., Quinlivan, J., Ryan, P. and the DOMInO Investigative Team (2010) Effect of DHA supplementation during pregnancy on maternal depression and neurodevelopment of young children: a randomized controlled trial. *Journal of the American Medical Association*, **304**, 1675–83.

McManus, A., Merga, M. and Newton, W. (2010) Omega-3 fatty acids: what consumers need to know. *Appetite*, **57**, 80–3.

Mokhber, N., Namjoo, M., Tara, F., Boskabadi, H., Rayman, M. P., Ghayour-Mobarhan, M., *et al.* (2011) Effect of supplementation with selenium on post-partum depression: a randomized double-blind placebo-controlled trial. *Journal of Maternal-Fetal and Neonatal Medicine*, **24**, 104–8.

Mozaffarian, D. and Rimm, E. B. (2006) Fish intake, contaminants, and human health: evaluating the risks and the benefits. *Journal of the American Medical Association*, **296**, 1885–99.

Myers, G. J., Davidson, P. W., Cox, C., Shamlaye, C. F., Palumbo, D., Cernichiari, E., *et al.* (2003) Prenatal methylmercury exposure from ocean fish consumption in the Seychelles child development study. *Lancet*, **361**, 1686–92.

Nawar, W. W. (1985) Lipids. In: *Food Chemistry*, 2nd edn (ed. O. R. Fennema). Marcel Dekker Inc, New York.

Noaghiul, S. and Hibbeln, J. R. (2003) Cross-national comparisons of seafood consumption and rates of bipolar disorders. *American Journal of Psychiatry*, **160**, 2222–7.

Pasco, J. A., Jacka, F. N., Williams, L. J., Evans-Cleverdon, M., Brennan, S. L., Kotowicz, M. A., *et al.* (2012) Dietary selenium and major depression: a nested case-control study. *Complementary Therapies in Medicine*, **20**(3), 119–23.

Patel, V., Flisher, A. J., Hetrick, S. and Mcgorry, P. (2007) Mental health of young people: a global public-health challenge. *Lancet*, **369**, 1302–13.

Ramakrishnan, U. (2011) Fatty acid status and maternal health. *Maternal and Child Nutrition*, **7**, 99–111.

Ramakrishnan, U., Imhoff-Kunsch, B. and Digirolamo, A. M. (2009) Role of docosahexaenoic acid in maternal and child mental health. *American Journal of Clinical Nutrition*, **89**, 958–62S.

Richardson, A. J. (2006) Omega-3 fatty acids in ADHD and related neurodevelopmental disorders. *International Review of Psychiatry*, **18**, 155–72.

Ruxton, C. H. S. and Derbyshire, E. (2009) Latest evidence on omega-3 fatty acids and health. *Nutrition and Food Science*, **39**, 423–38.

Sanchez-Villegas, A., Delago-Rodriguez, M., Alonso, A., Schlatter, J., Lahortiga, F., Majem, L. S. and Martinez-Gonzalez, M. A. (2009) Association of the Mediterranean dietary pattern with the incidence of depression. *Archives of General Psychiatry*, **66**, 1090–8.

Sanders, T., Mistry, M. and Naismith, D. (1984) The influence of a maternal diet rich in linoleic acid on brain and retinal docosahexaenoic acid in the rat. *British Journal of Nutrition*, **51**, 57–66.

Sawyer, M. G., Arney, F. M., Baghurst, P. A., Clark, J. J., Gratez, B. W., Kosky, R. J., *et al.* (2001) The mental health of young people in Australia: key findings from the child and adolescent component of the national survey of mental health and well-being. *Australian and New Zealand Journal of Psychiatry*, **35**, 806–14.

Shannon, S. (2009) Integrative approaches to pediatric mood disorders. *Alternative Therapies*, **15**, 48–53.

Stillwell, W. and Wassall, S. R. (2003) Docosahexaenoic acid: membrane properties of a unique fatty acid. *Chemistry and Physics of Lipids*, **126**, 1–27.

Tomlinson, D., Wilkinson, H. and Wilkinson, P. (2009) Diet and mental health in children. *Child and Adolescent Mental Health*, **14**, 148–55.

UNICEF (2011) *IDD: Achievements and challenges*. Available at: http://www.unicef.org/media/14946.html (accessed 19 January 2013).

Van Horn, L. (2011) Eating pattern analyses: the whole is more than the sum of its parts. *Journal of the American Dietetic Association*, **111**(2), 1.

Vogiatzoglou, A., Smith, A. D., Nurk, E., Berstad, P., Drevon, C. A., Ueland, P. M., Vollset, S. E., Tell, G. S. and Refsum, H. (2009) Dietary sources of vitamin B-12 and their association with plasma vitamin B-12 concentrations in the general population: the Hordaland Homocysteine Study. *American Journal of Clinical Nutrition*, **89**, 1078–87.

Weber, D. N., Connaughton, V. P., Dellinger, J. A., Klemer, D., Udvadia, A. and Carvan, M. J. (2008) Selenomethionine reduce visual deficits due to developmental methylmercury exposures. *Physiological Behaviour*, **93**, 250–60.

World Health Organization (2001) *Strengthening Mental Health Promotion* (Fact sheet no. 220). WHO, Geneva.

World Health Organization (2008) *The Global Burden of Disease. 2004 Update*. WHO, Geneva.

Index